Criminal Law in Lithuania

Criminal Law in Lithuania

Gintaras Švedas

This book was originally published as a monograph in the International Encyclopaedia of Laws/Criminal Law.

Founding Editor: Roger Blanpain
General Editor: Frank Hendrickx
Volume Editors: Frank Verbruggen & Vanessa Franssen

Wolters Kluwer

Published by:
Kluwer Law International B.V.
PO Box 316
2400 AH Alphen aan den Rijn
The Netherlands
E-mail: lrs-sales@wolterskluwer.com
Website: www.wolterskluwer.com/en/solutions/kluwerlawinternational

Sold and distributed by:
Wolters Kluwer Legal & Regulatory U.S.
7201 McKinney Circle
Frederick, MD 21704
United States of America
E-mail: customer.service@wolterskluwer.com

ISBN 978-94-035-4711-4

e-Book: ISBN 978-94-035-4472-4
web-PDF: ISBN 978-94-035-4902-6

The Author

Professor, habilitated doctor Gintaras Švedas (born 8 February 1964) studied Law at the Vilnius University, Lithuania where he graduated in 1989. G. Švedas has acquired the degree of Doctor of Law with thesis 'Theoretical Issues of the Punishment of Deprivation of Liberty and its Execution' in 1993 (Vilnius University) and post-doctoral degree (Dr Habil.) with thesis 'Basics and Tendencies of Criminal Policy in the Republic of Lithuania' in 2009 (Faculty of Law and Administration; University of Lodz (Poland).

G. Švedas – Head of Criminal Justice Department of Law Faculty of Vilnius University (from 2003), Professor of law at Law Faculty of Vilnius University (from 2009); Vice-Dean for Planning and Sciences of Law Faculty of Vilnius University (from 2006); Member of the Committee of the Criminal Code Supervision under the Ministry of Justice (from 2012); Contact point for Lithuania in the European Criminal Law Academic Network (ECLAN) (from 2006) and Member of Management Committee of ECLAN (from 2018); Member of the Committee on Legal Reform in Ukraine (from 2019), etc.

As a Lithuanian national expert, he took part in more than ten international scientific projects. As a short-term senior expert, he participated in the EU projects 'Support to the Government of Moldova in the field of anti-corruption, reform of Ministry of Internal Affairs, including police and personal data protection' (2011–2013), 'Support to Justice Sector Reforms in Ukraine' (2015–2017) and 'Support to Justice Sector Reforms in Ukraine-PRAVO-Justice' (from 2018).

G. Švedas was Vice Minister of Justice of Lithuania (1993–2006), Agent of the Government of the Republic of Lithuania to the European Court of Human Rights (1995–2003), Member of the Management Board of Fundamental Rights Agency (2007–2010), Public Adviser to the Minister of Justice in the fields of criminal law, enforcement of punishments, implementation of the EU law (2012–2016), etc.

G. Švedas is an author (co-author) of ten monographs, ninety-five scientific articles, twenty-two manuals, textbooks and educational works, eleven compendiums. He also was involved in preparation of, among others, the Criminal Code, Code of Punishment Enforcement and Code of Criminal Procedure of Lithuania.

The Author

Table of Contents

The Author 3

List of Abbreviations 17

General Introduction 19

§1. Lithuania's General Background 19
I. Geography and Climate 19
II. Population 19
III. Economy 20
IV. Political System and Administrative Structure 20
V. The Judicial System 21

§2. Criminal Law, Criminal Justice and Criminal Science 23
I. Definitions of Criminal Law 23
A. Criminal Law 23
B. Substantive Criminal Law 24
C. Criminal Procedure 24
D. Punishment Execution 25
II. Characteristics of Criminal Law 26
III. Overview of the Criminal Justice System 27
A. The Police and Other Law Enforcement Agencies 27
B. The Prosecution Service 28
C. Investigating Judges 30
D. Trial Jurisdictions 30
E. Prison System and After-Care 30
F. The Bar 31
G. Statistical Overview 32
IV. Trends Within Criminal Justice 33

§3. The Historical Background 35
I. Code of Casimir of 1468 35
II. Lithuanian Statutes of 1529, 1566 and 1588 36
III. Russian Criminal Laws in Lithuania 37
IV. Criminal Laws in Independent Lithuania (1918–1940) 38
V. Criminal Laws During the Soviet Occupation 39
VI. Criminal Laws after the Restoration of the Independence of Lithuania (1990–2000) 41
VII. Criminal Code of 2000 41

§4. Sources of Criminal Law 44
I. International Sources 44
II. National Sources 48
A. The Constitution and Constitutional Court Rulings 48
B. Statute Legislation 49
C. Statutory Delegated Legislation 50
D. Court Decisions 51

§5. Classifications and Technique of Criminal Law 53

Part I. Substantive Criminal Law 61

Chapter 1. General Principles 61

§1. The Principle of Legality 61
I. Limitation on Penalisation 61
II. Legality and Interpretation 63

§2. The Principle of the Individual Guilty Mind 63

§3. The Principle of Justice and Proportionality 64

Chapter 2. Scope of Application of Criminal Statutes 66

§1. Principles Concerning the Applicability of Criminal Statutes with Respect to Time 66
I. Prohibition of Retroactive Criminal Law 66
II. Retroactivity of the Milder Provision 67
III. Retroactivity of the Stricter Statute 67
IV. The Extent of the Prohibition Against Retroactive Criminal Law 68

§2. Principles Concerning the Applicability of Criminal Statutes with Respect to Space 68
I. The Territorial Principle 68
II. Extraterritorial Criminal Jurisdiction 70
A. Principle of Active Personality 70
B. Principle of Protection 71
C. Principle of Universality 72
D. Cases 73
E. The Effect of Foreign Adjudication and Execution 74

§3. Principles Concerning the Applicability of Criminal Statutes with Respect to Persons 75
I. Immunities Based on National Public Law 75
II. Immunities Based on International Public Law 76

Chapter 3. General Principles of Criminal Liability 79

§1. INTRODUCTION: THE BASIC ELEMENTS OF CRIMINAL OFFENCES 79

§2. THE MATERIAL OR PHYSICAL ELEMENT (*ACTUS REUS*) 80
I. Description 80
II. Acts, Omissions and Causation 81
A. Offences of Action 81
B. Offences of Omission 81
C. Commission by Omission 82
D. Causation Offences 82
III. Classification of Offences from the Point of View of the Material Element 83
A. Momentary and Continuous Offences 83
B. Occasional and Habitual Offences 84

§3. THE MORAL OR MENTAL ELEMENT (*MENS REA*) 85
I. Subjective Guilt or Culpability 85
II. Intent 85
A. Degrees of Intent 86
1. General Intent 86
2. Premeditated and Sudden Intent 86
B. Types of Intention with Reference to Their Consequences 87
1. Direct Intent (*Dolus Directus*) 87
2. Indirect or Eventual Intent (*Dolus Eventualis*) 87
3. Specified and Unspecified Intent 87
III. Negligence 88
A. Definition 88
B. The Evaluation of Negligence 88
C. Types of Negligence 88
IV. The Required Form of Guilt 89
V. Legal Entity as a Subject of the Criminal Act 90

Chapter 4. Justification, Excuse and Other Grounds of Impunity 92

§1. GENERAL PRINCIPLES 92

§2. GROUNDS OF JUSTIFICATION 92
I. Public Duty or Orders of the Authorities 92
II. (Self-) Defence 94
A. Posing the Problem 94
B. Position Within the National Law 94
C. Conditions 94
1. Conditions Relating to the Attack 94
2. Conditions Relating to the Defence 95

D. Excessive (Self-)Defence 95
E. Putative (Self-)Defence 96
III. Legitimate Resistance against Unlawful Acts of Civil Servants 96
IV. Necessity 96
A. Necessity as a Justification 96
B. Conditions 97
C. Putative Necessity 98
V. Consent of the Victim 98
VI. Apprehension of a Person Who Committed a Criminal Act 99
VII. Performance of an Assignment of a Law Enforcement Institution 99
VIII. Justifiable Professional or Economic Risk 100
IX. Scientific Experiment 100
X. Realisation of his/her Rights 101

§3. GROUNDS OF EXCUSE 101
I. Introduction 101
II. Minority 102
III. Insanity 103
A. Insanity at the Moment of the Act or Omission 103
B. Insanity at Time the Trial 104
C. Diminished Capacity 105
IV. Intoxication 106
V. Force Majeure and Coercion 106
VI. Ignorance or Mistake 107
A. Ignorance or Mistake of Law 107
B. Ignorance or Mistake of Fact 108
C. Special Cases 108

§4. OTHER GROUNDS OF IMPUNITY 109
I. Report of Some Criminal Offences to the Public Authority 109
II. Submission to the Public Authorities 109
III. Family Relationship 110

Chapter 5. Incomplete or Partly Perpetrated Criminal Offences 111

§1. PREPARATION FOR COMMISSION OF A CRIME 111
I. Describing the Problem 111
II. Lithuanian Preparation and Attempt Statutes 111
III. Conditions of Preparation 112
IV. The Punishment for Preparation 113

§2. CRIMINAL ATTEMPT 113
I. Conditions of Attempt 113
A. Intent to Commit a Crime or a Misdemeanour 113
B. Commencement of Execution 114

C. Incompletion of the Offence Independent of the Perpetrator's Will 114
II. Attempting the Impossible 115
III. The Punishment for Attempt 116

§3. COMPLICITY 116
I. General Remarks 116
II. Forms of Perpetrator Actions 117
A. Direct Perpetrator 117
B. Joint Perpetrators (Co-perpetrators) 117
C. Indirect Perpetrator 118
III. Organiser 118
IV. Instigator 118
V. Abettor 119
VI. Forms of Complicity 119
VII. Special Cases 121
A. Withdrawal from Participation 121
B. Entrapment 121
VIII. Peculiarities of Criminal Liability of Accomplices 122

Chapter 6. Classification and Survey of Criminal Offences 123

§1. GENERAL CLASSIFICATION OF CRIMINAL OFFENCES 123
I. Ordinary and Political Offences 123
II. Ordinary and Printing Press Offences 123

§2. SURVEY OF CRIMINAL OFFENCES 124
I. Criminal Offences of the Penal Code 124
II. Criminal Offences in the Special Criminal Laws 145

Chapter 7. The Sanctioning System 146

§1. THE GENERAL SANCTIONING SYSTEM 146

§2. RELEASE FROM CRIMINAL LIABILITY 147

§3. PUNISHMENTS 153
I. The System and Types of Punishments 153
A. The Death Penalty 154
B. Custodial Penalties 155
C. Fine 157
D. Restriction of Liberty 158
E. Community Service 159
F. Restriction of Operation of a Legal Entity 160
G. Liquidation of a Legal Entity 160

§4. MEASURES OF SECURITY AND REFORM 160

I. The System and Types of Penal Measures 160
A. Prohibition to Exercise a Special Right 162
B. Deprivation of Public Rights 162
C. Deprivation of the Right to be Employed in a Certain Position or to Engage in Certain Type of Activities 163
D. Compensation for or Elimination of Property Damage 163
E. Unpaid Work 163
F. Payment of a Contribution to the Fund of Violent Crime Victims 164
G. Confiscation of Property 164
H. Obligation to Reside Separately from the Victim and (or) Prohibition to Approach the Victim Closer than a Prescribed Distance, Obligation to Notify a Change of the Place of Residence or Departure of the Place of Residence 165
I. Obligation to Participate in Violence Correction Programmes 166
J. Extended Confiscation of Property 166
II. The System and Types of the Reformative Measures for Minors 168
A. Warning 168
B. Compensation for or Elimination of Property Damage 169
C. Unpaid Reformative Work 169
D. Placement for Upbringing and Care with Parents or Other Natural or Legal Persons Taking Care of Children 169
E. Restriction on Conduct 169
F. Placement in a Special Reformative Facility 170
III. The System and Types of the Compulsory Medical Measures 170

§5. Modes of Punishment 172
I. The Suspension of the Execution of a Punishment 172
A. The Suspension of the Execution of a Punishment for Adults 172
B. The Suspension of the Execution of a Punishment for Minors 174
II. Release from the Execution of the Punishment 174
A. Release from the Execution of the Punishment due to an Illness 174
B. Amnesty 175
C. Clemency 175

§6. Principles and Rules Concerning Sentencing 176
I. The General Principles 177
II. Grounds for Increasing Punishment 180
A. Aggravating Circumstances 180
B. Recidivism 181
III. Grounds for Mitigating Punishment 182
A. Mitigating Circumstances 183
B. Sentencing Rules Permitting to Mitigate the Punishment 184
1. Imposition of a More Lenient Punishment than Provided for by a Law 184

2. Imposition of a Punishment Upon Hearing a Case Under the Simplified Procedure or upon Conducting a Summary Examination of Evidence 186
3. Imposition of a Punishment Applying the Principle of Justice 186
IV. Concurrence of Offences 186
A. Concurrence by One Act 187
B. Real Concurrence of Offences 187
C. Continued or Collective Offences 187
D. Sentencing Rules for the Commission of Several Criminals Acts 188
V. Combination of Sentencing Rules 189

Part II. Criminal Procedure 191

Chapter 1. Principles, Institutions, Stages 191

§1. The Judicial Organisation 191
I. Trial Jurisdictions 191
II. Investigating Jurisdictions 194

§2. The Stages of the Penal Process 196
I. Two Basic Distinctions 196
II. The Preparatory Inquiry 197
A. Pretrial Investigation 197
1. The Police and the Prosecution Service 197
2. The Beginning and Closing of the Pretrial Investigation 199
III. The Prosecution 201
A. The Attribution and the Object of the Right to Prosecute 201
B. The Suspension of the Right to Prosecute 202
C. The Dissolution of the Right to Prosecute 203
1. Abolition of Penal Provision, Grant of Amnesty, Death of the Accused 205
2. Too long Duration of the Pretrial Investigation 205
3. Commission of the Several Criminal Acts 206
4. Limitation by Time 206
5. *Non bis in idem* (Provisions Against Double Jeopardy) 209

§3. The Legal Position of the Accused and the Civil Party 209
I. Introductory Remarks 209
II. The Legal Position of the Accused 211
A. The Provisions in the Code of Criminal Procedure 211
1. The Right to Know the Suspicion and the Charge 212
2. The Right to Legal Assistance 213
3. The Right to Lodge Requests, to Give Explanations or to Remain Silent in Pretrial Investigation 215

4. The Right to Access to the Case-File During Pretrial Investigation and Trial 216
5. The Right to have Another Person Informed About Arrest or Detention 217
B. Other Applicable Laws 218
III. The Legal Position of the Victim and the Civil Party 219
A. General Observations 219
B. The Rights of the Victim 220
C. The Rights of the Injured Party 221

§4. THE RULES OF EVIDENCE 222
I. The Principles of Evidentiary Law 223
II. The Means of Proof 225
A. The Testimony of the Suspect and Accused 225
B. The Testimony of the Witness and Victim 226
C. The Expert Report 229
D. The Specialist Conclusion 230
E. The Item (as an Evidence) 231
F. The Document (as an Evidence) 231
III. The Exclusion of Evidence 232

Chapter 2. Powers, Rights and Duties in the Pretrial Investigation 234

§1. POWERS, RIGHTS AND DUTIES OF THE PROSECUTOR AND PRETRIAL INVESTIGATOR 234
I. Introductory Remarks 234
II. Covert Policing Methods 235
III. The Powers to Check and Search 237
IV. The Powers of Entry, Search and Seizure 238
V. The Powers of Arrest 240
VI. The Powers for the Temporary Limitation of the Property Rights 241
VII. The Powers to Interview the Suspect and Witness 242
A. The Powers to Interview the Suspect 242
B. The Powers to Interview the Witness 242
C. The Powers for Confrontation, Identification Parade, Verification of the Testimonies on the Site and Experiment 243
VIII. Miscellaneous 244
A. The Powers at the Scene of the Offence 244
B. The Powers to Call in Experts 245

§2. POWERS, RIGHTS AND DUTIES WITHIN THE FRAMEWORK OF THE PRETRIAL DETENTION 247
I. Introductory Remarks 247
II. The Warrants of Attachment and of Arrest 247
A. The Warrant of Attachment 247
B. The Warrant of Pretrial Detention 248

III. The Continuation of Pretrial Detention 250
IV. The Lifting of the Warrant of Arrest or Pre-trial Detention 251
V. The Appeals to the Court of Appeal and the Court of Cassation 251
VI. The Committal the Suspect or Accused to the Medical Institution 252
VII. An Alternative to the Pretrial Detention: Freedom and Release Under Conditions 252

§3. THE POWERS AND DUTIES OF THE INVESTIGATING JUDGE IN THE PRE-TRIAL INVESTIGATION 255
I. Introductory Remarks 255
II. The Powers to Trace Telephonic Communications 255
III. The Powers to Interview the Accused and Witnesses 257
A. The Interviewing of the Accused 257
B. The Interviewing of Witnesses 258

Chapter 3. The Inquiry in Court 259

§1. THE TRIAL 259
I. The Preparation of the Hearing 261
II. The Attendance of the Parties 262
III. The Course of the Trial 263
A. The Preparation of the Hearing 264
B. The Examination of the Evidence 266
C. The Final Speeches and Last Word of the Accused 269
IV. The Judgment of the Case 270

§2. THE LEGAL REMEDIES 272
I. Introductory Remarks 272
II. The Ordinary Legal Remedies 273
A. Appeal Against the Judgment of the First Instance Court 273
B. Cassation Appeal Against the Judgment of the Second Instance Court 276
C. Appeal Against the Rulings of the Lower Courts to the Superior Courts 280
III. The Extraordinary Legal Remedies 281
A. Reopening the Criminal Case if New Circumstances are Discovered 281
B. Reopening the Criminal Case due to the Decision of the European Court on Human Rights or Human Rights Committee of the United Nations or Constitutional Court of Lithuania 282
C. Reopening the Criminal Case due to Clear Improper Application of the Criminal Law 284

Part III. Execution and Extinction of Sanctions 287

Chapter 1. Sources of Penitentiary Law and Nature of Regulations 287

Chapter 2. General Principles Concerning the Execution of Sentences and Orders 290

Chapter 3. The Prison System 292

§1. Organisational Structure 292
I. Prison Administration and Classification of Penitentiaries 292
II. Classification of Prisoners 293

§2. The Penitentiary Regime 294
I. Introduction 294
II. Aspects of Living Conditions 295
A. Visits, Correspondence and Telephone 295
B. Information and Media 297
C. Prison Labour 297
D. Disciplinary Measures 298
E. Leave from Prison 299
III. Forms of Alternative Execution of the Prison Sentence 300

§3. Prisoners' Rights, Complaints Procedures and Judicial Control 301

§4. Early Release 303
I. Conditional Release 303

Chapter 4. Extinction of Sanctions or Sentences 306

§1. Pardon, Amnesty, Illness 306

§2. The Limitation of the Penalty by Time 307

§3. Deletion of the Conviction and Rehabilitation of Offenders 309

§4. Revision of Sentences 310
I. Conditions Relating to the Nature of the Sanction Imposed 310
II. Circumstances Justifying Revision of the Sentence 310
A. Inconsistency Between Distinct Convictions 310
B. False Statement, New Facts or New Circumstances 311
C. Resolution of Doubts and Ambiguities Arising in the Course of Execution of Judgment 311

D. Resolution of Certain Issues Arising in the Course of Execution of Judgment 312
E. Resolution of the Application of the Milder Criminal Law 312
III. Procedure 312
General Conclusions 313

Selected Bibliography 315

Index 321

Table of Contents

List of Abbreviations

BAPP	Basic amount of punishment and penalty
CAO	Code of Administrative Offences
CC	Criminal Code
CCP	Code of Criminal Procedure
CJEU	Court of Justice of the European Union
CPE	Code of Punishment Execution
CPT	Council of Europe's Committee for the Prevention of Torture and Inhuman or Degrading Treatment or Punishment
EAW	European Arrest Warrant
ECHR	European Convention on Human Rights
ECtHR	European Court on Human Rights
EU	European Union
ICCPR	International Covenant on Civil and Political Rights
Para	Paragraph
TAR	Register of Legal Acts
UN	United Nations

List of Abbreviations

General Introduction

§1. Lithuania's General Background

I. Geography and Climate

1. Lithuania (officially the Republic of Lithuania) is a country in Northern Europe. Being one of the three Baltic States – the largest and most populous of them – it is situated along the south-eastern shore of the Baltic Sea, to the east of Sweden and Denmark. It is bordered by Latvia to the north, Belarus to the east and south, Poland to the south and Kaliningrad oblast (a Russian exclave) to the south-west. Lithuania covers an area of 65,200 square kilometres and the average density is 42.9 people per square kilometre as of January 2017.

2. Lithuania's climate, which ranges between maritime and continental, is relatively mild. Average temperatures on the coast are –2.5°C in January and 16°C in July.

II. Population

3. As of 1 January 2021, the population of Lithuania was estimated to be 2,795,700 people. The women ratio of the total population was 53% (1,000 males per 1,128 females). In 2016, the 69.3% of the population (1,987,499 people) lives in cities. The capital and largest city of Lithuania is Vilnius, which has a population of 526,000 inhabitants.

4. Lithuanians are a Baltic population. Ethnic Lithuanians account for five-sixths of the population, which makes the country one of the most homogeneous in the Baltic States. The 2020 census found that 85.5% of the population was ethnic Lithuanians who spoke Lithuanian. Poles made up 5.7%, followed by Russians (4.5%), Belarusians (1.9%) and Ukrainians (1.4%). Poles are mostly concentrated in south-east Lithuania, while Russians are mostly in Vilnius and Klaipėda. There are approximately 3,000 Roma in Lithuania, as well as a small community of Tatar. The official language, Lithuanian, along with Latvian, is one of only two living languages in the Baltic branch of the Indo-European language family.

5. Approximately 80% of the total population of Lithuania is Roman Catholic. Others include Orthodox, Old Believers, Lutherans, Reformats, Jewish and other communities.

6. In Lithuania, the average life expectancy for men is 71.5 years and for women 81 years (2019).

III. Economy

7. The gross national product in Lithuania was estimated to be worth USD 58.89 billion in 2020. This is equivalent to about USD 19,900 per inhabitant in 2020.

8. The top industries in Lithuania are metal-cutting machine tools, electric motors, television sets, refrigerators and freezers. The top exported goods in 2015 were oil and mineral fuels, industrial machinery and furniture. The main trade partners in 2015 were Russia, Poland and Germany. Lithuania was ranked 11 out of 190 states in the ease of doing business index (2020).

9. The most important sectors of Lithuania's economy in 2015 were wholesale and retail trade, transport, accommodation and food services (32.5%), industry (22.6%) and public administration, defence, education, human health and social work activities (14.3%).

10. The total labour force includes 1,358,000 employers (2020). Employment in agriculture was 9%, in industry 25% and in services 66% of all labour force in Lithuania (2014). In 2020, the unemployment rate was 8.5% in Lithuania.

IV. Political System and Administrative Structure

11. On 11 March 1990, Lithuania became the first Soviet Republic to declare itself an independent country. The Constitution of the Republic of Lithuania came into force on 2 November 1992. Article 1 of the Constitution states that 'The State of Lithuania shall be an independent democratic republic'.[1] According to the explanation by the Constitutional Court, Lithuania is a unitary democratic parliamentary republic with elements of a semi-presidential republic.

12. The Parliament, called '*Seimas*', has 141 members that are elected for a four-year term. About seventy-one of the members are elected in single-member districts, and the other seventy members are elected in the nationwide vote using proportional representation by party lists. A party must receive at least 5% of the national vote to be represented in the *Seimas*.

1. The Constitution of the Republic of Lithuania, Vilnius, 2016.

13. The President of Lithuania is the head of state of the country. The president is elected directly by the population for a five-year term and can serve a maximum of two terms consecutively. The president, with the approval of the *Seimas*, is first responsible for appointing the Prime Minister. Upon the Prime Minister's nomination, the president also appoints, under the recommendation of the Prime Minister, the government, as well as a number of other top civil servants and the judges for all courts. Among the duties specified in the Constitution, the president serves as the commander-in-chief, oversees foreign and security policy, addresses political problems of foreign and domestic affairs, proclaims states of emergency, signs and promulgates the laws adopted by the *Seimas*.

14. The Prime Minister of Lithuania is the head of the government of the country, appointed by the president and approved by the *Seimas*. The Prime Minister, within fifteen days of being appointed, is responsible for choosing the ministers, who will be approved by the president. The Prime Minister is in charge of the management of national affairs of the country, maintains homeland security, carries out the laws and resolutions of the *Seimas* and the decrees of the president, maintains diplomatic relations with foreign countries and international organisations, and performs other duties specified in the Constitution. The government consists of fourteen ministers chosen by the Prime Minister and appointed by the president.

15. Lithuania is divided into ten counties that are further subdivided into sixty municipalities of three types: forty-three district municipalities, eight city municipalities and nine municipalities. Municipalities consist of 546 elderships. Municipalities are the most important administrative units. The election of municipality councils occurs once every four years. Each municipality has its own elected government. Mayors are elected directly since 2015. The council appoints elders to govern the elderships.

16. Lithuania is a member of the United Nations (1991), the International Monetary Fund (1992), the Council of Europe (1993), the World Trade Organization (2001), NATO (2004), the European Union (2004).

V. The Judicial System

17. The system of courts, their competence, the system of court organisation, activity, administration; the system of autonomy of courts; the status of judges, their appointment, career, liability; other issues related to the judicial activities are regulated by the Constitution, the Law on Courts[2] and other legal acts. A court system of the Republic of Lithuania is made up of courts of general jurisdiction and courts of special jurisdiction.

18. The Supreme Court of Lithuania, the Court of Appeal of Lithuania, five regional courts and twelve district courts (with the territorial chambers) of general

2. Lietuvos Respublikos teismų įstatymas, *Valstybės žinios*, 2008, No. 81-3186.

jurisdiction dealing with civil and criminal cases. District courts also hear cases of administrative offences coming within their jurisdiction by law. The regional courts, the Court of Appeal, the Supreme Court of Lithuania have the Civil Division and the Criminal Division.

19. District courts are the courts of first instance for criminal, civil and administrative offence cases, cases assigned to the jurisdiction of mortgage judges, as well as cases relating to the enforcement of decisions and sentences. Judges of a district court also perform the functions of pretrial and enforcement judges, as well as any other functions assigned to a district court by law. Regional courts are first instance for criminal and civil cases assigned to its jurisdiction by law, and appeal instance for judgments, decisions, rulings and orders of district courts. The Court of Appeal is appeal instance for cases heard by regional courts as courts of first instance. It also hears requests for the recognition of decisions of foreign or international courts and foreign or international arbitration awards and their enforcement in the Republic of Lithuania, as well as performs other functions assigned to the jurisdiction of this court by law. The Supreme Court of Lithuania is the only court of cassation (third instance) for reviewing effective judgments, decisions, rulings and orders of the courts of general jurisdiction. It develops a uniform court practice in the interpretation and application of laws and other legal acts.

20. The Supreme Administrative Court of Lithuania and five regional administrative courts are courts of special jurisdiction hearing disputes arising from administrative legal relations.

21. A regional administrative court is the court of special jurisdiction established for hearing complaints (petitions) in respect of administrative acts and acts of commission or omission (failure to perform duties) by entities of public and internal administration. Regional administrative courts hear disputes in the field of public administration, deal with issues relating, for example, to the lawfulness of regulatory administrative acts and tax disputes. The Supreme Administrative Court is first and final instance for administrative cases assigned to its jurisdiction by law. It is appeal instance for cases concerning decisions, rulings and orders of regional administrative courts, as well as for cases involving administrative offences from decisions of district courts. The Supreme Administrative Court develops a uniform practice of administrative courts in the interpretation and application of laws and other legal acts.

22. The Constitutional Court ensures the supremacy of the Constitution within the legal system as well as constitutional justice by deciding whether the laws and other legal acts adopted by the *Seimas* are in conformity with the Constitution, and whether the acts adopted by the President of the Republic or the government are in compliance with the Constitution and laws.[3] The Constitutional Court decides the

3. Lietuvos Respublikos Konstitucinio Teismo įstatymas, *Valstybės žinios*, 1993, No. 6-120.

constitutionality issues of enacted laws and other legal acts (*a posteriori* control). The Constitutional Court of Lithuania consists of nine justices, each appointed for a single nine-year term office.

23. The right to file a petition with the Constitutional Court concerning the constitutionality of a legal act is vested in: (1) the government, groups consisting of at least one-fifth of all members of the *Seimas*, and the courts for cases concerning a law or other act adopted by the *Seimas*; (2) groups consisting of at least one-fifth of all members of the *Seimas* and the courts for cases concerning an act of the President of the Republic; and (3) groups consisting of at least one-fifth of all members of the *Seimas*, the courts and the President of the Republic for cases concerning governmental acts. Moreover, since 1 September 2019, every person has the right to apply to the Constitutional Court regarding the constitutionality of laws of the Republic of Lithuania and other legal acts adopted by parliament, also legal acts of the President of the Republic and Government, '*if the decision based on them violated the constitutional rights or freedoms of that person and that person has exhausted all legal remedies*'.[4] The Constitutional Court gives rulings on these issues. Rulings of the Constitutional Court are final, not subject to appeal, have the same power as law and are obligatory.

24. The Constitutional Court also gives the following conclusions: (1) whether there were violations of election laws during the elections of the President of the Republic and of members of the *Seimas*, (2) whether the state of health of the President of the Republic allows him to continue to hold office, (3) whether international treaties signed by the Republic of Lithuania are not in conflict with the Constitution, and (4) whether concrete actions of members of the *Seimas* and State officials against whom an impeachment case has been instituted are in conflict with the Constitution.

§2. Criminal Law, Criminal Justice and Criminal Science

I. Definitions of Criminal Law

A. Criminal Law

25. Criminal law is a branch of public law that has the purpose of defending human and citizen rights and freedoms as well as the public and State's interests against criminal acts. Lithuanian criminal law may be described as a system of legal norms defining criminal acts, penal sanctions (punishments as well as penal, reformative and compulsory medical measures), grounds for and conditions of criminal liability, the establishment of procedural rules for establishment of criminal liability (pretrial investigation, trial, appeal and cassation procedure, etc.) and rules on the execution of punishment.

4. Lietuvos Respublikos Konstitucijos 106 ir 107 straipsnių pakeitimo įstatymas, TAR, 2019, No. 2019-05330.

26. Lithuanian's criminal law consists of substantive criminal law, law on criminal procedure (including international assistance in criminal matters) and law on the execution of punishments.

B. Substantive Criminal Law

27. Substantive criminal law defines which acts are crimes and misdemeanours, prohibits them, establishes punishments, penal, reformative and compulsory medical measures for the criminal acts. Moreover, it establishes grounds for and conditions of criminal liability as well as the grounds for and conditions of releasing the persons who have committed criminal acts from criminal liability or a punishment. Lithuanian substantive criminal law is fully codified in the Criminal Code of Lithuania (2000).[5]

28. In Lithuania, substantive criminal law is combined with an autonomous law on administrative violations, which defines which acts are administrative offences and prohibits them, establishes penalties and administrative measures for the administrative offences. Moreover, it establishes grounds for and conditions of administrative liability as well as administrative procedure for offences. All these regulations can be found in the Code of Administrative Offences of Lithuania (2015).[6]

C. Criminal Procedure

29. Law on criminal procedure contains rules concerning the organisation of the courts, the prosecution, the police and other pretrial investigation institutions, and the bar, as well as rules for pretrial investigation, trial, appeal and cassation in criminal cases, etc. The most significant rules of criminal procedure are codified and contained in the Code of Criminal Procedure of Lithuania (2002).[7] However, the Code of Criminal Procedure does not regulate all procedural legal aspects. Certain provisions of the criminal procedural law are contained in other legal acts, which regulate the legal status of the institutions and individuals that implements the procedural functions (e.g., the Law of Courts,[8] the Law on Police,[9] the Law on the

5. Lietuvos Respublikos baudžiamasis kodeksas, *Valstybės žinios*, 2000, No. 89-2741.
6. Lietuvos Respublikos administracinių nusižengimų kodeksas, TAR, 2015, No. 11216.
7. Lietuvos Respublikos baudžiamojo proceso kodeksas, *Valstybės žinios*, 2002, No. 37-1341.
8. Lietuvos Respublikos teismų įstatymas, *Valstybės žinios*, 2008, No. 81-3186.
9. Lietuvos Respublikos policijos įstatymas, TAR, 2015, No. 10818.

Bar,[10] the Law on Prosecution Service,[11] the Law on Special Investigation Service,[12] the Law on Financial Crime Investigation Service[13]) or some other relationships which are related to criminal procedure (e.g., the Law on Electronic Communications,[14] Code of Civil Procedure,[15] Civil Code[16]). Moreover, some rules on the collection and use of probative information in criminal procedure are regulated by the Law on Criminal Intelligence.[17]

30. Regulations concerning international assistance in criminal matters may be found in the Code of Criminal Procedure or in a special separate Law on Mutual Recognition and Enforcement of the European Union Member States Court Decisions in Criminal Matters.[18]

D. Punishment Execution

31. Law on punishment execution contains rules concerning the execution of all punishments provided in the Criminal Code (CC) for physical and legal persons: imprisonment, life imprisonment, arrest, restriction of liberty, fine and community service as well as fine, restriction of operation and liquidation of legal persons respectively. The most significant rules of punishment's execution are contained in the Code of Punishment Execution of Lithuania (2002).[19] The Code of Punishment Execution does not regulate all aspects of the punishment's execution. Certain provisions of the punishment execution law are contained in other legal acts that regulate probation aspects – most notably, the Law on Probation (2012)[20] – as well as the legal status of the state and private institutions, which executes the punishments (e.g., the Law on Activities of Correctional Officers[21] and the Law on Bailiffs[22]).

32. Punishment execution is administered by the Prison department. The Ministry of Justice is politically responsible for it.

33. On prison system and probation in Lithuania, *see also* paragraphs 51–54.

---

10. Lietuvos Respublikos advokatūros įstatymas, *Valstybės žinios*, 2004, No. 50-1632.
11. Lietuvos Respublikos prokuratūros įstatymas, *Valstybės žinios*, 2003, No. 42-1919.
12. Lietuvos Respublikos specialiųjų tyrimų tarnybos įstatymas, TAR, 2017, No. 21647.
13. Lietuvos Respublikos finansinių nusikaltimų tyrimo tarnybos įstatymas, *Valstybės žinios*, 2002, No. 33-1250.
14. Lietuvos Respublikos elektroninių ryšių įstatymas, *Valstybės žinios*, 2004, No. 69-2382.
15. Lietuvos Respublikos civilinio proceso kodeksas, *Valstybės žinios*, 2002, No. 36-1340.
16. Lietuvos Respublikos civilinis kodeksas, *Valstybės žinios*, 2000, No. 74-2262.
17. Lietuvos Respublikos kriminalinės žvalgybos įstatymas, *Valstybės žinios*, 2012, No. 122-6093.
18. Lietuvos Respublikos įstatymas dėl Europos Sąjungos valstybių narių sprendimų baudžiamosiose bylose tarpusavio pripažinimo ir vykdymo, TAR, 2014, No. 17299.
19. Lietuvos Respublikos bausmių vykdymo kodeksas, *Valstybės žinios*, 2002, No. 73-3084.
20. Lietuvos Respublikos probacijos įstatymo Nr. 1860 pakeitimo įstatymas, TAR, 2019, No. 11184.
21. Lietuvos Respublikos pataisos pareigūnų veiklos įstatymas, TAR, 2018, No. 12055.
22. Lietuvos Respublikos antstolių įstatymas, *Valstybės žinios*, 2002, No. 53-2042.

II. Characteristics of Criminal Law

34. The main purpose of criminal law is to defend human and citizen rights and freedoms, public and the State interests against criminal acts. Lithuanian criminal law doctrine states that criminal law fulfils functions of repression, information, special and general prevention.[23] Having a repressive function means that offenders (physical persons or legal entities) who commit criminal acts are punished. The information function signifies that society should be informed about the prohibitions and obligations provided in criminal laws. Special prevention function means that offenders are kept from committing further criminal acts by realisation of criminal liability through release from criminal liability or imposition of punishment. General prevention function means that other members of the society are kept from committing criminal acts by imposing punishment.

35. State criminal policy is implemented through the adoption and application of criminal law. Lithuanian criminal policy is governed, *inter alia*, by the principles of *ultima ratio*, natural justice and proportionality. In particular, according to the principle of *ultima ratio*, only to the most dangerous behaviours should be criminalised. The Constitutional Court has emphasised that:

> [I]n a democratic state under the rule of law the legislator has the right and duty to prohibit by means of laws such deeds that may essentially harm the interests of persons, society or the state or there might be a threat of such harm to appear. The laws define as to what deeds are considered crimes and establish punishment for their commission. [...] The dangerousness of criminal acts are determined inter alia by the values which are encroached upon by means of these acts.[24]

The content of the principles of natural justice and proportionality in criminal policy was also disclosed in the case law of the Constitutional Court, which provides that:

- the principle of natural justice consolidated in the Constitution presupposes that punishments established by a penal law must be just; punishments and their sizes must be differentiated in a penal law, while taking account of the danger of criminal acts;[25]
- the constitutional principles of justice and a state under the rule of law imply that the measures established by the state for violations of law must be proportionate (adequate) to the violation of law, they must be in line with the

23. Baudžiamoji teisė: Bendroji dalis, Vilnius, Eugrimas, 2003, p. 25–28.
24. Decision of the Constitutional Court of Lithuania of 4 Jun. 2012, *Valstybės žinios*, 2012, No. 64-3246.
25. Decision of the Constitutional Court of Lithuania of 8 Jun. 2009, *Valstybės žinios*, 2009, No. 69-2798.

legitimate and generally important objectives sought, they may not restrict the person clearly more than it is necessary in order to reach these objectives;[26]

- it is not allowed to establish any such legal regulation (punishments or their sizes) in a penal law on the basis of which the court, while taking account of all circumstances of a case and applying the penal law, would not be able to individualise the punishment which is imposed on a concrete person for a concrete criminal act.[27]

III. Overview of the Criminal Justice System

A. The Police and Other Law Enforcement Agencies

36. The main police institution in Lithuania is the Lithuanian Police. The Lithuanian Police is a statutory organisation ensuring public safety and order, preventing, detecting and investigating criminal acts and other violations of law as well as rendering other social aid for the people. The police activity is regulated by the Law on Police.[28]

37. The general management and control of the Lithuanian Police is the responsibility of the Police Commissioner General of Lithuania, who is appointed for a period of five years and dismissed by the President of the Republic by the suggestion of the Minister of Interior and approved by the government. The Police Commissioner General is directly subordinated to the Minister of Interior and accountable to the President of the Republic.

38. The Lithuanian Police consists of the Police department, territorial police units, specialised police units and the police professional training institution. The Police department is a police agency assisting the Police Commissioner General of Lithuania to develop the strategy for the police activity and control its implementation, as well as to organise the management of the territorial police units. Police department ensures the implementation of the police functions; controls and coordinates the activity of subordinated police units; gives them recommendations and instructions; develops and implements common police activity and personnel policy of the subordinated police units, etc.

39. The territorial police units carry out the police functions in the established territory. The territory police units consist of ten County Police Headquarters and their subunits (forty-nine Local Police Units). The County Police Headquarters are

26. Decision of the Constitutional Court of Lithuania of 17 Sep. 2008, *Valstybės žinios*, 2008, No. 108-4136.
27. Decision of the Constitutional Court of Lithuania of 10 Jun. 2003, *Valstybės žinios*, 2003, No. 57-2552.
28. Lietuvos Respublikos policijos įstatymas, TAR, 2015, No. 10818.

established in the county centres and ensure the implementation of the police tasks in the whole county territory. Local Police Units are established in the administrative centres of municipalities to serve within the territory of appropriate municipalities. Among its functions, the Local Police Unit ensures public safety and order, prevent, detect and investigate criminal acts and other violations of law.

40. The specialised police units are the police units established on a non-territorial principle, which carry out certain special police functions. They are the Lithuanian Criminal Police Bureau, the Lithuanian Police Forensic Science Centre, the Lithuanian Police Antiterrorist Operations Team 'ARAS', the Lithuanian Road Police Service and the Lithuanian Police School.

41. There were 7,849 policemen/police officers (286 police officers for 100,000 inhabitants) in Lithuania on 1 January 2020.

42. Article 165 of the Code of Criminal Procedure prescribes that the main pre-trial investigation institution is the police. In respect of criminal acts, which come to their notice when discharging the primary functions provided for in the laws regulating their activities, the other specialised pretrial investigation institutions are the State Border Guard Service, the Special Investigations Service, the Military Police, the Financial Crimes Investigations Service, the State Fire Prevention Service, the Prison department and the Customs. The division of responsibilities among all pre-trial investigation institutions is prescribed in the law. Moreover, Prosecutor General Recommendation on the distribution of the pretrial investigation of criminal acts between pretrial investigation authorities[29] provides the lists of criminal acts, for which concrete institution is responsible for the pretrial investigation.

B. The Prosecution Service

43. Article 118 of the Constitution of Lithuania provides that:

> a pre-trial investigation shall be organised and directed, and charges on behalf of the State in criminal cases shall be upheld, by the prosecutors. In cases established by law, prosecutors shall defend the rights and legitimate interests of the person, society, and the State. When performing their functions, prosecutors shall be independent and shall obey only the law. The Prosecutor's Office of the Republic of Lithuania shall be the Office of the Prosecutor General and territorial prosecutor's offices.[30]

29. Generalinio prokuroro rekomendacija 'Dėl nusikalstamų veikų tyrimo paskirstymo ikiteisminio tyrimo įstaigoms', *Valstybės žinios*, 2008, No. 94-3712.
30. The Constitution of the Republic of Lithuania, Vilnius, 2016.

The prosecutors are, in accordance with the Code of Criminal Procedure, the Prosecutor General of Lithuania and subordinate prosecutors, as well as the European Delegated Prosecutor and European Prosecutor participating in criminal proceedings in the Republic of Lithuania for matters falling within their authority. The General Prosecutor shall be appointed for a term of five years and dismissed from office by the President of the Republic with the approval of the *Seimas*. The Prosecutor General may be appointed to the same office for not more than two successive terms. Deputy Prosecutors General shall be appointed and dismissed by the President of the Republic on the recommendation of the Prosecutor General.

44. The Prosecutor General's Office is comprised of departments (e.g., the Department of Organised Crime and Corruption Investigation; the Department of Criminal Prosecution) and divisions (e.g., the Division of the Protection of Public Interests, Division of Internal Investigations). The structure of the Prosecutor General's Office is determined by the Prosecutor General. The Prosecutor General's Office is headed by the Prosecutor General and Deputy Prosecutors General acting within their remit.

45. Territorial prosecutor's office consists of five regional prosecutor offices in Vilnius, Kaunas, Klaipėda, Šiauliai and Panevėžys and ten district prosecutor's offices. All district prosecutor's offices have forty-four local units. Territorial prosecutor's offices, their status, structure, remit and territories of jurisdiction (depending on the territories of jurisdiction of regional and district courts) are established by the Prosecutor General. A territorial prosecutor's office is headed by the chief prosecutor and deputy chief prosecutors. According to the Law on Prosecution Service,[31] territorial prosecutor's offices have several functions, most importantly they: (1) organise and lead a pretrial investigation; (2) conduct a pretrial investigation; (3) control activities of pretrial investigation officers in criminal proceedings; (4) prosecute on behalf of the State in criminal proceedings; (5) supervise the delivery of judgments for enforcement; (6) coordinate actions of pretrial investigation bodies in the investigation of criminal acts; (7) defend the public interest; (8) prepare requests for legal assistance to be submitted to foreign state and international institutions and respond to requests for legal assistance of foreign state and international institutions.

46. A person may be admitted to the Prosecution Service and appointed to a prosecutor's position, provided that he/she is a citizen of good repute of the Republic of Lithuania, is proficient in the State language, has higher university-based legal education and holds a bachelor's and master's degree in law or a lawyer's professional qualification degree, has three years' professional experience in law and has passed the qualification examination of candidates for the prosecutor's post.

47. There were 644 prosecutors in Lithuania on 1 January 2020.

---

31. Lietuvos Respublikos prokuratūros įstatymas, *Valstybės žinios*, 2003, No. 42-1919.

C. Investigating Judges

48. Lithuanian criminal procedure provides a pretrial judge. Article 19 of the Code of Criminal Procedure states that 'a pretrial judge shall be a judge of a district court, appointed by the Chairman of a district court to conduct procedural actions prescribed by law and render decisions'. According to Article 173 of the Code of Criminal Procedure, it is in the pretrial judge's functions: '(1) to impose and order the application of procedural coercive measures; (2) to swear and examine witnesses and victims; (3) to examine suspects; (4) to adopt or approve the prosecutor's decisions to terminate a pretrial investigation; (5) to approve the prosecutor's decisions to resume the terminated pretrial investigation; (6) to examine the complaints of the parties to the proceedings concerning the actions of the pretrial investigation officers and the prosecutor'. These procedural actions shall be performed by the pretrial judge subject to an appropriate request from the prosecutor who shall submit it either on its own initiative or on the initiative of a party to the proceedings. The pretrial judge may not decline to examine the prosecutor's requests. Where the pretrial judge declines to grant the prosecutor's request, he/she shall deliver a reasoned ruling pertaining to it. The pretrial judge shall also perform procedural actions upon a request of the trial court. The pretrial judge has no right to perform any actions on his/her own initiative.

D. Trial Jurisdictions

49. A district court is first instance for criminal cases. A regional court is first instance for criminal cases assigned to its jurisdiction by law, and appeal instance for judgments and rulings of district courts. The Court of Appeal is appeal instance for cases heard by regional courts as courts of first instance. The Supreme Court of Lithuania is the only court of cassation instance for reviewing effective judgments and rulings (*see also* paragraphs 18 and 19).

50. There were 682 judges of the courts of general jurisdiction in Lithuania on 1 January 2021.

E. Prison System and After-Care

51. On 1 September 2000, in the course of the reform of the legal system, the penal enforcement system was transferred from the jurisdiction of the Ministry of Interior to the Ministry of Justice. The Department of Correction Affairs regained the name it had had during the interwar period of the independent Lithuania: at present it bears the official name of the Prison department under the Ministry of Justice of the Republic of Lithuania.

52. There are eight penal institutions subordinate to the Prison department enforcing pretrial detention sanctions and custodial sentences imposed by court.

Penal institutions are divided into four correctional houses, one correctional house-open prison, one juvenile correctional house-remand prison, two remand prisons and one central prison hospital.

53. Since 2017, the Lithuanian probation service, which includes five regional probation services, is responsible for the execution of sentences alternative to imprisonment (including suspended imprisonment) and the supervision of persons released early from correctional institutions. The Training Centre of the Prison Department organises the training of a newly hired staff of the institutions subordinate to the Prison department.

54. There were 3,318 officials (2,754 of them in correctional institutions) working in the penal enforcement system in Lithuania on 1 January 2020.

F. The Bar

55. Legal services which include legal consultations (legal advice), drafting of legal documents, representation on legal matters, defence and representation in legal proceedings when these actions are carried out for remuneration may be provided by advocates (as well as lawyers who are nationals of Member States of the European Union, countries of the European Economic Area or the Swiss Confederation). The status, competence, rights and duties of the advocates are regulated by the mentioned Law on Bar.

56. A natural person shall be recognised as an advocate provided he/she: (1) is a national of the Republic of Lithuania or a Member State of the European Union; (2) holds a bachelor's or master's degree in law, or a lawyer's professional qualification degree (one-cycle university education in law); (3) has a record of at least five years of service in the legal profession or has served an apprenticeship as an advocate's assistant for a period of at least two years; (4) is of high moral character; (5) has proficiency in the state language; (6) has passed the advocate's qualification examination (this requirement is not applicable to persons who have a record of at least seven years of work as a judge or holds a degree of doctor or habilitated doctor in social sciences (law)); (7) has no health disorders that would prevent him from performing the advocate's duties. The right to practise as an advocate shall be enjoyed by advocates entered in the List of Practising Advocates of Lithuania. An advocate shall be entered on the List of Practising Advocates of Lithuania when he/she: (1) has sworn the oath; (2) is covered by insurance of an advocate or a professional partnership of advocates against professional civil liability; (3) is ready to practise as an advocate individually, on the basis of a partnership without establishing a legal person or by establishing a legal person (a professional partnership of advocates).

57. An advocate shall also be entitled to provide services for remuneration as an administrator of bankruptcy, a lobbyist, a liquidator, a curator, an executor of a will, a trustee of property, a patent trustee, an arbiter, a mediator, a conciliator, etc. An advocate may be a member of the managing or supervisory body of a legal person, but he/she cannot receive any remuneration, with the exception of bonuses.

58. Every advocate shall be a member of the Lithuanian Bar Association. The self-government bodies of the Lithuanian Bar Association are: (1) the General Meeting of Advocates; (2) the Council of the Lithuanian Bar; (3) the Court of Honour of Advocates; (4) the Auditing Commission.

59. The conditions of and the procedure for the provision of State-guaranteed legal aid are regulated by Law on State-guaranteed legal aid.[32]

60. There were 2,245 advocates in Lithuania on 1 January 2020.

61. Only advocates may act as defence counsel. Assistants of advocates also may act as a defence counsel, but only if there is no objection from the accused. On the status of the defence counsel, *see* paragraphs 727–732.

G. *Statistical Overview*

62. The crime statistics in Lithuania[33] indicate that 46,306 criminal acts (3,886 of which misdemeanours) were registered in 2020 (59,075 criminal acts, 3,125 of which misdemeanours, were registered in 2016).[34] Approximately, 50% of these criminal acts were all types of property crimes and misdemeanours (e.g., 10,671 thefts (21,348 in 2016), frauds – 2,685 (2,870 in 2016), robberies – 479 (1,342 in 2016), destruction or damage of property – 2,197 (2,399 in 2016)).

63. About 2,843 of the registered crimes were serious and grave (on serious and grave crime, *see* paragraphs 389, 390). Among them, 110 intentional murders with attempts (161 – in 2016), 150 intentional severe health impairments (216 – in 2016) and 72 rapes (110 – in 2016) were registered.

64. The clear-up rate was around 68.4% in 2020 (55% in 2015) but only 25% for thefts and 70% for murders in 2020 (23 and 70% in 2015 respectively).

65. In 2020, a total of 16,082 physical persons and 22 legal persons were sentenced in Lithuania (15,490 physical persons and 18 legal persons – in 2016). Physical persons were sentenced to: community service – 1,023 (1,122 in 2016), fine – 4,918 (3,655 in 2016), liberty restriction – 4,074 (4,040 in 2016), arrest – 2,934 (1,602 in 2016) and imprisonment – 3,389, of which imprisonment was suspended – 975 (5,090 in 2016 (of which imprisonment was suspended – 1,473).

32. Lietuvos Respublikos valstybės garantuojamos teisinės pagalbos įstatymas, *Valstybės žinios*, 2005, No. 18-572.
33. The statistics for 2020 was collected from the annual reports of the Supreme Court of Lithuania, the Prosecutor General Office and Prison Department under the Ministry of Justice.
34. On the statistics in 2016 *see*: Crime and Law Enforcement Activity in 2015, Vilnius, 2017.

66. There were 5,320 prisoners (581 of them were detainees, 22 – juveniles and 252 – women, 111 – serving life sentence) in Lithuania on 1 January 2020 (6,815 prisoners in 2016). In 2020, the number of prisoners was 220 per 100,000 inhabitants, which is one of the highest within the European Union Member States (255 in 2015). In 2020, the average sentence length imposed by court judgment was seven years three months and fourteen days (six years five months and twenty-eight days in 2015).

67. In 2020, 984 prisoners were granted early release from a correctional institution (826 in 2016).

68. In 2016, 851 prisoners (951 in 2015) had mental and behavioural disorders due to drugs or psychotropic substances, 247 (256 in 2015) were human immunodeficiency virus (HIV)-positive persons and 59 (52 in 2015) had AIDS.

69. In 2020, there were 15,417 sentenced persons under the supervision of the regional probation services (8,536 (of which 484 juveniles) in 2015).

IV. Trends Within Criminal Justice

70. During the period from 1 May 2003 until 1 January 2021, the *Seimas* passed eighty-eight laws amending and supplementing the CC: sixteen laws amended and supplemented only the provisions of the General Part of the CC, forty-six laws – only the provisions of the Special Part of the CC and twenty-six laws – the provisions of the General and Special Part of the CC.[35] Moreover, during 2003–2016, fifty Articles of the General Part (47.2% of all Articles of General Part) of the CC were modified (amended, supplemented or repealed) at least once; fifty-six Articles (52.8%) remained unchanged. Furthermore, 40% of all amendments and supplements of the General Part were made in the chapters regulating punishment in general.[36] The Special Part of the CC during 2003–2016 was modified even more: 186 articles out of 276 articles of the Special Part of the CC (two-thirds of the articles of the Special Part) were amended, supplemented or repealed at least once. In total, 62% of all articles of the CC were changed at least once. A significant number of the amendments and supplements of the CC were made in order to comply with the new requirements imposed by international and European Union (EU) laws, the decisions of the CJEU and European Court on Human Rights (ECtHR) as well as the case law of the Constitutional Court of Lithuania and the Supreme Court of Lithuania.

35. Prapiestis J., Švedas G., Prapiestis D. Teisėkūra ir konstitucinė jurisprudencija Lietuvos Respublikos baudžiamojo kodekso Specialiosios dalies klausimais, Teisė, 2021, No. 119, p. 34.
36. Švedas G., Veršekys P., Levon J., Prapiestis D. Lietuvos Respublikos baudžiamojo kodekso bendrosios dalies vientisumo ir naujovių suderinimo iššūkiai, Vilnius, Vilniaus universiteto leidykla, 2017, p. 80, 83.

71. The amendments and supplements related to the system and separate types of penal measures, punishment imposition rules and statute of limitation of a judgment of convictions can be considered the most significant ones.

72. The list of penal measures (which consisted of a prohibition to exercise a special right, compensation for or elimination of property damage, unpaid work, payment of a contribution to the fund of crime victims and confiscation of property) was amended several times: in 2008, – prohibition to approach the victim and participation in the programmes addressing violent behaviour;[37] in 2010, – extended confiscation of property, which may also be imposed on legal entities;[38] in 2011, – deprivation of public rights and deprivation of the right to be employed in a certain position or to engage in certain type of activities;[39] in 2020, – obligation to notify a change of place of residence or departure from the place of residence.[40] In 2015, the Seimas extended the content of the prohibition to approach the victim and renamed this penal measure into the obligation to live separately from the victim's and/or not approach the victim closer than a prescribed distance. [41]

73. In 2015, the *Seimas* changed the CC rules, under which punishment imposition rules for repeat offender were mitigated; provided a possibility to impose a non-custodial sentence not only for a person prosecuted for the first time for a minor or less serious premeditated crime, but also in case of all negligent crimes; extended possibilities to apply suspended sentence also to the person who has committed a serious offence.[42] It should be noted that in 2017, the possibility to apply a suspended sentence to the person who has committed a serious offence was abolished.[43]

74. In 2010, the statute of limitations of a judgment of conviction (Article 95 of the CC) was significantly extended. First, the terms of statute of limitations of a judgment of a conviction were extended: three years (instead of two years), in the event of commission of a misdemeanour; eight years (instead of five years) – in the event of commission of a negligent or minor premeditated crime; twelve years (instead of eight years) – in the event of commission of a less serious premeditated

---

37. Lietuvos Respublikos baudžiamojo kodekso 42, 67, 129, 135, 138 straipsnių pakeitimo ir papildymo bei Kodekso papildymo 72(1), 72(2) straipsniais įstatymas, *Valstybės žinios*, 2008, No. 73-2796.
38. Lietuvos Respublikos baudžiamojo kodekso 3, 67, 72, 190 straipsnių pakeitimo ir papildymo ir Kodekso papildymo 72(3), 189(1) straipsniais įstatymas, *Valstybės žinios*, 2010, No. 145-7439.
39. Lietuvos Respublikos baudžiamojo kodekso 7, 42, 67, 68, 74, 123(1), 125, 126, 134, 142, 144, 176, 177, 204, 205, 210, 211, 213, 220, 223, 225, 226, 227, 228, 228(1), 229, 230, 253(1), 255, 257, 263, 268, 278, 281, 297, 308(1) straipsnių pakeitimo ir papildymo, Kodekso papildymo 68(1), 68(2) straipsniais ir 44, 45 straipsnių pripažinimo netekusiais galios įstatymas, *Valstybės žinios*, 2011, No. 81-3959.
40. Lietuvos Respublikos baudžiamojo kodekso 42, 67 straipsnių pakeitimo ir Kodekso papildymo 72(4) straipsniu įstatymas, TAR, 2020-11-18, No. 2020-24238.
41. Lietuvos Respublikos baudžiamojo kodekso 42, 67, 72(1) straipsnių ir priedo pakeitimo įstatymas, TAR, 2015, No. 2015-07563.
42. Lietuvos Respublikos baudžiamojo kodekso 27, 38, 39, 55, 56, 60, 62, 75, 179 ir 187 straipsnių pakeitimo įstatymas, TAR, 2015, No. 2015-04087.
43. Lietuvos Respublikos baudžiamojo kodekso 43, 47, 54, 62, 63, 64, 68-1, 68-2, 71, 75, 90, 226 ir 227 straipsnių pakeitimo įstatymas, TAR, 2017, No. 2017-15859.

crime, etc.[44] Second, a provision was established that in case where a juvenile was a victim of crimes against human health (Chapter XVIII of the CC) and liberty (Chapter XX of the CC) and crimes and misdemeanours against freedom of personal sexual self-determination and inviolability (Chapter XXI of the CC), children and family (Chapter XXIII of the CC) or morality (Chapter XLIV of the CC), the term of statute of limitations of a judgment of conviction shall be prolonged until the victim reaches the age of twenty-five years.

75. Meanwhile, during 2003–2016, the Special Part of the CC was supplemented by the following new crimes, for example: enforced disappearance (Article 100(1) of the CC), separation of children (Article 100(2) of the CC), use for forced labour (Article 147(1) of the CC), satisfaction of sexual desires by violating a minor's freedom of sexual self-determination and/or inviolability (Article 151(1) of the CC), grooming of a person under the age of 16 years (Article 152(1) of the CC), creation and activities of the groups and organisations aiming at discriminating a group of persons or inciting against it (Article 170(1) of the CC), public condonation of international crimes committed by the USSR or Nazi Germany against the Republic of Lithuania or inhabitants thereof, denial or gross trivialisation of crimes (Article 170(2) of the CC), illegal enrichment (Article 189(1) of the CC), incitement of terrorism (Article 250(1) of the CC), piracy (Article 251(1) of the CC).

76. In recent years, there have been numerous reform proposals in the scholarship relating to substantive criminal law, for example, concerning the decriminalisation of the preparation to commit a serious or grave offence, introduction of new types of punishment for legal entity (such as exclusion from entitlement to public benefit or aid and judicial supervision),[45] revision of the concept of criminal association by including additional elements in it that would *inter alia* bring more conformity with the requirements of the EU legislation – (a) a pre-agreement to engage in joint criminal activity; (b) presence of a leader or leaders; (c) intention to obtain, directly or indirectly, a financial or other material benefits,[46] etc.

§3. The Historical Background

I. Code of Casimir of 1468

77. Across the Grand Duchy of Lithuania, the criminal act in force was the Code of Casimir (1468).[47] It consisted of twenty-five articles and was intended to protect

44. Lietuvos Respublikos baudžiamojo kodekso 95 straipsnio pakeitimo bei papildymo, Kodekso papildymo 170(2) straipsniu ir Kodekso priedo papildymo įstatymas, *Valstybės žinios*, 2010, No. 75-3792.
45. Švedas, G. Europos Sąjungos baudžiamoji teisė ir jos įtaka Lietuvos baudžiamosios teisės bendrosios dalies institutams // Europos Sąjungos teisės įtaka Lietuvos teisinei sistemai, Vilnius, 2014, p. 154.
46. Gutauskas, A. Organizuoto nusikalstamumo baudžiamasis teisinis vertinimas pagal naują baudžiamąjį kodeksą, Jurisprudencija, 2003, No. 45(37), p. 34.
47. Prepared according to Baudžiamoji teisė: Bendroji dalis, Vilnius, Eugrimas, 2003, p. 73–74.

property. The Code's criminal law norms provided for liability for theft, arbitrary logging and mugging. The concept of theft, in addition to stealing the usual items, also covered the appropriation of unfree peasants. Such cases like peasants fleeing from their nobles and being lodged by another person or lured away from their nobles were treated as theft. Theft was also considered to be the appropriation of a lost horse or items that after a public announcement were not withdrawn. According to the ancient perception, such things were considered to be the property of the Duke, and the person who would find and return them would be rewarded. To protect feudal forests, the Code of Casimir separately provided for liability for illegal logging.

78. According to the Code of Casimir, a person was proved guilty after being caught with stolen goods, after a voluntary confession, a confession by torture or after hearing the evidence of 'good witnesses'.

79. The Code of Casimir did not provide for the penalty for a feudal lord who committed a crime. Meanwhile, the punishment for a peasant consisted of two elements: compensation for damages and a penalty. The penalty amounted to a tribute to the court that was the stolen item, and, in case it was absent, a tribute of the value of the stolen item. Death penalty by hanging was practised in case of repeated crime or when the value of the stolen items was more than a half *kappa* of *groschen*. This amount consisted of a stolen cow, a horse and a steed.

II. Lithuanian Statutes of 1529, 1566 and 1588

80. The Lithuanian Statute plays a special role among the Lithuanian legal memorials. It underwent three editions in 1529, 1566 and 1588 (known as the First, the Second and the Third Lithuanian Statutes).[48] Altogether, they form a highly significant legislation body of the organisation of private and public life in Lithuania. From a criminal law perspective, the Statutes reflected a new stage of development that revealed the State's approach to an offence and penalty as the institution of public law.

81. From a criminal law perspective, the First Lithuanian Statute is close to the codes of a composition system. A victim had to find, prosecute and prove his offender guilty. On the contrary, the culprit was required to compensate for damages immediately. However, the concept of guilt is not directly linked with the liability of the offender. Therefore, the compensation for the damages was not only the responsibility of the offender but also of his/her family members: they were obligated to compensate for all the damages and then to seek redress from the offender. The victim was authorised to forgive the whole or part of the caused damage and to come to terms with the offender. Another evaluation of the offence is also revealed in the First Lithuanian Statute. The offence is perceived not only as a private interest or a collision of private interests but also as an act jeopardising the government

48. Prepared according to Baudžiamoji teisė: Bendroji dalis, Vilnius, Eugrimas, 2003, p. 74–76.

and society. Therefore, in addition to the private criminal damage, in certain cases, the Statute also recognises the offence as against the public interests. Accordingly, in addition to the compensation for the damages, this Statute also provides for compensation in favour of the government. The public nature of the offence is also testified by the criminal liability for crimes such as high treason, retreat from a battlefield and desertion of a sentry post if it was useful to an enemy. Some of the crimes' roots were linked to the Catholic beliefs and the perception of sin. The First Statute contains articles where the commission of a certain crime is associated with the opposition to God.

82. Meanwhile, in the Second and Third Lithuanian Statutes, it is emphasised that private damage is considered to be a crime against society, therefore, the government must ensure that these offences would not go unpunished. For instance, they provided for the criminal liability for sedition, encroachment on the health or life of the Duke, withdrawal of troops and militants to the land of the enemy, collusion with an enemy and murder. The murder of a husband, wife, father, mother or a relative was considered as most serious. For the murder of a child, the punishment for the parents was obviously softer. The Statutes regulated in detail the property-related offences. The penalty for a thief depended on the value of the stolen goods and the stealing frequency. If the theft was done for the third time, the offender had to be sentenced to death. A separate criminal liability was provided for horse thievery. As in the Code of Casimir, the withdrawal of unfree person was considered theft. For example, severe penalties were provided for an arson attack on the Grand Duke's castle or the houses of the nobles, rape, or forcing a girl into marriage.

83. The penalty system evidently changed with every edition of the statute. For example, the First Statute provided for the death penalty for twenty crimes, the Second Statute for sixty times and the Third Statute even for 100 times. Physical penalties in the First Statute were provided for four times, in the Second Statute eight, and in the Third Statute twenty-four. Imprisonment in the First Statute was provided only three times, in the Second Statute thirty, and in the Third Statute forty-five times.

III. Russian Criminal Laws in Lithuania

84. At the end of the eighteenth century, most of contemporary Lithuania was annexed to Russia. Hence, the Code of criminal and corrective penalties of Russia (*Уложение о наказаниях уголовных и исправительных 1845 года*) was adopted in 1845 by the State Council and came into force on 1 May 1846 in the entire territory of the Russian Empire (except for Finland and Poland). This Criminal Statute can be described as a sort of eclectic set of various legal theory claims of Western Europe, court practices of Russia and customary law norms. The casuistic nature of the Criminal Statute is testified by the fact that, at the time of its adoption, the Statute had 2,224 articles and, in 1,857, 2,304 articles. In the Criminal Statute, definitions of misdemeanours and offences were introduced, the different stages of crime were distinguished (preparation, attempt and completed crime), the types of accomplices were recognised (accomplice, assistant, instigator, helper and perpetrator), a complex penalty system was provided for (eleven types of punishments, thirty-seven degrees of punishments).

85. In 1864, the minor crimes defined in the Criminal Statute were taken and introduced into the new law – the Charter of Penalties (*Устав о наказаниях*) – and were assigned for the investigation of magistrates (judges of peace). The remaining part was edited, shortened and, in 1866, named the Statute of Penalties (*Уложение о наказаниях*) The Military Criminal Statute (*Воинский устав о наказаниях*) which was applied to military personnel, entered into force in 1869.

IV. Criminal Laws in Independent Lithuania (1918–1940)

86. After the declaration of independence in 1918, on 16 January 1919, the Presidium of the State Council of Lithuania adopted a Temporary Law on the Organization of Lithuanian Courts and Their Work[49] (*Laikinasis Lietuvos Teismų ir jų darbo sutvarkymo įstatymas*) that contained a provision of criminal laws under which 'the Criminal Statute adopted in Russia in 1903 is considered to be the legitimate penal code'. Besides, the law indicated the articles of this statute that were invalid in Lithuania and provided another penal system, including: (a) imprisonment with hard labour; (b) simple imprisonment; (c) arrest; (d) fine. The imprisonment with hard labour was supposed to replace capital punishment; deportation and fortress imprisonment was replaced by simple imprisonment.

87. In 1903, the Criminal Statute[50] created a modern image of the criminal law by reflecting the most significant achievements of the criminal legal science in Western Europe at the beginning of the twentieth century, maintaining some Russian penal traditions. In conformity with Continental Europe's tradition, the Criminal Statute was divided in General Part (one chapter, Articles 1–72) and Special Part (thirty-five chapters, Articles 73–687). The General Part regulates the formal definition of crime, the validity of criminal law in time and area, the forms of culpability, the stages of crime and complicity issues. According to the Criminal Statute, all crimes were classified into felonies, offences and misdemeanours.

88. The Special Part of the Criminal Statute regulates every crime specifically. The majority of crimes, in accordance with the ancient Russian traditions, were greatly differentiated by special features. For instance, in the Criminal Statute, theft, robbery and extortion of property had even two chapters consisting of approximately twenty articles. Whereas, Article 585 of the Criminal Statute separately regulated a horse theft, and the second part of this article a qualified horse theft done by

49. Laikinasis Lietuvos Teismų ir jų darbo sutvarkymo įstatymas, *Vyriausybės žinios*, No. 2-3.
50. Kavolis M.; Bieliackinas S. Baudžiamasis statutas su papildomaisiais baudžiamaisiais įstatymais ir komentarais, Kaunas, 1934.

a person who had been already convicted for this offence. The order of crimes provided in the Criminal Statute is interesting: the beginning consists of chapters intended to protect the interests of the state and state institutions, then crimes against the public order and peace follow. Only chapter 22 and later chapters deal with the liability for crimes against human life, health, sexual independence and so forth. The property-related crimes (e.g., theft, robbery, extortion of property, usury) are regulated in the last chapters of the Criminal Statute.

89. Along with the Criminal Statute, other criminal legal acts were in force in Lithuania. In the *Klaipėda* Region, the German Criminal Code of 1871 (*Strafgesetzbuch*) was in force together with some additional criminal laws enacted by the Parliament of the *Klaipėda* Region. Furthermore, with the aim to protect the interests of Lithuania, in 1919 the State Council of Lithuania adopted the Special Law on State Protection, where paragraph 14 stated that, in the places where the martial law was announced, individuals could have been sentenced to death for the following crimes: (1) preparation and premeditation of armed insurrection against the independent state of Lithuania; (2) anti-state incitement of troops and society; (3) damaging of communication devices; (4) destruction of military ammunition; (5) spying or helping the enemy by providing them with food, feed, horses and so forth; (6) crimes against human life and robbery; (7) concealing, carrying, possessing weapons illegally; (8) physical resistance to state officials on duty. These laws were replaced in 1938 by a new Law to Protect the Nation and the State[51] that provided for state offences, for example, anti-state agitation, sabotage, collaboration with foreign organisations that were forbidden in Lithuania.

V. Criminal Laws During the Soviet Occupation

90. After the Soviet Union had occupied Lithuania (15 June 1940), the USSR Supreme Council Presidium adopted the ordinance 'On the provisional application of the Russian SFSR criminal, civil and labour laws in Lithuania, Latvia and Estonia' (6 November 1940). Article 3 of the ordinance established that:

> the prosecution for the crimes committed in the territory of Lithuania [...] before the introduction of the Soviet authority as well as the completion and transfer of interrogation and court cases that were brought [...] by Lithuanian [...] representatives before the introduction of the Soviet government must be implemented pursuant the CC of the Russian SFSR.[52]

The ordinance, by violating the principle of *lex retro non agit,* legalised the reversible validity of the criminal law and authorised criminal liability for crimes that were committed in another independent state by performing certain duties (judges, prosecutors and police officers) or engaging in a political activity (political party and others).

---

51. Tautai ir valstybei saugoti įstatymas, *Vyriausybės Žinios*, No. 437-3044.
52. Rusijos TFSR baudžiamasis kodeksas su pakeitimais iki 1941 m. lapkričio 15 dienos, Kaunas, 1941.

91. During the first post-war years, the criminal laws of Russian SFRS that were also applied in Lithuania underwent principal modifications following the orders of the USSR Supreme Council Presidium. On 26 May 1947, the capital punishment was abolished but, on 12 January 1950, it was introduced again. Its application was provided for the crimes of 'high treason, espionage, sabotage and subversion'. On 4 June 1947, the following two ordinances of the Supreme Council of the USSR were enacted: 'On criminal liability for crimes against the state or public property' and 'On the enhancement of the security of the personal property of citizens', by which the liability for the offence against the state or societal property was strengthened. For example, for the robbery of the state property committed repeatedly by an organised group or in a large scale, an imprisonment from ten to twenty-five years was imposed. For the same kind of robbery of cooperative or collective property, the imprisonment from eight to twenty years was imposed. For the robbery of personal property related to violence dangerous for the life or health of a person, the imprisonment from fifteen to twenty years was imposed. It is also to be noted that under these 'draconian' laws, a great number of people were sentenced to long-time imprisonment solely for taking a bag of potatoes, hay or straw from a cooperative field, or a loaf of bread from a factory. Moreover, several peasants were convicted for a failure to perform their duties (delivery of agricultural products) that were impossible to truly accomplish. There is no accurate data on the number of the convicted persons, however, some sources suggest that, during the period of 1946–1952, around 150,000 of people were convicted in Lithuania.

92. In 1958, three main acts were adopted: (1) framework of the criminal laws of the Soviet Union and allied republics; (2) law on state crimes (3) law on military crimes. Each of the republics had to prepare their own CC consisting of the framework of the criminal laws – the General Part – and the laws on the state and military crimes – the Special Part. The framework of the criminal laws that forms the General Part of the CC had to ensure a unified criminal policy in the entire Soviet Union. The creation of other CC's chapters was formally assigned to the Supreme Counsels of the republics. However, in order to actually ensure a unified criminal legislation, the CC of the Russian SFSR was drafted and adopted, so that the other republics would draft their own CC based on this example. In later years, the application of the model of the Russian SFRS expanded: all of the corrections and modifications of the CC of the Russian SFSR were automatically adapted to all of the other republics' CCs.

93. The CC of the Soviet Lithuania[53] was adopted on 26 June 1961 and came into force on 1 September 1961. The CC included the General Part (5 chapters, 61 articles) and the Special Part (11 chapters, 221 articles). In later years, the CC was intensively supplemented and amended by providing for the criminal liability for new crimes. In order to diminish the number of the convicted to imprisonment, the possibility for the exemption from the criminal liability and penalty was broadened, e.g., in 1980, the CC provided for more than thirty cases of exemption.[54] When

53. Lietuvos TSR baudžiamasis kodeksas, Vilnius, 1978.
54. Baudžiamoji teisė: Bendroji dalis, Vilnius, Eugrimas, 2003, p. 83.

assessing the criminal laws of this period, it can be noted that the state, its apparatus and the state's economic foundation (state-owned property) were considered as the priority values to be defended. The most severe penalties, as well as capital punishment, were provided for the so-called crimes against State and crimes against state and public (socialist) property. The sanctions for crimes against the State or public property were stricter than the ones for the same type of crimes against private property. The state and public property were defended not only from crimes such as theft, robbery or fraud but also from other kinds of damage (e.g., falsification of work plan performance, the output of poor quality or non-standard products and speculation). Criminal laws were mostly oriented to impose one kind of punishment – imprisonment. For this reason, the number of people convicted to imprisonment accounted for the majority of the convicted for many years.

VI. Criminal Laws after the Restoration of the Independence of Lithuania (1990–2000)

94. After the restoration of independence of Lithuania (11 March 1990), a legal reform was launched. In the field of criminal law, the reform was carried out in two ways: (1) by amending and supplementing the CC of 1961 (adopted during the Soviet period) (2) by preparing a new CC of the Republic of Lithuania.

95. Especially broad and substantial amendments in the CC of 1961 were made by the law adopted by the *Seimas* of the Republic of Lithuania on 19 July 1994.[55] For example, the General Part of the CC contained seventy-three articles in force, thirty-five out of which were newly redrafted, seventeen articles were eliminated, four new articles were added (that is to say, 75% of articles of the General Part of the CC were changed). Meanwhile, the Special Part of the CC contained 219 articles in force, 19 out of which were eliminated completely. Instead of sixty eliminated articles, the legislator provided sixty-one new articles that regulated criminal liability for crimes against property, employment, justice and war crimes. According to this law, 133 articles were newly redrafted (i.e., 90% of the articles of the Special Part of the CC were changed).[56]

VII. Criminal Code of 2000

96. The new CC of Lithuania[57] was adopted on 26 September 2000, and came into force on 1 May 2003, along with the new Code of Criminal Procedure[58] and the Punishment Enforcement Code.[59] The CC was the first codified national law in

55. Lietuvos Respublikos įstatymas 'Dėl Baudžiamojo, Pataisos darbų ir Baudžiamojo proceso kodeksu pakeitimo ir papildymo', *Valstybės žinios*, 1994, No. 60-1182.
56. Švedas G. Baudžiamosios politikos pagrindai ir tendencijos Lietuvos Respublikoje, Vilnius, TIC, 2006, p. 124; Baudžiamoji teisė. Bendroji dalis, Vilnius, Eugrimas, 2003, p. 85.
57. Lietuvos Respublikos baudžiamasis kodeksas, *Valstybės žinios*, 2000, No. 89-2741.
58. Lietuvos Respublikos baudžiamojo proceso kodeksas, *Valstybės žinios*, 2002, No. 37-1341.
59. Lietuvos Respublikos bausmių vykdymo kodeksas, *Valstybės žinios*, 2002, No. 73-3084.

the legal framework of the Republic of Lithuania to reinforce the national legal fundamentals underpinning the criminal policy of the state.[60] The CC was in development for almost ten years. In the final period of its drafting, it was mostly influenced by the criminal law of Germany, Poland and Russia, the conventions of the Council of Europe, and by legal acts of the EU.

97. The General Part of the CC, which had consisted of ninety-eight articles, was supplemented by thirty-three entirely new articles, concerning, for example, the criminal liability for the crimes provided for in international treaties (Article 7 of the CC), the types of criminal acts (Article 10 of the CC), diminished capacity (Article 18 of the CC), discharge of professional duties (Article 30 of the CC), performance of an assignment of a law enforcement institution (Article 32 of the CC), justifiable professional or economic risk (Article 34 of the CC), release from criminal liability on bail (Article 40 of the CC), community service (Article 46 of the CC), restriction of liberty (Article 48 of the CC), purpose and types of penal measures (Articles 67–74 of the CC) and the peculiarities of criminal liability of minors (Articles 80–94 of the CC).

98. The main new feature of the CC is a complete classification of all the criminal acts. According to the CC, all criminal acts are divided into misdemeanours[61] and crimes. Crimes are committed with intent and through negligence. Intentional crimes are divided into minor, less serious, serious and grave crimes. The concept of a subject of a criminal act has been broadened because legal entities may also be the subjects of the criminal acts specifically provided for in the Special Part of the CC. The system of punishments has been supplemented by new non-custodial punishments, for example, community service and restriction of liberty. In addition to punishments, the CC also provides for the institution of penal measures that may be imposed on adult offenders who are released from criminal liability or penalty. It is now possible to ensure the principle of imminent liability for one's guilt in the commission of a criminal act. The punishment system of the CC starts from the most lenient punishment, consistently followed by other more stringent punishments. This principle has, in fact, also been applied in the design and structure of the sanctions provided for in the Special Part of the CC. It shows the position of the legislator: when selecting a punishment or other penal sanction for the offender, one should seek to apply the most rational, economic and, at the same time, effective punishment or penal sanction.

99. Other provisions of the General Part of the CC also consistently implement and develop principles such as the principles of liability's differentiation, humanity, individualised punishments and economy of punishments. For example, the CC

60. Lietuvos Respublikos baudžiamojo kodekso komentaras. Bendroji dalis (1–98 straipsniai), Vilnius, TIC, 2004, p. 11.
61. It should be noted that the Criminal Code has provided only thirty-eight misdemeanours on 1 Jan. 2017 and it was one of the reasons for which the necessity of such kind of a criminal act was discussed in the Lithuanian doctrine (*see*: Švedas G., Veršekys P., Levon J., Prapiestis D. Lietuvos Respublikos baudžiamojo kodekso bendrosios dalies vientisumo ir naujovių suderinimo iššūkiai, Vilnius, Vilniaus universiteto leidykla, 2017, p. 128–129).

shows clearly the legislator's intention to make liability more stringent, for example, for persons who commit serious or grave crimes, for recidivists (especially if dangerous), and for members of an organised group or a criminal association. Moreover, there are more possibilities provided in the CC to commute liability, to release persons from liability or to mitigate punishment for misdemeanours, negligent, minor and less serious intentional crimes.

100. Cardinal changes have been made to the Special Part of the CC. It consists of thirty-two chapters, including entirely new ones, for example, Chapter XV 'Crimes against Humanity and War Crimes', Chapter XVI 'Crimes against the Independence, Territorial Integrity and Constitutional Order of the State of Lithuania', Chapter XXIII 'Crimes and misdemeanours against a child and a family' and Chapter XLV 'Crimes and misdemeanours against the memory of the deceased'. The Special Part of the CC is more specific: its structure and classification is based on more precisely and specifically defined group objects (legal goods) and on the groups of criminal offences distinguished on the basis thereof. Furthermore, the classification of norms and their division into separate chapters in the Special Part of the CC is also underpinned by the value criterion revealing the importance, significance and value of the specific object of criminal offences, i.e., protected public (social) relations. Therefore, the system of the CC Special Part starts from the chapters joining together the provisions of criminal law that prohibit criminal offences threatening the principal and most valuable legal goods[62] (e.g., the first chapter of the Special part of CC deals with genocide, crimes against humanity and war crimes (*see* paragraph 126). This design of the Special Part also reveals the directions and priorities of the criminal policy of the State and forms the strategy and tactics of this policy.

101. The Special Part of the CC, which consists of 232 articles, includes thirty-one articles providing for the criminal liability for new criminal acts that did not exist before, for example aggression (Article 110 of the CC), unlawful collection of information about a person's private life (Article 167 of the CC), unlawful use of energy and communications services (Article 179 of the CC), violation of industrial property rights (Article 195 of the CC), credit fraud (Article 207 of the CC) and market manipulation (Article 218 of the CC). There were forty articles in the old CC that have not been transposed into the new CC. However, not all the criminal acts provided for in these articles have been decriminalised. In the author's opinion, only the criminal acts provided for in eight articles have been fully decriminalised (e.g., prosecution of citizens for criticism, violation of construction regulations, violation of regulations on the stay of foreigners in the Republic of Lithuania and avoidance of a military service record). The offences covered in six other articles of the old CC have been only partly decriminalised (e.g., failure to report a crime, concealment of a crime or a person who commits a crime, and unlawful transportation

62. Lietuvos Respublikos baudžiamojo kodekso komentaras. Bendroji dalis (1–98 straipsniai), Vilnius, TIC, 2004, p. 13.

of explosives by air transport). The elements of criminal acts provided in twenty-six articles have been moved to the *corpus delicti* of other criminal acts (e.g., the armament of criminal groups, unlawful engagement in medical treatment activities).[63]

§4. SOURCES OF CRIMINAL LAW

102. The sources of Lithuanian criminal law are both national and international. Moreover, the legal acts of the European Union play a special role in Lithuanian criminal law. The influence of international and European Union law on the Lithuanian criminal law is shown by the following example: in 2004–2016, thirty amendments and supplements of the General Part of the CC were adopted. The majority (even eighteen) of these amendments and supplements, in whole or in part, was caused by the implementation of the international and the EU legal requirements in the national criminal law.[64]

I. International Sources

103. The status of international law in the Lithuanian legal system is provided in paragraph 3 of Article 138 of the Constitution which determines that 'International treaties which are ratified by the *Seimas* of the Republic of Lithuania shall be the constituent part of the legal system of the Republic of Lithuania'. The ruling of the Constitutional Court of 17 October 1995 'On the compliance of Paragraph 4 of Article 7 and Article 12 of the Republic of Lithuania's Law On International Treaties of the Republic of Lithuania with the Constitution of the Republic of Lithuania'[65] emphasised that 'pursuant to the Constitution only the legislature by the way of ratification may decide which statute of international law shall be the constituent part of the legal system of the Republic of Lithuania having the force of law'. The ratified international treaty of the Republic of Lithuania shall not contradict the Constitution because Article 7 of the Constitution and the case law of the Constitutional Court[66] emphasise that 'any law or other act that contradicts the Constitution shall be invalid'.

104. In the conclusion of the Constitutional Court of 24 January 1995 'On the compliance of Articles 4, 5, 9, 14 as well as Article 2 of Protocol No. 4 of the Convention for the Protection of Human Rights and Fundamental Freedoms with the

63. Švedas G. Baudžiamosios politikos pagrindai ir tendencijos Lietuvos Respublikoje, Vilnius, 2TIC, 006, p. 137.
64. Švedas G., Veršekys P., Levon J., Prapiestis D. Lietuvos Respublikos baudžiamojo kodekso bendrosios dalies vientisumo ir naujovių suderinimo iššūkiai, Vilnius, Vilniaus universiteto leidykla, 2017, p. 46–47.
65. Decision of the Constitutional Court of Lithuania of 17 Oct., 1995, *Valstybės žinios*, 1995, No. 86-1949.
66. For example, *see*: decision of Constitutional Court of Lithuania of 5 Sep. 2012, *Valstybės žinios*, 2012, No. 105-5330.

Constitution of the Republic of Lithuania'[67] was stated that 'the [...] direct application of international treaties to decide the competition of norms shall not be applied in criminal proceedings. In such cases, criminal laws and laws of criminal procedure of the Republic of Lithuania shall be directly applied, whereas international treaties shall be applicable only in special cases prescribed by law'. The possibility of direct application of Lithuanian international treaties (if a treaty contains self-executing norms) are provided only in criminal procedure and punishment execution, since paragraph 3 of Article 4 of the CCP and Article 4 of the CPE states: 'where are international treaty of the Republic of Lithuania prescribes rule other than this Code, the rule of international treaty shall apply'.[68]

105. Lithuania has ratified several criminal law and international cooperation in criminal matters conventions of the Council of Europe, including the European Convention on Extradition of 1957 and its Additional Protocols of 1975 and 1978 (ratified in 1995); the European Convention on Mutual Assistance in Criminal Matters of 1959, including the Additional protocol of 1978 (1995) and the Second Additional Protocol of 2001 (2004); the European Convention on the International Validity of Criminal Judgments of 1970 (1997); the European Convention on the Transfer of Proceedings in Criminal Matters of 1972 (1997); the European Convention on the Suppression of Terrorism of 1977 (1997); the Convention on the Transfer of Sentenced Persons of 1983 (1995) and its Additional Protocol of 1997 (2000); the Convention on Laundering, Search, Seizure and Confiscation of the Proceeds from Crime of 1990 (1995); the Criminal Law Convention on Corruption of 1999 (2002); the Convention on Cybercrime of 2001 (2003); the Council of Europe Convention on the Prevention of Terrorism of 2005 (2014); the Council of Europe Convention on Action against Trafficking in Human Beings of 2005 (2012); the Additional Protocol to the Convention on Cybercrime, concerning the criminalisation of acts of a racist and xenophobic nature committed through computer systems of 2003 (2006); and Council of Europe Convention on the Protection of Children against Sexual Exploitation and Sexual Abuse of 2007 (2013).

106. Lithuania has ratified the following criminal law conventions of the United Nations, including the Convention on the Prevention and Punishment of the Crime of Genocide of 1948 (ratified in 1992); the Convention on the non-applicability of statutory limitations to war crimes and crimes against humanity of 1968 (1992); the United Nations Convention against Illicit Traffic in Narcotic Drugs and Psychotropic Substances of 1988 (1998); the International Convention for the Suppression of the Financing of Terrorism of 1999 (2003); the United Nations Convention against Corruption of 2003 (2006); the United Nations Convention against Transnational Organized Crime of 2000 (2002); the Protocol to Prevent, Suppress and Punish Trafficking in Persons, Especially Women and Children, supplementing the United

67. Conclusion of the Constitutional Court of Lithuania of 24 Jan. 1995, *Valstybės žinios*, 1995, No. 9-199.
68. More on the international law's influence on Lithuanian criminal law, *see*: Švedas G. Tarptautinės teisės reikšmė ir įgyvendinimas Lietuvos baudžiamojoje teisėje // Nepriklausomos Lietuvos teisė: praeitis, dabartis ir ateitis, Vilnius, 2012, p. 100–112.

Nations Convention against Transnational Organized Crime of 2000 (2003); the Protocol against the Smuggling of Migrants by Land, Sea and Air, supplementing the United Nations Convention against Transnational Organized Crime 2000 (2003); the Protocol against the Illicit Manufacturing of and Trafficking in Firearms, Their Parts and Components and Ammunition, supplementing the United Nations Convention against Transnational Organized Crime of 2001 (2005); the Rome Statute of the International Criminal Court of 1998 (2003); the Amendment to Article 8 of the Rome Statute of the International Criminal Court of 2010 (2015); and the Amendments on the crime of aggression to the Rome Statute of the International Criminal Court of 2010 (2015).

107. The status of the EU law in the Lithuanian legal system is defined in a Constitutional act 'On membership of the Republic of Lithuania in the European Union',[69] which states:

> The norms of the European Union law shall be a constituent part of the legal system of the Republic of Lithuania. Where it concerns the founding Treaties of the European Union, the norms of European Union law shall be applied directly, while in the event of the collision of legal norms, they shall have supremacy over the laws and other legal acts of the Republic of Lithuania.

108. Lithuania has to implement the EU secondary law, namely directives (and also framework decisions). The implementation of these legal acts in most cases requires new laws. For example, the implementation of Directive 2014/57/EU of the European Parliament and of the Council of 16 April 2014 on criminal sanctions for market abuse ('Market abuse directive') required to modify the definition of trade in securities by using non-public information (Article 217 of the CC) and manipulation of the market of financial instruments (Article 218 of the CC).[70] Similarly, the implementation of the Council Framework Decision 2008/909/JHA of 27 November 2008 on the application of the principle of mutual recognition to judgments in criminal matters imposing custodial sentences or measures involving deprivation of liberty for the purpose of their enforcement in the European Union led to the adoption of the law on mutual recognition and enforcement of European Union Member States courts decisions in criminal matters.[71] Besides, Lithuania has ratified the following criminal law and mutual assistance in criminal matters conventions of the European Union, including the Convention, on the protection of the European Communities' financial interests of 1995 (ratified in 2004); the Protocol to the Convention on the protection of the European Communities' financial interests of 1996 (2004); the Convention on Mutual Assistance in Criminal Matters

69. Lietuvos Respublikos Konstitucijos papildymo Konstituciniu aktu 'Dėl Lietuvos Respublikos narystės Europos Sąjungoje' ir Lietuvos Respublikos Konstitucijos 150 straipsnio papildymo į statymas, *Valstybės žinios*, 2004, No. 111-4123.
70. Lietuvos Respublikos baudžiamojo kodekso 7, 213, 217, 218, 224(1) straipsnių ir Priedo pakeitimo įstatymas, TAR, 2016, No. 2016-20291.
71. Lietuvos Respublikos įstatymas dėl Europos Sąjungos valstybių narių sprendimų baudžiamosiose bylose tarpusavio pripažinimo ir vykdymo, TAR, 2014-11-21, No. 17299.

between the Member States of the European Union adopted by the Council in accordance with Article 34 of the Treaty on European Union of 2000 (2004); and the Protocol to the Convention on Mutual Assistance in Criminal Matters between the Member States of the European Union adopted by the Council in accordance with Article 34 of the Treaty on European Union of 2001 (2004).

109. Lithuanian courts must follow the decisions of the ECtHR and CJEU when applying national law, since paragraph 3 of Article 33 of mentioned Law on Courts establishes that 'when hearing cases, courts shall apply the legislation of the European Union and be guided by the resolutions of judicial institutions of the European Union as well as their prejudicial decisions on the issues of interpretation and validity of legal acts of the European Union'. The Constitutional Court has also emphasised that 'the jurisprudence of the European Convention on Human Rights (ECHR) (and CJEU) as a source of construction of law is also important to construction and application of Lithuanian law'.[72] It should be mentioned that the Lithuanian courts have the right or obligation to request a preliminary ruling or an advisory opinion from the CJEU or ECtHR. For example, Article 40(1) of the Law on Courts provides, that:

> the court to which the issue of interpretation or application of the legal provisions of the acts of the European Union arise when applying the law of the European Union the examination of which is mandatory in order to adopt the decision in the case shall be entitled to apply to a competent judicial institution of the European Union with a request to give a preliminary ruling thereon. The Supreme Court and the Supreme Administrative Court as well as the court which is the last instance in the action pending before the court (when the decision cannot be further appealed against), in the referred cases must request the competent judicial institution of the European Union for a preliminary ruling on the issues of interpretation or validity of legal acts.

In addition, Article 40(2) of the above-mentioned Law on Courts states that:

> the Supreme Court and the Supreme Administrative Court, when arises questions of principle relating to the interpretation or application of the rights and freedoms defined in the Convention or the protocols thereto, may apply to the European Court on Human Rights with request of an advisory opinion.

110. It should be mentioned that on 11 July 2008 the European Court of Justice delivered a preliminary ruling in the first case C–207/08 concerning Lithuanian criminal law. The European Court of Justice stated in its preliminary ruling that the provisions of Article 265 of the CC imposing criminal liability for the cultivation of any type of hemp without exception are contrary to Council Regulation (EC) No.

---

72. For example, decision of the Constitutional Court of Lithuania of 9 Jun. 2011, *Valstybės žinios*, 2011, No. 156-7405.

1782/2003 of 29 September 2003, which establishes common rules for direct support schemes under the common agricultural policy and establishes certain support schemes for farmers. Therefore, the provisions of Article 265 of the CC were to be precluded from the application.

II. National Sources

A. *The Constitution and Constitutional Court Rulings*

111. The Constitution of the Republic of Lithuania was adopted by the citizens of the Republic through the referendum on 25 October 1992 and came into force on 2 November 1992.

112. The Constitution – as an integral and directly applicable act – is a supreme source of Lithuanian law. All subordinated sources of law must comply with constitutional requirements. Paragraph 1 of Article 33 of the Law on Courts provides that 'when hearing cases courts shall be guided by the Constitution of the Republic of Lithuania'. The Constitution as the fundamental legal act proclaims that 'human rights and freedoms shall be innate', regulates conditions under which certain constitutional rights may be restricted, for example, the right to human liberty in the case of detention, or the right to respect private life in the case of a search of a home. The Constitution furthermore provides fundamental principles of criminal law and criminal procedure, such as the presumption of innocence, the right to a fair and public hearing of the case by an independent and impartial court, the principle of *non bis in idem*, the right to defence, as well as the right to an advocate (paragraphs 1, 2, 5, 6 of Article 31), etc. These principles are then concretised in the norms of the CC and CCP.

113. The Constitution contains provisions, *inter alia*, on the organisation of the judicial power and the public prosecution service and regulates the powers and duties of public prosecutors in criminal proceedings.

114. Paragraph 2 of Article 33 of the Law on Courts states: 'When hearing cases courts shall also be guided by the officially reported decisions of the Constitutional Court of the Republic of Lithuania'. Until 1 January 2021, the Constitutional Court adopted sixteen rulings on various aspects of substantive criminal law.[73] Seven rulings of the Constitutional Court analyse the constitutionality of institutions of the General Part of the CC, two rulings of the institutions of the Special Part of the CC and two rulings of the institutions of both the General and the Special Part of the CC. Even six rulings of the Constitutional Court were dedicated to the constitutionality of punishments and sentencing rules. In three rulings, the Constitutional Court found contradictions against the Constitution, for example, concerning the death

73. Prapiestis J., Švedas G., Prapiestis D. Teisėkūra ir konstitucinė jurisprudencija Lietuvos Respublikos baudžiamojo kodekso Specialiosios dalies klausimais, Teisė, 2021, No. 119, p. 34.

penalty,[74] the rules on the imposition of a more lenient punishment than the one provided for by the law[75] and the rules on the retroactive validity of the law concerning genocide.[76] Meanwhile, in other rulings, the Constitutional Court decided that the punishment of property confiscation,[77] the rules on the retroactive validity of the law,[78] the criminal liability of legal persons,[79] the definition of aggravated murder[80] and genocide[81] did not contradict the requirements of the Constitution.

115. Moreover, during 2000–2017, the Constitutional Court adopted twelve rulings on various aspects of criminal procedure. In eight rulings, the Constitutional Court found contradictions against the Constitution, for example on the compensation for damages inflicted by unlawful actions of pretrial investigation bodies, the prosecutor's office, and a court;[82] the drawing up and announcement of the reasoning of court decisions; the change of charges in court;[83] the dismissing of criminal proceedings after the expiration of a statutory limitation period for criminal liability[84] and the consideration of criminal cases under the appeal procedure upon coming into light of essentially different factual circumstances.[85] Meanwhile, in other four rulings, the Constitutional Court has declared that, for example, the institutions of private accusation,[86] the competence of the prosecutor to start a pretrial investigation[87] did not contradict the Constitution.

B. *Statute Legislation*

116. The main sources enacted on a legislative level by the *Seimas* are the CC for substantive criminal law, the Code of Criminal Procedure and the Code of Punishment Execution.

---

74. Decision of the Constitutional Court of Lithuania of 9 Dec., 1998, *Valstybės žinios*, 1998, No. 109-3004.
75. Decision of the Constitutional Court of Lithuania of 10 Jun. 2003, *Valstybės žinios*, 2003, No. 57-2552.
76. Decision of the Constitutional Court of Lithuania of 18 Mar., 2014, TAR, 2014, No. 03226.
77. Decision of the Constitutional Court of Lithuania of 13 Dec., 1993, *Valstybės žinios*, 1993, No. 70-1320.
78. Decision of the Constitutional Court of Lithuania of 9 Jul. 1998, *Valstybės žinios*, 1998, No. 63-1827.
79. Decision of the Constitutional Court of Lithuania of 8 Jun. 2009, *Valstybės žinios*, 2009, No. 69-2798.
80. Decision of the Constitutional Court of Lithuania of 4 Jun. 2012, *Valstybės žinios*, 2012, No. 64-3246.
81. Decision of the Constitutional Court of Lithuania of 18 Mar. 2014, TAR, 2014, No. 03226.
82. Decision of the Constitutional Court of Lithuania of 19 Aug. 2006, *Valstybės žinios*, 2006, Nr. 90-3529, No. 137-0.
83. Decision of the Constitutional Court of Lithuania of 15 Nov. 2013, *Valstybės žinios*, 2013, No. 119-6005.
84. Decision of the Constitutional Court of Lithuania of 27 Jun. 2016, TAR, 2016, No. 17705.
85. Decision of the Constitutional Court of Lithuania of 26 Jun. 2017, TAR, 2017, No. 10749.
86. Decision of the Constitutional Court of Lithuania of 16 Jan. 2006, *Valstybės žinios*, 2006, No. 7-254.
87. Decision of the Constitutional Court of Lithuania of 15 Jun. 2006, *Valstybės žinios*, 2006, No. 68-2514.

Besides these main legislative sources of criminal law, there are numerous secondary laws that concern criminal law *largo sensu*, for example the Law on Courts, the Law of Police, the Law on Criminal Intelligence, the Law on Mutual Recognition and Enforcement of the European Union Member States Court Decisions in Criminal Matters and the Law on Probation, but even *stricto sensu,* for example in 1994, 1999, 2000 and 2006 several temporary laws on voluntary submission and legalisation of firearms, ammunition and explosive materials were adopted and created legal preconditions for withdrawing firearms, ammunition and explosive materials from illegal civil circulation without applying criminal and administrative liability for persons who submit firearms, ammunition or explosive materials.[88] Moreover, several laws on amnesty[89] may be assigned to the group of criminal law.

C. Statutory Delegated Legislation

117. Statutory delegated legislation in criminal justice may be adopted only on the ground of the law and within the scope that the law itself determines. Statutory delegated legislation in the area of substantive criminal law usually performs only an auxiliary function.

118. Statutory delegated legislation in criminal justice may come through different legal instruments. In substantive criminal law, the statutory delegated legislation usually consists of regulations issued on the ground of the CC by the competent ministers, for example, Article 141 of the CC provides that:

> characteristics of the cases of health impairment (Articles 135, 138 and 140 of the CC) shall be defined by the rules for determining the extent of health impairment as approved by the Minister of Justice, Minister of Health Protection and Minister of Social Security and Labour' or Article 269 of the CC states that 'the narcotic and psychotropic substances [...] shall be the substances entered in the lists of narcotic and psychotropic substances approved by the Ministry of Health. The quantity of narcotic or psychotropic substances to be considered as small, large and very large shall be determined on the basis of the recommendations approved by the Ministry of Health.[90]

In criminal procedure, recommendations were issued on the ground of the CCP by the Prosecutor General on various aspects of criminal procedure, for example,

88. Lietuvos Respublikos ginklų, šaudmenų, sprogmenų, sprogstamųjų medžiagų savanoriško atidavimo bei ginklų ir šaudmenų įteisinimo laikinieji įstatymai, *Valstybės žinios*, 1994, No. 5-66; No. 1999, No. 55-1769, 2000, No. 42-1193; 2006, No. 77-2962, etc.
89. Lietuvos Respublikos įstatymas 'Dėl amnestijos pažymint Lietuvos Respublikos Konstitucijos priėmimą', *Valstybės žinios*, 1990, No. 25-580; Lietuvos Respublikos įstatymas 'Dėl dalinės amnestijos akto', *Valstybės žinios*, 1999, No. 1-1; Lietuvos Respublikos įstatymas 'Dėl amnestijos akto', *Valstybės žinios*, 2000, No. 35-973, etc.
90. Sveikatos apsaugos ministro 2003 m. balandžio 23 d. įsakymas No. V-239 'Dėl Narkotinių ir psichotropinių medžiagų nedidelio, didelio ir labai didelio kiekio nustatymo rekomendacijų', *Valstybės žinios*, 2003, No. 41-1899.

the Recommendation on control of the term of pretrial investigation[91] and the Recommendation on registration of pretrial investigation.[92] In punishment execution, the rules were issued on the ground of CPE by the Minister of Justice on various aspects of punishment execution, for example, Prison rules.[93]

119. It should be noted that the legality principle in substantive criminal law, criminal procedure and punishment execution requires that all the restrictions on human rights and freedoms (including *corpus delicti* of a criminal act) must be regulated on the legislative level. Meanwhile, the statutory delegated legislation may provide only a procedure of implementation of restrictions on human rights and freedoms established by the law.

D. Court Decisions

120. The decisions of courts became a binding precedent on 28 March 2006, when the Constitutional Court decided that:

> under the Constitution, court practice is formed only when courts decide cases themselves. A different construction of the provisions of the Constitution [...] would deny the independence of courts entrenched in the Constitution, would violate the provision of paragraph 2 of Article 109 of the Constitution that while administering justice, the court and judges shall be independent, and the provision of paragraph 3 of this Article that when considering cases, judges shall only obey the law.[94]

In 2008, Article 33 of the Law on Courts was amended by paragraph 4, which provides:

> When taking decisions in cases of appropriate categories the courts shall be bound by the rules of interpretation of law created by them, formed in analogous or similar cases. The courts of lower instance when taking decisions in cases of appropriate categories shall be bound by the rules of interpretation formulated in analogous or conceptually similar cases. The court practice in cases of appropriate categories must be amended and new rules for the interpretation of the law in analogous or similar cases may be created only in cases when it is inevitable or objectively necessary.

---

91. Generalinio prokuroro įsakymas 'Dėl ikiteisminio tyrimo terminų kontrolės tvarkos aprašo patvirtinimo', *Valstybės žinios*, 2010, No. 124-6363.
92. Generalinio prokuroro įsakymas 'Dėl Rekomendacijos dėl ikiteisminio tyrimo pradžios ir jos registravimo tvarkos patvirtinimo', TAR, 2014, No. 2014-09479.
93. Pataisos įstaigų ir tardymo izoliatorių vidaus tvarkos taisyklės, TAR, 2020, No. 911.
94. Decision of the Constitutional Court of Lithuania of 28 Mar. 2006, *Valstybės žinios*, 2006, Nr. 36-1292.

Meanwhile, the Supreme Court of Lithuania noted that precedents are applicable in those cases where the facts are identical or very similar to and the same law applies.[95]

121. The Supreme Court of Lithuania has the function to develop a uniform court practice in the interpretation and application of Statutes and other legal acts. The rulings of the plenary sessions, as well as the rulings of the extended panel of seven judges of the Supreme Court of Lithuania, have a major influence on court practice. According to paragraph 1 of the Article 378 of the CCP, the criminal case may be referred to the 'extended panel of seven judges if the appropriate application in the case of criminal law or law of criminal procedure would mean the establishment for court practice of a novel example of interpretation of the legal norm'. Paragraph 2 of the Article 378 of CCP provides that the criminal case may be referred to the 'plenary session if the appropriate application in the case of the criminal law or law of criminal procedure would mean the deviation from the established practice of the Supreme Court of Lithuania'. The Supreme Court of Lithuania, during the period of 2003–2016, issued 180 rulings (38 by the plenary session of the Criminal division and 142 by the extended panel of seven judges) that addressed substantive criminal law issues.[96]

122. Furthermore, the Supreme Court of Lithuania has the function to prepare Senate rulings (until 2006) and summary-reviews of the Criminal Division of the Supreme Court of Lithuania, when ensuring the uniform interpretation and application of legal acts. These rulings and summary-reviews are not formally binding from 2006, but they function as a model of 'best practice', indirectly influencing the case law of the lower courts. The Senate and the Criminal Division of the Supreme Court of Lithuania, during the period of 1995–2016, adopted thirty-four rulings and summary-reviews[97] on various aspects of the general part of the criminal law (e.g., on extradition, European Arrest Warrant and surrender to the International Criminal Court,[98] sentencing rules,[99] suspended sentence[100] and confiscation[101]) and special part of criminal law (e.g., on theft and robbery,[102] rape and sexual

95. Ruling of the Supreme Court of Lithuania in criminal case No. 2K-P-100/2008.
96. Švedas G., Veršekys P., Levon J., Prapiestis D. Lietuvos Respublikos baudžiamojo kodekso bendrosios dalies vientisumo ir naujovių suderinimo iššūkiai, Vilnius, Vilniaus universiteto leidykla, 2017, p. 85.
97. Švedas G., Veršekys P., Levon J., PRAPIESTIS D. Lietuvos Respublikos baudžiamojo kodekso bendrosios dalies vientisumo ir naujovių suderinimo iššūkiai, Vilnius, Vilniaus universiteto leidykla, 2017, p. 72–76.
98. Decision of the Senate of the Supreme Court of Lithuania of 29 Dec., 2003, Teismų praktika, No. 20.
99. Review of the Criminal division of Supreme Court of Lithuania of 28 Jun. 2007, Teismų praktika, No. 27.
100. Review of the Criminal division of Supreme Court of Lithuania of 15 Feb. 2008, Teismų praktika, No. 28.
101. Review of the Criminal division of Supreme Court of Lithuania of 18 Feb. 2010, Teismų praktika, No. 32.
102. Decision of the Senate of the Supreme Court of Lithuania of 23 Jun. 2005, Teismų praktika, No. 23.

assault,[103] crimes against humanity and war crimes[104]).

123. Meanwhile, the Senate and the Criminal Division of the Supreme Court of Lithuania, during the period 2000–2016, adopted twelve rulings and summary-reviews on various aspects of the criminal procedure, for example, on the content of the judgment,[105] simplified procedure,[106] pretrial detention and home arrest,[107] appeal procedure,[108] evidentiary procedure[109] and suspect and accused rights.[110]

§5. Classifications and Technique of Criminal Law

124. The Lithuanian CC is divided into two parts: General and Special. The General Part consists of provisions that can be applied to all the criminal acts, while the Special Part of the CC covers single misdemeanours and offences.

125. The General Part of the CC (Articles 1–98) consists of fourteen chapters:

I Chapter. General provisions;
II Chapter. Validity of criminal law;
III Chapter. Crime and misdemeanour;
IV Chapter. Stages and forms of criminal acts;
V Chapter. Circumstances eliminating criminal liability;
VI Chapter. Release from criminal liability;
VII Chapter. Punishment;
VIII Chapter. Imposition of punishment (sentencing);
IX Chapter. Penal measures and their imposition;
X Chapter. Suspended sentence and release from punishment;
XI Chapter. Peculiarities of criminal liability of juveniles;
XII Chapter. Statute of limitations of criminal liability;
XIII Chapter. Previous conviction;
XIV Chapter. Compulsory medical measures.

126. The Special Part of the CC (Articles 99–330) consists of thirty-two chapters:

---

103. Decision of the Senate of the Supreme Court of Lithuania of 30 Dec., 2004, Teismų praktika, No. 22.
104. Decision of the Senate of the Supreme Court of Lithuania of 29 Jun. 2012, Teismų praktika, No. 37.
105. Decision of the Senate of the Supreme Court of Lithuania of 20 Jun. 2003, Teismų praktika, No. 20.
106. Decision of the Senate of the Supreme Court of Lithuania of 17 Sep. 2004, Teismų praktika, No. 22.
107. Decision of the Senate of the Supreme Court of Lithuania of 30 Dec. 2004, Teismų praktika, No. 22.
108. Decision of the Senate of the Supreme Court of Lithuania of 23 Jun. 2005, Teismu praktika, No. 23.
109. Decision of the Senate of the Supreme Court of Lithuania of 28 Jun. 2007, Teismų praktika, No. 27.
110. Review of the Criminal division of Supreme Court of Lithuania of 15 Dec., 2016, Teismų praktika, No. 45; Review of the Criminal division of Supreme Court of Lithuania of 6 Apr., 2017, Teismų praktika, No. 46.

XV Chapter. Crimes against humanity and war crimes;
XVI Chapter. Crimes against the independence, territorial integrity and constitutional order of the state of Lithuania;
XVII Chapter. Crimes against human life;
XVIII Chapter. Crimes against human health;
XIX Chapter. Crimes endangering human health and life;
XX Chapter. Crimes and misdemeanours against human liberty;
XXI Chapter. Crimes and misdemeanours against the freedom of a person's sexual self-determination and inviolability;
XXII Chapter. Crimes and misdemeanours against a person's dignity and honour;
XXIII Chapter. Crimes and misdemeanours against a child and a family;
XXIV Chapter. Crimes against the inviolability of a person's private life;
XXV Chapter. Crimes and misdemeanours against a person's equal rights and freedom of conscience;
XXVI Chapter. Crimes against persons' voting rights and the procedure of elections of the President of the Republic of Lithuania, elections to the *Seimas*, the European Parliament and municipal councils or the procedure for conducting referendums, crimes against political parties and political campaigns funding order;
XXVII Chapter. Crimes and misdemeanours against a person social rights;
XXVIII Chapter. Crimes and misdemeanours against property, property rights and property interests;
XXIX Chapter. Crimes against the intellectual and industrial property;
XXX Chapter. Crimes against the security of electronic data and information systems;
XXXI Chapter. Crimes and misdemeanours against the economy and business order;
XXXII Chapter. Crimes and misdemeanours against the financial system;
XXXIII Chapter. Crimes and misdemeanours against civil service and public interest;
XXXIV Chapter. Crimes and misdemeanours against justice;
XXXV Chapter. Crimes against public security;
XXXVI Chapter. Crimes and misdemeanours relating to the possession of weapons, ammunition, explosives, explosive or radioactive materials or military equipment;
XXXVII Chapter. Crimes and misdemeanours relating to the possession of narcotic or psychotropic, toxic or highly active substances;
XXXVIII Chapter. Crimes and misdemeanours against the environment and human health;
XXXIX Chapter. Crimes and misdemeanours against traffic safety;
XL Chapter. Crimes and misdemeanours against public order;
XLI Chapter. Crimes and misdemeanours against the activities of a civil servant or a person performing the functions of public administration;
XLII Chapter. Crimes and misdemeanours against the government's order;
XLIII Chapter. Crimes and misdemeanours against the government's order relating to forgery of documents or measuring devices;
XLIV Chapter. Crimes and misdemeanours against morality;
XLV Chapter. Crimes and misdemeanours against the memory of deceased people;

XLVI Chapter. Crimes and misdemeanours against the national defence service and mobilisation.

127. The CC has Annex which consists of the European Union legal acts implemented by the CC.

128. The Lithuanian CCP is divided into eleven Parts and thirty-five chapters (some chapters have sections):

Part 1. General provisions (Articles 1–106):

I Chapter. The aim of criminal procedure and main rules;
II Chapter. Main definitions;
III Chapter. Securing the rights of the parties of procedure:

1 section. Basics of ensuring respect to the individual's rights;
2 section. Defence;
3 section. Representation;
4 section. Disqualification;
5 section. Complaints during the pretrial investigation;

IV Chapter. Communication between courts and prosecution office of Lithuania with foreign and international institutions;
V Chapter. Witnesses, Experts and Specialists:

1 section. Witnesses;
2 section. Experts;
3 section. Specialists;

VI Chapter. Tangible objects and documents:

1 section. Tangible objects;
2 section. Documents;
3 section. Recovery of tangible objects and documents relevant for the investigation;

VII Chapter. Terms of criminal procedure;
VIII Chapter. Procedural expenses and reimbursement.

Part 2. Compensation for damage resulting from criminal acts (Articles 107–118):

IX Chapter. Compensation for damage without a civil action in a criminal case;
X Chapter. Compensation for damage by entering a civil action in a criminal case.

Part 3. Procedural coercive measures (Articles 119–163):

XI Chapter. Remand measures;
XII Chapter. Other procedural coercive measures.

Part 4. Pretrial investigation (Articles 164–220):

XIII Chapter. General principles of pretrial investigation;
XIV Chapter. Actions of pretrial investigation:

1 section. Basics of actions of pretrial investigation;
2 section. Questioning during a pretrial investigation;
3 section. Actions of verification of testimonies;
4 section. Peculiarities of actions of pretrial investigation in respect of the victim or the witness who are subject to non-disclosure of their identity;
5 section. Examination and inspection of the objects;
6 section. Expert examination.

XV Chapter. Termination of pretrial investigation;
XVI Chapter. Conclusion of the pretrial investigation by drawing up the indictment.

Part 5. Procedure in the Court of First Instance (Articles 221–310):

XVII Chapter. Composition and jurisdiction of the court;
XVIII Chapter. Preparation of the case for the hearing;
XIX Chapter. General principles of the hearing;
XX Chapter. Preparatory stage of hearing;
XXI Chapter. Examination of evidence;
XXII Chapter. The final speech and the final statement of the accused;
XXIII Chapter. Rendering of the judgment.

Part 6. Procedure in the court of the appeal instance (Articles 311–334):

XXIV Chapter. Appeal against judgment or ruling before it becomes effective;
XXV Chapter. Appeals procedure.

Part 7. Execution of judgment and ruling (Articles 335–365(4)).

Part 8. Procedure in the court of the cassation instance (Articles 366–386):

XXVI Chapter. Appeal against effective judgment or ruling and preparation of cassation case;
XXVII Chapter. Cassation procedure.

Part 9. Peculiarities of criminal procedure in investigating and hearing cases of certain categories (Articles 387–438):

XXVIII Chapter. Criminal procedure in respect of crimes committed by legal persons;
XXIX Chapter. Procedure in respect of the application of compulsory medical measures;
XXX Chapter. Procedure in respect of private indictment cases;
XXXI Chapter. Summary procedure:

1 section. Procedure for penal order of the court;
2 section. Expedited procedure;

XXXII Chapter. Criminal procedure in the absence of the accused (*in absentia*).

Part 10. Appealing to superior courts against the rulings of lower courts and hearing of appeals (Articles 439–442).

Part 11. Reopening of a criminal case (Articles 443–461):

XXXIII Chapter. Reopening of a criminal case due to newly disclosed circumstances;
XXXIV Chapter. Reopening of a criminal case due to clearly inappropriate applications of criminal law;
XXXV Chapter. Reopening of a criminal case due to a decision of the Human Rights Committee of United Nations or European Court of Human Rights, or Constitutional Court of Lithuania.

129. The Code of Criminal Procedure has Annex, which consists of the European Union legal acts implemented by the Code of Criminal Procedure.

130. The Code of Punishment Execution is divided into five parts and fifteen chapters (some chapters have sections):

Part 1. General provisions (Articles 1–21):

I Chapter. Statutes of punishment execution;
II Chapter. Principles of punishment execution;
III Chapter. Legal status of the sentenced person;
IV Chapter. Institutions of punishment execution.

Part 2. Procedure and conditions of execution of the punishments restricting property rights (Articles 22–31):

V Chapter. Procedure and conditions of the execution of fines;

VI Chapter. Procedure and conditions for the execution of restriction of legal person operation and legal person liquidation punishments.

Part 3. Procedure and conditions for the execution of the punishments restricting personal rights (Articles 39–45) (abolished):

VII Chapter. Procedure and conditions for deprivation of public rights and deprivation of the right to be employed in a certain position or to engage in certain type of activities;
VIII Chapter. Procedure and conditions for community service.

Part 4. Procedure and conditions of the execution of the punishments restricting the right to freedom (Articles 46–175):

IX Chapter. Procedure and conditions for the execution of restriction of liberty and arrest:

1 section. Procedure and conditions of the execution of the restriction of liberty;
2 section. Procedure and conditions of the execution of the arrest;

X Chapter. Procedure and conditions of the execution of imprisonment:

1 section. Types of correctional institutions, the procedure of transmission and custody of prisoners;
2 section. Correctional houses;
3 section. Correctional houses for juveniles;
4 section. Prisons;
5 section. Open colonies;
6 section. Special rights and duties of prisoners.

XI Chapter. Correctional measures of prisoners:

1 section. Regime of correctional institutions;
2 section. Employment of prisoners;
3 section. Social rehabilitation of prisoners;
4 section. Education and professional training of prisoners;
5 section. Peculiarities of execution of imprisonment for pregnant women and mothers with children under 3 years;
6 section. Prisoners' right to leave correctional institutions without guard or unaccompanied;
7 section. Early release from correctional institutions;
8 section. Abolition of partially suspended execution of punishment.

XII Chapter. Peculiarities of the execution of life imprisonment;
XIII Chapter. Compensation of pecuniary damage caused during punishment execution;

XIV Chapter. Material welfare and healthcare of prisoners.

Part 5. Final provisions (Articles 176–183):

XV Chapter. Release from punishment execution, support to persons released from punishment execution. Appeal against actions and decisions of the correctional institutions and officials:

1 section. Release from punishment execution;
2 section. Support to persons released from punishment execution;
3 section. Appeal against actions and decisions of the correctional institutions and officials.

131. The Code of Punishment Execution has Annex, which consists of the European Union legal acts implemented by the Code of Punishment Execution.

Part I. Substantive Criminal Law

Chapter 1. General Principles

132. Traditionally, principles in the Lithuanian criminal law are divided into general (i.e., common for all branches of law), such as the principles of justice, proportionality, humanity and equality and special (i.e., common only to the branch of criminal law), such as principles of legality, culpability, personal liability and *non bis in idem.*

133. Recently, the doctrine of Lithuanian criminal law[111] attributed the principle of subsidiarity of criminal law (*ultima ratio*) to the group of special principles. This principle means that criminal law prohibitions and sanctions should be adopted only when it is absolutely necessary, i.e., it is impossible to protect the legal interest at stake through other legal and social measures. Also, the case law of the Supreme Court of Lithuania has recognised this principle, by stating in several criminal cases that 'the purpose and subsidiarity of criminal law (*ultima ratio*) implies that personal behaviour which only violates purely civil legal relationships, cannot be regarded as a criminal act'.[112]

§1. The Principle of Legality

I. Limitation on Penalisation

134. The principle of legality (*nullum crimen, nulla poena sine lege*) is declared in the CC, which provides that 'a person shall be held liable under the CC only when the act committed by him/her is forbidden by a criminal law in force at the time of commission of the criminal act'. Furthermore, in the Constitution, it is stated that 'punishments may be imposed or applied only on the grounds established by law'. This rule is extended in the CC providing that 'punishments, penal or reformative measures and compulsory medical measures shall be imposed only in accordance with the law'. Explaining the meaning of this constitutional rule, the

111. Fedosiuk O. Baudžiamoji atsakomybė kaip kraštutinė priemonė (*ultima ratio*): teorija ir realybė, Jurisprudencija, 2012, No. 19(2), p. 717.
112. Rulings of the Supreme Court of Lithuania in criminal cases No. 2K-409/2011, No. 2K-P-267/2011, No. 2K-36/2012, No. 2K-69/2014.

Constitutional Court of Lithuania has emphasised that 'the legislature must establish punishments for criminal acts and sizes of these punishments by law only; punishments must be established for each criminal act'.[113]

135. The principle of legality is traditionally implemented through four requirements. The first is the requirement that the regulation of the criminal acts and punishments, as well as penal, reformative and compulsory medical measures, shall be reserved to written laws (*nullum crimen, nulla poena sine lege scripta*). The law prohibiting certain conducts and determining the definition of the punishable conduct has to be written and adopted by the *Seimas*. No criminal liability can be based on a decree issued by the President of the Republic or a legal act of the government or a minister.

136. The second is the requirement that the criminal law in force at the time of commission of the criminal act shall be applied and the retroactive application of more stringent laws is prohibited (*nullum crimen nulla poena sine lege praevia*) (on the principles concerning the temporal applicability of criminal law, *see* paragraphs 150–160).

137. The third is the requirement of specificity of criminal law (*nullum crimen, nulla poena sine lege certa*), which implies that all criminal acts must be defined in a clear and precise language. When explaining this requirement, the Supreme Court of Lithuania has noted that 'the definition of the criminal act is sufficiently clear, if the individual has the ability to know from the text of the law or, where appropriate, through judicial interpretation of the law what his/her actions or omissions may result in criminal liability'.[114]

138. The last requirement is the prohibition of analogy in the application of the law when establishing the criminality and (or) punishability of an act (*nullum crimen, nulla poena sine lege stricta*).

139. The Constitution, the CC and the Code of Criminal Procedure determine the principle of *non bis in idem,* which means that no person can be punished for the same violation of law twice. When explaining this constitutional principle, the Constitutional Court of Lithuania has noted in several cases that this prohibition:

> means a prohibition on punishing twice for the same act that is contrary to law, i.e., for the same crime, as well as for the same violation of law which is not a crime. The above-mentioned constitutional principle does not mean that different kinds of liability may not be applied to the person for the violation of the law. In itself, the constitutional principle non bis in idem does not deny the possibility of applying more than one sanction of the same kind (i.e., defined

113. Decision of the Constitutional Court of Lithuania of 10 Jun. 2003, *Valstybės žinios*, 2003, No. 57-2552.
114. Ruling of the Supreme Court of Lithuania in criminal case No. 2K-P-218/2004.

by the norms of the same branch of law) to a person for the same violation, i.e., the main and additional punishment or the main and additional administrative penalty.[115]

Furthermore, the Constitutional Court of Lithuania has emphasised that 'the constitutional principle *non bis in idem* also means, *inter alia,* that if a person, who has committed an act which is contrary to law, has been held administratively but not criminally liable, he/she cannot be held criminally liable for the said act'.[116]

II. Legality and Interpretation

140. The application of every provision of criminal law requires to interpret and reveal the meaning of the legal norm, as well as the essence and content of the definitions used in the law. In Lithuanian criminal law, only interpretations that reveal the meaning, essence and content of the law are consistent with the requirements of the principle of legality. Interpretations that expand legal provisions and create new legal norms for filling legal gaps are contrarily evaluated as an analogy, which is prohibited.

141. The doctrine of the Lithuanian criminal law recognises a number of types of interpretation (such as authentic, casuistic and doctrinal) and methods of interpretation (such as grammatical, logical, systematic, historical, teleological and comparative). Also, the interpretation may be divided into expanded or narrowed interpretation.

§2. The Principle of the Individual Guilty Mind

142. The principle of the individual guilty mind (or the principle of culpability) is one of the most fundamental principles of the Lithuanian criminal law. The CC establishes that 'a person shall be held liable under a criminal law only when he/she is guilty of committing a criminal act and only if at the time of the commission of the act the conduct of the person could have been reasonably expected to conform to the requirements of law'. In order to hold criminal liability for the offender, it must be established that he/she was culpable in the commission of the criminal act. This rule also means that the Lithuanian criminal law does not recognise the concept of strict liability (liability based for mere actions, regardless of the *mens rea*) as well as of vicarious liability (liability for the acts of others).

143. The individual guilt (which may be intentional or negligent) is a basic feature of the concept of a criminal act and the main element of the *corpus delicti* of

115. Decision of the Constitutional Court of Lithuania of 7 May, 2001, *Valstybės žinios*, 2001, No. 39-1373.
116. Decision of the Constitutional Court of Lithuania of 10 Nov. 2005, *Valstybės žinios*, 2005, No. 134-4819.

criminal act: the unlawful conduct cannot constitute a criminal act and the *corpus delicti* of criminal act without individual guilt (*nullum crimen sine culpa*). It should be noted that culpability is only a condition for punishment (*nulla poena sine culpa*), but not for some penal measures (e.g., property confiscation and extended confiscation of property) and compulsory medical measures that may be imposed even on a non-culpable person since compulsory medical measures are based on the dangerousness of the person and not on his/her guilt.

144. The principle of the individual guilty mind also requires that the person, in the situation in which he/she committed a criminal act, has had the possibility to act in accordance with the requirements of the law.

145. It should be noted that the principle of culpability must be applicable even in case of criminal liability of legal entities. The Constitutional Court of Lithuania has stated that the 'legal regulation established in […] the CC, under which the liability of the legal person is linked to the criminal act committed by the natural person, does not mean that the guilt of the legal person should not be proved according to the procedure established by law and recognised by a court judgment'.[117]

§3. The Principle of Justice and Proportionality

146. Proportionality is a constituent part of one of the most important constitutional principles – the principle of natural justice. The content of the principle of natural justice in criminal law has been endorsed by the Constitutional Court of Lithuania, which has emphasised that:

> the principle of natural justice consolidated in the Constitution presupposes that punishments established by a criminal law must be just; punishments and their sizes must be differentiated in criminal law, taking account the danger of criminal acts. This principle implies that the measures established by the state for violations of law must be proportionate (adequate) to the violation of law, they must be in line with the legitimate and generally important objectives sought, they may not restrict the person more than it is necessary in order to reach these objectives. It is not allowed to establish any legal regulation (punishments or their sizes) in a criminal law on the basis of which the court, while taking into account all circumstances of a case and applying the criminal law, would not be able to individualise the punishment which is imposed on a concrete person for a concrete criminal act.[118]

147. Hence, the principle of natural justice (and proportionality) is addressed at both the legislator, who should use criminal law only as *ultima ratio* and limit the

117. Decision of the Constitutional Court of Lithuania of 8 Jun. 2009, *Valstybės žinios*, 2009, No. 69-2798.

118. Decision of the Constitutional Court of Lithuania of 4 Jun. 2012, *Valstybės žinios*, 2012, No. 64-3246.

maximum duration or size of punishments, penal, reformative and compulsory medical measures *in abstracto*, and judges, who should abide by this principle when imposing sanctions *in concreto*.

148. Meanwhile, when explaining the significance of the principle of justice (and proportionality), the Supreme Court of Lithuania has stated that:

> imposed punishment must be proportionate to the committed crime: the punishment must comply with the nature and degree of the dangerousness of the criminal act, and in addition, it is necessary to take into account the convict's personality, behaviour of the victim and his/her opinion as well as public interest in execution of the justice.[119]

119. Rulings of the Supreme Court of Lithuania in criminal cases No. 2K-7-45/2007; 2K-428/2009; 2K-39-788/2021.

Chapter 2. Scope of Application of Criminal Statutes

§1. Principles Concerning the Applicability of Criminal Statutes with Respect to Time

149. The Law on Legislative Procedure[120] provides that the criminal law (as well as other normative legal acts) shall enter into force on the day following its official publication in the register of legal acts if the law itself does not provide for a later effective date. The criminal law will expire when it is replaced or repealed.

I. Prohibition of Retroactive Criminal Law

150. The Lithuanian criminal law in principle has no retroactive force since the CC provides for a general rule according to which 'the criminalisation of an act and punishability of a person shall be determined by a criminal law in force at the time of the commission of that act'. The prohibition of the retroactivity of the criminal law derives from the principle of legality which, *inter alia*, requires that a person may be held liable under the CC only when the act committed by him/her is forbidden by a criminal law in force at the time of commission of the criminal act and only if at the time of the commission of the act the conduct of the person could have been reasonably expected to conform to the requirements of law (on the principle of legality, *see* paragraphs 134–138).

151. The time of the commission of a criminal act depends on the type of the committed criminal act. All criminal acts in Lithuania are classified as either material or formal.[121] Criminal acts whose *actus reus* includes only the act are called 'formal'. In this case, the time of the commission of the criminal act is related to the completion of the act or omission. Criminal acts whose *actus reus* includes both the act and the consequences of the act are called 'material'. In this case, the time of the commission of the criminal act is related to the occurrence of the consequences provided for by a criminal law (e.g., death or bodily harm), where the occurrence of those consequences was desired at a different time.

152. The penal or reformative measures and compulsory medical measures may be imposed, if they are provided for by a criminal law in force at the time of passing of a court judgment. Meanwhile, the extended confiscation of property shall be imposed, if it is provided for by a criminal law in force at the time of the commission of a criminal act.

153. The general prohibition of applying criminal law retroactively has two exceptions in the Lithuanian criminal law: one concerns milder criminal law and the other stricter criminal law.

120. Lietuvos Respublikos teisėkūros pagrindų įstatymas, *Valstybės žinios*, 2012, No. 110-5564.
121. Lietuvos baudžiamoji teisė, Bendroji dalis, 1 knyga, Vilnius, Vilniaus universiteto leidykla, 2019, p. 181.

II. Retroactivity of the Milder Provision

154. The CC provides that 'a criminal law nullifying the criminality of an act, commuting a punishment or otherwise mitigating the legal circumstances for the person who committed the criminal act shall have a retroactive effect'. The Supreme Court of Lithuania has noted that criminal law nullifying the criminality of an act (decriminalising) is the law which does not provide completely for the former *corpus delicti* or narrows *corpus delicti* by providing for new or refusing old features *of corpus delicti.*[122]

155. The criminal law commuting a punishment is the law which, for example, reduces the minimum or maximum, or both of these limits of the punishment or provides a new milder punishment for a particular crime.[123] Meanwhile, the criminal law otherwise mitigating legal circumstances for the person who committed the criminal act is the law that (a) removes an act from the groups of the serious or grave crimes, (b) expands the possibilities to release the person from criminal liability and punishment or to suspend the execution of the punishment and (c) reduces the terms of statute of limitations of the criminal liability or previous conviction.

156. It should be noted that the Supreme Court of Lithuania did not allow a combined application of the new and old criminal law, not even if it benefits the accused.[124]

157. The criminal law nullifying the criminalisation of an act, commuting a punishment or in otherwise mitigating legal circumstances for the person who committed the criminal act must be applied to the persons who committed the criminal act prior to the coming into force of such a law, also to the persons serving punishments and those with previous convictions.

III. Retroactivity of the Stricter Statute

158. The CC provides for a general rule that 'a criminal law establishing the criminalisation of an act, imposing a more severe punishment upon or otherwise aggravating legal circumstances of the person who has committed the criminal act shall have no retroactive effect'. The Supreme Court of Lithuania has noted that a stricter criminal law is the law that establishes criminal liability for the new criminal act; provides for stricter types of punishment; increases the minimum or maximum or both of these limits of the punishment; restricts the possibilities to release

122. Decision of the Senate of the Supreme Court of Lithuania of 20 Dec. 2002 // Lietuvos Respublikos baudžiamasis kodeksas ir lydimoji medžiaga pastraipsniui, Vilnius, 2009, p. 53.
123. Švedas G. Švelnesnis baudžiamasis įstatymas ir jo taikymo ribos Lietuvos teismų jurisprudencijoje, Teisė, 2015, No. 97, p. 30.
124. Decision of the Senate of the Supreme Court of Lithuania of 20 Dec. 2002 // Lietuvos Respublikos baudžiamasis kodeksas ir lydimoji medžiaga pastraipsniui, Vilnius, 2009, p. 55.

from criminal liability and the punishment or suspend the execution of the punishment; extends the terms of statute of limitations of the criminal liability or previous conviction.[125]

159. In accordance with the requirements of the international treaties which Lithuania ratified (e.g., the Rome Statute of the International Criminal Court[126]), the provisions of the CC establishing liability for the following crimes constitute an exception to the prohibition of the retroactivity of a stricter criminal law: genocide (Article 99 of the CC), treatment of persons in a way prohibited under international law (Article 100 of the CC), the killing of persons protected under international humanitarian law (Article 101 of the CC), the deportation or transfer of civilians (Article 102 of the CC), the causation of bodily harm to, torture or other inhuman treatment of persons protected under international humanitarian law or violation of protection of their property (Article 103 of the CC), the forcible use of civilians or prisoners of war in the armed forces of the enemy (Article 105 of the CC), the destruction of protected objects or national valuable properties (Article 106 of the CC), aggression (Article 110 of the CC), the prohibited military attack (Article 111 of the CC), the use of prohibited means of warfare (Article 112 of the CC), the negligent performance of the commander's duties (Article 113(1) of the CC). The doctrine of the Lithuanian criminal law has stated that such exception may be applicable for the person who has not been prosecuted and convicted for the crime or released from the criminal liability or punishment.[127]

IV. The Extent of the Prohibition Against Retroactive Criminal Law

160. The prohibition of retroactive criminal law is applicable only in the substantive criminal law of Lithuania. The CCP provides for a general rule according to which the criminal procedure shall be established pursuant to the law effective at the moment of carrying out the procedural action. The CPE also states that the execution of punishments shall be governed pursuant to punishment's execution law effective at the moment the of authorities' acts.

§2. Principles Concerning the Applicability of Criminal Statutes with Respect to Space

I. The Territorial Principle

161. The CC states that persons who have committed criminal acts within the territory of the State of Lithuania or on board of the ships or aircraft flying the flag

125. Decision of the Senate of the Supreme Court of Lithuania of 20 Dec. 2002 // Lietuvos Respublikos baudžiamasis kodeksas ir lydimoji medžiaga pastraipsniui, Vilnius, 2009, p. 54.
126. Romos Tarptautinio baudžiamojo teismo statutas, *Valstybės žinios*, 2003, No. 49-2156; 49-2165; etc.
127. Lietuvos Respublikos baudžiamojo kodekso komentaras. Bendroji dalis (1-98 straipsniai), Vilnius, TIC, 2004, p. 42.

or displaying marks of registry of the State of Lithuania shall be held liable under the CC. The principle of territoriality is fundamental in the criminal law of Lithuania. The doctrine of Lithuanian criminal law has noted that the extraterritorial jurisdiction of the State is complementary to the territorial jurisdiction.[128] Moreover, the case law of the courts does not allow for the unambiguous conclusion that primacy has been given to the principle of territoriality.

162. The territory of the Republic of Lithuania is defined by the State borders of Lithuania. According to the Law on State Borders and Protection thereof,[129] the State border of the Republic of Lithuania refers to the line, and the vertical surface extending along this line, that delineates the limits of the Republic of Lithuania on land, in the interior of the earth, in the space above, in inland waters, and in the territorial sea and the depths thereof. The sea region and the inland waters of the frontier zone are: (1) the waters of the Republic of Lithuania located on the dry land side of the territorial sea base connecting the furthest seaport jetty points that extend into the sea; (2) the waters of the Couronian Lagoon, rivers, lakes and other water bodies situated along the frontier zone of the Republic of Lithuania.

163. The place of commission of a criminal act depends on the type of the committed criminal act. The place of commission of a formal criminal act is the place in which a person acted or ought to have acted or could have acted. The place of commission of a material criminal act is the place in which the consequences provided for by a criminal law occurred. The criminal act of omission is characterised by the offender having not taken certain actions in the appropriate time and place that he/she could and ought to have taken. The location of such a criminal act is therefore in that location where the obligation to act occurs. The place of commission of a criminal act by accomplices shall be the place in which the criminal act was committed or, if one of the accomplices acted elsewhere, the place where he/she acted.

164. The CC states that a single criminal act committed both in the territory of the State of Lithuania and abroad shall be considered to have been committed in the territory of the Republic of Lithuania if it was commenced or completed or discontinued in this territory. The essence of this rule is that if the criminal act was being committed in Lithuania and abroad, it is sufficient for criminal liability to arise according to the CC of Lithuania, that at least one part of criminal act (the beginning, the end, or the continuation and the end of the act) would have been committed in Lithuania. The doctrine of Lithuanian criminal law deems that 'this rule deliberately pre-programmes a clash between criminal statutes of several states and intends to prevent that a person who commits a criminal act in several states could avoid criminal liability. In which state criminal liability will take place depends on

---

128. Nevera A. Valstybės baudžiamosios jurisdikcijos principai, Vilnius, TIC, 2006, p. 12.
129. Lietuvos Respublikos valstybės sienos ir jos apsaugos įstatymo Nr. VIII-1666 pakeitimo įstatymas, TAR, 2017, No. 12168.

various circumstances as defined in the international treaties of Lithuania, for example, citizenship of the offender or victim or the place where the evidence can be found'.[130]

165. The Lithuanian criminal law extends the scope of the territorial principle to conducts committed on board the ships or aircraft flying the flag or displaying marks of registry of the State of Lithuania. The application of Lithuanian criminal law is foreseeable for all persons when boarding ships or aircraft displaying the flag or marks of registry of the State of Lithuania.

166. Ships or aircraft operating in a foreign country are subject to the laws of that foreign country but this does not mean that the foreign law will automatically be applied if a criminal act is committed on that ship or aircraft.

II. Extraterritorial Criminal Jurisdiction

167. The Lithuanian criminal law provides the principles of jurisdiction of active personality, State protection and universality.

168. It should be noted that the principles of passive personality and representational jurisdiction (in which a crime is prosecuted and sentenced on behalf of another State[131]) are not recognised in the criminal law of Lithuania. Currently, the doctrine of the Lithuanian criminal law is discussing the possibility of adopting the principle of passive personality in the CC.[132]

A. Principle of Active Personality

169. The CC provides that 'citizens of the Republic of Lithuania and other permanent residents of Lithuania shall be held liable for the crimes committed abroad under this Code'. The validation of this principle is found in the constitutional ban on the extradition of Lithuanian citizens (except for those cases provided for in the international treaties that the Republic of Lithuania has ratified) and the provisions of international agreements of mutual assistance in criminal matters, which allow the State to refuse extradition of its citizen, to not provide legal aid and so forth. The doctrine of Lithuanian criminal law states that the principle of active personality is based on the permanent relationship between a person and a State.[133]

130. Lietuvos Respublikos baudžiamojo kodekso komentaras. Bendroji dalis (1-98 straipsniai), Vilnius, TIC, 2004, p. 48–49.
131. Bose M., Meyer F., Schneider A. Conflicts of Jurisdiction in Criminal Matters in the European Union, Volume II: Rights, Principles and Model rules, Nomos, Baden-Baden, 2014, p. 103.
132. Švedas G., Veršekys P., Levon J., Prapiestis D. Lietuvos Respublikos baudžiamojo kodekso bendrosios dalies vientisumo ir naujovių suderinimo iššūkiai, Vilnius, Vilniaus universiteto leidykla, 2017, p. 123.
133. Nevera A. Valstybės baudžiamosios jurisdikcijos principai, Vilnius, TIC, 2006, p. 98–99.

170. The principle of active personality may be applied under the following conditions: (a) the crime (and not just a misdemeanour under the CC) has been committed; (b) the crime has started, has been acted and completed or terminated in a foreign country; (c) the crime is considered a crime in both Lithuania and the country where the crime was committed (double criminality clause); (d) the crime has been committed by a citizen of the Republic of Lithuania or any other person permanently residing in Lithuania; (e) the offender is present in the territory of the Republic of Lithuania; (f) there is no legal basis to surrender a citizen from the Republic of Lithuania or any other person permanently residing in Lithuania to the State in which the crime has been committed; and (g) the offender has not been prosecuted and convicted for the crime, or released from criminal liability or punishment in another country.

171. Lithuanian citizens are those persons who meet the requirements of the Law on Citizenship.[134] The doctrine of the Lithuanian criminal law has noted that the principle of active personality can also be applied to those citizens of the Republic of Lithuania who did not have that status during the commission of the criminal act.[135]

B. Principle of Protection

172. The CC provides that 'the aliens who do not have a permanent residence in the Republic of Lithuania shall be liable under a criminal law where they commit crimes abroad against the State of Lithuania as provided for in Articles 114–128 of this Code'.

173. The principle of protection may be applied under the following conditions: (a) the crime has been committed by a foreigner (a foreign national, a stateless person or a person who does not have permanent residence in the Republic of Lithuania); (b) the crime has been committed abroad; (c) the crime is covered under Chapter VI of the CC, establishing liability for crimes against Lithuania's independence, territorial integrity and constitutional order; (d) crime is considered a crime in both Lithuania and the country where the crime was committed (double criminality clause); (e) the offender is in the territory of the Republic of Lithuania; and (f) the offender has not been prosecuted and convicted for the crime, or released from the criminal liability or punishment, in another country.

174. Chapter VI 'Crimes against the independence, territorial integrity and constitutional order of the state of Lithuania' of the CC provides criminal liability for coups (Article 114 of the CC), attempt on the life of the President of the Republic of Lithuania (Article 115 of the CC), attempt on the life of a representative of another state or international public organisation (Article 116 of the CC), treason (Article 117 of the CC), assistance to another State in carrying out activities hostile

134. Lietuvos Respublikos pilietybės įstatymas, *Valstybės žinios*, 2010, No. 144-7361.
135. Nevera A. Valstybės baudžiamosios jurisdikcijos principai, Vilnius, TIC, 2006, p. 106.

to the Republic of Lithuania (Article 118 of the CC), espionage (Article 119 of the CC), collaboration (Article 120 of the CC), creation of anti-constitutional groups or organisations and participation therein (Article 121 of the of the CC), public incitement to infringe upon sovereignty of the Republic of Lithuania by using violence (Article 122 of the CC), abuse of authority (Article 123 of the CC), violation of international sanctions (Article 123(1) of the CC), unlawful possession of information constituting a State secret (Article 124 of the CC), disclosure of a State secret (Article 125 of the CC), loss of a State secret (Article 126 of the CC), desecration of State symbols (Article 127 of the CC) and desecration of symbols of a foreign State, the European Union or an international public organisation (Article 128 of the CC). This is a comprehensive list of crimes. Therefore, the commission of a crime that harms the essential interests of the State of Lithuania, but which is not included in the list, will not result in criminal liability. The foreigner who commits one of these crimes is to be prosecuted in Lithuania.

C. *Principle of Universality*

175. The CC provides that:

> persons shall be liable under this Code regardless of their citizenship and place of residence, also of the place of commission of a crime and whether the act committed is subject to punishment under laws of the place of commission of the crime where they commit the following crimes subject to liability under treaties: 1) crimes against humanity and war crimes (Articles 99–113(1) of the CC); 2) trafficking in human beings (Article 147 of the CC); 3) purchase or sale of a child (Article 157 of the CC); 4) production, storage or handling of counterfeit currency or securities (Article 213 of the CC); 5) property laundering (Article 216 of the CC); 6) bribery (Article 225 of the CC); 7) trading in influence (Article 226 of the CC); 8) graft (Article 227 of the CC); 9) piracy (Para 1 and 2, Article 251(1) of the CC); 10) acts of terrorism and crimes related to terrorist activity (Article 252(1) of the CC; 11) unlawful handling of nuclear or radioactive materials or other sources of ionising radiation (Articles 256, 256(1) and 257 of the CC); 12) crimes related to possession of narcotic or psychotropic, toxic or highly active substances (Articles 259–269 of the CC); 13) crimes against the environment (Articles 270, 270(1), 270(2), 270(3), 271, 272 and 274 of the CC).

176. Lithuania applies the principle of universal jurisdiction only to those crimes provided in the international treaties ratified by Lithuania and in the EU legal acts, for example, crimes against humanity and war crimes – in the mentioned Rome Statute of the International Criminal Court or trafficking in human beings and the purchase or sale of a child – in The Protocol on Trafficking in Persons, Especially Women and Children to Prevent, Suppress and Punish Trafficking in Persons, supplementing the United Nations Convention against Transnational Organized

Crime,[136] etc. There is an exhaustive list of the crimes covered in the international treaties of Lithuania and EU legal acts, to which the principle of universal jurisdiction must be applied. One of the key features of this principle is that the person who has committed an international or cross-border crime is liable under the CC of Lithuania, even if the act is not subject to punishment under the laws of the place of its commission.

D. Cases

177. A person who has committed crimes abroad shall be held criminally liable under the CC of Lithuania on the grounds of the principles of active personality and protection, only where the committed act is recognised as a crime and is punishable under the criminal laws of the state of the place of commission of the crime and the CC of Lithuania (double criminality clause). The double criminality clause is understood as a requirement that an individual may not be held criminally liable for an act committed abroad if the criminal act he/she is accused of is not punishable under the laws of the State where that criminal act was committed (i.e., if the laws of that foreign country do not provide for an analogous of the criminal act) or if, in that State, the particular criminal act is not penalised (i.e., if foreign criminal law provides for a similar criminal act, but there exist particular circumstances that eliminate criminal liability for such a person, for example, the situation of necessity). The double criminality clause does not require that rules establishing criminal liability are the same in the Republic of Lithuania and the State where the crime was committed. For prosecution to be carried out it is sufficient that criminal liability for the person's acts is recognised by the laws of both countries.[137]

178. Although the CC does not require that the normative definitions of the acts for which a person is being prosecuted be the same in the state of the crime and in the Republic of Lithuania, the level of danger that the acts represent must be classified similarly in both countries. A person can be prosecuted only for conduct that is recognised as a crime (i.e., not a misdemeanour or an offence of criminal law), not only in Lithuania but also in the State of the criminal act.

179. The features of the crimes, which are prosecuted on the ground of the principle of protection, require that, when determining the criminal nature of an act according to the local laws of the State, it must be decided whether the act would

---

136. Protokolas dėl prekybos žmonėmis, ypač moterimis ir vaikais, prevencijos, sustabdymo bei baudimo už vertimąsi ja, papildantis Jungtinių Tautų Organizacijos Konvenciją prieš tarptautinį organizuotą nusikalstamumą, *Valstybės žinios*, 2003, No. 49-2157, No. 49-2166.

137. Švedas G. Country report 'Lithuania' // Bose M., Meyer F., Schneider A. (eds.) Conflicts of Jurisdiction in Criminal Matters in the European Union. Volume I. National Reports and Comparative Analysis, Baden-Baden, Nomos, 2013, p. 305, 308–309.

be considered criminal if it had not been directed against the interests of the Republic of Lithuania, but against the interests of the State where the crime was committed.[138]

180. Implementing the requirements of Directive 2011/92/EU of the European Parliament and of the Council of 13 December 2011 on combating the sexual abuse and sexual exploitation of children and child pornography, and replacing Council Framework Decision 2004/68/JHA,[139] the CC provides for the special rule that a citizen of the Republic of Lithuania or another person permanently residing in Lithuania who has committed abroad one or more crimes shall be punishable regardless of whether the committed act is punishable under the criminal law of the state of commission of the crime. The crimes include rape of a child (paragraphs 3 and 4, Article 149 of the CC), sexual assault in respect of a child (paragraphs 3 and 4, Article 150 of the CC), sexual abuse in respect of a child (paragraph 2, Article 151 of the CC), sexual relationship with a person under the age of 16 (Article 151(1) of the CC), grooming of a person under the age of 16 (Article 152(1) of the CC), etc.

181. Where a person who has committed a crime abroad is prosecuted in Lithuania, but a different punishment is provided for this crime in each country, the person shall be subject to a punishment according to laws of Lithuania. However, in this case it may not exceed the maximum limit of punishment specified in the criminal laws of the State of the place of commission of the crime. The maximum punishment's limit under the particular article of the Special Part of the CC should not be the only criterion for determining the maximum punishment limit for the specific criminal act specified in the criminal laws of the State. The maximum punishment's limit and its imposition should also take into account other rules of foreign criminal law governing, for example, the types of punishment, the rules of the imposition of punishments, the release from the criminal liability and punishment and the suspension of the execution of the punishment.

E. The Effect of Foreign Adjudication and Execution

182. Lithuanian citizens, other permanent residents of Lithuania or foreigners may be convicted and punished by the local court of the State where the crime was committed. In this case, the rule of the CC applies, under which 'no one may be punished for the same criminal act twice', as does the rule of the CC, under which a person who has committed the crimes abroad shall not be held liable under the CC of the Republic of Lithuania, when he/she:

138. Lietuvos Respublikos baudžiamojo kodekso komentaras. Bendroji dalis (1-98 straipsniai), Vilnius, TIC, 2004, p. 59.
139. Directive 2011/92/EU of the European Parliament and of the Council of 13 Dec. 2011 on combating the sexual abuse and sexual exploitation of children and child pornography, and replacing Council Framework Decision 2004/68/JHA, *OJ L 335, 17.12.2011, p. 1–14.*

(1) has served the sentence imposed by a foreign court (the term 'foreign court' must be interpreted broadly; it includes, for example, the International Criminal Court, the International Criminal Tribunal for the Former Yugoslavia);
(2) has been released from serving the entire sentence (or a part of it) imposed by a foreign court;
(3) has been acquitted or released from criminal liability or punishment by a foreign court's judgment, or no punishment has been imposed by reason of the statute of limitation or on other legal grounds provided for in that State.

§3. Principles Concerning the Applicability of Criminal Statutes with Respect to Persons

I. Immunities Based on National Public Law

183. The Constitution sets out the immunity for the members of the *Seimas* (the Parliament), the President of the Republic, the Prime Minister and ministers, judges (including judges of the Constitutional Court). Immunity is granted only during the time in office.

184. According to the Law on the Status and Working Conditions of the Members of the European Parliament Elected in the Republic of Lithuania,[140] a member of the European Parliament shall enjoy the same personal immunity in the territory of the Republic of Lithuania as a member of the Seimas of the Republic of Lithuania, unless otherwise provided for in the European Union legislation. Furthermore, laws on elections set out the immunity also for the candidates to the position of member of the European Parliament,[141] the *Seimas*,[142] local councils[143] as well as for president.[144] The candidates to the European Parliament, the *Seimas*, local councils as well as the president may not be held criminally liable or be detained, or have their liberty restricted otherwise without the prior consent of the Central Electoral Commission.

185. According to the Constitution, a member of the *Seimas* may neither be held criminally liable, arrested, nor may his/her liberty be otherwise restricted without the consent of the *Seimas*. A member of the *Seimas* may not be persecuted for his/her voting or speeches at the *Seimas*. However, he/she may be held liable according to the general procedure for personal insult or slander.

186. Judges of the Constitutional Court have the same rights concerning the inviolability of their person as members of the *Seimas*.

---

140. Lietuvos Respublikos Lietuvos Respublikoje išrinktų Europos Parlamento narių statuso ir darbo sąlygų įstatymas, *Valstybės žinios*, 2004, No. 32-1009.
141. Lietuvos Respublikos rinkimų į Europos Parlamentą įstatymas, *Valstybės žinios*, 2003, No. 115-5192.
142. Lietuvos Respublikos Seimo rinkimų įstatymas, *Valstybės žinios*, 2000, No. 59-1760.
143. Lietuvos Respublikos savivaldybių tarybų rinkimų įstatymas, TAR, 2014, No. 10139.
144. Lietuvos Respublikos Prezidento rinkimų įstatymas, *Valstybės žinios*, 2013, No. 120-6055.

187. According to the Constitution, the person of the President of the Republic shall be inviolable: while in office, he/she may be neither detained nor held criminally or administratively liable. The President of the Republic may be removed from office only for a gross violation of the Constitution or a breach of the oath, or when he/she is found to have committed a crime. The issue of the removal of the President of the Republic from office shall be decided by the Seimas according to the procedure for impeachment.

188. According to the Constitution, the Prime Minister, ministers and judges may not be held criminally liable or be detained, or have their liberty restricted otherwise, without the prior consent of the *Seimas* or, in the period between the sessions of the *Seimas*, without the prior consent of the President of the Republic.

189. The Constitution provides that the President of the Republic, the president and judges of the Constitutional Court, the president and judges of the Supreme Court, the president and judges of the Court of Appeal, as well as any members of the *Seimas*, who grossly violate the Constitution or breach their oath, or are found to have committed a crime, may be removed from office or have the mandate of a Member of the *Seimas* revoked by a three-fifth majority vote of all the members of the *Seimas*. This shall be performed according to the procedure for impeachment proceedings, which is established by the Statute of the *Seimas*. [145]

190. The prior consent of the *Seimas*, the President of the Republic, or the Central Election Commission suspends the immunity. The impeachment procedure is a legal decision of politicians and not a part of the criminal procedure.

191. The immunity is not absolute since the CCP allows to start the criminal procedure. However, the prosecutor and court cannot write a notice of suspicion, question a person as a suspect or recognise him/her as a suspect, arrest or otherwise restrict his/her liberty. Other procedural coercive measures may be applicable to the extent not prohibited by the laws of Lithuania or international law. If, after the execution of all non-prohibited procedural actions, the competent authority does not permit a person to prosecute, the criminal procedure should be discontinued. The criminal procedure may be renewed when there is the permission of the competent authority to prosecute or when the immunity was deprived otherwise, or it is necessary to carry out the procedural actions, which are not prohibited by the laws of Lithuania or international law.

II. Immunities Based on International Public Law

192. The criminal liability of the persons who enjoy immunity under international legal norms and commit a criminal act in the territory of the Republic of Lithuania is decided in accordance with the international treaties of Lithuania and

145. Lietuvos Respublikos Seimo statutas, *Valstybės žinios*, 1999, No. 5-97.

the laws of Lithuania. In accordance with the Vienna Convention on Diplomatic Relations,[146] the Law on the Status of Diplomatic Missions of Foreign States in the Republic of Lithuania[147] states that:

> heads of diplomatic missions and diplomatic agents, together with members of their families, shall enjoy personal inviolability and inviolability of the private residence. Diplomats who are not citizens of the Republic of Lithuania enjoy immunity from criminal, civil, and administrative liability in the Republic of Lithuania. Administrative and technical personnel and their family members who are not citizens of the Republic of Lithuania enjoy privileges and immunities. Service staff members who are not citizens of the Republic of Lithuania and diplomats who are citizens of the Republic of Lithuania enjoy immunity only for the actions carried out in the performance of official duties, unless otherwise agreed between the states.

193. The Republic of Lithuania has ratified bilateral and multilateral international treaties dealing with immunities. As a result of these treaties, for instance, the officials in the United Nations in accordance with the United Nations Convention on the Privileges and Immunities,[148] the representatives of the Member States and officials of various United Nations and other specialised agencies (e.g., the International Labour Organisation and the World Health Organisation) according to the Convention for officials of the specialised agencies of the Privileges and Immunities,[149] the representatives of the Member States and the Council of Europe officials in accordance with the Statute of the Council[150] and the Council of Europe on the Privileges and Immunities of the basic agreement,[151] the European Court of Human Rights judges under the European Convention on Human Rights and Fundamental Freedoms,[152] the International Criminal Court judges, prosecutors, and deputy and secretary, according to the mentioned Rome Statute of the International Criminal Court, the members of the Commission against the Torture and Other Cruel, Inhuman or Degrading Treatment or Punishment, according to the Convention against Torture and Other Cruel, Inhuman or Degrading Treatment or Punishment.[153]

---

146. Vienos konvencija dėl diplomatinių santykių, *Valstybės žinios*, 1999, No. 83-2455.
147. Lietuvos Respublikos įstatymas dėl užsienio valstybių diplomatinių atstovybių Lietuvos Respublikoje statuso, *Valstybės žinios*, 1991, No. 29-791; 1992, No. 22-634.
148. Konvencija dėl Jungtinių Tautų privilegijų ir imunitetų, *Valstybės Žinios*, 1999, No. 83-2457.
149. Konvencija dėl specializuotų agentūrų privilegijų ir imunitetų, *Valstybės Žinios*, 1999, No. 83-2458.
150. Europos Tarybos statutas, *Valstybės Žinios*, 2002, No. 40-987.
151. Europos Tarybos privilegijų ir imunitetų pagrindinį susitarimas, *Valstybės Žinios*, 1998, No. 59-1658.
152. Europos žmogaus teisių ir pagrindinių laisvių apsaugos konvencija, *Valstybės Žinios*, 2000, No. 96-3016.
153. Konvencija prieš kankinimus ir kitokį žiaurų, nežmonišką ar žeminantį elgesį ir baudimą, *Valstybės Žinios*, 1998, No. 86-2393.

194. In each case that raises the question of whether a person has immunity from the criminal jurisdiction of the Republic of Lithuania, one must accurately identify the personal status, its legal basis (international treaty of Lithuania) and the possible immunity enjoyed by that person.[154]

154. Lietuvos Respublikos baudžiamojo kodekso komentaras. Bendroji dalis (1-98 straipsniai), Vilnius, TIC, 2004, p. 50.

Chapter 3. General Principles of Criminal Liability

§1. Introduction: The Basic Elements of Criminal Offences

195. Lithuanian criminal law uses both a material and formal definition of criminal acts.

196. The CC of Lithuania divides all criminal acts into crimes and misdemeanours. A crime shall be a dangerous act (act or omission) forbidden under the CC and punishable with imprisonment. A misdemeanour shall be a dangerous act (act or omission) forbidden under the CC, which is punishable by a non-custodial punishment, with the exception of arrest. These statutory concepts of crime and misdemeanour allow to specify four mandatory features of the criminal act:

(1) every criminal act must be a conduct. It means that criminal acts must be fruit of a conscious and wilful human behaviour, which may be an action or omission;
(2) every criminal act must be a dangerous act. The Constitutional Court of Lithuania has noted that 'in a democratic state under the rule of law the legislator has the right and duty to prohibit by means of laws such acts that may essentially harm the interests of persons, society or the State or there might be a threat of such harm'.[155] The dangerousness of a criminal act is described by the nature and degree of the dangerousness. The nature of the dangerousness of criminal acts is determined, *inter alia*, by the values which are encroached upon by means of these acts, the consequences of these acts and so forth. The degree of dangerousness shows the size of the dangerousness, which is important in cases where the criminal acts are of the same nature of dangerousness. Crimes are considered to be more dangerous than a misdemeanour;
(3) every criminal act must be unlawful. It means that (a) every criminal act shall be unlawful when the committed act is forbidden by a criminal law in force at the time of commission of the criminal act, and (b) every criminal act must have all the elements of the *corpus delicti* of the criminal act provided in the CC (*see* paragraph 198); and
(4) every criminal act must punishable by imprisonment (in case of crime) or by a non-custodial punishment (in case of misdemeanour).

197. The CC provides an exhaustive classification of the crimes. First of all, the crimes are divided into crimes committed with intent and crimes committed through negligence. Negligent crimes are not further divided into groups and compose one group of criminal acts. Intentional crimes are divided into minor, less serious, serious and grave crimes. A minor crime shall be an intentional crime punishable, under the criminal law, by an imprisonment for the maximum duration of three years. A less serious crime shall be an intentional crime punishable, under the criminal law,

155. Decision of the Constitutional Court of Lithuania of 4 Jun. 2012, *Valstybės žinios*, 2012, No. 64-3246.

by an imprisonment for the maximum duration in excess of three years, but not exceeding six years. A serious crime shall be an intentional crime punishable, under the criminal law, by an imprisonment for the duration in excess of six years, but not exceeding ten years. A grave crime shall be an intentional crime punishable, under the criminal law, by an imprisonment for the maximum duration in excess of ten years or by a life imprisonment.

198. The formal definition of criminal act is disclosed through the *corpus delicti* of the criminal act, which consists of four elements:

(1) object: the protected values and victim;
(2) objective side: criminal act (act or omission), consequences, causal relation, as well as time, place, way and means of the criminal act;
(3) subject: the age and legal capacity of the natural person; the conditions for the criminal liability of a legal entity;
(4) subjective side: guilt (intention and negligence), motive and purpose of the criminal act.

199. The protected value, criminal act, age and legal capacity of a natural person and guilt are necessary elements of the *corpus delicti* of each criminal act provided in the CC. Other elements (e.g., victim or consequences) are necessary solely in the cases provided for separately in the *corpus delicti* of the concrete criminal act (e.g., the consequences in the *corpus delicti* of the killing of a newborn child).

200. Taking into account the above-mentioned differences, these elements of the *corpus delicti* of the criminal act may be only conditionally attributed with a common law classification of *actus reus* and *mens rea.*

§2. The Material or Physical Element (*Actus Reus*)

I. Description

201. The criminal act (which may take two forms: act or omission), consequences and causal relation, also time, place, way and means of the criminal act may be attributed with the material or physical element (*actus reus*).

202. As mentioned, the criminal act must be a conscious and wilful human behaviour, which may be an action or omission. The criminal act must be a human behaviour and not human thoughts or emotions (if they are not converted into action). For criminal law, it is only relevant that human behaviour (or those movements of the body) which was conscious and led by the will. Movements of the body that result, for example, from a reflex shall not be recognised as a criminal act.

II. Acts, Omissions and Causation

203. Criminal acts in the Lithuanian criminal law can be classified in: (a) criminal act committed by action and by omission; (b) material criminal act and formal criminal act; (c) continued criminal act and continuous criminal act.

A. *Offences of Action*

204. According to the CC of Lithuania, the action is the main form of commission of criminal acts. Action means an active behaviour of the person by carrying out various body movement(s). The Lithuanian criminal law describes it in two ways. First, the criminal law requires that the action is carried out with certain modalities; thus, an act will be relevant only if it has been committed in accordance with the model described by the criminal law. Second, criminal law also covers human behaviour, which has caused certain consequences, regardless in which manner it was realised.

205. Actions may be committed in many ways, therefore, the legislator, when defining the features of the criminal act, often does not specify concrete actions, but uses more generalised concepts, for example, 'murder', 'destruction' or 'damage'.

B. *Offences of Omission*

206. Certain criminal acts may be carried out by omission, which is, according to the CC of Lithuania, the other form through which criminal acts can be committed. Omission means a passive behaviour of a person, i.e., failing to do what should have been done or failing to act, when one has both the opportunity and the capability to do what should have been done.[156]

207. The doctrine of the Lithuanian criminal law divides all criminal acts of omission into two groups: 'real criminal act by omission' (*delictum ommissionis*) and 'unreal criminal act by omission' (*delictum commissionis per omissionem*).[157]

208. In case of a real criminal act of omission, the perpetrator is held responsible only for the act of omission, and not for any potential consequences. The *corpora delicti* of these criminal acts do not describe any consequences as a necessary element.

156. Lietuvos Respublikos baudžiamojo kodekso komentaras. Bendroji dalis (1-98 straipsniai), Vilnius, TIC, 2004, p. 88.
157. Baudžiamoji teisė : Bendroji dalis, Vilnius, Eugrimas, 2003, p. 293.

209. Meanwhile, the *corpus delicti* of unreal criminal acts of omission include the occurrence of consequences and the perpetrator is not punished solely for the failure to act, but for the failure to avert such consequences although the perpetrator was legally bound to do so.

C. Commission by Omission

210. As it was mentioned before, the essence of the unreal criminal acts of omission lies in the breach of duty to avert the occurrence of the consequences prescribed in the criminal law. This means that this type of omission liability may exist only in the context of the so-called material (or causation) criminal acts, whose statutory definitions describe a consequence as a necessary element of the *corpus delicti* of the criminal act.

211. The unreal criminal acts by omission may be committed only by a person legally bound to prevent the occurrence of the prescribed consequences. The doctrine of the Lithuanian criminal law traditionally provides the following legal grounds for obligation to act: (a) profession or official duties (e.g., doctor or policemen), (b) family relationship (e.g., parents towards their children), (c) a prior dangerous act of a person (e.g., the driver who caused an accident must provide medical assistance to the victims), etc.[158]

D. Causation Offences

212. For some criminal acts, the causation of consequences is either a necessary element of the *corpus delicti* of the criminal act or an aggravating circumstance. In the light of this, the Lithuanian criminal law also draws a distinction between: (1) formal criminal acts, which do not require consequences; and (2) material (or causation) criminal acts, in which the consequences and causal relation between an action or omission and the consequences are constitutive elements of the *corpus delicti* of the criminal act. In formal criminal acts, the criminal law punishes the commission of an action or an omission. If a consequence occurs, it may be considered as an aggravating circumstance of a criminal act that was already punishable without any consequences occurring. In the case of material (causation) criminal acts, neither action nor failure to act are punishable as such; the act or omission will only be punishable if it causes a certain consequence as defined by criminal law (e.g., death of the victim). The mere conduct of a person can only constitute responsibility for attempt to commit material (causation) criminal act.

158. Lietuvos Respublikos baudžiamojo kodekso komentaras. Bendroji dalis (1-98 straipsniai), Vilnius, TIC, 2004, p. 90.

213. Consequences according to the doctrine of the Lithuanian criminal law may be physical (e.g., bodily injuries) and material (e.g., damage of the property).[159] Material consequences also may be divided into those which may be financially measurable (e.g., in case of car theft) and immeasurable in money (e.g., in case of air pollution).

214. The CC of Lithuania traditionally describes consequences in a concrete, detailed form (e.g., murder of another person) or in general, without specifying concrete consequences (e.g., violation of the requirements of safety or health protection at work, where it 'causes other serious consequences' (Article 176 of the CC)).

215. The causal relation is a necessary element only of the *corpus delicti* of the material (causation) criminal act, which is completed when the described consequences have occurred. The causal relation according to the doctrine of Lithuanian criminal law is such a relationship between the facts in which one of them (the act) consistently determines the appearance of the other (the consequences).[160] The causal relationship is not defined in the CC of Lithuania, but it has been developed by the court's jurisprudence. The Supreme Court of Lithuania has stated that starting point for the examination of the causal relationship is the determination of the formula *conditio sine qua non*, according to which a relevant cause is an act (which is prohibited in criminal law and committed by a perpetrator) without which the consequence would not have occurred.[161] Meanwhile, the next step is the setting up of the nature of the causal relationship. The criminal liability can be based only on a mandatory (and not accidental) causal relationship,[162] which means that the consequences are adequate or typical consequences of the conduct of the perpetrator.

216. The causal relationship is a necessary element of the *corpus delicti* of the material (causation) criminal acts of omission as well. In the case of these criminal acts, however, determination of the causal relationship should find an answer to the question of what would have happened had the perpetrator carried out the omitted conduct. If the consequences occurred, the omission would be its cause.

III. Classification of Offences from the Point of View of the Material Element

A. *Momentary and Continuous Offences*

217. The Lithuanian criminal law did not provide the definition of a momentary criminal act. On the contrary, the jurisprudence of the Supreme Court of Lithuania

159. Lietuvos baudžiamoji teisė, Bendroji dalis, 1 knyga, Vilnius, Vilniaus universiteto leidykla, 2019, p. 210–211.
160. Baudžiamoji teisė. Bendroji dalis: Vilnius, Eugrimas, 2003, p. 180–181.
161. Ruling of the Supreme Court of Lithuania in criminal case No. 2K-450/2003.
162. Ruling of the Supreme Court of Lithuania in criminal case No. 2K-250/2005.

and the doctrine of the Lithuanian criminal law distinguish the types of continued and continuous criminal acts and reveal their features.

218. According to the jurisprudence of the Supreme Court of Lithuania, a continued criminal act is a situation when the offender commits the same criminal act through several identical or homogeneous acts, every act of which corresponds to the *corpus delicti* of the same article of the Special Part of the CC, but only with unified intent.[163] A continued criminal act is also a situation when several acts are not identical or homogeneous, but they implement the same feature of the criminal act[164] or alternative features of the criminal act.[165]

219. A continuous criminal act is characterised by the creation and maintenance of an unlawful situation, which comprises one *corpus delicti* of the criminal act.[166] An example of the continuous criminal act when the unlawful situation comes from non-fulfilment of the legal obligation is *corpus delicti* of the evasion of a child's maintenance (Article 164 of the CC), unlawful possession of firearms, ammunition, explosives or explosive materials (Article 253 of the CC), etc.

220. The continued and continuous criminal act is only one, single criminal act and does not constitute concurrence of criminal acts.

B. Occasional and Habitual Offences

221. Under the Lithuanian criminal law, criminal acts traditionally are not classified into occasional and habitual criminal acts. On the contrary, some of the *corpus delicti* of the criminal acts presuppose a long-term perpetration, for example, *corpus delicti* of the unauthorised engagement in economic, commercial, financial or professional activities (Article 202 of the CC) requires that a person should 'undertake economic, commercial, financial or professional activities in the form of a business or on a large scale without holding a licence/authorisation to engage in the activities for which it is required', etc. The doctrine of Lithuanian criminal law and court's jurisprudence such habitual criminal act shall consider a continuous criminal act.

222. Also, it should be mentioned that habitual criminal acts may constitute a repeat offence and dangerous repeat offence that significantly influence the imposition of the punishment (*see* paragraphs 603–610).

163. Rulings of the Supreme Court of Lithuania in criminal cases No. 2K-474/2010, No. 2K-650/2010.
164. Ruling of the Supreme Court of Lithuania in criminal case No. 2K-269/2011.
165. Ruling of the Supreme Court of Lithuania in criminal case No. 2K-322/2008.
166. Ruling of the Supreme Court of Lithuania in criminal case No. 2K-P-267/2011.

§3. The Moral or Mental Element (*Mens Rea*)

I. Subjective Guilt or Culpability

223. The principle of culpability is one of the most fundamental principles in the Lithuania criminal law. In order to hold criminal liability on the offender, it must be established that he/she was culpable in the commission of a criminal act. This rule must be applicable even in case of criminal liability of the legal entity. This rule also means that the Lithuanian criminal law does not recognise the concept of strict liability as well as vicarious liability.

224. The doctrine of the Lithuanian criminal law has stated that guilt is a personal mental relationship to his/her act and the consequences of his/her act.[167] The individual guilt (which may be intentional or negligent) is a basic feature of the concept of a criminal act and the main element of the *corpus delicti* of the criminal act: unlawful conduct cannot constitute a criminal act and *corpus delicti* of the criminal act without individual guilt.

225. The Lithuanian criminal law provides two forms of guilt: intent and negligence. Intention is the main form of guilt. Meanwhile, a person shall be punishable for the commission of a criminal act through negligence solely in the cases provided for separately in the article of the Special Part of the CC.

II. Intent

226. The Lithuanian criminal law provides two definitions of the intent: one – for formal criminal act, and one – for material (causal) criminal act. The formal criminal act shall be done intentionally when the person was aware of the dangerous nature of the criminal act and desired to engage therein. The material criminal act shall be done intentionally, when the person was aware of the dangerous nature of the criminal act, anticipated that his/her criminal act might cause dangerous consequences provided for by the CC and desired that they arise or consciously allow them to occur.

227. The doctrine of the Lithuanian criminal law emphasised that intent has two components: cognitive and volitional elements. Both elements of intent are explicitly laid down in the CC. The cognitive element of intent means that the perpetrator (1) was aware of the dangerous nature of the criminal act, and (2) anticipated that his/her criminal act might cause the dangerous consequences provided for by the

167. Prapiestis J., Prapiestis D. Kaltės institutas baudžiamojoje kasacijoje // Baudžiamoji justicija ir verslas, Vilnius, 2016, p. 61.

CC. The volitional element of the intent means that the perpetrator (1) desired to engage in an act, or (2) desired that dangerous consequences arise or consciously allow them to occur.[168]

228. It should be noted that as a general rule of the Lithuanian criminal law the perpetrator must be aware of the dangerousness of his/her act. Also, there are several special *corpus delicti* of the criminal acts in the CC of Lithuania, who required the awareness of the unlawfulness of the act, for example, unlawful deprivation of liberty (Article 146 of the CC), unlawful violation of inviolability of a person's dwelling (Article 165 of the CC), etc.

A. *Degrees of Intent*

229. The Lithuanian criminal law did not distinguish between the degrees of intent. The CC provides two types of intent: direct intent and indirect intent. Meanwhile, the doctrine of Lithuanian criminal law, as well as court jurisprudence divide intent into (1) premeditated and sudden intent; (2) specified and unspecified intent.[169] Furthermore, the doctrine of the Lithuanian criminal law also points out the general intent.

1. General Intent

230. According to the doctrine of Lithuanian criminal law,[170] the general intent means that the perpetrator is aware of the dangerous nature of the criminal act and anticipates that his/her criminal act might cause the dangerous consequences, but the consequences he/she reaches by another act than the planned actions (e.g., the perpetrator believes that victim has already died by his/her prior shooting and bury the 'body', whereupon the still living victim suffocates).

2. Premeditated and Sudden Intent

231. Premeditated intent means the perpetrator's mental relationship with the criminal act which takes more time to consider the circumstances of the criminal act, manner of the action and results to be achieved. The premeditated intent is generally considered to be more dangerous.

168. Lietuvos Respublikos baudžiamojo kodekso komentaras. Bendroji dalis (1-98 straipsniai), Vilnius, TIC, 2004, p. 106–107.
169. Lietuvos Respublikos baudžiamojo kodekso komentaras. Bendroji dalis (1-98 straipsniai), Vilnius, TIC, 2004, p. 108–109.
170. Lietuvos baudžiamoji teisė, Bendroji dalis, 1 knyga, Vilnius, Vilniaus universiteto leidykla, 2019, p. 266.

232. In case of sudden intent, the time period between the criminal idea and its implementation through a criminal act is very short or almost imperceptible. The sudden intent is generally considered to be less dangerous. The kind of sudden intent is affective intent, which is characterised by the fact that the person has committed a criminal act in a state of sudden passion due to the unlawful or particularly offensive conduct of the victim's. The affective intent is generally considered as the least dangerous.

B. Types of Intention with Reference to Their Consequences

1. Direct Intent (*Dolus Directus*)

233. A formal criminal act shall be committed with a direct intent where, when committing it, the person was aware of the dangerous nature of the criminal act and desired to engage therein. A material (causal) criminal act shall be committed with the direct intent where, when committing it, the person was aware of the dangerous nature of the criminal act, anticipated that his/her act or omission might cause the dangerous consequences provided for by the CC and desired that they arise.

2. Indirect or Eventual Intent (*Dolus Eventualis*)

234. A material (causal) criminal act shall be committed with an indirect intent where, when committing it, the person was aware of the dangerous nature of the criminal act, anticipated that his/her act or omission might cause dangerous consequences provided for by the CC and, though he/she did not desire that they arise, consciously allowed the consequences to arise. The volitional element of the indirect intent means that the perpetrator does not want the consequences, but he/she is indifferent to them and does nothing to avoid it.

3. Specified and Unspecified Intent

235. An unspecified intent means that the perpetrator is aware of the dangerous nature of the criminal act, but did not specify the dangerous consequences of his/her act or omission (in other words, the perpetrator is satisfied with the consequences of any degree, regardless of their severity). In case of the unspecified intent, the perpetrator shall be held liable for the caused consequences.

236. A specified intent means that the perpetrator is aware of the dangerous nature of the criminal act and specifies the dangerous consequences of his/her act or omission. The specified intent may be simple – when the perpetrator specifies one concrete result of his/her act or omission (e.g., the death of the victim), or alternative – when the perpetrator specifies that his/her act or omission may cause two alternative results from which he/she shall be satisfied with any of them (e.g., the death or serious health impairment of the victim).

237. In the case of the specified intent, if the results were not achieved for reasons beyond the will of the perpetrator, the criminal act shall be qualified as an attempt to cause the results that have been specified. The specified intent could become unspecified, when the real result exceeds the designed results and in that case, the perpetrator shall be held liable for the caused (but not designed) consequences.

III. Negligence

A. Definition

238. The Lithuanian criminal law provides two types of negligence: a criminal recklessness or criminal carelessness. The CC of Lithuania lays down the definition of both types of negligence.

239. A crime or a misdemeanour is committed through a criminal recklessness 'if the person who committed the act had anticipated that his/her act or omission may cause the consequences provided for by the CC, but recklessly expected to avoid them'.

240. A crime or a misdemeanour is committed through criminal carelessness 'if the person who committed the act had not anticipated that his/her act or omission might cause the consequences provided for by the CC, although the person could and ought to have anticipated such a result based on the circumstances of the act and his/her personal traits'.

B. The Evaluation of Negligence

241. Both types of negligence – a criminal recklessness or criminal carelessness are treated equally by the CC of Lithuania. Nevertheless, the court jurisprudence considers these types of negligence during the imposition of the punishment.

C. Types of Negligence

242. The criminal recklessness means that the perpetrator perceives that in general such an act can lead to dangerous consequences, but unreasonably believes that in his/her concrete situation they will not occur due to certain specific circumstances, for example, perpetrator's personal physical or psychological abilities or experiences, behaviour of the third persons or even circumstances beyond his/her control, etc.[171] The real (objective) nature of circumstances is the ground for distinction between criminal recklessness and indirect intent which presupposes confidence with no real basis.

243. The criminal carelessness means that the perpetrator has not anticipated that his/her act or omission might cause the dangerous consequences (intellectual element), although the person could and ought to have anticipated such a result (volitional element). Unforeseeability of consequences occurs when the perpetrator has acted contrary to the written or non-written precautionary rules relating to his/her activity or profession. A volitional element of the criminal carelessness consists of the perpetrator's duty (objective criterion) and opportunity (subjective criterion) to foresee the consequences of his/her act or omission.[172] The Supreme Court of Lithuania has noted that 'duty to foresee the consequences is an objective criterion, which determines the existence of the obligation to be cautious. Such an obligation stems from the law, professional activity, etc. An opportunity to foresee the consequences is a subjective criterion, which establishes the possibility for a specific person to foresee the consequences in a particular situation'.[173] The possibility that a specific person in a particular situation foresees the consequences depends on the perpetrator's personal traits (e.g., knowledge, experience, physical or psychological conditions, etc.) or the circumstances of the act (e.g., night time, etc.).

244. If a concrete person has no duty or was not able to foresee the consequences of his/her act or omission, he/she shall not be held criminally liable for the negligence.

IV. The Required Form of Guilt

245. Intent is a general requirement of all criminal acts. Meanwhile, negligence may only be punished if the article of the Special Part of the CC expressly prescribes that the commission of the concrete criminal act by negligence is punishable. If the commission of a certain criminal act by negligence is punishable, the range of punishment is lower compared to the same criminal act committed intentionally.

246. Currently, the Lithuanian criminal law did not foresee the *corpus delicti* of the criminal act with a mixed form of guilt. In case when the act or omission was intentional while consequences were covered by negligence, the whole criminal act shall be regarded as committed by negligence.

---

171. Lietuvos Respublikos baudžiamojo kodekso komentaras. Bendroji dalis (1-98 straipsniai), Vilnius, TIC, 2004, p. 110.
172. Prapiestis J., Prapiestis D. Kaltės institutas baudžiamojoje kasacijoje // Baudžiamoji justicija ir verslas, Vilnius, 2016, p. 66, 69.
173. Ruling of the Supreme Court of Lithuania in criminal case No. 2K-565/1999.

V. Legal Entity as a Subject of the Criminal Act

247. Corporate criminal liability was introduced in 2002 for several crimes when Lithuania ratified the Council of Europe Criminal Law Convention on Corruption.[174] The prerequisites for the criminal liability of legal entities stem directly from the aforementioned Convention and the EU legislation. The Constitutional Court decision of 8 June 2009[175] should be noted as being of special importance – the court recognised that corporate criminal liability does not expostulate with the Constitution of Lithuania. Also, the Constitutional Court has recognised that corporate criminal liability derives from the liability of a physical person and this leads to the conclusion that a legal entity and a physical person may be subject to criminal liability only for one and the same crime, committed by a physical person.[176]

248. A legal entity shall be held liable solely for the criminal acts the commission whereof is subject to the liability of a legal entity as provided for in the Article of the Special Part of the CC. In 1 June 2019, the criminal liability was provided in 135 articles of the CC of Lithuania for 242 *corpora delicti* of criminal acts.[177] This list has been composed mostly as a result of the national implementation of the requirements of the international treaties Lithuania and EU legal acts.

249. The CC provides two grounds for the criminal liability of legal entity – mandatory and discretionary. A legal entity shall be held mandatorily liable for the criminal acts committed by a physical person solely where a criminal act was committed for the benefit or in the interests of the legal entity by a natural person acting independently or on behalf of the legal entity, provided that he/she, while occupying a managing position in the legal entity, was entitled: (1) to represent the legal entity, or (2) to take decisions on behalf of the legal entity, or (3) to control activities of the legal entity.

250. The discretionary ground of the criminal liability of legal entity may be realised in two instances. First, a legal entity may be held liable for criminal acts also where they have been committed by an employee or an authorised representative of the legal entity as a result of insufficient supervision or control by the person occupying a managing position in the legal entity. Second, a legal person also may be held liable for the criminal act committed by another legal person representing him/her or being under control, when a criminal act was committed for the benefit of the

174. 1999 m. Europos baudžiamosios teisės konvencija dėl korupcijos, *Valstybės žinios*, 2002, No. 23-851; 23-853.
175. Decision of the Constitutional Court of Lithuania of 8 Jun. 2009, *Valstybės žinios*, 2009, No. 69–2798.
176. Švedas G. Kai kurie probleminiai juridinio asmens baudžiamosios atsakomybės aspektai Lietuvos konstitucinėje jurisprudencijoje ir baudžiamosios justicijos doktrinoje // Lietuvos Respublikos baudžiamajam kodeksui – 10 metų, Vilnius, Registrų centras, 2011, p. 98.
177. Švedas G., Abramavičius A. Tendencies and Problematical Aspects of Criminal Liability of a Legal Person in Lithuania // *In Legal Developments During 30 Years of Lithuanian Independence. Overview of Legal Accomplishments and Challenges in Lithuania* 302 (Gintaras Švedas & Donatas Murauskas eds., Springer 2021).

above-mentioned legal entity as a result of an order or permission, or insufficient supervision or control by the person occupying a managing position in the legal entity. In these cases, a legal entity may be prosecuted only when it is held that such liability is reasonable. The prosecutor and the court, when ascertaining whether it is possible to prosecute, should take account of the entity's organisational culture, management principles applicable to the prevention of criminal acts, the acceptance of the consequences of the criminal act, the relationship between the legal entity and the employee who has committed the criminal act, indicating whether the criminal act and consequences may be associated with the legal person, etc. It should be noted that the Constitutional Court has stressed that, although the legal entity's guilt is closely related to the individual's guilt, they are not identical. This separation of guilt allowed the Constitutional Court to conclude that the legal entity's guilt should be established by law and recognised by an effective court sentence. The Supreme Court of Lithuania has also emphasised that a legal entity's guilt should be proved by the methods mentioned in the Code of Criminal Procedure.[178] In order to hold a legal entity guilty, two elements should be present: (1) a relationship between the criminal act of the head of the legal entity and the legal entity's business strategy (e.g., all appropriated money was used for unreported payments, etc.) and (2) the legal entity's owner, who is responsible for the strategy formulation and compliance with the duty of care, should promote the illegal conduct, be aware of or at least tolerate such behaviour (e.g., recognise crime results *ex post facto*, etc.).[179]

251. Criminal liability of a legal entity did not release from criminal liability a physical person who has committed, organised, instigated or assisted in the commission of the criminal act as well as the fact that a physical person shall be released from criminal liability or not be held liable for any other reason.

252. The State, a municipality, a State and municipal institution and agency (e.g., the Ministry of Economy, Prison department under the Ministry of Justice, etc.) as well as international public organisation (e.g., NATO, Council of Europe, etc.) shall not be held liable under the CC of Lithuania.

253. It should be noted that State and municipal enterprises, public institutions, which are owned or shared/jointly owned by a state or municipality, as well as joint-stock companies and limited liability companies whose all shares or part of the shares are owned by the State or municipality may be held liable under the CC of Lithuania.

---

178. Ruling of the Supreme Court of Lithuania in criminal case No. 2K–269/2010.
179. ŠVEDAS G. Kai kurie probleminiai juridinio asmens baudžiamosios atsakomybės aspektai Lietuvos konstitucinėje jurisprudencijoje ir baudžiamosios justicijos doktrinoje // Lietuvos Respublikos baudžiamajam kodeksui – 10 metų, Vilnius, Registrų centras, 2011, p. 100.

Chapter 4. Justification, Excuse and Other Grounds of Impunity

§1. General Principles

254. The Lithuanian criminal law provides that two main features of the criminal act are dangerousness and unlawfulness of the act. Also, the criminal law establishes the circumstances in which an act may be foreseen in the CC, but it shall not be recognised as dangerous. These circumstances in the Lithuanian criminal law are called circumstances eliminating criminal liability. Chapter V 'Circumstances eliminating criminal liability' of the CC determines the system of the circumstances eliminating criminal liability: self-defence (Article 28 of the CC), apprehension of a person who has committed a criminal act (Article 29 of the CC), discharge of a professional duty (Article 30 of the CC), necessity (Article 31 of the CC), performance of an assignment of a law enforcement institution (Article 32 of the CC), execution of an order (Article 33 of the CC), justifiable professional or economic risk (Article 34 of the CC) and scientific experiment (Article 35 of the CC). This list of the circumstances eliminating criminal liability is not exhaustive, since some of the circumstances may be found in other laws, for example, blood donation – in Law on Blood Donation[180] or donation of human organ or tissue – in Law on Donation and Transplantation of Human Organ or Tissue.[181]

255. Also it should be noted that the doctrine of the Lithuanian criminal law refers to additional circumstances eliminating criminal liability, which are not directly provided in the laws, such as a consent of the victim, participation in sporting events,[182] realisation of his/her rights[183] or even force majeure and coercion.[184] It is noteworthy that, although the Lithuanian criminal law provides eight circumstances eliminating criminal liability, only four of them – self-defence, discharge of public duty, apprehension of a person who has committed a criminal act and necessity are met in the courts' practice.

§2. Grounds of Justification

I. Public Duty or Orders of the Authorities

256. Discharge of professional duty and execution of an order are two separate circumstances eliminating criminal liability in the Lithuanian criminal law. It should

180. Lietuvos Respublikos kraujo donorystės įstatymas, *Valstybės žinios*, 1996, No. 115-2666.
181. Lietuvos Respublikos žmogaus audinių, ląstelių, organų donorystės ir transplantacijos įstatymas, *Valstybės žinios*, 1996, No. 116-2696; 2013, No. 120-6057.
182. Žalnieriūnas L., Gutauskas A. Fizinio smurto sporte baudžiamasis teisinis vertinimas, Jurisprudencija, 2014, No. 21(3), p. 885–906.
183. Lietuvos Respublikos baudžiamojo kodekso komentaras. Bendroji dalis (1-98 straipsniai), Vilnius, TIC, 2004, p. 181.
184. Lietuvos baudžiamoji teisė, Bendroji dalis, 1 knyga, Vilnius, Vilniaus universiteto leidykla, 2019, p. 287.

be emphasised that both circumstances are associated with the execution of the legal duty (and not the right as in case of other circumstances eliminating criminal liability) of the person.

257. Discharge of professional duty is a situation where a damage provided in the criminal law is caused by a person, who is in charge of a professional duty. Such a person may be a policeman, doctor, firefighter, etc.[185] A person shall not be held liable under the Code Criminal for the damage caused in charge of a professional duty, provided he/she has not exceeded the authority granted to him/her by laws or other legal acts. Usually, laws and other legal acts provide the limits of the authority, which cannot be exceeded during the discharge of a professional duty. The doctrine of the Lithuanian criminal law has stated that the damage caused during the discharge of a professional duty should be as low as possible.[186] On the contrary, the Supreme Court of Lithuania has stressed that, according to the essence of the discharge of a professional duty, an official must not be prosecuted for having caused more damage (e.g., severe health impairment) if, in the discharge of his/her professional duties, he/she does not exceed the limits laid down by law.[187] Where a person has exceeded the authority granted to him/her by laws or other legal acts, he/she shall be held liable under the CC, however a punishment imposed upon him/her may be commuted (*see* paragraphs 613, 617–620, 622, 623).

258. Execution of an order is a situation where an act or damage provided in the criminal law is committed or caused by a person while executing a lawful order, ordinance or instruction of the superior. A person shall be held criminally liable where he/she executed an order, ordinance or instruction known to be unlawful. A person who refuses to execute an order, ordinance or instruction which is unlawful shall not be held criminally liable for non-execution of an order, ordinance or instruction. Such a person may be held liable under the CC only if the act committed by him/her constitutes the *corpus delicti* of another criminal act. It should be noted that the rules are applicable for the execution of an order, ordinance or instruction in the civil area.

259. In the military area, a failure or refusal to execute a commander's order creates a *corpus delicti* of crime. This rule should not be applicable only in the case where a soldier or other serviceman fails or refuses to execute a clearly unlawful (or even criminal) order of a commander.

185. KUJALIS P. Profesinių pareigų vykdymas kaip baudžiamąją atsakomybę šalinanti aplinkybė // Globalizacijos iššūkiai baudžiamjai justicijai, Vilnius, Registrų centras, 2014, p. 98–99.
186. Lietuvos Respublikos baudžiamojo kodekso komentaras. Bendroji dalis (1-98 straipsniai), Vilnius, TIC, 2004, p. 196.
187. Ruling of the Supreme Court of Lithuania in criminal case No. 2K-P-1/2014.

II. (Self-) Defence

A. *Posing the Problem*

260. The State defines human rights and guarantees their protection. However, the State is not able to protect human rights in all instances, so the criminal law provides a person with the right to defend himself/herself. The person's right to self-defence is every person's natural right, but not the obligation, so failure to exercise it does not incur any legal liability. Self-defence is socially valuable since it is directed against a dangerous attack. The person may exercise this right regardless of whether he/she had the possibility of avoiding the attack or applying for assistance to other persons or authorities.

B. *Position Within the National Law*

261. Self-defence is a situation where a person commits an act formally having the features of a crime or misdemeanour provided for in the criminal law when defending himself/herself or another person, property, inviolability of a dwelling, other rights, interests of society or the State against an initiated or imminent dangerous attack. The damage caused to aggressor shall be recognised as a legitimate self-defence only where it is made subject to certain conditions which are related to the attack and defence.

C. *Conditions*

1. Conditions Relating to the Attack

262. An attack is described by three conditions: an attack must be (1) dangerous; (2) evident and (3) real. Self-defence is possible only against actions which are dangerous. Actions shall be dangerous if they are directed against human life, health, personal integrity, sexual inviolability, property, inviolability of dwelling, other rights, also interests of the society and the State. The Supreme Court of Lithuania has noted that dangerousness of the attack depends on the intensity of the attack, the tools and means used, the number of attackers and the retreating forces, the size of the possible damage, etc.[188] Furthermore, the doctrine of the Lithuanian criminal law[189] stresses that a dangerous attack may be considered only as the criminal act. Dangerous attack presupposes only an active behaviour.

188. Ruling of the Supreme Court of Lithuania in criminal case No. 2K-7-326/2013.
189. Lietuvos baudžiamoji teisė, Bendroji dalis, 1 knyga, Vilnius, Vilniaus universiteto leidykla, 2019, p. 289–290.

263. Dangerous attack shall be considered also as actions of such persons who, for whatever reason, cannot be held liable under the criminal law. This rule allows self-defence from dangerous actions that are committed by a legally incapable person or a child under the age of 14.

264. The doctrine of the Lithuanian criminal law[190] has stated that it cannot be recognised as dangerous acts of the officials which limit human rights and freedoms, for example, administrative detention or arrest of the criminal procedure. On the contrary, a person does not lose the right to the defence, if the official's actions are clearly illegal. The illegality of the official's actions must be an objective fact, and not the result of imagination, because, otherwise, responsibility for the resistance against the civil servant or a person performing functions of the public administration may arise.

265. An attack shall be considered evident if it has been started or imminent. The self-defence is restricted in duration; it may last during the attack and also after it if the defender did not understand that attack has been finished. According to the Lithuanian criminal law, the use of the preventive defence means is not recognised as self-defence since there is no evident and dangerous attack.

266. According to the jurisprudence of the Supreme Court of Lithuania, an attack shall be considered real if it is an objective fact, and not an imagination of the defender.[191]

2. Conditions Relating to the Defence

267. The defence is described by three conditions: (1) damage must be done to the offender; (2) damage must be done by defending from the dangerous attack; and (3) defence cannot go beyond the limits of the self-defence. The defence will be lawful if it complies with the nature and dangerousness of the attack, which depends on the significance of the object of the attack, intensity, time and place of the attack, the number of the aggressors, used means and arms, age and physical condition of the aggressor and defender, etc.

D. Excessive (Self-)Defence

268. According to the CC of Lithuania, the limits of self-defence shall be exceeded when (a) a murder or a serious health impairment is committed; (b) this damage is caused with a direct intent and (c) where defence has been clearly disproportionate to the nature and dangerousness of an attack. The jurisprudence of the Supreme Court of Lithuania[192] and doctrine of the Lithuanian criminal

190. Baudžiamoji teisė: Bendroji dalis, Vilnius, Eugrimas, 2003, p. 224.
191. Ruling of the Supreme Court of Lithuania in criminal case No. 2K-7-326/2013.
192. Ruling of the Supreme Court of Lithuania in criminal case No. 2K-31-788/2015.

law[193] has stated that the meaning of clearly disproportionate defence may be disclosed by two criteria: objectively – defence does not comply with the nature and dangerousness of an attack externally; subjectively – it is evident for the defender.

269. It should be noted that the limits of self-defence shall not be considered to have been exceeded by the reason of extreme confusion or fright caused by the dangerous attempt or an act committed in the course of defence against breaking into a dwelling.

270. A person who has exceeded the limits of self-defence shall be held criminally liable under the CC, however a punishment imposed upon him/her may be commuted (*see* paragraphs 613, 617–620, 622, 623).

E. Putative (Self-)Defence

271. Where a person believes that he/she is the object of a dangerous attack and defends himself/herself against the assumed attack although no attack in fact existed, the case is of a putative self-defence. The issue of the criminal liability in case of a putative self-defence shall be solved by the rules governing the institute of mistake: if a defender could and ought to have anticipated that an attack did not exist in reality, he/she will be held liable for the criminal act committed through the negligence (if the CC of Lithuania provides liability for such criminal act committed through the negligence).

III. Legitimate Resistance against Unlawful Acts of Civil Servants

272. The CC of Lithuania has no general provision on the legitimate resistance against unlawful acts of civil servants. It should be noted that unlawful acts of civil servants may be considered as a dangerous attack from which self-defence is possible (*see* paragraph 264).

IV. Necessity

A. Necessity as a Justification

273. Necessity is a situation where a person commits an act provided in the criminal law for an attempt to avert the danger which threatens him/her, other persons or their rights, public or State interests, where this danger could not have been averted by other means and where the damage caused is less than the damage attempted to be averted. The person's right to act in a state of necessity is a person's

193. Lietuvos Respublikos baudžiamojo kodekso komentaras. Bendroji dalis (1-98 straipsniai), Vilnius, TIC, 2004, p. 186–187.

right, but not the obligation, so failure to exercise it does not incur any legal liability. The main difference between self-defence and necessity is that the necessity legalises violation of the rights of the innocent third party.

274. It should be noted that a person (e.g., firefighter, etc.) cannot justify a failure to perform a duty by invoking the provisions of necessity, where he/she is under the obligation to act under the conditions of an increased degree of danger according to his/her profession, the position held or due to other circumstances.

B. Conditions

275. Necessity should be lawful if it complies with all these conditions at the same time:

(a) legal interests (person or other persons or their rights, public or State interests) are in imminent danger. The danger may occur from the lawful or unlawful behaviour of another person, a natural phenomenon (e.g., earthquake, flooding, etc.), an accident, an attack by an animal, operation of mechanisms, etc. Even behaviour of a person who afterwards may behave in the state of necessity may create a danger, since the CC provides the rule that 'a person who creates a dangerous situation by his actions may invoke the provisions of necessity only when the dangerous situation arose through negligence';
(b) the danger must be evident and real. The danger shall be considered as evident if it arises and poses a direct threat to the legal interests. Future or past danger do not constitute the situation of necessity. The danger shall be considered as real if it is an objective fact, and not an imagination of the person;
(c) the danger could not have been averted by other means, but only inflicting damage. If the danger can be averted by the conduct which does not cause the damage provided in the criminal law, the necessity rule is not applicable;
(d) the damage caused is less than the damage attempted to be averted. This proportion of the caused and averted damages should be evaluated in a qualitative and quantitative manner. It should be noted that neither the CC of Lithuania nor jurisprudence of the courts did not respond to the question of whether it is possible to rescue one life by killing another human. Meanwhile, the doctrine of the Lithuanian criminal law would accept such a situation as a lawful necessity.[194]

276. A person who has exceeded the limits of necessity shall be held criminally liable under the CC, however a punishment imposed upon him/her may be commuted (*see* paragraphs 613, 617–620, 622, 623).

---

194. Lietuvos Respublikos baudžiamojo kodekso komentaras. Bendroji dalis (1-98 straipsniai), Vilnius, TIC, 2004, p. 201.

C. Putative Necessity

277. Where a person believes that he/she is acting in the state of necessity but no danger, in fact, existed, the case is of a putative necessity. The issue of the criminal liability in case of a putative necessity shall be solved by the rules governing the institute of mistake: if a person could and ought to have anticipated that a danger did not exist in reality, he/she will be held liable for the criminal act committed through the negligence (if the CC of Lithuania provides liability for such a criminal act committed through the negligence).

V. Consent of the Victim

278. The CC of Lithuania has no general provision on the consent of the victim. Currently, the content and conditions of lawfulness of the consent of the victim describe the doctrine of the Lithuanian criminal law,[195] since there is no court jurisprudence on this issue. It should be noted that the consent of the victim may be a constituent part of other circumstances eliminating criminal liability, for example, discharge of a professional duty by medical staff, scientific experiment, etc.

279. The consent of the victim is a situation where a damage provided in the criminal law is caused with the consent of the victim. The consent of the victim shall be lawful when there are all the conditions at the same time. First, the consent may be given only by a capable person who has reached 18 years of age. Second, the consent should be voluntary and must be given before or during the commission of the act. The consent should not be considered as lawful if it was obtained by deceit or using violence. Third, the person may give the consent to violate the rights that he/she has the right to dispose of such as a right of sexual or physical integrity and property rights. It should be noted that the age limits protecting minors in the case of sexual criminal acts are absolute and no lawful consent on modifying them is allowed. According to the CC of Lithuania, it is possible to give consent for causing a non-severe health impairment through negligence (Article 139 of the CC), physical pain or a negligible health impairment (Article 140 of the CC), sexual harassment (Article 152 of the CC), unlawful violation of inviolability of a person's dwelling (Article 165 of the CC), simple theft (paragraphs 1 and 4, Article 178 of the CC), destruction of or damage of property (Article 187 of the CC), etc.

280. According to the Lithuanian criminal law, a person cannot give a lawful consent to being killed. Mercy killing (*euthanasia*) committed at the request of the victim shall be considered as intentional murder. Meanwhile, the request of the victim shall influence the sentencing as a mitigating circumstance.

281. Also, the CC of Lithuania provides criminal liability for abetting, aiding or procuring of suicide (Articles 133 and 134 of the CC).

---

195. Lietuvos baudžiamoji teisė, Bendroji dalis, 1 knyga, Vilnius, Vilniaus universiteto leidykla, 2019, p. 323–324.

VI. Apprehension of a Person Who Committed a Criminal Act

282. Apprehension of a person who has committed a criminal act is a situation where a damage provided in the criminal law is caused by a person during the apprehension of a person who has committed a criminal act. It should be noted that this circumstance is associated with the right of the person (and not a legal duty). The actions of the person who has a legal duty to apprehend the person who commits a criminal act (e.g., a policeman, prosecutor, etc.), shall create another circumstance eliminating criminal liability – the discharge of a professional duty[196] (*see* paragraphs 256–259). A person shall not be held liable under the CC for his/her actions when there are all conditions at the same time: (a) an offender is actively attempting to escape detention; (b) a person causes property damage, a minor health impairment or a serious health impairment through negligence by chasing, attempting to stop, preventing the escape or by other actions or an intentional serious health impairment when detaining on the spot of a crime a person who has committed or attempted to commit an intentional murder; and (c) it was not otherwise possible to detain the person who has committed the criminal act.

283. Actions of a person restraining the resistance of a person who has committed a criminal act shall be subject to the rules for self-defence (*see* paragraph 260–271).

284. Where a person has exceeded the conditions of the apprehension of a person who has committed a criminal act, he/she shall be held liable under the CC however a punishment imposed upon him/her may be commuted (*see* paragraphs 613, 617–620, 622, 623).

VII. Performance of an Assignment of a Law Enforcement Institution

285. Performance of an assignment of a law enforcement institution is a situation where a person commits an act provided in the CC while carrying out (a) actions imitating a criminal act, (b) controlled delivery or (c) performs another assignment of a law enforcement institution. 'Law enforcement institutions' means the police, other bodies of pretrial investigation (e.g., Special Investigation Service, Financial Crime Investigation Service, etc.) and the prosecutor's office, also institutions of criminal intelligence (e.g., Criminal Service of Customs, etc.).

286. A person shall not be held liable under the CC, if he/she carries out lawful actions imitating a criminal act or controlled delivery. The conditions of lawfulness of the actions imitating a criminal act and controlled delivery are established in the Law on Criminal Intelligence[197] and the CCP, for example, actions imitating a criminal act and controlled delivery must be sanctioned by the prosecutor or pretrial

196. Ruling of the Supreme Court of Lithuania in criminal case No. 2K-P-1/2014.
197. Lietuvos Respublikos kriminalinės žvalgybos įstatymas, *Valstybės žinios*, 2012, No. 122-6093.

investigation judge, they may not last more than six months, it is forbidden to perform such actions if they pose a direct threat to human life or health, or if they can lead to other serious consequences, etc. It should be noted that controlled delivery can be carried out only in accordance with the international treaties of Lithuania.

287. A person shall not be held criminally liable under the CC where he/she participated in the activities of a criminal association (*see* paragraph 371–379) or an organised group (*see* paragraph 376) and in the criminal acts committed by it while performing another lawful assignment of a law enforcement institution and did not exceed the limits of this assignment. The conditions of lawfulness and limits of another assignment of a law enforcement institution are established in the Law on Criminal Intelligence, for example, assignment of a law enforcement institution must be sanctioned by the chairman or authorised judge of the regional court (in urgent cases, sanction may be given by the prosecutor, but this sanction within 24 hours must be confirmed by the judge); assignment of a law enforcement institution may not last more than six months, it is forbidden to perform actions that pose a direct threat to human life, health or can lead to other serious consequences, etc. The sanction for performing an assignment of a law enforcement institution should indicate the actions and their limits under the criminal acts provided in the CC.

288. A person shall be held criminally liable where, while carrying out actions imitating a criminal act or controlled delivery as well as performing another assignment of a law enforcement institution, he/she exceeded the limits of this assignment, however a punishment imposed upon him/her may be commuted (*see* paragraphs 613, 617–620, 622, 623).

VIII. Justifiable Professional or Economic Risk

289. Justifiable professional or economic risk is a situation where a person commits an act or causes damages provided in the CC while carrying out a justifiable professional or economic risk and for a publicly beneficial purpose. The risk shall be deemed justifiable when there are all conditions at the same time: (a) the committed act is in line with the contemporary science and technology, and (b) it was not possible to attain the specified objective by carrying out the actions not involving risk, and (c) where the person taking the risk has taken the necessary precautions to prevent damage to the interests protected by the law.

290. Where a person has exceeded the conditions of the justifiable professional or economic risk, he/she shall be held liable under the CC, however a punishment imposed upon him/her may be commuted (*see* paragraphs 613, 617–620, 622, 623).

IX. Scientific Experiment

291. Scientific experiment is a situation where a person commits an act or causes damages provided in the CC while conducting a lawful scientific experiment. The scientific experiment shall be lawful when there are all conditions at the same time: (a) the experiment was conducted in compliance with scientifically approved methods, (b) the problem under investigation is of an exceptional scientific significance, and (c) the researcher has taken the necessary precautions to prevent damage to the interests protected by the law.

292. It should be noted that scientific experiment with the human is forbidden without the voluntary consent of the person participating in the experiment, who must be informed of the possible consequences.

293. A pregnant woman, her foetus, young child, a mentally ill person and a person in confinement may not be subjected to scientific experiments, with the exception of the cases provided for by the law.

294. Where a person has exceeded the conditions of the scientific experiment, he/she shall be held liable under the CC, however a punishment imposed upon him/her may be commuted (*see* paragraphs 613, 617–620, 622, 623).

X. Realisation of his/her Rights

295. The CC of Lithuania has no general provision on the realisation of his/her rights. Currently, the content and conditions of lawfulness of the realisation of his/her rights describe the doctrine of the Lithuanian criminal law[198] since there is no court jurisprudence on this issue.

296. The realisation of his/her rights is a situation where a person commits an act or causes damages provided in the CC while realising his/her own rights. Usually the realisation of his/her rights is associated with the person's rights that he/she has the right to dispose of such as property rights (e.g., to damage his/her property) and parental rights (e.g., to limit the child's freedom of movement).

§3. Grounds of Excuse

I. Introduction

297. The intoxication, force majeure, coercion and mistake may be conditionally attributed to the grounds of excuse in the Lithuanian criminal law.

298. It should be noted that the minority, insanity (legal incapacity) and diminished capacity in the Lithuanian criminal law are dealt with as part of general conditions for criminal liability in connection with the requirement for 'unlawfulness of the criminal act'.

---

198. Baudžiamoji teisė: Bendroji dalis, Vilnius, Eugrimas, 2003, p. 241–242.

II. Minority

299. The age and legal capacity are the main features of a physical person as a subject of the criminal act. The physical person may be held criminally liable if he/she prior to the time of the commission of a criminal act has reached the age provided in criminal law and at the time of commission of a criminal act was legally capable.

300. The Lithuanian criminal law sets up a few age limits for criminal liability. The main rule states that a person who, prior to the time of commission of a crime or misdemeanour, had attained the age of 16 shall be considered liable under the CC. It should be noted that some *corpus delicti* of the criminal acts may require a higher age limit for the subject of the criminal act, for example, the age of majority, etc. Meanwhile, an exceptional rule is established for a person who, prior to the time of commission of a crime or misdemeanour, had attained the age of 14. Such a person shall be held criminally liable only for ten crimes: (1) murder (Article 129 of the CC), (2) serious impairment to health (Article 135 of the CC), (3) rape (Article 149 of the CC), (4) sexual assault (Article 150 of the CC), (5) theft (Article 178 of the CC), (6) robbery (Article 180 of the CC), (7) extortion of property (Article 181 of the CC), destruction of or damage to property (paragraph 2 of Article 187 of the CC), (8) seizure of a firearm, ammunition, explosives or explosive materials (Article 254 of the CC), (9) theft, racketeering or other illicit seizure of narcotic or psychotropic substances (Article 263 of the CC) and (10) damage to vehicles or roads and facilities thereof (Article 280 of the CC).

301. A person who, prior to the time of the commission of a dangerous act provided for by the CC, had not attained the age of 14 may be subject to reformative sanctions or other measures in accordance with the procedure laid down by laws of the Republic of Lithuania.[199]

302. The CC provides some peculiarities of the criminal liability of minors. These peculiarities have the following purpose: (1) to ensure the correspondence of liability to the age and social maturity of these persons; (2) to restrict the possibilities of imposition of imprisonment and broaden the possibilities of imposition of reformative sanctions against these persons; (3) to help a minor to alter his/her manner of living and conduct by coordinating a punishment for the committed criminal act with the development and education of his/her personality and elimination of reasons for the unlawful conduct; (4) to prevent a minor from committing new criminal acts. These peculiarities concern the punishments imposed upon minors and sentencing rules, conditions of the suspension of the execution of the punishment and release from criminal liability as well as reformative measures. For example, a minor may be subject solely to the following punishments: (1) community service, which may not be imposed for more than 240 hours of work; (2) a fine in the amount from 5 up to 50 BAPP, which may be imposed only against a minor

199. Lietuvos Respublikos vaiko minimalios ir vidutinės priežiūros įstatymas, TAR, 2016, No. 20656.

already employed or possessing his/her own property; (3) restriction of liberty; (4) arrest for a period from five to forty-five days; and (5) fixed-term imprisonment, which may not exceed ten years; etc.

III. Insanity

303. The physical person may be held criminally liable if he/she at the time of commission of a criminal act was legally capable. The CC did not describe the concept of legal capacity. Meanwhile, the doctrine of the Lithuanian criminal law and jurisprudence of the courts state that the person has the legal capacity if he/she is capable to recognise the dangerous nature of his/her act and to control his/her behaviour.[200]

304. The physical person who cannot recognise the dangerous nature of the act or to control his/her behaviour may be considered as legally incapable. The Lithuanian criminal law foresees legal incapacity (or insanity at the moment of the act or omission), insanity after the commission of the act or omission as well as diminished capacity.

A. Insanity at the Moment of the Act or Omission

305. The CC provides that a person shall be considered legally incapacitated where, at the time of commission of an act forbidden under the CC, he/she was unable to recognise the dangerous nature of the act or to control his/her behaviour as a result of a mental disorder. If mental disorders do not undermine the person's ability to understand his/her actions and to control them, it is not recognised as a legally incapacitated person.

306. The legal incapacity consists of medical (biological) and legal criteria, which must exist both at the time of the commission of a dangerous act. Medical criterion may consist solely of mental disorders caused by a disease (e.g., schizophrenia, brain syphilis, etc.), dementia or other mental dysfunctions. Mental disorders are defined by the order of Ministry of Health Protection of Lithuania on 23 February 2011 No. V-164 'On the implementation of the international statistical classification of diseases and related health problems. 10 revision.'[201] The medical criterion cannot be founded, if a person's mental activity is disrupted for other reasons, such as excitement, anger, character, social degradation, etc. The medical criterion is only a precondition to recognise a person legally incapacitated, because not

---

200. Lietuvos Respublikos baudžiamojo kodekso komentaras. Bendroji dalis (1-98 straipsniai), Vilnius, TIC, 2004, p. 113.
201. Lietuvos Respublikos sveikatos apsaugos ministro 2011 m. vasario 23 d. įsakymas No. V-164 'Dėl Tarptautinės statistinės ligų ir sveikatos sutrikimų klasifikacijos dešimtojo pataisyto ir papildyto leidimo 'Sisteminis ligų sąrašas' (Australijos modifikacija, TLK-10-AM) įdiegimo', *Valstybės žinios*, 2011, No. 23-1108.

every case of a mental disease caused the state, in which the person is unable to understand his/her actions or control them.

307. The legal criteria describe the severity of a person's mental disorder that takes away the ability to recognise the nature of the act or the ability to control the actions (even understanding their essence). Inability to recognise the essence of his/her act is called intellectual, and the inability to control them – volitional feature of the legal criterion. The intellectual feature is limited to those actions (omission) that the criminal law describes as criminal. This feature means that the person does not recognise the dangerousness of his/her actions (omission) or consequences, or a causal relationship between the actions (omission) and the consequences. The inability to control the person's actions (omission) is a situation, when the mental disorder violates the person's will. In this case, the person even recognising dangerousness of the actions (omission) cannot defeat his/her desire to do so, such as kleptomania (desire to steal), pyromania (desire to set fire), etc.

308. The court shall recognise a person legally incapacitated when at least one aspect of the medical criterion (e.g., dementia) and at least one feature of the legal criterion (e.g., inability to recognise the essence of his/her act) are established. The person who did not commit a dangerous act, although suffering from a mental disorder, for which he/she did not recognise the essence of his/her actions (omission) or control them, shall not be considered as legally incapacitated.

309. A person found legally incapacitated by a court shall not be held liable under the CC for a committed dangerous act. The court may apply the compulsory medical measures to him/her (*see* paragraphs 564–570).

B. Insanity at Time the Trial

310. The offender may become mentally insane after the commission of the criminal act. According to the Lithuanian criminal law, there is no legal significance when the person becomes mentally insane: it may be during the criminal procedure or even during the execution of the punishment. If a physical person who, following the commission of a criminal act or imposition of a punishment, starts to suffer from a mental disorder rendering him/her incapable of understanding the nature of his/her actions or controlling them, he/she shall be released from serving for the undischarged term of the sentence. In releasing this person from punishment, the court shall decide whether to impose a compulsory medical measure upon him/her. In the event of convalescence of this person, he/she may be ordered to serve the undischarged term of the sentence. In such a case, the period during which the person was undergoing a compulsory medical measure shall be included in the term of imprisonment on a day-to-day basis.

C. Diminished Capacity

311. According to the CC of Lithuania, a court shall find a person to be of diminished capacity where, at the time of commission of an act forbidden under the CC, he/she lacked a capacity sufficient to fully recognise the dangerous nature of the criminal act or to control his/her behaviour as a result of a mental disorder, even though the disorder is not a sufficient ground for finding him/her legally incapacitated. The diminished capacity consists of medical (biological) and legal criteria, which must exist both at the time of the commission of a dangerous act. The medical criterion (also as in case of legal incapacity) may consist solely of mental disorders caused by a disease, dementia or other mental dysfunctions. On the contrary, the intensity of the mental disorder must not be sufficient to declare a person legally incapacitated. It should be noted that the doctrine of the Lithuanian criminal law has proposed that medical criterion of diminished capacity should include not only mental disorders but also congenital or acquired mental abnormality.[202] Meanwhile, the legal criterion describes a person's mental disorder severity, who takes away the ability to recognise only in part the essence of his/her act (omission) or the ability to control the actions.

312. A person who has committed a misdemeanour, a negligent or minor or less serious intentional crime and whom a court finds to be of diminished capacity shall be liable under a criminal law, however, a punishment imposed upon him/her may be commuted or he/she may be released from criminal liability and be subject to the penal measures or the compulsory medical measures.

313. A person who has committed a serious or grave crime and is found by a court to be of diminished capacity shall be held liable under a criminal law, however a punishment imposed upon him/her may be commuted.

314. Also, the doctrine of the Lithuanian criminal law[203] has noted that the CC of Lithuania provides criminal liability for three crimes, whose main (mandatory) feature of the perpetrator is diminished capacity, that is to say, a murder in a state of passion (Article 130 of the CC), infanticide (Article 131 of the CC) and severe health impairment caused in a state of passion (Article 136 of the CC).

---

202. MEŠKA A. Riboto pakaltinamumo samprata // Lietuvos Respublikos baudžiamajam kodeksui – 10 metų, Vilnius, 2011, p. 255.
203. Lietuvos Respublikos baudžiamojo kodekso komentaras. Specialioji dalis (99-212 straipsniai), Vilnius, Registrų centras, 2009, p. 120, 123, 138.

IV. Intoxication

315. Lithuanian criminal law distinguishes (a) physiological and pathological intoxication, and (b) voluntary and compulsory intoxication. Pathological intoxication is a temporary mental disorder, which creates the medical criterion for the incapacity[204] (*see* paragraph 306). Physiological intoxication is a mental condition in which a person due to the consumption of the alcohol, narcotic, psychotropic or other psychotropic substances distortedly perceives the reality and weakens self-control processes, etc.[205] Voluntary intoxication is when a person is aware of and voluntarily consumes alcohol, narcotic, psychotropic or other psychoactive substances. Compulsory intoxication is when a person is intoxicated involuntarily against his/her will by using violence or deceit.[206]

316. The CC of Lithuania provides that a person who has committed a criminal act under the physiological voluntary intoxication of alcohol, narcotic, psychotropic or other psychoactive substances (e.g., drugs, glue, petrol, etc.) shall not be released from criminal liability. The Supreme Court of Lithuania has noted that this rule does not mean that a person who has committed the criminal act under the influence of alcohol, narcotic, psychotropic or other psychoactive substances, cannot be released from the criminal liability, for example, on the ground of the reconciliation of the offender and the victim[207] (about the release from criminal liability *see* paragraphs 457–479).

317. Also, the CC establishes a special rule for the physiological compulsory intoxication. This rule states that a person who has committed a misdemeanour, a negligent or minor or less serious intentional crime as a result of intoxication against his/her will and hence lacked a sufficient capacity to fully evaluate the dangerous nature of the criminal act or to control his/her behaviour at the time of his/her conduct shall be released from criminal liability. The person who has committed a serious or a grave crime under the same conditions shall be held liable under the CC, however the punishment imposed upon him/her may be commuted.

V. Force Majeure and Coercion

318. The CC does not set up special rules concerning force majeure and coercion as a ground of justification or release from criminal liability. It should be noted that irresistible force, which causes an immediate danger to a person, property or other protected interests, may be avoided by necessity (*see* paragraphs 273–277).

---

204. Ruling of the Court of Appeal of Lithuania in criminal case No. 1A-311/2014.
205. Ruling of the Court of Appeal of Lithuania in criminal case No. 1A-437-307/2016.
206. Lietuvos Respublikos baudžiamojo kodekso komentaras. Bendroji dalis (1-98 straipsniai), Vilnius, TIC, 2004, p. 119.
207. Ruling of the Supreme Court of Lithuania in criminal case No. 2K-250/2014.

319. The doctrine of the Lithuanian criminal law[208] states that a person who has acted in the state of irresistible force or under the influence of physical coercion which breaks the resistance of the person, cannot be held criminally liable, since his/her act was out of his/her control. The psychological coercion (threats) as a rule did not break the will of the person, so he/she can be responsible for the act. In the cases when the irresistible force or coercion only restricts the person in acting to his/her will, the criminal liability is not eliminated, however the punishment imposed upon him/her may be commuted.

VI. Ignorance or Mistake

320. The CC does not regulate mistakes in law and (or) in fact. This task is left up to the courts' jurisprudence, and the doctrine of criminal law. Unfortunately, significant court jurisprudence of these aspects does not exist. The doctrine of the Lithuanian criminal law[209] separates the mistake in law and the mistake in fact.

A. Ignorance or Mistake of Law

321. A mistake in law may lead to an incorrect evaluation of the prohibitedness of an act. In particular, a person may believe that his/her conduct is prohibited, although the law does not classify the act as a criminal act (an alleged crime or misdemeanour). In this case, criminal liability does not arise. Conversely, a person may believe that his/her conduct is not prohibited, although the law classifies it as a criminal act. In this case, the mistake does not preclude criminal liability, because the perception of the prohibitedness of the act is not the content of intent. This interpretation is based on Article 7 of the Constitution of Lithuania, which provides that 'ignorance of the law shall not exempt a person from responsibility'. This type of mistake may preclude criminal liability, however, when the feature of unlawfulness is provided in the Special Part of the CC and the criminal act can be committed only with intent, as with, for example, unlawful influence on an information system (Article 197 of the CC). In some cases, this mistake may have an impact on culpability, for example, the unlawful actions of an official. When a mistake in law exists, it cannot be seen as intentional abuse of office (Article 228 of the CC), because it contains only the features of a negligent failure to perform official duties (Article 229 of the CC).[210]

208. Lietuvos Respublikos baudžiamojo kodekso komentaras. Bendroji dalis (1-98 straipsniai), Vilnius, TIC, 2004, p. 87.
209. Baudžiamoji teisė : Bendroji dalis, Vilnius, Eugrimas, 2003, p. 216.
210. Švedas G. Country Report 'Lithuania' // Bose M., Meyer F., Schneider A. Conflicts of jurisdictions in criminal matters in the European Union. Volume I. National reports and comparative analysis, Baden-Baden, Nomos, 2013, p. 313.

B. Ignorance or Mistake of Fact

322. A mistake about the nature of an act can lead to the presence or absence of an incorrect assessment of the facts, which constitutes the objective side of the elements of a criminal act. The mistake of the circumstances, which are not part of the *corpus delicti* of the criminal act, is not relevant. The doctrine of the Lithuanian criminal law[211] provides these types of the mistake of fact: (a) mistake related to the object and victim; (b) mistake related to the nature of the act; (c) mistake related to the means; (d) mistake related to the causal relation; and (e) mistake related to the time and place as well as qualifying features of the *corpus delicti* of criminal act.

323. For example, a mistake related to the object means that a person makes a mistake as to the object of an act. This mistake should be decided on the category of the protected interest and the type of intent. If a person wanted to attempt to the less important object, but, in fact, attempted to the more important object, the act shall be qualified as a finished attempt to the more important object. In case the person wants to attempt to the more important object, but, in fact, attempted to the less important object, the decision shall depend on the type of intent: (a) if intent was specific (defined) – the act shall be qualified as an attempt to the more important object; (b) if intent was general (non-defined) – the act shall be qualified as a finished attempt to a less important object.

324. Meanwhile, the mistake related to the nature of the act means that a person mistakenly believes that his/her actions represent the facts constituting a crime on the objective side, then this mistake does not affect the form of guilt. Rather, the act can be regarded only as an attempt to commit a criminal act. If a person mistakenly believes that his/her actions do not represent the facts constituting a criminal act on the objective side, then such a person can be prosecuted for the criminal act committed through the negligence (if the CC provides such a form of guilt), because it is necessary to understand all the facts for the guilt form of intent.

C. Special Cases

325. It should be noted that the Supreme Court of Lithuania has established rules for the qualification of the aggravating features of the *corpus delicti* of the murder, rape and sexual assault, which differs from the rules established in the doctrine of the Lithuanian criminal law. The Senate of the Supreme Court has stated that the murder shall be qualified as a murder of a pregnant woman, if a perpetrator knew or, according to the circumstances of the situation and his/her personal qualities, had to and was able to realise that the woman was pregnant.[212] Also, the Senate of the

211. Lietuvos baudžiamoji teisė, Bendroji dalis, 1 knyga, Vilnius, Vilniaus universiteto leidykla, 2019, p. 278–282.
212. Decision of the Senate of the Supreme Court of Lithuania of 18 Jun. 2004 // Lietuvos Respublikos baudžiamasis kodeksas ir lydimoji medžiaga pastraipsniui, Vilnius, 2009, p. 6.

Supreme Court has recognised that the rape and sexual assault shall be qualified as a rape and sexual assault of a juvenile or minor, if a perpetrator, according to the circumstances of the situation (particularly physical features of the victim) and his/her personal qualities, had to and was able to realise that the victim was juvenile or minor.[213]

§4. Other Grounds of Impunity

326. Report of some criminal acts to the public authority, submission to the public authorities and family relations may be conditionally attributed to the other ground of impunity in the Lithuanian criminal law.

I. Report of Some Criminal Offences to the Public Authority

327. Lithuanian criminal law did not provide a general rule concerning the impunity of the reporting the criminal act to the public authority. It should be noted that reporting the criminal act to the public authority may be one of the conditions for the release from the criminal liability when a person actively assisted in detecting the criminal acts committed by members of an organised group or a criminal association (Article 39(1) of the CC) or one of the circumstances for the rules for imposition of a milder punishment (Article 61, 62 of the CC), or mitigating circumstance which influence sentencing (Article 59 of the CC), etc.

328. Also, it is necessary to have in mind that Article 238 of the CC provides criminal liability for 'a person who, without a valid reason, fails to report to a law enforcement agency or to a court a grave crime known to him/her, either in progress or already committed'. The failure to report to a law enforcement agency or to a court a misdemeanour, negligent crime, minor, non-serious and serious intentional crime does not create the *corpus delicti* of this crime.

II. Submission to the Public Authorities

329. Lithuanian criminal law did not provide a general rule concerning the impunity of the submission to the public authorities. Also, separate articles of the Special Part of the CC provide special rules when submission to the public authorities creates the grounds for the release of a person from criminal liability who:

(1) participates in a coup d'etat and if he/she voluntarily provides to a state institution significant information about the coup d'etat being prepared (Article 114 of the CC);

213. Decision of the Senate of the Supreme Court of Lithuania of 30 Dec. 2004 // Lietuvos Respublikos baudžiamasis kodeksas ir lydimoji medžiaga pastraipsniui, Vilnius, 2009, p. 473.

(2) commits a use of a person's forced labour or services crime and if he/she, prior to his/her identification as the suspect, voluntarily notifies thereof a law enforcement institution and actively cooperates in identifying the victim of trafficking in human beings (Article 147 of the CC) or purchase or sale of a child (Article 157 of the CC) and detecting any of these criminal acts (147(2) of the CC);
(3) commits grafting and if he/she was demanded or provoked to give a bribe and he/she, upon offering or promising to give or giving the bribe voluntarily notifies a law enforcement institution thereof within the shortest possible time, but in any case before the delivery of a notice of suspicion raised against him/her, also where he/she promises to give or gives the bribe with the law enforcement institution being aware thereof (Article 227 of the CC);
(4) commits production, acquisition or storage of the consumed or submitted narcotic or psychotropic substances and if he/she voluntarily addresses a State institution in order to submit the narcotic or psychotropic substances which have been unlawfully produced, acquired, stored for the purpose other than distribution (Article 259 of the CC), etc.

III. Family Relationship

330. Article 31 of the Constitution states that 'persons cannot be compelled to give evidence against themselves or against their family members or close relatives'. Under criminal law, close relatives are parents (adoptive parents), children (adopted children), brothers, sisters, grandparents and grandchildren. Family members of the perpetrator are the parents (adoptive parents), children (adopted children), brothers, sisters and their spouses living together with him/her, the spouse of the perpetrator or the person living with him/her in common law (partnership), parents of the spouse, person with whom the marriage had been agreed, and also former spouses. The Special Part of the CC of Lithuania provides that close relatives and family members of the perpetrator shall not be held liable for a failure to report a crime (Article 238 of the CC) and concealment of a crime or the perpetrator (Article 239 of the CC).

Chapter 5. Incomplete or Partly Perpetrated Criminal Offences

§1. Preparation for Commission of a Crime

I. Describing the Problem

331. Lithuanian criminal law provides criminal liability not only for a completed criminal act, but also for the preliminary stages of a criminal act – preparation to commit a serious or grave crime and an attempt to commit the criminal act. Only intentional criminal acts may have preliminary stages. Criminal liability for criminal acts committed through negligence shall arise only if completed (it should be noted that a negligent criminal act always requires the emergence of physical or material consequences).

II. Lithuanian Preparation and Attempt Statutes

332. Preparation to commit an intentional serious or grave crime and an attempt to commit an intentional criminal act are dealt with by the CC, the jurisprudence of the Supreme Court of Lithuania and the doctrine of the Lithuanian criminal law. The preparation is punishable only if the offender intends to commit a serious or grave crime; the criminal liability shall not arise in case of preparation to commit the misdemeanour, minor or less serious crime.

333. Some of the EU legal acts impose an obligation on the EU Member States to criminalise, as a completed criminal act, certain conduct whose substance constitutes only an attempt or even preparation to commit a certain criminal act, for example, Article 4 of Council Framework Decision 2001/413/JHA of 28 May 2001 combating fraud and the counterfeiting of non-cash means of payment requires the Member State to establish as a criminal offence 'the intentional fraudulent making, receiving, obtaining, sale or transfer to another person or possession of computer programmes the purpose of which is the commission of any of the offences described under Article 3',[214] etc. In this case, criminal liability, in principle, should be set for the preparation to commit fraud by using non-cash payment instruments. It should be noted that at present there are even thirteen articles of the Special Part of the CC, which establish criminal liability for separate criminal acts the substance whereof is preparation to commit another criminal act,[215] for example, 'production, transportation, import, selling, providing access to or other distribution, acquisition or storing the installations or software directly intended or adapted for the commission of criminal acts' (Article 198(2) of the CC), 'production, acquisition, storing or

214. Council Framework Decision 2001/413/JHA of 28 May 2001 combating fraud and counterfeiting of non-cash means of payment, *OJ L 149, 2.6.2001, p. 1–4.*

215. ŠVEDAS G. European Union criminal law and its influence on the institutes of the General Part of Lithuanian criminal law // Lithuanian legal system under the influence of European Union law, Vilnius, 2014, p. 158.

handling of the equipment, software or special materials for the production of counterfeit currency or securities or for the forgery of genuine currency or securities' (Article 213 of the CC), etc. The doctrine of the Lithuanian criminal law, taking into account these requirements of the EU legislation, have expressed an opinion that it should be considered whether it is necessary to leave in the CC the general rule that the preparation to commit a serious and grave crime shall be punishable.[216]

334. Therefore, criminal liability for the preparatory stages is exceptional, attempt is punishable generally – for all kinds of intentional criminal acts (e.g. misdemeanour, minor, less serious, serious and grave crime).

III. Conditions of Preparation

335. The Lithuanian criminal law provides that preparation for the commission of a serious or grave crime shall be (1) a search for or (2) adaptation of means and instruments, (3) development of an action plan, (4) engagement of accomplices or (5) other intentional creation of the conditions facilitating the commission of serious or grave crimes. All five actions of preparation are alternative; criminal liability shall arise even for the commission of one of them. Also, each of these actions must be carried out in order to commit a concrete serious or grave crime. The offender must have a special purpose to commit the crime and behave with direct intent. These subjective features are the main criterion for distinguishing a stage of preparation from the non-criminal behaviour.

336. The doctrine recognises that such a description of preparation as 'any other intentional facilitation of the commission of a crime' means that the criminal law does not provide for all potential ways (forms) of preparation to commit crimes.[217] Other facilitation of crimes can include any intentional acts (omissions), if they make it possible to implement a criminal intention or significantly facilitate the commission of the intended crime. This definition of one of the forms of preparation in criminal law raises serious doubts, as it is completely unclear which acts or omissions form the basis for the criminal liability.

337. It should be noted that if the actions of preparation in itself constitute the *corpus delicti* of another criminal act (e.g., illegal acquisition of the firearm for the commission of the armed robbery in the future, etc.), the offender shall be liable also for that criminal act.

338. The distinctive feature separating the preparation and attempt stages, is the fact that actions of preparation cannot be an act of the *corpus delicti* of the intention to commit a serious or grave crime; otherwise, the crime is already attempted.

216. Švedas G., Veršekys P. The Tendencies and Issues of Transposing EU law to the General Part of Lithuanian Criminal Code, Studia Prawno-Ekonomiczne, T. 99, Lodz, 2016, p. 104.
217. Lietuvos Respublikos baudžiamojo kodekso komentaras. Bendroji dalis (1–98 straipsniai), Vilnius, TIC, 2004, p. 134.

IV. The Punishment for Preparation

339. A person shall be held liable for preparation to commit a serious or grave crime according to an article of the Special Part of the CC providing liability for an appropriately completed crime. A punishment for preparation for commission of a serious and grave crime shall be imposed according to the general sentencing procedure and having regard to the dangerousness of the actions performed by the offender, the degree of accomplishment of the criminal intent and the reasons for which the criminal act was not accomplished. Preparation for the commission of a serious and grave crime may be subject to a more lenient punishment than the one provided for the completed criminal act (Article 62 of the CC).

§2. Criminal Attempt

I. Conditions of Attempt

340. The Lithuanian criminal law defines an attempt to commit a criminal act as an intentional act or omission, which marks the direct commencement of a crime or misdemeanour where the act has not been completed by reason of the circumstances beyond the control the offender. It should be noted that, according to the CC, an attempt to commit a criminal act shall also occur when the offender is not aware that his/her act cannot be completed, because his/her attempt is directed at an inappropriate object or he/she is applying improper means.

341. The doctrine of the Lithuanian criminal law[218] and jurisprudence of the Supreme Court of Lithuania[219] distinguish two kinds of attempt: a complete and an incomplete attempt. Complete attempt means that in the view of the offender he/she did everything was expected (in case of formal criminal act) and necessary for the achievement of criminal consequences (in case of material criminal act). Incomplete attempt means that in the view of the offender, the act was not completed, since he/she failed to carry out all was expected (in case of formal criminal act) and necessary for the achievement of criminal consequences (in case of material criminal act). The kind of attempt has influence in sentencing for the individualisation of the punishment for the commission of the incomplete criminal act.

A. *Intent to Commit a Crime or a Misdemeanour*

342. An attempt to commit a criminal act presupposes an intention since the concrete criminal act that will be attempted must be intentional, and the attempt

---

218. Lietuvos Respublikos baudžiamojo kodekso komentaras. Bendroji dalis (1–98 straipsniai), Vilnius, TIC, 2004, p. 142–143.
219. Ruling of the Supreme Court of Lithuania in criminal case No. 2K-7-48/2009.

itself can be carried out as a rule with direct intent.[220] Criminal acts by negligence or mixed form of guilt cannot be attempted.

B. *Commencement of Execution*

343. The doctrine of the Lithuanian criminal law[221] and jurisprudence of the Supreme Court of Lithuania,[222] when interpreting the feature of the attempt – 'the direct commencement of a crime or misdemeanour' requires that the execution of the offender's conduct (act or omission) provided in the *corpus delicti* of the criminal act must be started.

C. *Incompletion of the Offence Independent of the Perpetrator's Will*

344. The definition of the attempt requires that 'the act has not been completed by reason of the circumstances beyond the control of the offender'. This feature means that the offender's behaviour may not be carried out entirely (in case of formal criminal acts) or the criminal consequences may not occur (in case of material criminal acts) due to the reason of the circumstances beyond the will of the offender. The circumstances may be very different, but in particular they prevent from the completion of the criminal act.

345. In case where an attempt to commit a criminal act constitutes a separate *corpus delicti* of the criminal act, the offender shall be liable for that criminal act, except the situation when the attempted criminal act is more serious.

346. Meanwhile, if the incompletion of the criminal act depends on the offender's will, he/she may not be liable for the attempted criminal act due to the voluntary renunciation of a criminal act. Voluntarily renounce completion of a crime or a misdemeanour means an active or passive voluntarily termination of an initiated criminal act by the offender while he/she is aware that it can be completed. The Supreme Court of Lithuania has stated that 'voluntary renounce shall be a conscious and free-will decision of the offender who was not forced into it by other persons or faced with insurmountable obstacles preventing the completion of a criminal act'.[223]

347. The doctrine of the Lithuanian criminal law requires that voluntary termination has three conditions to fulfil: (1) termination of the completion of the criminal act was conscious and free-will decision of the offender; (2) this decision was

220. Lietuvos Respublikos baudžiamojo kodekso komentaras. Bendroji dalis (1–98 straipsniai), Vilnius, TIC, 2004, p. 141; Baudžiamoji teisė: Bendroji dalis, Vilnius, Eugrimas, 2003, p. 250.
221. Lietuvos Respublikos baudžiamojo kodekso komentaras. Bendroji dalis (1–98 straipsniai), Vilnius, TIC, 2004, p. 140.
222. Ruling of the Supreme Court of Lithuania in criminal case No. 2K-7-48/2009.
223. Ruling of the Supreme Court of Lithuania in criminal case No. 2K-175/2012.

not based on the external circumstances which prevented the completion of the criminal act; (3) this decision was final and unconditional.[224]

348. The Lithuanian criminal law establishes special conditions for the voluntarily renounce completion of a crime or a misdemeanour of the organiser, abettor and accessory. The organiser or abettor who voluntarily renounces completion of the act shall not be liable under the CC if he/she has made every effort within his/her reasonable power to prevent commission by his/her accomplices of the criminal act which he/she has organised or instigated, and this act has not been committed or has not caused any consequences. Moreover, an accessory shall not be held liable under the CC if he/she voluntarily refused to participate in a criminal act, informed thereof other accomplices or law enforcement institutions and that act has not been committed or it has been committed without his/her assistance.

349. The Lithuania criminal law provides that a person who voluntarily renounces completion of a crime or misdemeanour shall be held liable under the CC solely in cases where the committed act constitutes the *corpus delicti* of another crime or misdemeanour.

350. If a person who attempted to voluntarily renounce completion of a crime or misdemeanour, has failed to avoid the criminal act or its consequences, he/she shall be held liable under the CC, however, a punishment imposed upon him/her may be commuted due to active repentance as a mitigating circumstance (Article 59 of the CC).

II. Attempting the Impossible

351. The law foresees two kinds of the impossible attempt: an attempt at an inappropriate object or an attempt by applying improper means. Both kinds of impossible attempt mean that the attempted criminal act cannot be completed due to the unsuitability of the object or means (methods, instruments) used by the offender.

352. The doctrine distinguishes between an absolutely and relatively impossible attempt.[225] However, these theoretical provisions have not yet been approved by the Supreme Court.

224. Baudžiamoji teisė: Bendroji dalis, Vilnius, Eugrimas, 2003, p. 258–259.
225. Lietuvos Respublikos baudžiamojo kodekso komentaras. Bendroji dalis (1–98 straipsniai), Vilnius, TIC, 2004, p. 144–145; Baudžiamoji teisė: Bendroji dalis, Vilnius, Eugrimas, 2003, p. 251–253.

III. The Punishment for Attempt

353. A person shall be held liable for an attempt to commit a criminal act according to the article of the Special Part of the CC providing liability for an appropriately completed crime. A punishment for the attempt to commit a criminal act shall be imposed according to the general sentencing procedure and having regard to the dangerousness of the actions performed by the offender, the degree of accomplishment of the criminal intent, the kind of the attempt and the reasons for which the criminal act was not accomplished. The attempt to commit a criminal act may be subject to a more lenient punishment than the one provided for in the completed criminal act (Article 62 of the CC).

§3. Complicity

I. General Remarks

354. The General Part of the CC lays down provisions on complicity, types of accomplices, forms of complicity as well as peculiarities of criminal liability of accomplices. Article 24 of the CC provides that complicity shall be the intentional joint participation in the commission of a criminal act of two or more conspiring legally capable persons who have attained the age for criminal liability.

355. Accomplices in a criminal act include a perpetrator, an organiser, an instigator and an abettor.

356. The concept of complicity requires that the same criminal act shall be completed at least by two legally capable physical persons who have attained the age for criminal liability. It should be noted that the Supreme Court has stated that, in some cases, the courts must recognise the complicity even if the person of the perpetrator was not identified.[226] Legal persons cannot be accomplices.

357. Accomplices must mutually agree on the commission of the criminal act. The agreement between accomplices may be expressed in any form – orally, in writing, by conclusive actions, for example, by gesture, mime, etc. According to the Supreme Court, 'the mutual agreement between accomplices may be concluded in any stage of the criminal act until the criminal consequences shall be reached'.[227]

358. The criminal liability of the accomplices is bound to the principal criminal act. The criminal liability for the organiser, instigator and abettor cannot be realised, since the principal criminal act is not committed. The perpetrator's criminal act must be an intentional criminal act and must have been committed intentionally. Furthermore, the criminal liability of accomplices requires an intentional participation in the commission of criminal act; participation by negligence is excluded.

---

226. Ruling of the Supreme Court of Lithuania in criminal case No. 2K-P-9/2009.
227. Ruling of the Supreme Court of Lithuania in criminal case No. 2K-279/2011.

359. Complicity is possible at any stage of the criminal act.

360. The complicity may be considered as aggravating circumstance (*see* paragraphs 599–600), qualified feature of the *corpus delicti* of the criminal act, for example, commission the theft, robbery, swindling and extortion of property by participating in an organised group (Articles 178, 180, 181 and 182 of the CC), or even as separate completed crime, for example, creation of anti-constitutional groups or organisations and participation in their activities (Article 121 of the CC), criminal association and participation in his activity (Article 249 of the CC), establishment and activities of groups having the aim of committing terrorist crimes (Article 249(1) of the CC).

II. Forms of Perpetrator Actions

361. As perpetrators are considered: direct perpetrators, joint perpetrators (co-perpetrators) and indirect perpetrator.

A. Direct Perpetrator

362. A direct perpetrator is a person who has committed a criminal act by himself/herself. The Article of the Special Part of the CC which establishes a*ctus reus* of a concrete criminal act is typically worded such that there is one perpetrator, for example, in case of theft: 'a person who seizes another's property', etc. This means that all *corpus delicti* of the criminal act independently are completed by one single person.

363. It should be noted that, for some criminal acts, the perpetrator must have a certain special feature, for example, State official, doctor, accountant, etc. In these cases, an organiser, an instigator or an abettor is not exempted from criminal liability if they do not comply with this special feature, since the Supreme Court has stated that 'only the perpetrator must comply with the special feature of the subject of the criminal act; such requirement is not applicable to the organiser, instigator or abettor'.[228]

B. Joint Perpetrators (Co-perpetrators)

364. If the criminal act has been committed by several physical persons acting together, each of them shall be considered a joint perpetrator (co-perpetrator). This legal definition means that joint perpetrator (co-perpetrator) can only be the one who realises at least one element of *actus reus* of the jointly committed criminal act. Joint perpetration requires that each perpetrator participates in the commission of

228. Ruling of the Supreme Court of Lithuania in criminal case No. 2K-400/2011.

the criminal act with united intent. United intent means that each participant must perceive joint commission of the *actus reus* of the criminal act and must be aware of each other's activity.[229]

C. Indirect Perpetrator

365. An indirect perpetrator is a person who has committed a criminal act by involving (1) legally incapacitated person (*see* paragraphs 303–310), or (2) person who have not yet attained the age for criminal liability under the CC (*see* paragraphs 299–301), or (3) other person who is not guilty of that act.

366. In the case of commission of the criminal act by involving another person who is not guilty of that act, the essential fact is that the immediate perpetrator has the intent and knowledge of the situation in which the criminal act has been committed that the agent lacks.

III. Organiser

367. An organiser is a person who has formed an organised group or a criminal association, has been in charge of an organised group or a criminal association, or has coordinated the activities of its members or has prepared a criminal act or has been in charge of the commission of a criminal act. The essential feature of the organiser is that he/she unites and directs the actions of another accomplice, establishes interrelations between accomplices, creates the criminal act plans, provides ways and means for their implementation, etc.

368. The Supreme Court of Lithuania has stated that 'an organiser as a rule is in an organised group or criminal association in the crimes under commission; he/she may also be in a group of accomplices in the crimes under commission, if their actions are complex, multilayered, multifaceted and related to the preparation or management of the criminal act'.[230]

IV. Instigator

369. An instigator is a person who has incited another person to commit a criminal act. Incitement must always be specific; it means that the person should be induced to commit the concrete crime. The Lithuanian criminal law did not specify

229. Lietuvos Respublikos baudžiamojo kodekso komentaras. Bendroji dalis (1-98 straipsniai), Vilnius, TIC, 2004, p. 158.
230. Ruling of the Supreme Court of Lithuania in criminal case No. 2K-391/2011.

the methods of incitement – they can be varied. However, the incitement, even disguised, is recognised as active actions (e.g., invitation, persuasion or even threat, etc.) that cause a person's conscious desire to commit a criminal act.[231]

370. It should be mentioned that the Special Part of the CC provides a few crimes where incitement compose a completed *corpus delicti* of the criminal act, for example, public incitement to infringe upon the sovereignty of the Republic of Lithuania by using violence (Article 122 of the CC) or incitement to terrorism (Article 250(1) of the CC).

V. Abettor

371. An abettor is a person who has aided in the commission of a criminal act through counselling, issuing instructions, providing means or removing obstacles, protecting or shielding other accomplices, who has promised in advance to conceal the offender, hide the instruments or means of commission of the criminal act, the traces of the act or the items acquired by criminal means, also a person who has promised in advance to handle the items acquired or produced in the course of the criminal act. Abetting may be intellectual (counselling, issuing instructions) or physical (providing means, removing obstacles, etc.). It can take the form of action or omission, the latter occurring, when the person fails to comply with the legal obligation to act (e.g., the guard leaves the key in the doors, etc.).[232]

372. Actions of abetting may be committed prior to or during the principal criminal act. If it occurs when the criminal act has already been committed, these actions become one of harbouring an offender, which are criminalised separately as a concealment of a crime or the perpetrator (Article 237 of the CC), or a failure to report a crime (Article 238 of the CC).

373. It should be mentioned that the Special Part of the CC provides a few crimes where abetting constitutes a completed *corpus delicti* of the criminal act, for example, recruitment for terrorism (Article 250(2) of the CC), financing and support of terrorist activities (Article 250(4) of the CC), training of terrorism (Article 250(5) of the CC).

VI. Forms of Complicity

374. Lithuanian criminal law establishes three forms of complicity: a group of accomplices, an organised group or a criminal association. The doctrine of the

231. Ruling of the Supreme Court of Lithuania in criminal case No. 2K-506/2010.
232. Lietuvos Respublikos baudžiamojo kodekso komentaras. Bendroji dalis (1-98 straipsniai), Vilnius, TIC, 2004, p. 155, 163.

Lithuanian criminal law specifies that, in practice, the features of complicity, which do not meet the requirements of any form of complicity, may be encountered.[233]

375. A group of accomplices shall be one in which two or more persons agree, at any stage of the commission of a criminal act, on the commission, continuation or completion of the criminal act, where at least two of them are perpetrators. This form of complicity is the least dangerous. A group of accomplices is a qualified feature of the *corpus delicti* of rape (Article 149 of the CC) and sexual assault (Article 150 of the CC). In all other situations, a group of accomplices may be treated as an aggravating circumstance (*see* paragraphs 602–604).

376. An organised group shall be one in which two or more persons agree, at any stage of the commission of a criminal act, on the commission of several crimes or of one less serious, serious or grave crime, and, in committing the crime, each member of the group performs a certain task or is given a different role. This form of complicity is on an average dangerous. When explaining the differences between a group of accomplices and an organised group, the Supreme Court of Lithuania has underlined that 'organised group should be created for the commission of several crimes or of one less serious, serious or grave crime; each member of the group must perform a certain task or must be given a different role in the commission of the crimes'.[234] An organised group is a qualified feature of the *corpus delicti* of theft (Article 178 of the CC), robbery (Article 180 of the CC), swindling (Article 181 of the CC) and extortion of property (Article 182 of the CC). In all other situations, the organised group is treated as an aggravating circumstance (*see* paragraphs 602–604).

377. A criminal association shall be one in which three or more persons linked by permanent mutual relations and division of roles or tasks join together for the commission of a joint criminal act – one or several less serious, serious and grave crimes. An anti-state group or organisation and a terrorist group shall be considered equivalent to a criminal association. This form of complicity is the most dangerous.

378. When interpreting the essential characteristics of a criminal association, the Supreme Court has supplemented the above indicated characteristics with the constant character of a group, the long-term close relations between its members, internal discipline maintained by authority, intimidation and other means, the distribution of roles and tasks, the possession of communication and other technical equipment, weapons, etc. All these features 'highlight and describe more precisely' the elements necessary for a criminal association[235] and eliminate the risk that a group having nothing in common with the organised crime will be considered a

233. Švedas G., Veršekys P., Levon J., Prapiestis D. Lietuvos Respublikos baudžiamojo kodekso bendrosios dalies vientisumo ir suderinimo iššūkiai, Vilnius, Vilniaus universiteto leidykla, 2017, p. 147.

234. Ruling of the Supreme Court of Lithuania in criminal case No. 2K-7-96/2012.

235. LAT Senato 1995 m. spalio 10 d. nutarimas No. 16 'Dėl teismų praktikos nagrinėjant nusikalstamo susivienijimo (BK 227(1) str.) baudžiamąsias bylas' // Lietuvos Respublikos baudžiamasis kodeksas ir lydimoji medžiaga pastraipsniui, Vilnius, 2009, p. 643, 654–659.

criminal association.[236] In the doctrine of the Lithuanian criminal law,[237] it was also proposed to revise the concept of criminal association by including in it additional elements that would *inter alia* bring more conformity with the requirements of Council Framework Decision 2008/841/JHA of 24 October 2008 on the fight against organised crime[238] – (a) a pre-agreement to engage in joint criminal activity; (b) presence of a leader or leaders; (c) intention to obtain, directly or indirectly, a financial or other material benefit.

379. This form of complicity is criminalised as a separate completed crime: a criminal association (Article 249 of the CC), an anti-state group or organisation (Article 122 of the CC) and a terrorist group (Article 249(1) of the CC).

VII. Special Cases

A. *Withdrawal from Participation*

380. As it was mentioned before, the Lithuanian criminal law establishes special conditions for the voluntarily renounce completion of a crime or a misdemeanour of the organiser, instigator and abettor. The organiser or instigator who voluntarily renounces the completion of the act shall not be liable under the CC if he/she has made every effort within his/her reasonable power to prevent commission by his/her accomplices of the criminal act which he/she had organised or instigated, and this act has not been committed or has not caused any consequences. Moreover, an abettor shall not be held liable under the CC if he/she voluntarily refuses to participate in a criminal act, and informs thereof other accomplices or law enforcement institutions and that act has not been committed or it has been committed without his/her assistance.

B. *Entrapment*

381. Entrapment, which in Lithuanian legal system includes actions imitating a criminal act, controlled delivery and performance of an assignment of a law enforcement institution, is regulated by the CC as a circumstance eliminating criminal liability (*see* paragraphs 285–288). Meanwhile, the CCP and the Law on Criminal Intelligence mentioned above, establish the grounds and procedural rules for the application of actions imitating a criminal act, controlled delivery and performance of an assignment of a law enforcement institution.

236. Fedosiuk, O. Turto prievartavimas ir jo kvalifikavimas, Vilnius, 2002, p. 185.
237. Švedas G., Veršekys P., Levon J., Prapiestis D. Lietuvos Respublikos baudžiamojo kodekso bendrosios dalies vientisumo ir suderinimo iššūkiai, Vilnius, Vilniaus universiteto leidykla, 2017, p. 148, 152.
238. Council Framework Decision 2008/841/JHA of 24 Oct. 2008 on the fight against organized crime, *OJ L 300, 11.11.2008, p. 42–45.*

VIII. Peculiarities of Criminal Liability of Accomplices

382. An organiser, an instigator or an abettor shall be held liable under the article of the Special Part of the CC which provides for liability for an act committed by a perpetrator. It may happen that the realisation of the criminal act partially or totally differs from the accomplices' agreement (*excessus*). The Supreme Court of Lithuania has stated that 'perpetrator's excess is the overstepping of the limits of an accomplices' agreement when the perpetrator commits actions, which by their nature, extent or committed manner are inconsistent with the agreement content'.[239] In case of perpetrator's excess, the accomplices shall be held liable solely for the criminal acts as committed by the perpetrator, which are covered by their intent.

383. Where a perpetrator's criminal act was discontinued at the stage of preparation for commission of or an attempt to commit it, an organiser, an instigator and an abettor shall be held liable for complicity in preparation or attempt to commit the criminal act.

384. Where there are the circumstances eliminating, mitigating or aggravating the liability of one of the accomplices, they shall not be taken into account when determining the criminal liability of other accomplices.

385. Members of a criminal association shall be held liable for commission of the *corpus delicti* of criminal association (Article 249 of the CC) as perpetrators regardless of their roles in the commission of a criminal act which is covered by their intent.

386. It should be mentioned that a person who actively assists in detecting the criminal acts committed by members of an organised group or a criminal association may be released from criminal liability (*see* paragraphs 467, 468).

387. A punishment shall be imposed upon accomplices in a crime or misdemeanour in accordance with the general sentencing procedure and taking into consideration the type and form of participation of the person as an accomplice in the commission of the criminal act as well as the role and nature of participation therein. Members of an organised group for the commission of a crime shall be generally imposed a more severe punishment than to members of a group of accomplices.

239. Ruling of the Supreme Court of Lithuania in criminal case No. 2K-279/2011.

Chapter 6. Classification and Survey of Criminal Offences

§1. General Classification of Criminal Offences

388. Under Lithuanian criminal law, criminal acts can be classified in a variety of ways, for example, intentional and negligent criminal acts, qualified and non-qualified criminal acts, or criminal acts of action and criminal acts of omission, etc.

389. The main new feature of the CC is a complete classification covering all criminal acts. According to Article 10 of the CC, all criminal acts are divided into misdemeanours and crimes. This distinction is based on the gravity of the crime and, in particular, on the severity of the punishment and different types of punishments envisaged in the CC. A misdemeanour shall be a dangerous act (act or omission) forbidden under the CC which is punishable by a non-custodial sentence, with the exception of arrest. According to Article 11 of the CC 'a crime shall be a dangerous act (act or omission) forbidden under the CC and punishable with a custodial sentence'. Crimes may be committed with intent and through negligence. All negligent crimes compose one group of criminal acts.

390. As it was mentioned before, intentional crimes are divided into minor, less serious, serious and grave crimes. A minor crime is an intentional crime punishable, under the criminal law, apply everywhere of the maximum duration of three years. A less serious crime is an intentional crime punishable, under the criminal law, by an imprisonment for the maximum duration in excess of three years, but not exceeding six years of imprisonment. A serious crime is an intentional crime punishable, under the criminal law, by an imprisonment for the duration in excess of six years, but not exceeding ten years of imprisonment. A grave crime is an intentional crime punishable, under the criminal law, by an imprisonment for the maximum duration in excess of ten years or by life imprisonment.

391. This division of criminal acts is important as it has consequences in the field of substantive criminal law. For example, application of the institutes of release from criminal liability or the suspended sentence depends on whether the criminal act is a misdemeanour or crime (and on the category of the crime).

I. Ordinary and Political Offences

392. Crimes having political content (crimes against the Independence, Territorial Integrity and Constitutional Order of the State of Lithuania) do not have a special status in the Lithuanian criminal law.

II. Ordinary and Printing Press Offences

393. Press crimes do not have a special status in the Lithuanian criminal law.

§2. Survey of Criminal Offences

394. Since it is impossible to provide an extensive and full survey of all criminal acts under the Lithuanian criminal law, the following survey is limited to a brief representation of the structure and the content of the Chapters of the Special Part of the CC of Lithuania.

I. Criminal Offences of the Penal Code

395. On 1 June 2019, the Special Part of the CC consisted of 32 Chapters (273 articles).[240] The structure and classification in the Special Part of the CC is based on more precisely and specifically defined group objects (legal goods) and on the groups of criminal offences distinguished on the basis thereof. Furthermore, the classification of norms and their division into separate chapters in the Special Part of the CC are also underpinned by the value criterion revealing the importance, significance and value of the specific object of criminal offences, i.e., protected public (social) relations. Therefore, the order of sequence of the chapters of the CC Special Part has, in principle, been determined by the significance of the legal goods encroached by the relevant group of criminal acts. The framework of the CC Special part was constructed according to the following principle – from most dangerous to less dangerous groups of criminal acts.[241]

Criminal Code Chapter XV 'Crimes against Humanity and War Crimes' (Articles 99–113(1) of the CC)

396. Chapter XV provides criminal liability for the most dangerous criminal offences – crimes against humanity and war crimes. Genocide (Article 99 of the CC), Killing of Persons Protected under International Humanitarian Law (Article 101 of the CC), Forcible Use of Civilians or Prisoners of War in the Armed Forces of the Enemy (Article 105 of the CC), Aggression (Article 110 of the CC), Prohibited Military Attack (Article 111 of the CC) are examples of such crimes. Definitions of these crimes fully correspond to the requirements of The Rome Statute of the International Criminal Court and amendments to the Rome Statute of the International Criminal Court, which was ratified by Lithuania.[242] It should be noted that the concept of genocide under Lithuanian criminal law is broader because it includes not only national, ethnic, racial or religious, but also social and political groups. Punishments for crimes against humanity and war crimes range from imprisonment not exceeding three years (e.g., for delay in repatriation of prisoners

---

240. Švedas G., Abramavičius A. Tendencies and Problematical Aspects of Criminal Liability of a Legal Person in Lithuania // *In Legal Developments During 30 Years of Lithuanian Independence. Overview of Legal Accomplishments and Challenges in Lithuania* 302 (Gintaras Švedas & Donatas Murauskas ed Springer 2021).
241. Abramavičius A., Prapiestis J. The influence of European Union law on the institutes of the Special Part of Lithuanian criminal law // Lithuanian legal system under the influence of European Union law, Vilnius, 2014, p. 174.
242. Lietuvos Respublikos įstatymas Dėl Tarptautinio baudžiamojo teismo Romos statuto pakeitimų dėl agresijos nusikaltimo ratifikavimo, TAR, 2015, No. 2015-18319, No. 2015-19274.

of war (Article 107 of the CC), etc.) up to life imprisonment (e.g., for genocide (Article 99 of the CC), aggravating military attack (Article 111 of the CC), etc.).

Criminal Code Chapter XVI 'Crimes against the Independence, Territorial Integrity and Constitutional Order of the State of Lithuania' (Articles 114–128 of the CC)

397. Chapter XVI provides criminal liability for the crimes against the Independence, Territorial Integrity and Constitutional Order of the State of Lithuania, which may be considered as political crimes. Attempt on the life of the President of the Republic of Lithuania, Representative of another State or International Public Organisation (Articles 115 and 116 of the CC), Treason (Article 117 of the CC), Assistance to Another State in Carrying out Activities Hostile to the Republic of Lithuania (Article 118 of the CC), Espionage (Article 119 of the CC), Collaboration (Article 120 of the CC) are examples of such crimes. Punishments for crimes against independence, territorial integrity and constitutional order of the State of Lithuania range from imprisonment not exceeding two years (e.g., for loss of a State secret (Article 126 of the CC), etc.) up to life imprisonment (e.g., for attempt on the life of the President of the Republic of Lithuania (Article 115 of the CC), etc.). A legal entity can be held liable for the Violation of International Sanctions (Article 123(1) of the CC).

Criminal Code Chapter XVII 'Crimes against Human Life' (Articles 129–134 of the CC)

398. Lithuanian criminal law provides two kinds of homicide: intentional murder (paragraph 1, Article 129 of the CC), which may be punished by imprisonment from five to fifteen years, and killing committed through negligence – Negligent Homicide (Article 132 of the CC), which may be punished by imprisonment up to eight years. It should be noted that Article 132 of the CC is of general nature, since special situations in which a person's death may be caused are provided in other articles of the CC, for example, paragraph 5 of Article 281 of the CC provides liability for 'a person who, while driving a road vehicle, violates the regulations governing road traffic safety or operation of vehicles, where this results in an accident causing a person's death', etc.

399. Paragraph 2 of Article 129 of CC establishes situations of intentional murder under aggravating circumstances: murder of (1) a young person; (2) a person in a helpless state; (3) his close relative or family member; (4) a pregnant woman; (5) two or more persons; (6) by torturing or in another particularly cruel manner; (7) in a manner endangering other persons' lives; (8) by reason of disorderly conduct; (9) for mercenary reasons; (10) by reason of performance of official or citizen's duties by the victim; (11) in order to conceal another crime; (12) in order to acquire the victim's organ, tissue or cells; (13) in order to express hatred towards a group of persons or a person belonging thereto on grounds of age, sex, sexual orientation, disability, race, nationality, language, descent, social status, religion, convictions or views. Murder under aggravating circumstances may be punished by imprisonment from eight up to twenty years or by life imprisonment. Articles 130 and 131 of the CC deal with situations that might be regarded as intentional murder under mitigating circumstances – murder in state of passion, which may be punished by imprisonment up to six years, and infanticide, which may be punished by imprisonment up to five years. Finally, this CC Chapter criminalises abetting a suicide or procuring a suicide (Article 133 of the CC) and aiding a suicide (Article 134 of the CC), which may be punished *inter alia* by imprisonment up to four years. Lithuania has no special legislation on euthanasia. A legal entity can be held liable for Negligent Homicide (Article 132 of the CC).

Criminal Code Chapter XVIII 'Crimes against Human Health' (Articles 135–141 of the CC)

400. Chapter XVIII provides criminal liability for health impairment, distinguishing it on the basis of its severity and *mens rea* of a crime. It separates Severe and Non-Severe Health Impairment (accordingly Articles 135 and 138 of the CC), Severe Health Impairment Caused in a State of Passion (Article 136 of the CC), Severe and Non-Severe Health Impairment Caused through Negligence (accordingly Articles 137 and 139 of the CC) and Causing Physical Pain or a Negligible Health Impairment (Article 140 of the CC). Severe health impairment (Article 135 of the CC) is related to causing a dangerous bodily harm or an illness to a person, which results in three types of consequences: (1) the victim's loss of eyesight, hearing, ability to speak, ability to reproduce, pregnancy or other serious mutilation, contracting of a terminal illness or a long-lasting illness posing a threat to his life or seriously affecting his mental health or (2) in the loss of a considerable part of professional or general capacity for work or (3) in a permanent disfigurement of the victim's body.

401. Aggravating circumstances of Severe and Non-Severe health impairment (accordingly, paragraph 2 of Articles 135 and 138 of the CC) comply with aggravating circumstances of Intentional Murder (paragraph 2 of Article 129 of the CC), which include causing a serious bodily injury or illness: (1) to a young child; (2) to a person in a helpless state; (3) to his close relative or family member; (4) to a pregnant woman; (5) to two or more persons; (6) by torturing or in another particularly cruel manner; (7) in a manner endangering other persons' lives; (8) by reason of disorderly conduct; (9) for mercenary reasons; (10) by reason of performance of official or citizen's duties by the victim; (11) in order to conceal another crime; (12) in order to acquire the victim's organ, tissue or cells; (13) in order to express hatred towards a group of persons or a person belonging thereto on grounds of age, sex, sexual orientation, disability, race, nationality, language, descent, social status, religion, convictions or views.

402. Punishments for intentional crimes against human health, depending on the severity, range from *inter alia* imprisonment not exceeding one year for Physical Pain or a Negligible Health Impairment (Article 140 of the CC), up to three years for Non-Severe Health Impairment (Article 138 of the CC) or up to ten years for

Severe Health Impairment (Article 135 of the CC). Accordingly, under aggravating circumstances, these crimes may be punished by imprisonment up to two, five or twelve years.

403. Punishments for negligent impairment of human health are *inter alia* imprisonment for a term not exceeding one year for Non-Severe Health Impairment through Negligence (Article 139 of the CC) or three years for Severe Health Impairment Caused through Negligence (Article 137 of the CC); the latter, committed under aggravating circumstances, for example, in violation of the special conduct security rules as specified by legal acts, can be punished by imprisonment up to seven years. A legal entity can be held liable for Severe Health Impairment Caused through Negligence (Articles 137 of the CC).

Criminal Code Chapter XIX 'Crimes endangering Human Health and Life' (Articles 142–145 of the CC)

404. Chapter XIX criminalises various acts, endangering human health and life: Illegal Abortion (Article 142 of the CC), Compelling a Woman to Have an Illegal Abortion (Article 143 of the CC), Leaving a Person in a Life-Threatening Situation Without Providing Assistance (Article 144 of the CC), Threatening to Murder or Cause a Severe Health Impairment to a Person or Terrorisation of a Person (Article 145 of the CC).

405. Leaving a Person in a Life-Threatening Situation Without Providing Assistance (Article 144 of the CC) is considered a criminal offence when a person who, having raised a threat or while having the duty to take care of the victim, fails to provide assistance to him/her in a situation posing a threat to this person's life, although he was in a position to provide him/her with assistance. Threatening to Murder or Cause a Severe Health Impairment to a Person or Terrorisation of a Person (Article 145 of the CC) is considered a criminal offence only when there is a sufficient basis for believing that the threat may be fulfilled. Crimes endangering Human Health and Life may be punished *inter alia* by imprisonment for a term not exceeding two years (Articles 142, 144, 145 of the CC) or three years (Article 143 of the CC). It should be noted, that a legal entity can be held liable for Threatening to Murder or Cause a Severe Health Impairment to a Person or Terrorisation of a Person (Article 145 of the CC).

Criminal Code Chapter XX 'Crimes and Misdemeanours against Human Liberty' (Articles 146–148 of the CC)

406. Criminal liability for crimes against human liberty is provided in Chapter XX, which includes Unlawful Deprivation of Liberty (Article 146 of the CC), Trafficking in Human Beings (Article 147 of the CC), Use for Forced Labour or Services (Article 147(1) of the CC), Use of a Person's Forced Labour or Services (Article 147(2) of the CC) and Restriction of Freedom of a Person's Actions (Article 148 of the CC). Definitions of trafficking in human beings, use for forced labour or services and use of a person forced labour or services correspond to the requirements of Directive 2011/36/EU of the European Parliament and of the Council of 5 April 2011 on preventing and combating trafficking in human beings and protecting its victims, and replacing Council Framework Decision 2002/629/JHA.[243] Crimes against human liberty without aggravating or mitigating circumstances may be punished by *inter alia* imprisonment not exceeding two years (e.g., for Use of a Person's Forced Labour or Services (Article 147(2) of the CC), etc.) up to ten years (e.g., for trafficking in human beings (Article 147 of the CC), etc.). Aggravating circumstances, for example, endangering human life while committing a crime against human liberty, increases the punishment by imprisonment up to twelve years (e.g., for trafficking in human beings (Article 147 of the CC)). Legal entity can be held liable for all the crimes in this chapter, except Unlawful Deprivation of Liberty (Article 146 of the CC).

Criminal Code Chapter XXI 'Crimes and Misdemeanours against Freedom of a Person's Sexual Self-Determination and Inviolability' (Articles 149–153 of the CC)

407. Chapter XXI provides criminal liability for Rape (Article 149 of the CC), Sexual Assault, Abuse or Harassment (Articles 150, 151, 152 of the CC), Satisfaction of Sexual Desires by Violating a Minor's Freedom of Sexual Self-Determination and/or Inviolability (Article 151(1) of the CC) and others. In this chapter only sexual harassment (Article 152 of the CC) is considered to be a misdemeanour and may be punished by a punishment, not related to imprisonment. Other crimes against freedom of a person's sexual self-determination and inviolability without aggravating or mitigating circumstances may be punished *inter alia* by imprisonment for a term, not exceeding one year (e.g., for Grooming of a Person under the Age of Sixteen Years (Article 152(1) of the CC)) up to seven years (e.g., for Rape (Article 149 of the CC), Sexual Assault (Article 150 of the CC), etc.). Aggravating circumstances for rape and sexual assault include cases, when the crime is committed with a group of accomplices, also if the victim is a minor or a young child (paragraphs 2–4 of Articles 149–150 of the CC); in these cases, punishment includes only imprisonment which reaches up to fifteen years. It should be noted, that a legal entity can also be held liable for the majority of the crimes in this chapter, if the victim is a child or a minor.

Criminal Code Chapter XXII 'Crimes and Misdemeanours against Dignity and Honour' (Articles 154–155 of the CC)

408. Until the CC amendment No. XII-1888, enforced on 10 July 2015,[244] Chapter XXII contained two articles: Libel (Article 154 of the CC) and Insult (Article

243. Directive 2011/36/EU of the European Parliament and of the Council of 5 Apr. 2011 on preventing and combating trafficking in human beings and protecting its victims, and replacing Council Framework Decision 2002/629/JHA, *OJ L 101, 15.4.2011, p. 1–11.*

244. Lietuvos Respublikos baudžiamojo kodekso 155 ir 290 straipsnių pripažinimo netekusiais galios i ̧statymas, TAR, 2015-07-09, No. 11179.

155 of the CC), which both, if committed under no aggravating or mitigating circumstances, could be punished *inter alia* by imprisonment for a term not exceeding one year. For both of them, a person could be held liable only under a complaint filed by the victim or a statement by the legal representative thereof or at the prosecutor's request. Article 155 of the CC was repealed, by decriminalising Insult – a crime, committed when a person publicly humiliates another person in an abusive manner by an action, word of mouth or in writing, as it was acknowledged to be only a matter of civil liability. Currently, the chapter consists only of one article – Libel (Article 154 of the CC), which is committed when a person spreads false information about another person that could arouse contempt for this person or humiliate him/her or undermine trust in him/her. If a person who libels a person, accusing him of commission of a serious or grave crime or in the media or in a publication, the crime is considered to be committed under aggravating circumstances and the punishment rises *inter alia* up to two years of imprisonment.

Criminal Code Chapter XXIII 'Crimes and Misdemeanours against a Child and a Family' (Articles 156–164 of the CC)

409. Crimes and misdemeanours against child and family are provided in Chapter XXIII, which includes Abduction of a Child or Exchange of Children (Article 156 of the CC), Purchase or Sale of a Child (Article 157 of the CC), Desertion of a Child (Article 158 of the CC), Involvement of a Child in a Criminal Act (Article 159 of the CC), Exploitation of a Child for Pornography (Article 162 of the CC) and others. Only one act in this chapter is considered to be a misdemeanour – Involvement of a Child in Abuse of Alcohol (Article 161 of the CC), which may be punished by a punishment, not related to imprisonment. Other crimes against a child and a family, committed under no aggravating or mitigating circumstances, may be punished by *inter alia* imprisonment for a term, not exceeding two years (e.g., for Desertion of a Child or Evasion of a Child's Maintenance (accordingly Articles 158 and 164 of the CC), up to twelve years (e.g., for Purchase or Sale of a Child (Article 157 of the CC), etc.). A legal entity can be held liable for Purchase or Sale of a Child (Article 157 of the CC), and Use of a Child for Pornography (Article 162 of the CC).

410. It should be noted that the definitions of Satisfaction of Sexual Desires by Violating a Minor's Freedom of Sexual Self-Determination and/or Inviolability (Article 151(1) of the CC, Grooming of a Person under the Age of Sixteen Years (Article 152(1) of the CC), Exploitation of a Child for Pornography (Article 162 of the CC), Gaining Profit from Another Person's Prostitution (Article 307 of the CC), Involvement in Prostitution (Article 308 of the CC) and Possession of Pornographic Material (Article 309 of the CC) correspond to the requirements of Directive 2011/92/EU of the European Parliament and of the Council of 13 December 2011 on combating the sexual abuse and sexual exploitation of children and child pornography, and replacing Council Framework Decision 2004/68/JHA.[245]

Criminal Code Chapter XXIV 'Crimes against Inviolability of a Person's Private Life' (Articles 165–168 of the CC)

411. Chapter XXIV provides criminal liability for several crimes against a person's private life: Unlawful Violation of Inviolability of a Person's Dwelling (Article 165 of the CC), Violation of Inviolability of a Person's Correspondence (Article 166 of the CC), Unlawful Collection of Information about a Person's Private Life (Article 167 of the CC) and Unauthorised Disclosure or Use of Information about a Person's Private Life (Article 168 of the CC). Punishments for these crimes range from *inter alia* imprisonment not exceeding two years (Articles 165, 166 of the CC) up to three years (Articles 167, 168 of the CC). These crimes do not have aggravating or mitigating circumstances. A legal entity can be held liable for crimes, established in Articles 166–168 (i.e., excluding Article 165 of the CC).

Criminal Code Chapter XXV 'Crimes and Misdemeanours against a Person's Equal Rights and Freedom of Conscience' (Articles 169–171 of the CC)

412. Criminal liability for crimes against a person's equal rights and freedom of conscience is provided in Chapter XXV, which includes Discrimination on Grounds of Nationality, Race, Sex, Descent, Religion or Belonging to Other Groups (Article 169 of the CC), Incitement against Any National, Racial, Ethnic, Religious or Other Group of Persons (Article 170 of the CC), Public Condonation of International Crimes, Crimes Committed by the USSR or Nazi Germany against the Republic of Lithuania or Inhabitants Thereof, Denial or Gross Trivialisation of the Crimes (Article 170(2) of the CC), etc. The definition of this crime corresponds to the requirements of Council Framework Decision 2008/913/JHA of 28 November 2008 on combating certain forms and expressions of racism and xenophobia by means of criminal law.[246] Punishments for crimes against a person's equal rights and freedom of conscience without aggravating or mitigating circumstances range from *inter alia* imprisonment not exceeding one year (e.g., for Incitement against Any National, Racial, Ethnic, Religious or Other Group of Persons (Article 170 of the CC), etc.) up to three years (e.g., for Discrimination on Grounds of Nationality, Race, Sex, Descent, Religion or Belonging to Other Groups (Article 169 of the CC), etc.). A legal entity can be held liable for Incitement against Any National, Racial, Ethnic, Religious or Other Group of Persons (Article 170 of the CC), Creation and Activities of the Groups and Organisations Aiming at Discriminating a Group of Persons or Inciting against It (Article 170(1) of the CC) and for Public Condonation

245. Directive 2011/92/EU of the European Parliament and of the Council of 13 Dec. 2011 on combating the sexual abuse and sexual exploitation of children and child pornography, and replacing Council Framework Decision 2004/68/JHA, *OJ L 335, 17.12.2011, p. 1–14.*

246. Council Framework Decision 2008/913/JHA of 28 Nov. 2008 on combating certain forms and expressions of racism and xenophobia by means of criminal law, *OJ L 328, 6.12.2008, p. 55–58.*

of International Crimes, Crimes Committed by the USSR or Nazi Germany against the Republic of Lithuania or Inhabitants Thereof, Denial or Gross Trivialisation of the Crimes (Article 170(2) of the CC).

Criminal Code Chapter XXVI 'Crimes against Person's Voting Rights and the Procedure of Elections of the President of the Republic of Lithuania, Elections to the Seimas, the European Parliament and Municipal Councils or the Procedure for Conducting Referendums, Crimes against Political Parties and Political Campaigns Financing Order' (Articles 172–175 of the CC)

413. Chapter XXVI currently consists of five articles, criminalising intentional crimes against person's voting rights and the procedure of elections or the procedure of conducting referendums: Hindering the Exercise of the Right of Elections or Referendums (Article 172 of the CC), Forgery of an Election or Referendum Document or Use of a Forged Election or Referendum Document (Article 173 of the CC), Incorrect Counting of Election Votes (Article 174 of the CC), Destruction, Spoiling, Seizure or Concealment of an Election or Referendum Document (Article 175 of the CC) and Illegal Funding of Political Parties and Political Campaigns (Article 175(1) of the CC). Punishments for these crimes range from *inter alia* imprisonment for a term, not exceeding two years (e.g., for Incorrect Counting of Election Votes (Article 174 of the CC)), up to three years (e.g., for Hindering the Exercise of the Right of Elections or Referendums (Article 172 of the CC)). A legal entity can be held liable for most of the crimes, provided in this chapter.

Criminal Code Chapter XXVII 'Crimes and Misdemeanours against a Person's Social Rights' (Articles 176–177 of the CC)

414. Chapter XXVII contains only two articles, providing criminal liability for criminal acts against a person's social rights: Violation of Requirements of Safety and Health Protection at Work (Article 176 of the CC), Hindering the Activities of Trade Unions (Article 177 of the CC); the latter is considered to be a misdemeanour and can be punished by a penalty, not related to imprisonment. The former – Violation of Requirements of Safety and Health Protection at Work (Article 176 of the CC) – is considered to be a crime, committed either intentionally or through negligence, by an employer or a person authorised by him/her who violates the requirements of safety or health protection at work as stipulated in the Law on Safety and Health at Work or other legal acts, where this results in an accident at work, a breakdown or causes other serious consequences. A person, who committed the crime, may be punished *inter alia* by imprisonment for a term not exceeding eight years.

Criminal Code Chapter XXVIII 'Crimes and Misdemeanours against Property, Property Rights and Property Interests' (Articles 178–190 of the CC)

415. Chapter XXIII provides criminal liability for various criminal acts against property, which include Theft (Article 178 of the CC), Robbery (Article 180 of the CC), Extortion of Property (Article 181 of the CC), Swindling (Article 182 of the

CC), Misappropriation of Property (Article 183 of the CC), Causing Property Damage by Deceit (Article 186 of the CC), Illegal Enrichment (Article 189(1) of the CC) and others.

416. Paragraphs 2 and 3 of Article 178 of the CC establish theft under aggravating and particularly aggravating circumstances. Theft is considered to be committed under aggravating circumstances when a person: (1) openly seizes another's property or (2) seizes another's property by intruding into a room, a communications cable duct system, storage facility or guarded area or (3) seizes another person's property in a public place from the person's clothing, bag or another item (pickpocketing) or (4) a vehicle or (5) seizes a property comprising the infrastructure of legal persons of strategic or considerable importance to national security or a part thereof (paragraph 2, Article 178 of the CC). In these cases, a person may be punished by imprisonment for a term not exceeding six years. Theft is considered to be committed under particularly aggravating circumstances, when: (1) a person seizes another's property of a high value or the valuables of a considerable scientific, historical or cultural significance or (2) seizes another's property by participating in an organised group (paragraph 3, Article 178 of the CC); in these cases, a person may be punished by imprisonment for a term not exceeding eight years. Theft is considered to be committed under mitigating circumstances when a person seizes another's property of a low value. Any use of physical violence against a victim while committing a theft, transforms the crime into a robbery (Article 180 of the CC).

417. Anyone, who uses psychological violence without a lawful ground therefore, openly or secretly for his/her own benefit or for the benefit of other persons demands property from another person, asks to grant a property right or to release from a property obligation or to carry out other property related actions or to refrain from such actions, commits an Extortion of Property (Article 181 of the CC). It should be noted that Extortion of Property, committed with a lawful ground, is considered to be another crime – Self-Willed Conduct (Article 294 of the CC).

418. Punishments for crimes against property, property rights and property interests in Chapter XXVIII, committed under no aggravating or mitigating circumstances, range from *inter alia* imprisonment not exceeding two years (e.g., for destruction of or damage to property (Article 187 of the CC), etc.) up to six years (e.g., for robbery or extortion of property (accordingly Articles 180 and 181 of the CC). Aggravating circumstances for most of the crimes against property, property rights and property interests are considered to be a high value of the property, as well as the object – valuables of a considerable scientific, historical or cultural significance while being aware that the property or the valuable properties have been obtained by criminal means, and others. A legal entity can be held liable for most of the crimes against property, property rights and property interests.

419. It should be noted that the definitions of Swindling (Article 182 of the CC), Misappropriation of Property (Article 183 of the CC), Causing Property Damage by Deceit (Article 186 of the CC), Support not in Accordance with its Purpose or the

Established Procedure (Article 206 of the CC), Credit Fraud (Article 207 of the CC) and some other crimes against property, property rights and property interests as well as crimes against the economy and business order was influenced by the Convention Drawn up on the basis of Article K.3 of the Treaty on European Union, on the protection of the European Communities' financial interests which was ratified by Lithuania[247], Directive (EU) 2017/1371 of the European Parliament and of the Council of 5 July 2017 on the fight against fraud to the Union's financial interests by means of criminal law[248] and Directive (EU) 2019/713 of the European Parliament and of the Council of 17 April 2019 on combating fraud and counterfeiting of non-cash means of payment and replacing Council Framework Decision 2001/413/ JHA.[249]

Criminal Code Chapter XXIX 'Crimes against Intellectual and Industrial Property' (Articles 191–195 of the CC)

420. Chapter XXIX provides criminal liability for five criminal acts against Intellectual and Industrial Property: Misappropriation of Authorship (Article 191 of the CC), Unlawful Reproduction of a Literary, Scientific or Artistic Work or an Object of Related Rights, Distribution, Transportation or Storage of Illegal Copies Thereof (Article 192 of the CC), Destruction or Alteration of Information about Management of Author's Rights or Related Rights (Article 193 of the CC), Unlawful Removal of Technical Protection Means of Author's Rights or Related Rights (Article 194 of the CC) and Violation of Industrial Property Rights (Article 195 of the CC). One of the crimes, which by its nature is a crime against industrial property – Illegal Use of Another's Trademark or Service Mark (Article 204 of the CC) – is placed in another chapter as it is considered to be a crime more endangering the economy and business order than one's intellectual property rights. Punishments for all these crimes without aggravating or mitigating circumstances range from *inter alia* imprisonment not exceeding one year e.g., for Destruction or Alteration of Information about Management of Author's Rights or Related Rights (Article 193 of the CC) up to two years e.g., for Misappropriation of Authorship (Article 191 of the CC); if committed under aggravating circumstances, penalty may rise up to *inter alia* three years of imprisonment (e.g., paragraph 2 of Articles 191 and 192 of the CC). A legal entity can be held liable for all of the crimes against intellectual and industrial property.

---

247. Lietuvos Respublikos įstatymas dėl Konvencijos dėl Europos Bendrijų finansinių interesų apsaugos, parengtos vadovaujantis Europos Sąjungos sutarties K.3 straipsniu, ir jos protokolų, parengtų vadovaujantis Europos Sąjungos sutarties K.3 straipsniu, ratifikavimo, *Valstybės žinios*, 2004, No. 67-2354; No. 112-4178.
248. Directive (EU) 2017/1371 of the European Parliament and of the Council of 5 Jul. 2017 on the fight against fraud to the Union's financial interests by means of criminal law, *OJ L 198, 28.7.2017, p. 29–41.*
249. Directive (EU) 2019/713 of the European Parliament and of the Council of 17 Apr. 2019 on combating fraud and counterfeiting of non-cash means of payment and replacing Council Framework Decision 2001/413/JHA, PE/89/2018/REV/3, *OJ L 123, 10.5.2019, p. 18–29.*

Criminal Code Chapter XXX 'Crimes against Security of Electronic Data and Information Systems' (Articles 196–198(2) of the CC)

421. Crimes against security of electronic data and information systems are provided in Chapter XXX, and include, for example, Illegal Data or System Interference (Articles 196 and 197 of the CC), Unlawful Interception and Use of Electronic Data (Article 198 of the CC), etc. The system and definitions of the crimes against security of electronic data and information systems ware influenced by the Council of Europe Convention on cybercrime which was ratified by Lithuania[250] and Directive 2013/40/EU of the European Parliament and of the Council of 12 August 2013 on attacks against information systems and replacing Council Framework Decision 2005/222/JHA.[251]

422. Punishments for all these crimes, if there are no aggravating or mitigating circumstances, range from *inter alia* imprisonment not exceeding two years (e.g., for Illegal Access to an Information System (Article 198(1) of the CC) up to imprisonment for four years e.g., for Unlawful Disposal of Installations, Software, Passwords, Login Codes, Codes and Other Data (Article 198(2) of the CC). If committed under aggravating circumstances, punishment for these crimes may rise up to *inter alia* six years of imprisonment e.g., for Illegal System Interference if it's related to information system of strategic importance for national security, etc. (paragraph 2 of Article 197 of the CC). If committed under mitigating circumstances, criminal liability decreases and criminal offence is considered to be a misdemeanour, which can be punished by a punishment, not related to imprisonment (e.g., for Illegal Data or System Interference, incurring minor damage (paragraph 3 of Articles 196 and 197 of the CC)). A legal entity can be held liable for all of the crimes provided in this chapter.

Criminal Code Chapter XXXI 'Crimes and Misdemeanours against the Economy and Business Order' (Articles 199–212 of the CC)

423. Chapter XXXI provides criminal liability for various criminal offences against the economy and business order: Smuggling (Article 199 of the CC), Deceit of the Customs (Article 199(1) of the CC), Unlawful Failure to Bring Goods or Products outside the Republic of Lithuania (Article 200 of the CC), Unauthorised Engagement in Economic, Commercial, Financial or Professional Activities (Article 202 of the CC), Unlawful Activities of a Legal Entity (Article 203 of the CC), Criminal Bankruptcy (Article 209 of the CC) and others. Punishments for crimes against the economy and business order, committed under no aggravating or mitigating circumstances, range from *inter alia* imprisonment not exceeding one year (e.g., for Unlawful Activities of a Legal Entity (Article 203 of the CC), etc.) up to

---

250. Lietuvos Respublikos įstatymas dėl Konvencijos dėl elektroninių nusikaltimų ratifikavimo, *Valstybės žinios*, 2004, No. 36-1178; No. 36-1188.

251. Directive 2013/40/EU of the European Parliament and of the Council of 12 Aug. 2013 on attacks against information systems and replacing Council Framework Decision 2005/222/JHA, *OJ L 218, 14.8.2013, p. 8–14.*

imprisonment for eight years (e.g., for Smuggling (Article 199 of the CC), Deceit of the Customs (Article 199(1) of the CC, etc.). Most of them are considered to be crimes, but, in certain mitigating circumstances, they become misdemeanours (e.g., use of another's trademark or service mark, when a person illegally identifies a small number of goods with another's trademark (paragraph 2, Article 204 of the CC)). A legal entity can be held liable for most of the crimes provided in this chapter.

Criminal Code Chapter XXXII 'Crimes and Misdemeanours against Financial System' (Articles 213–224(1) of the CC)

424. Unlawful acts against financial system are criminalised in Chapter XXXII, which includes Production, Storage or Handling of Counterfeit Currency or Securities (Article 213 of the CC), Unlawful Use of an Electronic Means of Payment or Data Thereof (Article 215 of the CC), Legalisation of Property Obtained by Criminal Means (in other words, money or property laundering (Article 216 of the CC), Failure to Pay Taxes (Article 219 of the CC), Provision of Inaccurate Data on Income, Profit or Assets (Article 220 of the CC), Fraudulent or Negligent Management of Accounts (accordingly Articles 222 and 223 of the CC), etc. The definition of the production, storage or handling of counterfeit currency or securities correspond to the requirements of Directive 2014/62/EU of the European Parliament and of the Council of 15 May 2014 on the protection of the euro and other currencies against counterfeiting by criminal law, and replacing Council Framework Decision 2000/383/JHA.[252] The definition of the fencing of property obtained by criminal means (money or property laundering) corresponds to the requirements of the 1990 European Convention on laundering, search, seizure and confiscation of the proceeds from crime,[253] Directive (EU) 2018/1673 of the European Parliament and of the Council of 23 October 2018 on combating money laundering by criminal law and Directive (EU) 2015/849 of the European Parliament and of the Council of 20 May 2015 on the prevention of the use of the financial system for the purposes of money laundering or terrorist financing, amending Regulation (EU) No. 648/2012 of the European Parliament and of the Council, and repealing Directive 2005/60/EC of the European Parliament and of the Council and Commission Directive 2006/70/EC.[254] The definition of the trade in securities by using non-public information and

252. Directive 2014/62/EU of the European Parliament and of the Council of 15 May 2014 on the protection of the euro and other currencies against counterfeiting by criminal law, and replacing Council Framework Decision 2000/383/JHA, *OJ L 151, 21.5.2014, p. 1–8.*

253. 1990 m. Europos Konvencija dėl pinigų išplovimo ir nusikalstamu būdu įgytų pajamų paieškos, arešto bei konfiskavimo, *Valstybės žinios*, 1995, No. 12-263.

254. Directive 2015/849/EU of the European Parliament and of the Council of 20 May 2015 on the prevention of the use of the financial system for the purposes of money laundering or terrorist financing, amending Regulation No. 648/2012/EU of the European Parliament and of the Council, and repealing Directive 2005/60/EC of the European Parliament and of the Council and Commission Directive 2006/70/EC, *OJ L 141, 5.6.2015, p. 73–117* Directive (EU) 2018/1673 of the European Parliament and of the Council of 23 Oct. 2018 on combating money laundering by criminal law, PE/30/2018/REV/1, *OJ L 284, 12.11.2018, p. 22–30.*

manipulating the price of securities corresponds to the requirements of the Directive 2014/57/EU of the European Parliament and of the Council of 16 April 2014 on criminal sanctions for market abuse (market abuse directive).[255]

425. Punishments for the crimes against financial system, committed under no aggravating or mitigating circumstances, range from *inter alia* imprisonment not exceeding two years (e.g., for Negligent Management of Accounts (Article 223 of the CC), etc.) up to imprisonment for seven years (e.g., for Legalisation of Property Obtained by Criminal Means (Article 216 of the CC)). There is only one misdemeanour in this chapter – a Failure to Pay Taxes on mitigating circumstances, referring to a small amount of unpaid taxes (paragraph 3, Article 219 of the CC), which may be punished by a punishment, not related to imprisonment. A legal entity can be held liable for nearly all of the crimes provided in this chapter.

Criminal Code Chapter XXXIII 'Crimes and Misdemeanours against Civil Service and Public Interest' (Articles 225–230 of the CC)

426. Chapter XXXIII provides criminal liability for criminal acts against Civil Service and Public Interests. Bribery (Article 225 of the CC), Trading in Influence (Article 226 of the CC), Graft (Article 227 of the CC), Abuse of Office (Article 228 of the CC), Unlawful Registration of Rights to an Item (Article 228(1) of the CC), Failure to Perform Official Duties (Article 229 of the CC) are examples of such crimes. The system and definitions of the crimes and misdemeanours against civil service and public interest were influenced by the Council of Europe Criminal Law Convention on corruption, which was ratified by Lithuania[256] and Council Framework Decision 2003/568/JHA of 22 July 2003 on combating corruption in the private sector.[257]

427. The Lithuanian criminal law covers all the parties taking part in any form of bribery, committed by directly or indirectly offering a bribe, promising or agreeing to give and accept a bribe, demanding or provoking to give it, as well as giving or accepting it (Articles 225–227 of the CC). These criminal acts are considered to be misdemeanours in cases of a bribe in small amounts of money (paragraph 4 of Articles 225 (Bribery), 227 (Graft); paragraph 5 of Article 226 (Trading in Influence) of the CC). Punishments for crimes against civil service and public interest, committed under no aggravating or mitigating circumstances, range from imprisonment not exceeding two years (e.g., for Failure to Perform Official Duties (Article 229 of the CC), etc.) up to imprisonment for five years (e.g., for Bribery (Article 225 of the CC), Abuse of Office (Article 228 of the CC), etc.). If a person commits

255. Directive 2014/57/EU of the European Parliament and of the Council of 16 Apr. 2014 on criminal sanctions for market abuse (market abuse directive), *OJ L 173, 12.6.2014, p. 179–189.*
256. Lietuvos Respublikos įstatymas dėl Baudžiamosios teisės konvencijos dėl korupcijos ratifikavimo, *Valstybės žinios*, 2002, No. 23-851; No. 23-853.
257. Council Framework Decision 2003/568/JHA of 22 Jul. 2003 on combating corruption in the private sector, *OJ L 192, 31.7.2003, p. 54–56.*

these crimes under aggravating circumstances, he/she may be punished by imprisonment for a term not exceeding eight years (e.g., if a bribe is of a high value (paragraph 3 of Article 225 of the CC), etc.). A legal entity can be held liable for most of the crimes provided in this chapter.

Criminal Code Chapter XXXIV 'Crimes and Misdemeanours against Justice' (Articles 231–248 of the CC)

428. Chapter XXIV provides criminal liability for criminal acts against justice. Hindering the Activities of a Judge, Prosecutor, Pretrial Investigation Officer, Lawyer or Bailiff (Article 231 of the CC), Contempt of Court (Article 232 of the CC), Influence on a Witness, Victim, Expert, Specialist or Translator (Article 233 of the CC), False Complaint, Statement, Report, Testimony, Conclusions and Translation (Article 235 of the CC), Concealment of a Crime or the Perpetrator (Article 237 of the CC), Failure to Report a Crime (Article 238 of the CC), Freeing a Prisoner (Article 240 of the CC) are examples of crimes against justice.

429. Failure to Report a Crime (Article 238 of the CC) is considered to be a crime, when a person who, without a valid reason, fails to report to a law enforcement agency or to a court a grave crime known to him/her, either in progress or already committed. Punishments for this crime *inter alia* may be imprisonment for a term not exceeding one year. The close relatives and family members of the perpetrator are not held liable for a failure to report a crime (paragraph 2 of Article 238 of the CC). Punishments for other crimes against justice, committed under no aggravating or mitigating circumstances, range from *inter alia* imprisonment not exceeding two years (e.g., for Contempt of Court (Article 232 of the CC), etc.) up to imprisonment for six years (e.g., for Disruption of the Work of a Place of Detention (Article 239 of the CC). A legal entity can be held liable for most of the crimes against justice provided in this chapter.

Criminal Code Chapter XXXV 'Crimes against Public Security' (Articles 249–252(1) of the CC)

430. Chapter XXXV provides criminal liability for dangerous crimes, anyhow related to organised crime or terrorism: Criminal Association (Article 249 of the CC), Act of Terrorism (Article 250 of the CC), Hijacking of an Aircraft, Ship or Fixed Platform on a Continental Shelf (Article 251 of the CC), Piracy (Article 251(1) of the CC), Hostage Taking (Article 252 of the CC) and others.

431. Definition of criminal association was influenced by the United Nations Convention on organised crime, which was ratified by Lithuania[258] and Council

258. Lietuvos Respublikos įstatymas dėl Jungtinių Tautų organizacijos konvencijos prieš tarptautinį organizuotą nusikalstamumą ratifikavimo, *Valstybės žinios*, 2002, No. 51-1929; No. 51-1933.

Framework Decision 2008/841/JHA of 24 October 2008 on the fight against organised crime.[259] The Lithuanian criminal law condemns any person who merely participates in the activities of a criminal association, and provides criminal liability for a term of up to fifteen years of imprisonment (paragraph 1, Article 249 of the CC). If such person also participates in the activities of a criminal association armed with firearms, explosives or explosive materials, the punishment rises up to life imprisonment (paragraph 2, Article 249 of the CC).

432. This chapter was considerably supplemented in 2013 on the basis of implementation of Council Framework Decision 2008/919/JHA of 28 November 2008 amending Framework Decision 2002/475/JHA on combating terrorism,[260] criminalising Incitement to Terrorism (Article 250(1)), Recruitment for Terrorism (Article 250(2) of the CC), Threatening to Commit a Terrorist Crime (Article 250(3) of the CC), Financing and Support of Terrorist Activities (Article 250(4) of the CC), Training for Terrorism (Article 250(5) of the CC). This chapter also was supplemented in 2017 on the basis of implementation of Directive (EU) 2017/541 of the European Parliament and of the Council of 15 March 2017 on combating terrorism and replacing Council Framework Decision 2002/475/JHA and amending Council Decision 2005/671/JHA[261], criminalising Travelling for the purpose of terrorism (Article 250(6) of the CC).

433. Punishments for crimes against public security without aggravating or mitigating circumstances range from *inter alia* imprisonment not exceeding four years for example, for Incitement to Terrorism (Article 250(1) of the CC), up to imprisonment for fifteen years (e.g., for Criminal Association (Article 249) of the CC). Committing these crimes under aggravating circumstances considerably increases the punishment and in many cases a person may be punished by life imprisonment (e.g., Establishment and Activities of Groups Having the Aim of Committing Terrorist Crimes, if a person participates in the activities of a terrorist group armed with firearms, explosives, explosive, radioactive, biological or chemical harmful substances, preparations or microorganisms (paragraph 3, Article 249(1) of the CC), etc.). A legal entity can be held liable for all the crimes provided in this chapter.

Criminal Code Chapter XXXVI 'Crimes and Misdemeanours Relating to Possession of Weapons, Ammunition, Explosives, Explosive or Radioactive Materials or Military Equipment' (Articles 253–258 of the CC)

434. Chapter XXXVI criminalises Unlawful Possession of a Non-Firearm (Article 258 of the CC), Firearms, Ammunition, Explosives or Explosive Materials (Article 253 of the CC) as well as Nuclear or Radioactive Materials or Other

259. Council Framework Decision 2008/841/JHA of 24 Oct. 2008 on the fight against organised crime, *OJ L 300, 11.11.2008, p. 42–45.*
260. Council Framework Decision 2008/919/JHA of 28 Nov. 2008 amending Framework Decision 2002/475/JHA on combating terrorism, *OJ L 330, 9.12.2008, p. 21–23.*
261. Directive 2017/541/EU of the European Parliament and of the Council of 15 Mar. 2017 on combating terrorism and replacing Council Framework Decision 2002/475/JHA and amending Council Decision 2005/671/JHA, *OJ L 88, 31.3.2017, p. 6–21.*

Sources of Ionising Radiation (Article 256 of the CC), Unlawful Intermediation in the Transfer of Military Equipment (Article 253(1) of the CC), Threat to Use or Otherwise Influence or Unlawfully Acquire Nuclear or Radioactive Materials or Other Sources of Ionising Radiation (Article 256(1) of the CC) and other crimes and misdemeanours relating to possession of weapons, ammunition, explosives, explosive or radioactive materials or military equipment. Punishments for these crimes, committed under no aggravating or mitigating circumstances, range from *inter alia* imprisonment not exceeding three years for examplee.g., for Unlawful Intermediation in the Transfer of Military Equipment (Article 253(1) of the CC) up to imprisonment for seven years e.g., for Seizure of a Firearm, Ammunition, Explosives or Explosive Materials (Article 254 of the CC); if the crime is committed under aggravating circumstances (e.g., causing serious consequences) – punishment can increase *inter alia* up to imprisonment for a term not exceeding ten years Unlawful Possession of Nuclear or Radioactive Materials or Other Sources of Ionising Radiation (paragraph 2, Article 256 of the CC). A legal entity can be held liable for most of the crimes provided in this chapter.

Criminal Code Chapter XXXVII 'Crimes and Misdemeanours Relating to Possession of Narcotic or Psychotropic, Toxic or Highly Active Substances' (Articles 259–269 of the CC)

435. Chapter XXXVII provides criminal liability for Unlawful Possession of Narcotic or Psychotropic Substances for the Purpose Other than Distribution (Article 259 of the CC), as well as for the Purpose of Distribution Thereof or Unlawful Possession of a Large Quantity of Narcotic or Psychotropic Substances (Article 260 of the CC), Creation or Unlawful Possession of Biological Weapons (Article 267(1) of the CC) and other crimes and misdemeanours relating to possession of narcotic or psychotropic, toxic or highly active substances. The system and definitions of the crimes and misdemeanours relating to possession of narcotic or psychotropic substances were influenced by Council Framework Decision 2004/757/JHA of 25 October 2004 laying down minimum provisions on the constituent elements of criminal acts and penalties in the field of illicit drug trafficking.[262] Punishments for these crimes, committed under no aggravating or mitigating circumstances, range from *inter alia* imprisonment not exceeding two years (e.g., for Unlawful Possession of Narcotic or Psychotropic Substances for the Purpose Other than Distribution (Article 259 of the CC)), up to imprisonment not exceeding twelve years (e.g., for Distribution of Narcotic or Psychotropic Substances among Minors (Article 261 of the CC)). If the crime is committed under aggravating circumstances (e.g., involving large or very large quantities of these substances) – punishments can increase *inter alia* up to imprisonment for a term not exceeding fifteen years for examplee.g., for Unlawful Possession of Narcotic or Psychotropic Substances for the Purpose of Distribution Thereof or Unlawful Possession of a Large Quantity of Narcotic or Psychotropic Substances (paragraph 3, Article 260 of the

262. Council Framework Decision 2004/757/JHA of 25 Oct. 2004 laying down minimum provisions on the constituent elements of criminal acts and penalties in the field of illicit drug trafficking, *OJ L 335, 11.11.2004, p. 8–11.*

CC). There is only one misdemeanour in this chapter (paragraph 2, Article 259 of the CC), which is committed when a person unlawfully produces, processes, acquires, stores, transports or forwards a small quantity of narcotic or psychotropic substances for the purpose other than selling or otherwise distributing them, which may be punished by a punishment, not related to imprisonment. A legal entity can be held liable for most of the crimes, provided in this chapter.

Criminal Code Chapter XXXVIII 'Crimes and Misdemeanours Against the Environment and Human Health' (Articles 270–277(1) of the CC)

436. Chapter XXXVIII provides criminal liability for crimes and misdemeanours against the environment and human health. Unlawful Transportation of Waste across the State Border (Article 270(2) of the CC), Marine Pollution from Ships (Article 270(3) of the CC), Destruction or Devastation of Protected Areas or Objects of Natural Heritage (Article 271 of the CC), Unauthorised Forest Felling or Destruction of Marshes (Article 273 of the CC), Unauthorised Pharmaceutical Activities (Article 275 of the CC), Production of or Trading in the Products Harmful to Human Health or Life (Article 276 of the CC), Violation of the Regulations Governing Control of Epidemics or Contagious Diseases (Article 277 of the CC) are examples of these criminal acts. The system and definitions of the crimes against environment were influenced by the Directive 2008/99/EC of the European Parliament and of the Council of 19 November 2008 on the protection of the environment through criminal law,[263] Directive 2005/35/EC of the European Parliament and of the Council of 7 September 2005 on ship-source pollution and on the introduction of penalties for infringements,[264] Directive 2009/123/EC of the European Parliament and of the Council of 21 October 2009 amending Directive 2005/35/EC on ship-source pollution and on the introduction of penalties for infringements.[265]

437. Punishments for crimes provided in this chapter, committed under no aggravating or mitigating circumstances, range from *inter alia* imprisonment for a term not exceeding one year (e.g., for Unlawful Transportation of Waste across the State Border (Article 270(2) of the CC) up to imprisonment for six years (e.g., for Infringement of Provisions of Legal Acts Regulating Construction (Article 271(1) of the CC). If the crime is committed under aggravating circumstances, for example, if the crime results in a person's death or a serious impairment to a person's health, the punishment rises up to eight years of imprisonment Production of or Trading in the Products Harmful to Human Health or Life (paragraph 2, Article 276 of the CC), Unauthorised Pharmaceutical Activities (paragraph 2, Article 275 of the CC), etc.). Many of the crimes can be committed through negligence (e.g., Violation of the

263. Directive 2008/99/EC of the European Parliament and of the Council of 19 Nov. 2008 on the protection of the environment through criminal law, *OJ L 328, 6.12.2008, p. 28–37.*
264. Directive 2005/35/EC of the European Parliament and of the Council of 7 Sep. 2005 on ship-source pollution and on the introduction of penalties for infringements, *OJ L 255, 30.9.2005, p. 11–21.*
265. Directive 2009/123/EC of the European Parliament and of the Council of 21 Oct. 2009 amending Directive 2005/35/EC on ship-source pollution and on the introduction of penalties for infringements, *OJ L 280, 27.10.2009, p. 52–55.*

Regulations Governing Control of Epidemics or Contagious Diseases (paragraph 3, Article 277 of the CC), Production of or Trading in the Products Harmful to Human Health or Life (paragraphs 3 and 4, Article 276 of the CC), etc. A legal entity can be held liable for nearly all of the crimes, provided in this chapter.

Criminal Code Chapter XXXIX 'Crimes and Misdemeanours Against Traffic Safety' (Articles 278–282 of the CC)

438. Chapter XXXIX currently contains six articles, criminalising unlawful acts against traffic safety: Improper Maintenance or Repair of Vehicles or Roads and the Facilities Located Thereon (Article 278 of the CC), Violation of International Flight Regulations (Article 279 of the CC), Violation of Regulations Governing Road Traffic Safety or Operation of Vehicles (Article 281 of the CC) and others. Nearly all of the illicit acts within this chapter are criminalised only if they result in certain dangerous consequences: in a person's death or a severe impairment to a person's health (e.g., Improper Maintenance or Repair of Vehicles or Roads and the Facilities Located Thereon (Article 278 of the CC), etc.) or was likely to result in other serious consequences (e.g., Damage to Vehicles or Roads and the Facilities Located Thereon (Article 280 of the CC)). Punishments for these crimes, committed under no aggravating or mitigating circumstances, range from *inter alia* imprisonment for a term not exceeding two years (e.g., for Regulations Governing Road Traffic Safety or Operation of Vehicles (Article 281 of the CC), etc.), up to imprisonment for five years (e.g., for Improper Maintenance or Repair of Vehicles or Roads and the Facilities Located Thereon (Article 278 of the CC)). If the crime is committed under aggravating circumstances, for example, if the crime results in a person's death or causes serious bodily harm to persons or incurs massive property damage, punishment rises up to imprisonment for a term not exceeding ten years (e.g., for Damage to Vehicles or Roads and the Facilities Located Thereon (Article 280 of the CC), etc.). There is only one misdemeanour in this chapter: Improper Maintenance or Repair of Vehicles or Roads and the Facilities Located Thereon if the crime is committed under mitigating circumstances – when the crime does not result in serious consequences, but there exists a real risk thereof; in this case, a person can be punished by a punishment, not related to imprisonment (paragraph 3, Article 278 of the CC). All of the crimes in this chapter, except Violation of International Flight Regulations (Article 279 of the CC), can also be committed through negligence. A legal entity can be held liable only for Damage to Vehicles or Roads and the Facilities Located Thereon (Article 280 of the CC).

Criminal Code Chapter XL 'Crimes and Misdemeanours against Public Order' (Articles 283–285 of the CC)

439. Chapter XL currently contains three articles, criminalising unlawful acts against public order: Riots (Article 283 of the CC), Violation of Public Order (Article 284 of the CC) and False Report about a Danger Threatening the Community or Occurred Disaster (Article 285 of the CC).

440. Article 284 of the CC establishes a general norm, criminalising Violation of Public Order, which condemns a person who, by defiant conduct, threats, vicious taunting or acts of vandalism, demonstrates disrespect to the surrounding people or the environment in a public place and thereby disrupts public peace or order. This crime is punished by *inter alia* up to two years of imprisonment.

441. Punishments for other crimes against public order, committed under no aggravating or mitigating circumstances, range from *inter alia* imprisonment not exceeding one year (False Report about a Danger Threatening the Community or Occurred Disaster (Article 285 of the CC)) up to imprisonment for five years (Riots (Article 283 of the CC). Despite the fact, that the chapter is called Crimes *and Misdemeanours* against Public Order, at the present time, there are no misdemeanours in this chapter.

Criminal Code Chapter XLI 'Crimes against the Activities of a Civil Servant or a Person Performing the Functions of Public Administration' (Articles 286–290 of the CC)

442. Chapter XLI provides criminal liability for Resistance Against a Civil Servant or a Person Performing the Functions of Public Administration (Article 286 of the CC), Threatening and Interference with the Activities of such persons (Articles 287 and 288 of the CC) and Adoption of the Name of a Civil Servant or a Person Performing the Functions of Public Administration (Article 289 of the CC). Punishments for these crimes range from *inter alia* imprisonment for a term not exceeding two years (e.g., for Threatening a Civil Servant or a Person Performing the Functions of Public Administration (paragraph 1, Article 287 of the CC), etc.) up to imprisonment for five years, if the crime is committed under aggravating circumstances (e.g., using physical violence while threatening a civil servant or a person performing the functions of public administration (paragraph 2, Article 287 of the CC).

Criminal Code Chapter XLII 'Crimes and Misdemeanours against Government Order' (Articles 291–299 of the CC)

443. Chapter XLII provides criminal liability for crimes and misdemeanours against government order: Illegal Crossing of the State Border (Article 291 of the CC), Unlawful Transportation of Persons across the State Border (Article 292 of the CC), Self-Willed Conduct (Article 294 of the CC), Unlawful Installation of Special Equipment or Use Thereof for the Collection of Information (Article 295 of the CC), Disclosure of an Official Secret (Article 297 of the CC) and others. The system and definition of the crimes connected to illegal migration ware influenced by Council Directive 2002/90/EC of 28 November 2002 defining the facilitation of unauthorised entry, transit and residence[266] and Council Framework Decision 2002/

266. Council Directive 2002/90/EC of 28 Nov. 2002 defining the facilitation of unauthorised entry, transit and residence, *OJ L 328, 5.12.2002, p. 17–18.*

946/JHA of 28 November 2002 on the strengthening of the penal framework to prevent the facilitation of unauthorised entry, transit and residence.[267] This chapter was supplemented in 2011 on the basis of implementation of Directive 2009/52/EC of the European Parliament and of the Council of 18 June 2009 providing for minimum standards on sanctions and measures against employers of illegally staying third-country nationals,[268] criminalising Employment of Third-Country Nationals Illegally Staying in the Republic of Lithuania (Article 292(1) of the CC).

444. Punishments for these crimes, committed under no aggravating or mitigating circumstances, range from *inter alia* imprisonment for a term not exceeding two years (e.g., for Employment of Third-Country Nationals Illegally Staying in the Republic of Lithuania (Article 292(1) of the CC), etc.) up to imprisonment for seven years (e.g., for Organisation of Travels of Citizens of the Republic of Lithuania Abroad for the Purpose of Staying There Illegally or Abandoning Them without Assistance (Article 293 of the CC)). A legal entity can be held liable for three crimes provided in this Chapter: Unlawful Transportation of Persons across the State Border (Article 292 of the CC), Employment of Third-Country Nationals Illegally Staying in the Republic of Lithuania (Article 292(1) of the CC) and Staying There Illegally or Abandoning Them without Assistance (Article 293 of the CC).

Criminal Code Chapter XLIII 'Crimes and Misdemeanours against Government Order Relating to Forgery of Documents or Measuring Devices' (Articles 300–306(2) of the CC)

445. Criminal liability for unlawful acts against government order relating to forgery of documents or measuring devices is provided in Chapter XLIII, which includes Forgery of a Document or Possession of a Forged Document (Article 300 of the CC), Forgery of a Seal, Stamp or Form (Article 301 of the CC), Production, Storage, Transportation, Forwarding or Handling of Equipment for the Forgery of Seals, Stamps, Documents or Special Accounting Document Forms (Article 302(1) of the CC), Odometer Fraud (Article 306(2) of the CC) and others. Punishments for crimes against government order relating to forgery of documents or measuring devices, committed under no aggravating or mitigating circumstances, range from *inter alia* imprisonment for a term not exceeding two years (e.g., for Forgery, Unlawful Destruction or Alteration of a Number Plate of a Vehicle (Article 306(1) of the CC, etc.) up to imprisonment for six years (e.g., for Seizure of a Seal, Stamp or Document or Use of the Seized Seal, Stamp or Document (Article 302 of the CC), etc.). A legal entity can be held liable for all of the crimes, provided in this chapter.

---

267. Council Framework Decision 2002/946/JHA of 28 Nov. 2002 on the strengthening of the penal framework to prevent the facilitation of unauthorised entry, transit and residence, *OJ L 328, 5.12.2002, p. 1–3.*
268. Directive 2009/52/EC of the European Parliament and of the Council of 18 Jun. 2009 providing for minimum standards on sanctions and measures against employers of illegally staying third-country nationals, O*J L 168, 30.6.2009, p. 24–32.*

Criminal Code Chapter XLIV 'Crimes and Misdemeanours against Morality' (Articles 307–310 of the CC)

446. Chapter XLIV provides criminal liability for five crimes and misdemeanours against morality: Gaining Profit from Another Person's Prostitution (Article 307 of the CC), Involvement in Prostitution (Article 308 of the CC), Prohibited Biomedical Research Involving a Human Being or Human Embryo (Article 308(1) of the CC), Possession of Pornographic Material (Article 309 of the CC) and Cruel Treatment of Animals (Article 310 of the CC). Punishments for crimes against morality, committed under no aggravating or mitigating circumstances, range from *inter alia* imprisonment not exceeding one year (e.g., for Cruel Treatment of Animals (Article 310 of the CC)) up to imprisonment for four years (Gaining Profit from Another Person's Prostitution (Article 307 of the CC)). A legal entity can be held liable for most of the crimes against morality, provided in this chapter.

Criminal Code Chapter XLV 'Crimes and Misdemeanours against the Memory of the Deceased' (Articles 311–313 of the CC)

447. Chapter XLV protects the memory of the deceased and provides criminal liability for Desecration of the Remains of the Deceased (Article 311 of the CC), Desecration of a Grave or Another Place of Public Respect (Article 312 of the CC), Contempt for the Memory of the Deceased (Article 313 of the CC); the latter is considered to be a misdemeanour. For example, a person who unlawfully takes the remains of the deceased or a part thereof or ridicules the remains of the deceased or desecrates them can be punished *inter alia* by imprisonment for a term not exceeding two years (Desecration of the Remains of the Deceased (Article 311 of the CC). Punishments for crimes against the memory of the deceased, committed under no aggravating or mitigating circumstances, are *inter alia* imprisonment not exceeding one year for Desecration of a Grave or Another Place of Public Respect (Article 312 of the CC)) or two years for Desecration of the Remains of the Deceased (Article 311 of the CC). If the crime is committed under aggravating circumstances, criminal liability can rise up to three years of imprisonment (paragraph 2, Articles 311, 312 of the CC).

Criminal Code Chapter XLVI 'Crimes and Misdemeanours against National Defence Service and Mobilisation' (Articles 314–330 of the CC)

448. Chapter XLVI provides criminal liability for crimes and misdemeanours against national defence service: Evasion of a Draft into Mandatory Military Service (Article 314 of the CC), Evasion of Military Service (Article 316 of the CC), Failure to Execute an Order (Article 317 of the CC), Unlawful Order and Execution Thereof (Article 321 of the CC), Desertion (Article 323 of the CC), and others. Punishments for these crimes, committed under no aggravating or mitigating circumstances, range from *inter alia* imprisonment not exceeding two years (e.g., for Loss or Dishonouring the Flag of a Military Unit (Article 329 of the CC)) up to imprisonment for eight years (for Unlawful Order and Execution Thereof (Article 321 of the CC). Imprisonment for a term not exceeding eight years can also be imposed for less dangerous crimes, which are committed on certain aggravating circumstances, for example, if the crime causes serious consequences (Violent Actions against a Subordinate (paragraph 2, Article 319 of the CC), Terrorisation of a Serviceman (paragraph 3, Article 320 of the CC), etc.).

II. Criminal Offences in the Special Criminal Laws

449. There are no special criminal law norms containing criminal acts outside the CC of Lithuania; only the CC defines criminal acts.

Chapter 7. The Sanctioning System

§1. The General Sanctioning System

450. Lithuanian criminal law foresees three forms of realisation of the criminal liability of a physical person or legal entity for the commission of the criminal act:

(1) release from criminal liability with application of penal or reformative measures or without them;
(2) imposition of the punishment;
(3) suspension of the execution of punishment or release from the execution of punishment with application of penal or reformative measures or without them.

451. Lithuanian criminal justice system nowadays recognises four main types of criminal sanctions: punishments, penal measures, reformative measures and compulsory medical measures. The CC determines the legal content of each punishment, penal, reformative and compulsory medical measures, as well as the conditions of their application.

452. Punishments may be imposed on a physical person (adult and juvenile) and legal entity, who have committed a criminal act. Penal measures may be imposed on an adult person who was released from criminal liability or suspended execution of the imprisonment. Penal measures – prohibition to exercise a special right, deprivation of public rights, deprivation of the right to be employed in a certain position or to engage in certain type of activities, payment of a contribution to the fund of crime victims, confiscation of property, the obligation to reside separately from the victim and (or) prohibition to approach the victim closer than a prescribed distance, participation in the programmes addressing violent behaviour, extended confiscation of property and obligation to notify a change of the place of residence or departure from the place of residence may be imposed together with a punishment. It should be noted that the payment of a contribution to the fund for crime victims cannot be imposed together with a fine.

453. A legal entity may be subject to these penal measures – payment of a contribution to the fund of crime victims, confiscation of property or extended confiscation of property. The payment of a contribution to the fund for crime victims may be imposed only with restriction of operation of a legal entity.

454. Reformative measures may be imposed on a juvenile who was released from criminal liability or execution of the imprisonment. A minor released from criminal liability or execution of the punishment may be subject to these penal measures – payment of a contribution to the fund of crime victims, confiscation of property and extended confiscation of property. The payment of a contribution to the fund for crime victims cannot be imposed together with a fine.

455. Compulsory medical measures may be imposed on a person who was recognised as being legally incapacitated or a person of diminished capacity as well as a person who during the execution of the punishment starts to suffer from mental disorder rendering him/her incapable of understanding the nature of his/her action or controlling them.

456. It should be noted that the imposition of the punishment is a traditional consequence of the criminal act in Lithuania.

§2. Release from Criminal Liability

457. Release from criminal liability means that a person or legal entity, which has committed a criminal act release from main consequences of the criminal liability (e.g. imposition of the punishment). Chapter VI 'Release from Criminal Liability' and Chapter XI 'Peculiarities of Criminal Liability of Minors' of General Part of the CC provides seven types of release from criminal liability, which may be conditional or unconditional, for adult persons and one type of unconditional release from criminal liability for minors. A conditional type of release from criminal liability means that a released person or legal entity during probationary period must comply with the special obligations, which were imposed by the court, for example, compensate damage in case of release from criminal liability upon reconciliation between the offender and the victim, etc. Conditional types of release from criminal liability are release from criminal liability upon reconciliation between the offender and the victim (Article 38 of the CC) and release from criminal liability on bail (Article 40 of the CC). While unconditional types of release from criminal liability are release from criminal liability when a person or criminal act loses its dangerousness (Article 36 of the CC), release from criminal liability due to minor relevance of a crime (Article 37 of the CC), release from criminal liability on the basis of mitigating circumstances (Article 39 of the CC), release from criminal liability when a person actively assisted in detecting the criminal acts committed by members of an organised group or a criminal association (Article 39(1) of the CC), release of a whistle-blower from criminal liability (Article 39(2) of the CC) and release from criminal liability of a minor from criminal liability (Article 93 of the CC). It should be noted that the Supreme Court of Lithuania has emphasised that criminal law provides the possibility, but not the obligation for the court to apply all types of the release from criminal liability.[269]

458. Court for an adult person released from criminal liability may appoint one or few penal measures (on penal measures *see* paragraphs 518–549). Moreover, the court may appoint one or few reformative measures for a juvenile released from criminal liability (on reformative measures, *see* paragraphs 550–563).

269. Rulings of the Supreme Court of Lithuania in criminal cases No. 2K-7-84/2012, No. 2K-7-266-942/2015 and No. 2K-171-511/2016.

459. It should be noted that the CC did not provide an explicit possibility to apply all types of release from criminal liability for a legal entity. However, the Supreme Court of Lithuania (on the ground of the constitutional jurisprudence on criminal liability of legal entity[270]) has decided that release from criminal liability when a person or criminal act loses its dangerousness, provided in Article 36 of the CC may be also applicable to legal entity.[271] Moreover, in the opinion of the doctrine of the Lithuanian criminal law,[272] the legal entity may be subject to other forms of release from criminal liability such as release from criminal liability due to minor relevance of a crime (Article 37 of the CC), release from criminal liability upon reconciliation between the offender and the victim (Article 38 of the CC) and criminal liability on the basis of mitigating circumstances (Article 39 of the CC).

Release from Criminal Liability When a Person or Criminal Act Loses Its Dangerousness

460. Article 36 of the CC provides that 'a person who commits a criminal act shall be released from criminal liability where a court acknowledges that before the opening of the hearing of the case in the court this person or the act committed thereby had lost its dangerous character due to a change in circumstances'.

Release from Criminal Liability due to Minor Relevance of a Crime

461. Article 37 of the CC provides that 'a person who commits a crime may be released from criminal liability by a court where the crime is recognised as being of minor relevance due to the extent of the damage incurred, the object of the crime or other peculiarities of the crime'.

462. The Supreme Court of the Republic of Lithuania has emphasised that release from criminal liability due to minor relevance of a crime cannot be applied if a misdemeanour[273] or serious or grave crime or crime against human health was committed.[274]

Release from Criminal Liability upon Reconciliation between the Offender and the Victim

463. A person who commits a misdemeanour, a negligent crime or a minor or less serious intentional crime may be released by a court from criminal liability where: '(1) he has confessed to commission of the criminal act, and (2) voluntarily compensated for or eliminated the damage incurred to a natural or legal person or

270. Decision of the Constitutional Court of Lithuania of 8 Jun. 2009, *Valstybės žinios*, 2009, No. 69-2798.
271. Supreme Court of Lithuania ruling in criminal case No. 2K-7-84/2012.
272. Švedas G., Veršekys P., Levon J., Prapiestis D. Lietuvos Respublikos baudžiamojo kodekso bendrosios dalies vientisumo ir naujovių suderinimo iššūkiai, Vilnius, Vilniaus universiteto leidykla, 2017, p. 160.
273. Ruling of the Supreme Court of Lithuania in criminal case No. 2K-133/2011.
274. Ruling of the Supreme Court of Lithuania in criminal case No. 2K-139-507/2016.

agreed on the compensation for or elimination of this damage, and (3) reconciles with the victim or a representative of a legal person or a State institution, and (4) there is a basis for believing that he will not commit new criminal acts'. Interpreting the criminal law requirements, the Supreme Court of Lithuania has stated that 'in case where the criminal act victim dies, the reconciliation with the offender may be processed by the members of the victim's family or close relatives'.[275] It should be noted that this type of the release from criminal liability is most popular in court jurisprudence, since it was applied in 6,164 criminal cases in 2015.[276]

464. Dangerous repeat offenders may not be released from criminal liability on the basis of reconciliation with the victim. The same goes for a person who was already released from criminal liability on the basis of reconciliation with the victim, and less than four years had elapsed from the day of reconciliation until the commission of a new act.

465. If a person released from criminal liability commits a misdemeanour or a negligent crime within the period of one year or fails, without valid reasons, to comply with an agreement approved by a court on the terms and conditions of and procedure for compensating for the damage, the court may revoke its decision on the release from criminal liability and decide to prosecute the person for all the criminal acts committed. If a person released from criminal liability commits a new intentional crime within the period of one year, the previous decision releasing him from criminal liability shall become invalid and a decision shall be adopted on the prosecution of the person for all the criminal acts committed.

Release from Criminal Liability on the Basis of Mitigating Circumstances

466. Article 39 of the CC states that a person who commits a misdemeanour or a negligent or minor intentional crime may be released from criminal liability by a reasoned decision of the court where: (1) he/she commits a criminal act for the first time, and (2) there are at least two mitigating circumstances provided for in CC, and (3) there are no aggravating circumstances. Interpreting these requirements, the Supreme Court of Lithuania has noted that 'moreover, even if the whole of the conditions laid down in Article 39 of the CC is determined by the court, when considering the release from criminal liability, the court must provide a detailed statement of reasons for its decision, since release from criminal liability is the court's right and not a duty. This means that for such a solution only the existence of formal conditions is not sufficient – the court must thoroughly assess all circumstances of the case, describing the personality of the perpetrator and his/her criminal act'.[277]

---

275. Ruling of the Supreme Court of Lithuania in criminal case No. 2K-P-464/2005.
276. Švedas G., Veršekys P., Levon J., Prapiestis D. Lietuvos Respublikos baudžiamojo kodekso bendrosios dalies vientisumo ir naujovių suderinimo iššūkiai, Vilnius, Vilniaus Universiteto leidykla, 2017, p. 162.
277. Ruling of the Supreme Court of Lithuania in criminal case No. 2K-24-895/2017.

Release from Criminal Liability When a Person Actively Assisted in Detecting the Criminal Acts Committed by Members of an Organised Group or a Criminal Association

467. A person who is suspected of participation in the commission of criminal acts by an organised group or a criminal association or belonging to a criminal association may be released from criminal liability where he/she confesses his/her participation in the commission of such a criminal act or his/her membership of the criminal association and where he/she actively assists in detecting the criminal acts committed by members of the organised group or criminal association.

468. A person who participated in the commission of an intentional murder or who had already been released from criminal liability on such grounds, also an organiser or leader of an organised group or a criminal association shall not be released from criminal liability on this ground.

Release from Criminal Liability of a Whistle-blower

469. A person who commits a misdemeanour, negligent crime or a minor or less serious intentional crime may be released from criminal liability by a court reasoned decision where: (1) he/she is recognised as a whistle-blower under the Law on the Protection of Whistle-blowers,[278] and (2) he/she fully confess his/her guilt, and (3) actively assists in detecting the criminal acts committed by another person and (4) the criminal act which he/she has helped to disclose is more dangerous in nature than the criminal act which he/she himself/herself has committed.

470. A dangerous repeat offender, a person who has a criminal record, or a person who was the organiser of a criminal act to the detection of which he/she contributed, may not be released from criminal liability as a whistle-blower.

If a person released from criminal liability commits a misdemeanour or a negligent crime within a period of one year or fails, without valid reasons, to comply to an agreement approved by a court on the terms and conditions of and procedure for compensating for the damage, the court may revoke its decision on the release from criminal liability and decide to prosecute the person for all the criminal acts committed. If a person released from criminal liability commits a new intentional crime within the period of one year, the previous decision releasing him from criminal liability shall become invalid and a decision shall be adopted on the prosecution of the person for all the criminal acts committed.

Release from Criminal Liability on Bail

471. A person who commits a misdemeanour, negligent crime or a minor or less serious intentional crime may be released by a court from criminal liability subject to a request by a person worthy of a court's trust to transfer the offender into his/her

278. Lietuvos Respublikos pranešėjų apsaugos įstatymas, TAR, 2017-12-07, No. 19743.

responsibility on bail. Bail may be set with or without surety. This type of the release from criminal liability is one of the popular type of releases in court jurisprudence, since it was applied in 523 cases in 2015.[279]

472. A person may be released from criminal liability by a court on bail where: (1) he/she commits a criminal act for the first time, and (2) he/she fully confesses his/her guilt and regrets having committed the criminal act, and (3) at least partly compensates for or eliminates the damage incurred or undertakes to compensate for such where it has been incurred and (4) there is a basis for believing that he/she will fully compensate for or eliminate the damage incurred, will comply with laws and will not commit new criminal acts.

473. A bailsman may be parents of the offender, close relatives or other persons worthy of a court's trust. When taking a decision, the court shall take account of the bailsman's personal traits or nature of activities and a possibility of exerting a positive influence on the offender. The Supreme Court of Lithuania has noted that, in order to assess the bailsman suitability, the court may evaluate his/her characteristics: his/her personality, type of activity, previous bailsman's convictions or administrative liability cases, as well as the real abilities to positively influence the person who committed a criminal act, to ensure that he/she will comply with laws and will not commit new criminal acts.[280] The term of bail shall be set from one year up to three years.

474. When requesting to release a person on bail with a surety, a bailsman shall undertake to pay a surety in the amount specified by a court. Taking account of a bailsman's personal traits and his financial situation, the court shall specify the amount of the surety or decide on release from criminal liability on bail without surety. The bail bond shall be returned upon the expiry of the term of bail where a person subject to bail does not commit a new criminal act within the term of bail as laid down by the court.

475. A bailsman shall have the right to withdraw from bail. In this case, a court shall, taking account of the reasons for a withdrawal from bail, decide on the return of a surety, also on a person's criminal liability for the committed criminal act, appointment of another bailsman or the person's release from criminal liability.

476. If a person released from criminal liability on bail commits a new misdemeanour or negligent crime during the term of bail, a court may revoke its decision on the release from criminal liability and shall decide to prosecute the person for all the criminal acts committed. If a person released from criminal liability on bail commits a new intentional crime during the term of bail, the previous decision releasing

279. Švedas G., Veršekys P., Levon J., Prapiestis D. Lietuvos Respublikos baudžiamojo kodekso bendrosios dalies vientisumo ir naujovių suderinimo iššūkiai, Vilnius, Vilniaus Universiteto leidykla, 2017, p. 162.
280. Rulings of the Supreme Court of Lithuania in criminal cases No. 2K-P-82/2010 and No. 2K-86-895/2015.

him/her from criminal liability shall become invalid and the person must be prosecuted for all the criminal acts committed.

Release of a Minor from Criminal Liability

477. Article 93 of the CC provides special type of the release from criminal liability for minors. A minor who commits a misdemeanour, or a negligent crime, or a minor or less serious intentional crime for the first time may be released by the court from criminal liability where he/she: (1) has offered his/her apology to the victim and has compensated for or eliminated, fully or in part, the property damage incurred by his/her work or in monetary terms; or (2) is found to be of diminished capacity; or (3) pleads guilty and regrets having committed a criminal act or there are other grounds for believing that in the future the minor will abide by the law and will not commit new criminal acts.

478. Having released a minor from criminal liability, the court shall impose against him/her the reformative measures (*see* paragraphs 550–563).

479. It should be noted that the mentioned list of the types of release from criminal liability is not exhaustive, since the General and Special Parts of the CC additionally provide even thirteen special types of the release from criminal liability, for example: releasing a person from criminal liability who has committed a misdemeanour, negligent or minor or less serious intentional crime and whom a court finds to be of diminished capacity (Article 18 of the CC), releasing a person from criminal liability who has committed a misdemeanour, negligent or minor or less serious intentional crime as a result of intoxication against his/her will and hence lacked a capacity sufficient to fully appreciate the dangerous nature of the criminal act or to control his/her behaviour at the time of his/her conduct (Article 19 of the CC), releasing a person from criminal liability who participates in a coup d'etat and voluntarily provides to a State institution a significant information about the coup d'etat being prepared (Article 114 of the CC), releasing a victim of the trafficking in human beings from criminal liability for the criminal act which he/she was directly forced to commit as a result of the trafficking in human beings and committed against him/her (Article 147 of the CC), releasing a person from criminal liability for grafting where he/she was demanded or provoked to give a bribe and he/she, upon offering or promising to give or giving the bribe voluntarily notifies a law enforcement institution thereof within the shortest possible time, but in any case before the delivery of a notice of suspicion raised against him/her, also where he/she promises to give or gives the bribe with the law enforcement institution being aware thereof (Article 227 of the CC), releasing a person from criminal liability for the production, acquisition and storage of the consumed or submitted narcotic or psychotropic substances who voluntarily applies to a healthcare establishment for medical aid or addresses a State institution in order to submit the narcotic or psychotropic substances which have been unlawfully produced, acquired, stored for the purpose other than distribution (Article 259 of the CC), etc.

§3. PUNISHMENTS

480. Article 41 of the CC provides that 'a punishment (penalty) shall be a measure of compulsion applied by the State, which is imposed by a court's judgment upon a person who has committed a crime or misdemeanour'. The essence of the punishment consists of punishing the person who committed a criminal act, while the content of the punishment – restriction of certain freedoms and liberties as well as determination of certain special obligations.[281]

481. The purpose of a punishment shall be: (1) to prevent persons from committing criminal acts; (2) to punish a person who has committed a criminal act; (3) to deprive the convicted person of the possibility to commit new criminal acts or to restrict such a possibility; (4) to exert an influence on the persons who have served their sentence to ensure that they comply with laws and do not relapse into crime; (5) ensure the implementation of the principle of justice.

I. The System and Types of Punishments

482. Lithuanian criminal law sets different systems of punishments for crimes and misdemeanours as well as for legal entities. The systems consist of an exhaustive and compulsory list of punishments laid down in a certain order. The punishment systems start from the most lenient punishment, consistently followed by other more stringent punishments. This principle has, in fact, also been applied in the design and structure of the sanctions of the Articles in the Special Part of the CC. It shows the position of the legislator: when selecting a punishment for the offender, one should seek to apply the most rational, economic and, at the same time, effective punishment.[282]

483. Article 42 of the CC provides that the following punishments may be imposed on a person who commits a crime: (1) community service; (2) a fine; (3) restriction of liberty; (4) arrest; (5) fixed-term imprisonment; (6) life imprisonment. The following punishments may be imposed on a person who commits a misdemeanour: (1) community service; (2) a fine; (3) restriction of liberty; (4) arrest.

484. Article 90 of the CC provides peculiarities of the punishments imposed upon minors. A minor may be subject solely to the following punishments: (1) community service; (2) a fine; (3) restriction of liberty; (4) arrest; and (5) fixed-term imprisonment.

---

281. Lietuvos Respublikos baudžiamojo kodekso komentaras. Bendroji dalis (1-98 straipsniai). – Vilnius, TIC, 2004, p. 263.
282. Švedas G. European Union criminal law and its influence on the institutes of the General Part of Lithuanian criminal law // Lithuanian legal system under the influence of European Union law, Vilnius, 2014, p. 148.

485. Article 43 CC provides that the following punishments may be imposed upon a legal entity for the commission of a criminal act: (1) a fine; (2) restriction of operation of the legal entity; (3) liquidation of the legal entity. Having imposed a punishment upon a legal entity, a court may also decide to announce this judgment in the media. In 2017, *Seimas* established a special rule that a judgment by which a court imposes the legal person punishment for corruption crimes provided by Chapter XXXIII of the CC must be announced in the media.[283] Furthermore, in the doctrine of Lithuanian criminal law was stated that the CC must be supplemented with new types of punishments recommended by EU legal acts for legal entities: (a) exclusion from entitlement to public benefit or aid; (b) placing under judicial supervision. The inclusion of these punishments in the CC would enable the expansion of the list of punishments applicable to legal entities, by new and effective punishments meeting the principle of proportionality and the requirements of EU legal acts to impose effective, proportionate and dissuasive punishments (measures) on legal entities for the criminal acts committed.[284]

486. All punishments compose a single group. The division of punishments into principal (which was imposed independently) and additional (which was imposed only together with principal punishment) was repealed in the Lithuanian criminal law in 2000.

A. The Death Penalty

487. The death punishment in Lithuania was abolished by the ruling of the Constitutional Court on 9 December 1998.[285] It should be noted that the Constitution did not provide for an explicit prohibition of the death punishment, but the Constitutional Court decided that the death punishment contradicted the constitutional requirements concerning, *inter alia*, the right to life (Article 19 of the Constitution), prohibition to torture, injure, degrade, or maltreat a person, as well as to establish such punishments (Article 21 of the Constitution), etc.

488. The Seimas, on 22 June 1999 ratified Protocol No. 6 to the ECHR[286] and on 16 October 2003 – Protocol No. 13 to the ECHR on the abolition of the death punishment in all circumstances.[287]

283. Lietuvos Respublikos baudžiamojo kodekso 43, 47, 54, 62, 63, 64, 68(1), 68(2), 71, 75, 90, 226 ir 227 straipsnių pakeitimo įstatymas, TAR, 2017, No. 2017-15859.

284. Švedas G. European Union criminal law and its influence on the institutes of the General Part of Lithuanian criminal law // Lithuanian legal system under the influence of European Union law, Vilnius, 2014, p. 166.

285. Decision of the Constitutional Court of Lithuania of 9 Dec. 1998, *Valstybės žinios*, 1998, No. 109-3004.

286. Lietuvos Respublikos įstatymas dėl Europos žmogaus teisių ir pagrindinių laisvių apsaugos konvencijos 6 protokolo dėl mirties bausmės panaikinimo ratifikavimo, *Valstybės žinios*, 1999, No. 61-1975.

287. Lietuvos Respublikos įstatymas dėl Žmogaus teisių ir pagrindinių laisvių apsaugos konvencijos protokolo Nr. 13 dėl mirties bausmės panaikinimo visais atvejais ratifikavimo, *Valstybės žinios*, 2004, No. 77-2654.

B. Custodial Penalties

489. Arrest, fixed-term imprisonment and life imprisonment as a punishment are the custodial penalties in the Lithuanian criminal law.

490. Arrest is the offender's compulsory short-term isolation from the society served in a correctional institution. Article 49 of the CC provides that the arrest may be imposed by a court in the cases provided for in the Special Part of the CC. This punishment was provided in 226 sanctions of the articles of the Special Part of the CC.[288] The arrest shall be imposed for a period from fifteen up to ninety days for a crime and from ten to forty-five days for a misdemeanour. A minor may be subject to arrest for a period from five up to forty-five days.

491. The term of arrest for a criminal act shall be specified by a court when imposing the punishment.

492. The arrest shall not be imposed upon pregnant women and may not be imposed upon the persons raising a child under the age of 3 taking into consideration the interests of the child.

493. The fixed-term imprisonment is the offender's compulsory isolation from the society in the special State institutions. Article 50 of the CC provides that a fixed-term imprisonment may be imposed by a court in the cases provided for in the Special Part of the CC. This punishment was provided in 366 sanctions of the articles of the Special Part of the CC.[289] The fixed-term imprisonment may be imposed for a period from three months up to twenty years. In the case of imposing the punishment, when a new crime is committed before a sentence for the previous crime is served, an imprisonment for a period of up to twenty-five years may be imposed.

494. The court may impose a fixed-term imprisonment upon a minor where there is a ground for believing that another type of punishment is not sufficient to alter the minor's criminal dispositions, or where the minor has committed a serious or grave crime. In the event of imposition of the imprisonment upon the minor, the minimum punishment shall be equal to one-half of the minimum punishment provided for by the sanction of an article of the Special Part of the CC according to which the minor is prosecuted. The maximum period of an imprisonment in respect of a minor may not exceed ten years.

495. Convicted persons shall serve the imprisonment in open colonies, correctional houses and prisons. The place where the punishment is to be served shall be

288. Švedas G. Lietuvos Respublikos baudžiamojo kodekso specialiosios dalies straipsnių sankcijų sudarymo probleminiai aspektai, Teisė, 2011, No. 79, p. 12, 14.
289. Švedas G. Lietuvos Respublikos baudžiamojo kodekso specialiosios dalies straipsnių sankcijų sudarymo probleminiai aspektai, Teisė, 2011, No. 79, p. 12, 14.

selected by a court taking into consideration the personality of the offender, the nature and dangerousness of the committed crime. The Supreme Court of Lithuania has stated that:

> the court did not have an obligation for the person who committed a negligent or minor crime to select an open colony as a place for serving the imposed imprisonment. However, if the court in such a situation selects a correctional house for serving the imposed imprisonment, or in a case of serious crime selects the open colony, the court must motivate milder or more severe conditions for the enforcement of the imposed imprisonment.[290]

496. Life imprisonment is the most severe punishment in the Lithuanian criminal law. Article 51 of the CC provides that life imprisonment may be imposed by a court in the cases provided for in the Special Part of the CC. This punishment was provided in thirteen sanctions of the articles of the Special Part of the CC.[291] All these sanctions are alternative, e.g., life imprisonment is combined with fixed-term imprisonment. Life imprisonment may be imposed only if offender had reached the age of 18 by the time the crime was committed. In the opinion of the doctrine of the Lithuanian criminal law,[292] the life imprisonment should not be applicable to the person who was found to be of diminished capacity (*see* paragraphs 311–314).

497. Convicted persons shall serve the life imprisonment in a prison. Having served the first ten years of the life imprisonment, convicted persons may be transferred to a correctional house.

498. It should be noted that the Lithuanian criminal law was set up the so-called real life imprisonment, since the commutation of the life imprisonment was possible only on the ground of amnesty (*see* paragraphs 585, 1113, 1114) and clemency (*see* paragraphs 586, 1113, 1115). In the event of such commutation, the fixed-term imprisonment should be not less than twenty-five years. Considering the latest developments of the ECtHR case law that imposing a life punishment without any possibility of revision and conditional release violates Article 3 of the European Convention on Human Rights[293] (also a case from Lithuania[294]), such legal regulation was replaced.

499. Since 2019, Article 51 of the CC provides that after the sentenced person has served twenty years of life imprisonment, the question of replacement of his/her sentence by a fixed-term imprisonment shall be examined and resolved by a

290. Ruling of the Supreme Court of Lithuania in criminal case No. 2K-271/2010.
291. Švedas G. Lietuvos Respublikos baudžiamojo kodekso specialiosios dalies straipsnių sankcijų sudarymo probleminiai aspektai, Teisė, 2011, No. 79, p. 12, 14.
292. Lietuvos Respublikos baudžiamojo kodekso komentaras. Bendroji dalis (1-98 straipsniai), Vilnius, TIC, 2004, p. 298.
293. *Vinter and Others v. the United Kingdom* (No. 66069/09, 130/10 and 3896/10), *Lazlo Magyar v. Hungary* (No. 73593/10).
294. *K. Matijošaitis and Others v. Lithuania* (No. 22662/13, No. 51059/13, No. 58823/13, No. 59692/13, No. 59700/13, No. 60115/13, No. 69425/13 and 72824/13).

court. If the court decides to replace the life imprisonment with a fixed-term imprisonment, the term of imprisonment shall neither be less than five years and nor more than ten years from the date on which the judgment becomes effective. In deciding whether to replace a life imprisonment, the court shall take into account the risk posed by the convicted offender, the offender's conduct at the time of the sentence, the purpose of the punishment and the impact of the punishment on the offender, and also take into consideration whether the convicted person has compensated or eliminated a significant part of the damage caused by crime or undertakes to fully compensate or eliminate it.

C. Fine

500. A fine is a pecuniary punishment imposed by a court in the cases provided for in the Special Part of CC. This punishment was provided in 220 sanctions of the articles of the Special Part of the CC.[295] Article 47 of the CC provides that a fine is calculated in the basic amounts of punishments and penalties (BAPP). The minimum and maximum amount of a fine shall be determined as follows: (1) for a misdemeanour – from 15 up to the amount of 500 BAPP; (2) for a minor crime – from 50 up to the amount of 2.000 BAPP; (3) for a less serious crime – from 100 up to the amount of 4,000 BAPP; (4) for a serious crime – from 150 up to the amount of 6,000 BAPP; (5) for a negligent crime – from 20 up to the amount of 750 BAPP. The minimum and maximum amount of a fine for a legal entity shall be from 200 up to 100,000 BAPP. The concrete amount of a fine for a committed criminal act shall be specified by a court when imposing the punishment.

501. In 2017, Law No. XIII-653 established special rules concerning imposition of the fine for the corruption crimes. For the corruption crimes provided for in Chapter XXXIII of the CC, the fine shall not be less than the value of the bribe, or the property damage caused by the offender or the size of the obtained or it sought to obtain pecuniary benefit for offender or another person. Where there are several criteria for calculating the amount of the fine, the amount of the fine imposed is calculated on the basis of the highest value expressed in money. Where the fine is imposed in accordance with these rules, the final fine imposed by the court for the corruption crimes (Chapter XXXIII of the CC) may exceed the maximum amounts (paragraph 500) but may not be less than the minimum amounts (paragraph 500). This provision raises some doubts as to its discriminatory nature, as other property crimes in such a large fine cannot be applied.

502. A fine may be imposed only against a minor already employed or possessing his/her own property. A minor may be subject to a fine in the amount from 5 up to 50 BAPP.

---

295. Švedas G. Lietuvos Respublikos baudžiamojo kodekso specialiosios dalies straipsnių sankcijų sudarymo probleminiai aspektai, Teisė, 2011, No. 79, p. 12, 14.

503. Where a person does not possess sufficient funds to pay a fine imposed by a court, the court may (with the convict's consent) replace this punishment with community service. Where a person evades voluntary payment of a fine and it is not possible to recover it, a court may replace the fine with a restriction of liberty.

D. Restriction of Liberty

504. Restriction of liberty is one of the medium stringency punishments, which may be effective sanction for a person who has committed negligent crime, or misdemeanour, or minor intentional crime, or less serious crime as well as for a young offender. Article 48 of the CC states that the punishment of restriction of liberty may 'be imposed by a court in the cases provided for in the Special Part of the Criminal Code'. This punishment was provided in 123 sanctions of the articles of the Special Part of the CC.[296] The restriction of liberty may be imposed for a period from three months up to two years. The persons sentenced to the restriction of liberty shall be under the obligation: '(1) not to change their place of residence without giving a notice to the institution executing the punishment; (2) to comply with mandatory and prohibitive injunctions of the court; and (3) to give an account, in accordance with the established procedure, of compliance with the prohibitive and mandatory injunctions'.

505. When imposing a restriction of liberty, the court shall usually impose intensive supervision – i.e., control of the convict by the electronic means of surveillance. A court may impose one or more coordinated prohibitive or mandatory injunctions in respect of a person upon whom the restriction of liberty has been imposed.

506. A court may impose the following prohibitive injunctions: (1) to refrain from visiting certain places; (2) to refrain from communicating with certain individuals or groups of individuals; (3) not to own, use, acquire, store on one's own or transfer for safekeeping to other person certain items; (4) to use psychoactive substances.

507. A court may impose the following mandatory injunctions: (1) to stay at home at a certain time; (2) to compensate, fully or in part, for the property damage incurred by a criminal act or to eliminate such damage with his own work; (3) to take up employment or register at a labour exchange, to study; (4) to undergo a treatment against alcohol addiction, drug addiction, addiction to toxic substances or a sexually transmitted disease, where the convict agrees therefore; (5) to work for no remuneration for up to 200 hours within a period laid down by a court, but not exceeding the term of restriction of liberty at healthcare, social care and guardianship establishments or non-state organisations caring for the disabled, the aged or other persons in need of assistance.

296. Švedas G. Lietuvos Respublikos baudžiamojo kodekso specialiosios dalies straipsnių sankcijų sudarymo probleminiai aspektai, Teisė, 2011, No. 79, p. 12, 14.

508. At the request of a person or other participants in criminal proceedings, a court may impose other prohibitive or mandatory injunctions upon him/her, where, in the opinion of the court, this would have a positive effect on his/her behaviour.

509. Where, for objective reasons, the convict is not able to comply with the specified mandatory injunctions, a court may, on the recommendation of the institution executing the punishment, release him/her from the restriction of liberty and replace it with a penal or reformative measure. Where a person evades the serving of the restriction of liberty, this punishment shall be replaced with arrest.

E. Community Service

510. Community service is one of the lenient punishments, which may be an effective sanction for a person who has committed a negligent crime, or a misdemeanour, or a minor intentional crime. Article 46 of the CC provides that community service may be 'ordered by a court in the cases provided for in the Special Part of the Criminal Code'. This punishment was provided in 83 sanctions of the articles of the Special Part of the CC.[297] A person sentenced to perform community service shall be under the obligation to work for the community without remuneration from 10 to 40 hours per month during the time period set by the court.

511. Community service may be imposed for a period from one month up to one year. The time of performance and a number of hours of community service shall be determined by a court when imposing the punishment, however this time may not exceed 480 hours for a crime and 240 hours for a misdemeanour. Minors may not receive more than 240 hours of community service.

512. Community service may be imposed only with the consent of the convict. Where, for objective reasons, a person is not able to perform the community service imposed on him/her, a court may release him/her from this punishment and impose *in lieu* thereof a penal measure provided for in the CC.

513. Where a person fails, for valid reasons, to perform the required number of hours of community service within a time limit laid down by a court, the court may extend the time limit for performing community service until the person performs the required number of hours.

514. Where a person evades the performance of community service, the institution executing the punishment shall warn the convict of possible legal consequences. Where the person continues evading the serving of the community service upon receiving the warning, a court may, on the recommendation of the institution executing the punishment, replace community service with a fine or a restriction of liberty.

---

297. Švedas G. Lietuvos Respublikos baudžiamojo kodekso specialiosios dalies straipsnių sankcijų sudarymo probleminiai aspektai, Teisė, 2011, No. 79, p. 12, 14.

F. Restriction of Operation of a Legal Entity

515. Restriction of operation of a legal entity is one of the medium stringency punishments, which may be imposed on a legal entity. Article 52 of the CC provides that 'when imposing the restriction of operation of a legal entity, a court shall prohibit the legal entity from engaging in certain activities or order it to close a certain division of the legal entity'. Operation of a legal entity may be restricted for a period from one year up to five years.

516. The doctrine of the Lithuanian criminal law has emphasised that the restriction of operation of a legal entity may not be applicable for inner division of a legal entity, which is designated to serve for the legal person (e.g., finance or personal management department, etc.).[298]

G. Liquidation of a Legal Entity

517. Liquidation of a legal entity is the most severe punishment applicable for a legal entity. The doctrine of the Lithuanian criminal law has emphasised that this punishment should be imposed in exceptional cases, where a legal entity, for example, act as a cover for criminal activity.[299] Article 53 of the CC provides that 'when imposing the liquidation of a legal entity, a court shall order the legal entity to terminate, within the time limit laid down by the court, the entire economic, commercial, financial or professional activity and to close all divisions of the legal entity'.

§4. Measures of Security and Reform

I. The System and Types of Penal Measures

518. Penal measures as an alternative to former additional punishments were introduced in the Lithuanian criminal law in 2000. The main differences between punishments and penal measures can be summarised as follows: (a) the ground of application – penal measure may be imposed only in case when an adult person is released from criminal liability or punishment or conditionally released from a correctional institution, also an adult person in respect of whom the execution of the punishment has been suspended; (b) application of some penal measures (property confiscation, extended property confiscation) does not presuppose the personal guilt; (c) the aim of penal measures – assistance in implementing the purposes of

298. Lietuvos baudžiamoji teisė, Bendroji dalis, 2 knyga, Vilnius, Vilniaus universiteto leidykla, 2020, p. 100.
299. Lietuvos Respublikos baudžiamojo kodekso komentaras. Bendroji dalis (1-98 straipsniai), Vilnius, TIC, 2004, p. 301.

punishment; (d) the enforcement of penal measures is usually not limited by the statute of limitations of criminal liability; (e) penal measures are not divided according to their severity, etc.

519. Penal measures may be divided into (a) preventative measures (e.g., the prohibition to exercise a special right, deprivation of a public rights, deprivation of the right to be employed in a certain position or to engage in certain type of activities, property confiscation, etc.), (b) victim's rights protection measures (e.g., payment of a contribution to the fund of crime victims, obligation to reside separately from the victim and (or) prohibition to approach the victim closer than a prescribed distance, etc.) and (c) rehabilitative measures (e.g., unpaid work, obligation to participate in violence correction programmes).[300]

520. An adult person released from criminal liability or punishment or conditionally released from a correctional institution, also an adult person in respect of whom the execution of the punishment has been suspended may be subject to the following penal measures: (1) prohibition to exercise a special right; (2) deprivation of public rights; (3) deprivation of the right to be employed in a certain position or to engage in certain type of activities; (4) compensation for or elimination of property damage; (5) unpaid work; (6) payment of a contribution to the fund of crime victims; (7) confiscation of property; (8) the obligation to reside separately from the victim and (or) prohibition to approach the victim closer than a prescribed distance; (9) participation in the programmes addressing violent behaviour; (10) extended confiscation of property and (11) obligation to notify a change in the place of residence or departure from the place of residence.

521. Prohibition to exercise a special right, deprivation of public rights, deprivation of the right to be employed in a certain position or to engage in certain type of activities, payment of a contribution to the fund of crime victims, confiscation of property, the obligation to reside separately from the victim and (or) prohibition to approach the victim closer than a prescribed distance, participation in the programmes addressing violent behaviour, extended confiscation of property and obligation to notify a change in the place of residence or departure from the place of residence may be imposed together with a punishment.

522. A minor released from criminal liability or punishment may be subject to payment of a contribution to the fund of crime victims, confiscation of property and extended confiscation of property.

523. A legal entity may be subject to payment of a contribution to the fund of crime victims, confiscation of property or extended confiscation of property. The

300. Lietuvos Respublikos baudžiamojo kodekso komentaras. Bendroji dalis (1-98 straipsniai), Vilnius, TIC, 2004, p. 376–377.

doctrine of the Lithuanian criminal law has emphasised that a legal entity could also be subject to such penal measures as compensation for or elimination of property damage,[301] etc.

524. When imposing a punishment together with penal measures, also two or more penal measures, the compatibility of the punishments, measures and the possibility of their corrective effect upon the convicted person must be taken into consideration.

A. Prohibition to Exercise a Special Right

525. Article 68 of the CC provides that 'a court may prohibit a person from exercising special rights (the right to drive land vehicles, air- or water-borne vehicles, the right to hold and carry a weapon, the right to hunt, the right to fish, etc.) in the cases when a person committed a criminal act while exercising these rights'. It should be noted that the list of the special rights is not exhaustive, e.g. the court has the right to prohibit an exercise a special right which is not directly provided in criminal law.[302] The Supreme Court of Lithuania has noted that 'prohibition to drive land vehicle may be imposed even in case when offender was already deprived of the right to drive land vehicle in administrative case',[303] also that 'the court, in all cases when person drives a road vehicle under the influence of alcohol, narcotic, psychotropic or other psychoactive substances and violates regulations governing road traffic safety or operation of vehicles, has an obligation to consider the application of prohibition to exercise a special right'.[304]

526. The duration of the prohibition to exercise special rights may be determined for a period from one year up to three years. When prohibiting a person from exercising special rights, a court shall specify which right or rights he/she is prohibited from exercising as well as the term of validity of such a prohibition.

B. Deprivation of Public Rights

527. The deprivation of public rights means the deprivation of the right to be elected or appointed to an elected or appointed position at State or municipal institutions and agencies, undertakings or non-state organisations. The court may impose deprivation of public rights in the cases when a criminal act is committed in abuse of public rights.

---

301. Soloveičikas D. Juridiniams asmenims taikomos bausmės, baudžiamojo poveikio priemonės ir jų ypatumai: analizė, Teisė, 2006, No. 59, p. 122–125.
302. Lietuvos Respublikos baudžiamojo kodekso komentaras. Bendroji dalis (1-98 straipsniai), Vilnius, TIC, 2004, p. 381.
303. Ruling of the Supreme Court of Lithuania in criminal case No. 2K-7-49-788/2016.
304. Ruling of the Supreme Court of Lithuania in criminal case No. 2K-252-677/2015.

528. The duration of the deprivation of public rights may be determined for a period from one year up to five years. Public rights for less serious and serious corruption crimes (Chapter XXXIII of the CC) may be deprived of a term from three up to seven years. When imposing deprivation of public rights, the court shall indicate the right, which is derived as well as the term of validity of such a prohibition.

C. Deprivation of the Right to be Employed in a Certain Position or to Engage in Certain Type of Activities

529. An offender may be deprived of the right to be employed in a certain position or to engage in certain type of activities in the cases when a person commits a criminal act in the field of his occupational or professional activities or where, having regard to the nature of the criminal act committed, the court comes to the conclusion that the person may not preserve the right to be employed in a certain position or to engage in certain type of activities'. The Supreme Court of Lithuania has emphasised that 'the court, in all cases of corruption, has an obligation to consider the application of deprivation of the right to be employed in a certain position or to engage in certain type of activities'.[305]

530. This penal measure may be imposed for a period from one year up to five years. Right to be employed in a certain position or to engage in certain type of activities for less serious and serious corruption crimes (Chapter XXXIII of the of the CC) may be deprived of a term from three up to seven years. When ordering deprivation of the right to be employed in a certain position or to engage in certain type of activities, the court shall indicate the term of this penal measure.

D. Compensation for or Elimination of Property Damage

531. Article 69 of the CC provides that 'the court shall order compensation for or elimination of property damage when damage has been caused to a person, property or the natural environment as a result of a crime or misdemeanour'. The amounts received by the victim from insurance or other institutions to cover the damage incurred shall not be included in the amount of the damage to be compensated for. Damage must be compensated for or eliminated within a time limit laid down by the court.

E. Unpaid Work

532. Unpaid work means the offender obligation to perform a period from 20 up to 100 hours of unpaid work at healthcare, social care and guardianship or other State or non-state bodies and organisations. When imposing unpaid work, the court

---

305. Ruling of the Supreme Court of Lithuania in criminal case No. 2K-86-895/2015.

shall lay down a time limit for performance thereof. This term may not be longer than one year. Unpaid work shall be imposed only with the consent of a person.

F. Payment of a Contribution to the Fund of Violent Crime Victims

533. Article 71 of the CC provides that 'a court may order payment of a contribution in the amount from 10 up to 250 BAPP for adults and from 3 up to 25 BAPP for juveniles to the fund for victims of violent crime. The minimum and maximum amount of the payment of a contribution to the fund for victims of violent crime for a legal entity shall be from 100 up to 2,000 BAPP. A payment may be imposed only against a minor who is already employed or possessing his/her own property. The contribution must be paid within a time limit laid down by the court. This time cannot be longer than three years'.

534. It should be noted that Article 71 of the CC, law on damage of violent crimes victims compensation[306] as well as Council Directive 2004/80/EC of 29 April 2004 relating to compensation to crime victims[307] creates the system of legal acts, which regulates the issues of pecuniary and (or) non-pecuniary damage compensation for violent crime victims in Lithuania.

G. Confiscation of Property

535. In 1993, the Constitutional Court stated that confiscation of property of the offender as a supplementary punishment is 'one of legal means with the help of which attempts are made to put a stop to serious selfish crimes that threaten other persons' property which is protected by the Constitution' and recognised that this supplementary punishment is in compliance with the Constitution.[308] On the contrary, the legal concept of the confiscation of property was significantly changed from punishment to penal measure by restricting confiscation only to the instrument, means and results of the criminal act in Lithuania in 2000.[309]

536. The confiscation of property means a compulsory and uncompensated taking into the ownership of a state of any form of property subject to confiscation and held by the offender or other persons. Article 72 of the CC provides that 'an instrument or a means used to commit an act prohibited by the CC or the result of such

306. Lietuvos Respublikos smurtiniais nusikaltimais padarytos žalos kompensavimo įstatymo No. X-296 pakeitimo įstatymas, TAR, 2019, No. 858.
307. Council Directive 2004/80/EC of 29 Apr. 2004 relating to compensation to crime victims, *OJ L 261, 6.8.2004, p. 15–18.*
308. Decision of the Constitutional Court of Lithuania of 13 Dec. 1993, *Valstybės žinios*, 1993, No. 70-1320.
309. Lietuvos Respublikos baudžiamojo kodekso komentaras. Bendroji dalis (1-98 straipsniai), Vilnius, TIC, 2004, p. 375.

an act shall be considered as property subject to confiscation. The property of any form directly or indirectly obtained from the act prohibited by the CC shall be considered as the result of the act'.

537. The property held by the offender and being subject to confiscation must be confiscated in all cases.

538. The property held by another natural or legal person and being subject to confiscation shall be confiscated irrespectively of whether the person has been convicted of the commission of an act prohibited by the CC, where: (1) when transferring the property to the offender or other persons, he/she was, or ought to have been, aware that this property would be used for the commission of the act prohibited by the CC; (2) the property has been transferred thereto under a fake transaction; (3) the property has been transferred thereto as to a family member or close relative of the offender; (4) the property has been transferred to him/her as to a legal person, and the offender, his/her family members or close relatives is/are the legal person's manager, a member of its management body or participants holding at least 50% of the legal person's shares (member shares, contributions, etc.); (5) when acquiring the property, he/she or the persons holding managing positions in the legal person and being entitled to represent it, to make decisions on behalf of the legal person or to control the activities of the legal person was/were, or ought and could have been, aware that the property is an instrument or a means used to commit an act prohibited by the CC or the result of such an act.

539. When ordering confiscation of property, the court must specify the items subject to confiscation or the monetary value of the property subject to confiscation. Where the property which is subject to confiscation has been concealed, consumed, belongs to third parties or cannot be taken for other reasons or confiscation of this property would not be appropriate, the court shall recover from the offender or other persons a sum of money equivalent to the value of the property subject to confiscation.

H. Obligation to Reside Separately from the Victim and (or) Prohibition to Approach the Victim Closer than a Prescribed Distance, Obligation to Notify a Change of the Place of Residence or Departure of the Place of Residence

540. The penal measure – obligation to reside separately from the victim and (or) prohibition to approach the victim closer than a prescribed distance was introduced in 2008[310] and modified in 2015.[311]

310. Lietuvos Respublikos baudžiamojo kodekso 42, 67, 129, 135, 138 straipsnių pakeitimo ir papildymo bei Kodekso papildymo 72(1), 72(2) straipsniais įstatymas, *Valstybės žinios*, 2008, No. 73-2796.
311. Lietuvos Respublikos baudžiamojo kodekso 42, 67, 72(1) straipsnių ir priedo pakeitimo įstatymas, TAR, 2015-05-18, No. 2015-07563.

541. Article 72(1) of the CC provides that 'the court may impose the obligation to reside separately from the victim and (or) prohibition to approach the victim closer than a prescribed distance where this is necessary with a view to protecting the legitimate interests of the victim'. Upon imposition of this penal measure, the offender shall be prohibited, until the expiry of a time limit laid down by the court, from communicating in any form and seeking contacts with the victim and visiting the indicated places at which the victim is usually present.

542. The obligation to notify a change of place of residence or departure from the place of residence was introduced in 2020.[312] Article 72(4) of the CC provides that the obligation to notify a change of place of residence or departure from the place of residence is imposed by the court in cases, where the person has committed some kind of sexual crime (e.g., rape, sexual assault, sexual molestation of a person under the age of 16, etc.). This penal measure means that a person who intends to change his/her place of residence or to leave the place of residence for more than seven days, must notify the police authority before the change or leave no later than three days after leaving. This penal measure may be imposed from one up to five years.

I. Obligation to Participate in Violence Correction Programmes

543. The penal measure – obligation to participate in violence correction programmes was introduced in 2008.[313] Article 72(2) of the CC provides that 'the court shall place under the obligation to participate in violence correction programmes the persons who have committed criminal acts in respect of a close relative or family member. This obligation must be complied with within a time limit laid down by the court'.

J. Extended Confiscation of Property

544. Extended confiscation of property was introduced in the Lithuanian criminal law in 2010.[314] Extended confiscation of property together with *corpus delicti* of illegal enrichment (Article 189(1) of the CC) constitute the main measures of the system of the illegal enrichment control.

---

312. Lietuvos Respublikos baudžiamojo kodekso 42, 67 straipsnių pakeitimo ir Kodekso papildymo 72(4) straipsniu įstatymas, TAR 2020-11-18, No. 2020-24238.
313. Lietuvos Respublikos baudžiamojo kodekso 42, 67, 129, 135, 138 straipsnių pakeitimo ir papildymo bei Kodekso papildymo 72(1), 72(2) straipsniais įstatymas, *Valstybės žinios*, 2008, No. 73-2796.
314. Lietuvos Respublikos baudžiamojo kodekso 3, 67, 72, 190 straipsnių pakeitimo ir papildymo ir Kodekso papildymo 72(3), 189(1) straipsniais įstatymas, *Valstybės žinios*, 2010, No. 145-7439.

545. The extended confiscation of property means the taking into ownership of the state of the property of the offender or part thereof disproportionate to the legitimate income of the offender, where there are grounds for believing that the property has been obtained by criminal means.

546. Extended confiscation of property shall be imposed provided that all of the following conditions are met: (1) the offender has been convicted of a less serious, serious or grave premeditated crime from which he obtained, or could have obtained, material gain; (2) the offender holds the property acquired during the commission of an act prohibited by the CC, after the commission thereof or within the period of five years prior to the commission thereof, whose value does not correspond to the offender's legitimate income, and the difference is greater than 250 BAPP, or transfers such property to other persons within the period specified in this point; (3) the offender fails, in the course of criminal proceedings, to provide proof of the legitimacy of acquisition of the property.

547. This property, if it has been transferred to another natural or legal person, shall be confiscated from this person, where at least one of the following grounds exists: (1) the property has been transferred under a fake transaction; (2) the property has been transferred to the offender's family members or close relatives; (3) the property has been transferred to a legal person, and the offender, his/her family members or close relatives is/are the legal person's manager, a member of its management body or participants holding at least 50% of the legal person's shares (member shares, contributions, etc.); (4) the person whereto the property has been transferred or the persons holding managing positions in the legal person and being entitled to represent it, to make decisions on behalf of the legal person or to control the activities of the legal person was/were, or ought and could have been, aware that the property has been obtained by criminal means or with illicit funds of the offender.

548. When ordering extended confiscation of property, the court must specify the items subject to confiscation or the monetary value of the property or part thereof subject to confiscation. Where the property, or part thereof, which is subject to confiscation has been concealed, consumed, belongs to third parties or cannot be taken for other reasons or confiscation of this property would not be appropriate, the court shall recover from the offender or other persons a sum of money equivalent to the value of the property subject to confiscation.

549. It should be noted that in the doctrine of the Lithuanian criminal law an opinion was expressed that the institute of the extended confiscation of property is 'far beyond of any proportionality limits and creates preconditions for unreasonable repression'.[315]

---

315. FEDOSIUK O. Baudžiamųjų įstatymų prieš neteisėtas pajamas ir korupciją leidyba: tarp gerų siekių ir legitimumo, Jurisprudencija, 2012, No. 19(3); PIESLIAKAS V. Neteisėtu būdu gautų pajamų konfiskavimas Lietuvos baudžiamojoje teisėje: siekiai ir realybė, Jurisprudencija, 2011, No. 18 (2), etc.

II. The System and Types of the Reformative Measures for Minors

550. Chapter XI 'Peculiarities of the Criminal Liability of Minors' of the CC provides the reformative measures for minors. These measures, according to their content, application grounds and aims, fully comply with the penal measures for adults.

551. Reformative measures may be divided into (a) preventative measures (e.g., the warning, placement for upbringing and care parents or other natural or legal persons taking care of children; etc.), (b) victim's rights protection measures (e.g., the compensation for or elimination of property damage, etc.) and (c) rehabilitative measures (e.g., unpaid reformative work, restriction of conduct).[316]

552. A minor who has committed a misdemeanour or a crime and has been released from criminal liability or a punishment, also a minor in respect of whom the execution of the punishment has been suspended or who has been conditionally released from correctional institution may be subject to the following reformative measures: (1) a warning; (2) compensation for or elimination of property damage; (3) unpaid reformative work; (4) placement for upbringing and care with parents or other natural or legal persons taking care of children; (5) restriction on conduct; (6) placement in a special reformative facility.

553. The court may impose against a minor not more than three mutually compatible reformative measures.

554. The doctrine of the Lithuanian criminal law draws attention to a rare application of the reformative measures in court practice[317] or even compares them to the 'Sleeping Beauty' – they just look beautiful.[318]

A. *Warning*

555. Article 83 of the CC provides that 'a court may impose the warning upon a minor as an independent reformative measure or in conjunction with other such measures'. When imposing against a minor this reformative measure, the court shall state to him/her in writing the possible legal consequences ensuing from the commission of new criminal acts.

316. Lietuvos Respublikos baudžiamojo kodekso komentaras. Bendroji dalis (1-98 straipsniai), Vilnius, TIC, 2004, p. 428–455.
317. selė L. Jaunų pilnamečių (18-20 metų) socialinė branda – nepilnamečių baudžiamosios atsakomybės ypatumų jiems taikymo veiksnys, Teisės problemos, 2010, No. 68, p. 58–91.
318. Sakalauskas G. Nepilnamečių baudžiamosios atsakomybės ypatumų prasmė, Teisės problemos, 2013, No. 81, p. 22.

B. Compensation for or Elimination of Property Damage

556. The compensation for or elimination of property damage may be ordered only when a minor possesses resources which he/she can independently dispose of or when he/she is capable of eliminating the damage by his/her own work. Property damage must be compensated for or eliminated by a person's own work within a time limit laid down by the court.

C. Unpaid Reformative Work

557. The unpaid reformative work may be imposed on a minor for a period of 20 up to 100 hours to be performed at healthcare, curatorship and guardianship or other State or non-state bodies and organisations, where work thereat may be of a reformative character. Unpaid reformative work shall be imposed only with the consent of the minor. If the minor does not agree to work, the unpaid reformative work is replaced by another reformative measure.[319]

D. Placement for Upbringing and Care with Parents or Other Natural or Legal Persons Taking Care of Children

558. Article 86 of the CC provides that 'placement for upbringing and care with parents or other natural or legal persons taking care of children shall be ordered for a period from six months up to three years, but no longer than after a minor reaches the age of 18'. This reformative measure may be imposed in the cases when: (1) the parents or other persons agree to bring up and take care of the minor, have no negative influence on the minor themselves, have a possibility to provide favourable conditions for the development of his/her personality and agree to provide the necessary information to the institutions supervising the execution of this measure; (2) the minor agrees that the indicated persons bring him/her up and take care of him/her and promises to obey them and behave properly.

E. Restriction on Conduct

559. The restriction on conduct may be imposed for a term from thirty days up to twelve months. The court may impose the following mandatory injunctions upon a minor: (1) to be at home at a certain time; (2) to study, resume studies or take up employment; (3) to acquire certain knowledge or learn prohibitions (traffic safety regulations, school student's regulations, etc.); (4) to undergo a complete course of treatment against alcohol addiction, drug addiction, addiction to toxic substances or sexually transmitted diseases (this mandatory injunction shall be imposed at the

319. Lietuvos baudžiamoji teisė, Bendroji dalis, 2 knyga, Vilnius, Vilniaus universiteto leidykla, 2020, p. 324.

request of parents or guardians subject to the consent of the minor); (5) to participate in the social education or rehabilitation measures organised by State or non-governmental organisations.

560. The court may impose upon a minor the following prohibitive injunctions: (1) not to gamble; (2) not to engage in certain type of activities; (3) not to drive a motor vehicle (motorcycle, self-propelled vehicle, etc.); (4) not to visit the places that have a negative effect on the conduct of the minor, or not to communicate with the people who exert a negative influence on him/her; (5) not to change his/her place of residence without giving a notice to the institutions supervising execution of this measure.

561. The court may impose upon a minor, at the request of the minor or other participants of criminal proceedings, also at its own discretion, other mandatory or prohibitive injunctions, which, in the court's opinion, would have a positive impact on the conduct of the minor.

562. The court may impose one, two or more mandatory and prohibitive injunctions.[320] A minor must give an account of his/her compliance with mandatory and prohibitive injunctions.

F. Placement in a Special Reformative Facility

563. A minor may be placed in a special reformative facility for a period of six months up to three years, but no longer than until a minor reaches the age of 18. The specific term of placement in a special reformative facility shall be laid down by the court having regard to the personality of a minor, the repetitive character of his/her criminal conduct, the type of criminal sanctions previously applied and other circumstances of the case.

III. The System and Types of the Compulsory Medical Measures

564. According to the Lithuanian criminal law, compulsory medical measures are a certain combination of the medical and State coercion measures. These measures are intended to ensure the protection of health, treatment and other vital interests of those who have committed dangerous acts. At the same time, these measures must protect the society from other possible dangerous acts of mentally ill persons.[321]

565. The persons who are recognised by the court as being legally incapacitated or of diminished capacity as well as the persons who, after committing a criminal

320. Lietuvos Respublikos baudžiamojo kodekso komentaras. Bendroji dalis (1-98 straipsniai), Vilnius, TIC, 2004, p. 448.
321. Ruling of the Court of Appeal of Lithuania in criminal case No. 1A-448/2014.

act or having been imposed a punishment, start to suffer from a mental disorder rendering them incapable of understanding the nature of their actions or controlling them may be subjected by the court to the following compulsory medical measures: '(1) outpatient observation under the conditions of primary mental healthcare; (2) inpatient observation under the conditions of a general observation at specialised mental healthcare establishments; (3) inpatient observation under the conditions of an enhanced observation at specialised mental healthcare establishments; (4) inpatient observation under the conditions of a strict observation at specialised mental healthcare establishments'. The Supreme Court of Lithuania has noted that the court applies compulsory medical measures, taking into account the basic criteria established by the criminal law, i. e. the mental disorder and its severity, the nature of the dangerous act committed, the danger that a person may cause to himself/herself, also for other persons's health.[322]

566. The court shall impose an outpatient observation upon a person where it is not necessary to subject the person to observation and inpatient treatment due to the dangerousness of the committed act and his/her mental state or where this person may continue outpatient treatment after his/her mental state improves following inpatient treatment.

567. The court shall impose an inpatient observation under the conditions of a general observation upon a person who needs to be under observation and undergo treatment at a specialised inpatient treatment establishment due to his/her mental disorder.

568. The court shall impose an inpatient observation under the conditions of an enhanced observation upon a person who needs to be under observation and undergo treatment at a specialised inpatient treatment establishment due to the dangerousness of the committed act and his/her mental disorder.

569. The court shall impose an inpatient observation under the conditions of a strict observation upon a person who has committed an attempt against a person's life or health, is particularly dangerous to surrounding people due to his/her mental disorder and needs to be under observation and undergo treatment at a specialised inpatient treatment establishment.

570. The court shall not fix any period of time for compulsory medical treatment. It shall be applied until the person is cured or his/her mental state improves and he/she no longer represents a danger. At least once every six months, the court must make a determination on the basis of the findings of a healthcare establishment as regards extension of compulsory medical treatment, change of type thereof or discontinuation thereof.

---

322. Rulings of the Supreme Court of Lithuania in criminal cases No. 2K-793/2005 and No. 2K-121-976/2021.

§5. Modes of Punishment

I. The Suspension of the Execution of a Punishment

571. The Lithuanian criminal law provides a suspension of the execution of the punishment which means that court establishes the liability of the offender for committing a crime, pronounces his/her guilty and impose punishment – arrest or imprisonment, but the execution of the imposed punishment is suspended. When ordering the suspension of the execution of the punishment, the court considers: (a) abstract gravity of the crime; (b) form of guilt of the committed crime; (c) term of the imposed imprisonment; (d) possibility to achieve purposes of the punishment without the punishment actually being served. The Supreme Court of Lithuania has pointed a few aspects concerning the application of the suspension of the execution of the punishment. First of all, 'application of the suspension of the execution of the punishment is a discretionary right of the court',[323] second, 'it is particularly important in such cases to assess the nature and dangerousness of the committed crime,[324] the personality of the offender, because that's what leads to achieving the purpose of punishment provided in the CC'.[325]

572. If the period of suspension of the execution of the punishment has passed successfully, the execution of the imposed punishment will be automatically excluded. On the contrary, according to the requirements of the mentioned Law on Probation, if a person under suspended punishment has seriously violated the rules prescribed for him/her, without justified reasons does not fulfil imposed penal or reformatory measures and (or) obligations or has committed a new criminal act, the suspension of the execution of the punishment should be terminated and the suspended punishment must be executed.

573. The Lithuanian criminal law provides different conditions for the suspension of the execution of the punishment for adults and minors.

A. The Suspension of the Execution of a Punishment for Adults

574. Where a person is subject to an arrest for the first time, the court may suspend the execution of the imposed punishment for a period ranging from three months to one year and order intensive supervision – control of the convict by electronic means of surveillance. Moreover, together with intensive supervision, the court may impose on the convicted person one or more mutually compatible penal measures and (or) obligations. Where a person is subject to an imprisonment for a term of up to six years for one or several crimes committed through negligence or

323. Ruling of the Supreme Court of Lithuania in criminal case No. 2K-7-47-895/2016.
324. Ruling of the Supreme Court of Lithuania in criminal case No. 2K-61-895/2015.
325. Rulings of the Supreme Court of Lithuania in criminal cases No. 2K-7-554/2005 and No. 2K-7-8-788/2018.

to an imprisonment for a term of up to four years for the commission of one or several intentional crimes, (except for serious and grave crimes), the court may suspend the execution of the imposed punishment for a period ranging from one to three years. The execution of the punishment may be suspended where the court rules that there is a reasonable ground for believing that the purpose of the punishment will be achieved without the punishment actually being served.

575. Where a person is subject to an imprisonment for a term to more than six years for negligent crimes or more than four years for one or several minor or less serious intentional crimes, or up to five years for a serious crime (except for serious crimes provided for in Chapters XV, XVI, XVIII, XX, XXI, XXIII, XXXIII, XXXV, XXXVII and XLIV of the CC), the court may partially suspend the execution of the imposed punishment. In the case of partial suspension, the court shall determine the part of the custodial sentence to be served immediately after the entry into force of the sentence, a part which may not be less than six months and more than two years.

576. In suspending the execution of the punishment, the court shall impose upon the convict intensive supervision and one or more mutually compatible penal measures and (or) obligations, namely: (1) to offer an apology to the victim; (2) to provide assistance to the victim during the latter's medical treatment; (3) to undergo treatment of addiction diseases, where the convict agrees; (4) to educate and take care of his/her minor children, to take care of their health, to maintain them; (5) to take up employment or studies, continue employment or studies; (6) to participate in a programme addressing behaviour; (7) not to leave home at a certain time, unless this is related to work or studies; (8) not to leave the city/district of the place of residence without the authorisation of the institution supervising the convict; (9) not to visit certain places or to refrain from communicating with certain persons or groups of persons; (10) not to use psychoactive substances; (11) not to possess, use or acquire certain items or not engage in certain activities. The Supreme Court of Lithuania has ruled that 'the imposition of the penal measure is not obligatory; the court may select one of the alternatives: (a) one penal measure and one obligation; (b) one penal measure and few obligations; (c) one penal measure; (d) one obligation; or (e) few obligations'. [326]

577. The court also may impose upon a person, at the request of the person or other participants of criminal proceedings, also at its own discretion, other obligations not provided for by the criminal law, which, in the court's opinion, would have a positive impact on the conduct of the convict.

578. In imposing the penal measure and (or) the obligations, the court shall specify the time limit for complying therewith.

---

326. Rulings of the Supreme Court of Lithuania in criminal cases No. 2K-P-6/2010 and No. 2K-P-58-697/2019.

B. The Suspension of the Execution of a Punishment for Minors

579. Where a minor is subject to an arrest, the court may suspend the execution of the imposed punishment for a period ranging from one to nine months. Where an imprisonment is imposed on a minor for one or several crimes committed through negligence or an imprisonment for a term not exceeding five years for the commission of one or several intentional crimes, the court may suspend the execution of the imposed punishment for a period ranging from one to three years. The Supreme Court of Lithuania has underlined that the execution of the imposed punishment may be suspended even in cases when a minor was sentenced for the commission of a grave crime.[327] Moreover, where an imprisonment is imposed on a minor for a term of more than five years for the commission of one or more intentional crimes (except for grave crimes and serious crimes provided for in Chapters XV, XVI, XVII, XVIII, XX, XXI, XXIII, XXXIII, XXXV, XXXVII and XLIV of the CC), the court may partially suspend the execution of the imposed punishment. In the case of partial suspension, the court shall determine the part of the custodial sentence to be served immediately after the entry into force of the sentence, a part which may not be less than six months and more than one year. The execution of the punishment may be suspended where the court rules that there is a reasonable ground for believing that the purpose of the punishment will be achieved without the punishment actually being served.

580. When suspending the execution of a punishment, the court shall impose upon a minor intensive supervision (e.g., control of the convict by electronic means of surveillance) and one or few mutually compatible reformative measures, with the exception of placement in a special reformative facility. The court shall also lay down a time limit within which the minor must implement the reformative measures.

II. Release from the Execution of the Punishment

581. The Lithuanian criminal law provides following grounds of release from execution of the punishment: (a) release from the execution of the punishment due to an illness; (b) release from the execution of the punishment on the grounds of amnesty; and (c) release from the execution of the punishment on the grounds of clemency.

A. Release from the Execution of the Punishment due to an Illness

582. A person who committed a criminal act may be released from a punishment where, before a judgment is passed by the court, he/she contracts a serious

327. Rulings of the Supreme Court of Lithuania in criminal cases No. 2K-630-511/2015 and No. 2K-66-976/2019.

incurable illness[328] rendering him/her unable to serve the punishment. In such a case, the court shall, when passing a judgment of conviction, impose a punishment upon this person and release him/her from serving the punishment. The court shall decide on this issue taking into consideration the gravity of the committed criminal act, the personality of the convict and the nature of the illness.

583. A person who contracts a serious incurable illness following the passing of a judgment may be released from serving the undischarged term of the punishment. The court shall decide on this issue taking into consideration the gravity of the committed criminal act, the personality of the convicted person, his/her conduct while serving the punishment, the nature of the illness and the period of the sentence already served. The court also must assess the impact of the serious incurable disease on punishment execution as well as possibilities of such disease treatment in correctional institution.[329] The Supreme Court of Lithuania has ruled that release offender from punishment due to serious incurable illness is the discretionary right of the court, and not an obligation.[330]

584. A person who, following the commission of a criminal act or imposition of a punishment, starts to suffer from a mental disorder rendering him/her incapable of understanding the nature of his/her actions or controlling them shall be released from serving the undischarged term of the sentence. In releasing this person from a punishment, the court shall decide whether to impose upon him/her a compulsory medical measure. In the event of convalescence of this person, he/she may be ordered to serve the undischarged term of the sentence. In such a case, the period during which the person was undergoing compulsory medical measure shall be included in the term of an imprisonment on a day-to-day basis.

B. Amnesty

585. A person who commits a criminal act may be released from serving the entire length of the sentence or a part thereof by an amnesty act passed by the *Seimas*. The amnesty act lays down the grounds, conditions and procedure for granting amnesty.

C. Clemency

586. A convict may be released from serving the entire length of the sentence or a part thereof where the President of the Republic grants his/her clemency plea.

---

328. The list of serious incurable illnesses is provided by the order of the Minister of Health Protection and the Minister of Justice, *see*: Lietuvos Respublikos teisingumo ministro ir Lietuvos Respublikos sveikatos apsaugos ministro 2013 m. gruodžio 27 d. įsakymas No. 1R-308/V-1247 'Nuteistųjų, susirgusių sunkia nepagydoma ar psichikos liga, sveikatos būklės patikrinimo tvarkos aprašo patvirtinimo', *Valstybės žinios*, 2013, No. 139-7020; TAR 2013-12-31, No. 2013-00060.
329. Ruling of the Supreme Court of Lithuania in criminal case No. 2K-133-677/2015.
330. Ruling of the Supreme Court of Lithuania in criminal case No. 2K-524/2013.

§6. Principles and Rules Concerning Sentencing

587. Sentencing means the selection and imposition of the concrete type and size of the punishment after declaring the defendant guilty in commission of the criminal act. In a broader sense, according to the Lithuanian criminal law, sentencing also includes release from criminal liability or punishment, suspension of the execution of the punishment, imposition of the penal or reformative measures.[331] The framework for sentencing is laid down in the CC. A court shall impose a punishment according to the sanction of an article of the Special Part of the CC providing for liability for a committed criminal act and in compliance with provisions of the General Part of the CC. The sanction of an article of the Special Part of the CC determines the type(s) of punishment and the minimum and maximum or only maximum size of the imprisonment applicable to a concrete criminal act. It should be noted that, in case of community service, a fine, restriction of liberty and arrest, the sanctions do not provide the range of these punishments; in this case, the general minimum and maximum of the type of punishment provided in the General Part of the CC is applicable.

588. The sanctions of articles of the Special Part of the CC shall not specify the punishments for legal entities. In imposing a punishment upon a legal entity, a court shall refer to the list of punishments specified in the General Part of the CC (*see* paragraph 485).

589. Only one punishment may be imposed on a person or legal entity for the commission of one crime or misdemeanour. In the case of imposition of a punishment for the commission of several criminal acts (Articles 63 of the CC) and imposition of a punishment in the event of commission of a new criminal act before the sentence is served (Article 64 of the CC), two punishments may be imposed. If more than two punishments of different types are imposed for several committed crimes, a court shall, when imposing a final combined sentence, select two punishments from those imposed: one of them is to be the most severe punishment, and the other one selected at the discretion of the court.

590. On the imposition of punishment together with one or more penal measures, *see* paragraphs 452, 453.

591. Whereas, concrete type and size of the punishment has to be imposed by the court within this framework.

331. Švedas G. Baudžiamosios politikos pagrindai ir tendencijos Lietuvos Respublikoje, Vilnius, TIC, 2006, p. 169.

I. The General Principles

592. Every offender has the right to a just (fair) punishment, which must be ensured by the general principles of sentencing. The Constitutional Court in defining a just (fair) punishment has stated that:

> the principle of natural justice consolidated in the Constitution presupposes that punishments established by a penal law must be just; the measures established by the state for violations of law must be proportionate (adequate) to the violation of law, they must be in line with the legitimate and generally important objectives sought, they may not restrict the person clearly more than it is necessary in order to reach these objectives. It is not allowed to establish any such legal regulation (punishments or their sizes) in a penal law on the basis of which the court, while taking account of all circumstances of a case and applying the penal law, would not be able to individualise the punishment which is imposed on a concrete person for a concrete criminal act.[332]

Meanwhile, the Supreme Court of Lithuania has noted that 'a just (fair) punishment is the punishment, which meets the purposes of the punishment and basic principles of the imposition of the punishment'.[333] Meanwhile, the doctrine of the Lithuanian criminal law provides that the imposed punishment must be proportional and fair. The requirement that the punishment must be proportional is related to the attitude, that the punishment (its type and size) should match the dangerousness of the criminal act. The content of the fair punishment consists of the legality (only the punishment which is provided in the law could be imposed; its size should be provided in the law; it should be imposed by the requirements of the criminal procedure, etc.) and humanism (the punishment should not consist of the torment of human or the humiliation of the dignity, etc.) and individualisation (the type and size of the punishment should be imposed on the particular person considering to his/her internal; it should be imposed in pursuance of the purposes of the punishment, etc.) and economy (the minimal punishment for the achievement of the necessary purposes of the punishment, etc. should be imposed).[334]

593. According to the basic principles of imposition of a punishment, when imposing a punishment, a court shall take the following circumstances into consideration:

(1) the degree of dangerousness of a committed criminal act;
(2) the form and type of guilt;
(3) the motives and aims of the committed criminal act;

332. Decision of the Constitutional Court of Lithuania of 4 Jun. 2012, *Valstybės žinios*, 2012, No. 64-3246.
333. Rulings of the Supreme Court of Lithuania in criminal cases No. 2K-7-259/2011, No. 2K-87-976/2020 and 2K-7-32-719/2021.
334. Švedas G. Bausmės skyrimo asmeniui, pirmą kartą teisiamam už nesunkų arba apysunkį tyčinį nusikaltimą, nuostatos Lietuvos Aukščiausiojo Teismo jurisprudencijoje, Teisė, No. 90, 2014, pp. 18–19.

(4) the stage of the criminal act;
(5) the personality of the offender;
(6) the form and type of participation of the person as an accomplice in the commission of the criminal act;
(7) mitigating and aggravating circumstances;
(8) damage caused by a criminal act.

594. In imposing a punishment upon a minor, a court shall, in addition to the mentioned circumstances, take the following circumstances into consideration:

(1) the living and upbringing conditions of the minor;
(2) the state of health and social maturity of the minor;
(3) previously imposed sanctions and effectiveness thereof;
(4) the minor's conduct following the commission of a criminal act.

595. Explaining the significance of these circumstances, the Supreme Court of Lithuania has highlighted that 'in the process of the individualisation of a punishment, all the circumstances must be given the same legal value, none of them will be given the exclusive dominant value'.[335]

596. It should be noted that the CC did not provide the special rules for punishment imposition for the legal entity. The Constitutional Court of Lithuania has stated that criminal law did not:

> provide any criteria under which a certain punishment must be imposed on the legal person and the size (if it is a fine) or term and extent (if restriction of activity is imposed) of that punishment must be established. However, it does not mean ... that the court, while imposing a punishment on the legal person, may not follow other norms of the CC and the principles consolidated therein, *inter alia*, the basic principles of imposition of a punishment (to take account of the degree of dangerousness of the criminal act, the reasons and objectives of the act, etc.). Therefore, the legal regulation … does not prohibit the court from taking account of the basic requirements of imposition of punishments, *inter alia*, the rules of individualisation of punishments, the rules of summation of punishments, etc.[336]

597. The general principles of sentencing also include a few sentencing rules relevant to imprisonment: imposition of a punishment upon a person prosecuted for the first time for a negligent or minor or less serious intentional crime (Article 55 of the CC), imposition of a punishment in the presence of mitigating and (or) aggravating circumstances (so-called average rule) (Article 61 of the CC).

---

335. Rulings of the Supreme Court of Lithuania in criminal cases No. 2K-7-414-303/2015 and No. 2K-157-976/2018.
336. Decision of the Constitutional Court of Lithuania of 8 Jun. 2009, *Valstybės žinios*, 2009, No. 69-2798.

598. The doctrine of the Lithuanian criminal law has highlighted that, in the legislator's opinion, the criminal policy for the first time offender, who has committed a negligent, minor or less serious crime, is to be oriented to the imposition of non-custodial punishments.[337] This idea was implemented in the sentencing rule, which provides that 'the court shall generally impose a non-custodial punishment upon a person prosecuted for the first time for a negligent or minor or less serious intentional crime'. The Supreme Court of Lithuania has noted that 'this rule is not imperative; the court may choose an imprisonment, but in this event the court must justify its decision'[338] and 'court justification must be based on the circumstances relating to the dangerousness of the crime and the personality of the offender'.[339]

599. Imposition of a punishment in the presence of mitigating and (or) aggravating circumstances (the 'average rule') may be applicable only in the case of imprisonment. This rule means that a court, when imposing a punishment, shall take into consideration whether only mitigating circumstances or only aggravating circumstances, or both mitigating and aggravating circumstances have been established, and shall assess the relevance of each circumstance. Having assessed mitigating and (or) aggravating circumstances, the amount, nature and interrelation thereof, also other basic principles of the imposition of a punishment, a court shall make a reasoned choice of a more lenient or more severe type of the punishment as well as the size of the punishment with a reference to the average punishment. The average punishment provided for by the law shall be determined as the aggregate of the minimum and maximum size of a punishment provided for in the sanction of an article of the CC, which is subsequently divided by half. Where the sanction of the article of the CC prescribes no minimum size of a punishment for a committed criminal act, the average punishment shall be determined on the basis of the minimum size of a punishment fixed for that type of the punishment. The Supreme Court of Lithuania has noted that:

> the text of the law imperatively does not require to impose a punishment, which is higher than the average punishment – it is clear from systematic interpretation of the norms of the CC. The just (fair) punishment shall be imposed by not primarily focusing on the arithmetic average punishment provided for in the sanction, but by carefully assessing the committed crime and the offender.[340]

600. Where the offender voluntarily confesses to the commission of a crime, sincerely regrets it and actively assists in the detection of the crime as well as there are no aggravating circumstances, a court shall impose upon him an imprisonment not exceeding the average punishment provided for in the sanction of an article of the Special Part of the CC for the committed crime or a non-custodial punishment.

---

337. Lietuvos Respublikos baudžiamojo kodekso komentaras. Bendroji dalis (1-98 straipsniai), Vilnius, TIC, 2004, p. 310.
338. Rulings of the Supreme Court of Lithuania in criminal cases No. 2K-67/2005 and No. 2K-7-87/2014.
339. Ruling of the Supreme Court of Lithuania in criminal case No. 2K-7-358-303/2015.
340. Ruling of the Supreme Court of Lithuania in criminal case No. 2K-7-2/2007.

601. Moreover, a court may impose an imprisonment not exceeding the average punishment provided for in the sanction of an article of the Special Part of the CC for the committed crime upon a person who participated in the commission of an intentional murder, where he/she makes a confession regarding all the criminal acts committed by him/her and actively assists in the detection of the intentional murder committed by the members of an organised group or a criminal association. These rules are not applicable to the organiser or leader of an intentional murder, organised group or criminal association.

II. Grounds for Increasing Punishment

602. The Lithuanian criminal law provides only two grounds for an increasing punishment – aggravating circumstances, which influence the size of the punishment within the limits of the sanction of an article of the Special Part of the CC, and special sentencing rules for a dangerous repeat offender.

A. *Aggravating Circumstances*

603. Article 60 of the CC provides an exhaustive list of the aggravating circumstances:

(1) the act has been committed by a group of accomplices. Taking into consideration the nature and extent of participation of each accomplice in the commission of the criminal act, a court shall have the right not to recognise this circumstance as aggravating;
(2) the act has been committed by an organised group;
(3) the act has been committed by reason of disorderly conduct or for mercenary reasons;
(4) the act has been committed by torturing the victim or subjecting him/her to taunts;
(5) the act has been committed against a young child;
(6) the act has been committed against a person who, due to an illness, disability, old age or for other reasons, was in a helpless state, without his request, or the act has been committed against a minor taking advantage of his/her dependency or through abuse of trust, authority or influence;
(7) the act has been committed against a woman known to be pregnant;
(8) the act has been committed by taking advantage of a public or other person's disaster;
(9) the act has been committed by a person under the influence of alcohol, narcotic, psychotropic or other psychoactive substances, where these circumstances influenced the commission of the criminal act;
(10) the act has been committed in a publicly dangerous manner or by using explosives, explosive materials or firearms;
(11) the committed act has inflicted serious damage or a real threat to the victim's life;

(12) the act has been committed in order to express hatred towards a group of persons or a person belonging thereto on grounds of age, sex, sexual orientation, disability, race, nationality, language, descent, social status, religion, convictions or views;
(13) the act has been committed by a repeat offender;
(14) crimes of a sexual nature against minor, which were committed by a close relative or family member of the victim, or a person living together with victim.

604. When imposing a punishment, a court shall not take into consideration an aggravating circumstance, which is provided for in the law as a constituting element of the definition of the criminal act.

B. Recidivism

605. The Lithuanian criminal law sets two kinds of previous conviction – repeat offence and dangerous repeat offence.

606. Repeat offence means a situation when a person already was convicted for an intentional crime, which he/she had committed after attaining the age of majority, where his/her prior conviction has not expired yet or has not been expunged, repeatedly commits one or several intentional crimes. Such a person shall be considered a repeat offender. Repeat offender is an aggravating circumstance in sentencing.

607. A person having previous conviction means the person convicted of commission of a crime in respect of whom a judgment of conviction passed by a court of the Republic of Lithuania or another Member State of the EU has become effective. The person convicted of commission of a crime in a non-EU Member State, provided that a notice of the coming into effect of a judgment of conviction passed by a court of that state is received under international treaties of Lithuania, shall also be considered as person having previous conviction.

608. The rules for the recognition of a person as a repeat offender (even correctly implement the provisions of Council Framework Decision 2008/675/JHA of 24 July 2008 on taking account of convictions in the Member States of the European Union in the course of new criminal proceedings[341]), are very broad and raise certain doubts, as these rules preclude the court from assessing either the gravity of the crimes constituting a repeated crime (e.g., a repeat offender may include both a person who has committed two minor crimes and a person who has committed two

341. Council Framework Decision 2008/675/JHA of 24 Jul. 2008 on taking account of convictions in the Member States of the European Union in the course of new criminal proceedings, *OJ L 220, 15.8.2008, p. 32–34.*

grave crimes, etc.), or the type of the crimes (e.g., a repeat offender will also mean a person who has committed, for instance, two 'privileged' crimes), etc.[342]

609. Repeat offence shall be considered dangerous, and the offender may be recognised as a dangerous repeat offender by a court where this person: (1) commits a new grave crime while having an unexpired conviction for the commission of a grave crime; or (2) already being a repeat offender, commits a new grave crime; or (3) already being a repeat offender, where at least one of the crimes constituting a repeat offence is a grave crime, commits a new serious crime; or (4) commits a new serious crime while having three prior convictions for the commission of serious crimes.

610. When passing a judgment of conviction for the most recent crime committed, a court may recognise a person as a dangerous repeat offender having regard to the offender's personality, the extent to which criminal intentions have been accomplished, the nature of participation in the commission of the crimes and other circumstances of the case.

611. When deciding on the recognition of a person as a dangerous repeat offender, a court shall have no regard to prior convictions for the crimes committed by the person below the age of 18, the crimes committed through negligence, the crimes for which the conviction has expired or has been expunged, also the crimes committed abroad, if (1) such a crime is not regarded as a crime under the CC; or (2) the information received about the judgment of the conviction passed by the court of another State is not sufficient; etc.

612. The Lithuanian criminal law provides a special sentencing rule for a dangerous repeat offender. This rule determines that for the commission of an intentional crime, for a dangerous repeat offender, a punishment more severe than the average imprisonment prescribed by the sanction of an article of the Special Part of the CC for the committed crime shall be imposed. Another punishment may be imposed upon a dangerous repeat offender only on the grounds of the imposition of a more lenient punishment than provided for by the law (*see* paragraphs 613, 617–620, 622, 623).

III. Grounds for Mitigating Punishment

613. The Lithuanian criminal law provides four grounds for a mitigating punishment – mitigating circumstances, which influence the size of the punishment within the limits of the sanction of an article of the Special Part of the CC, and three special (exceptional) sentencing rules, which allow to impose a more lenient punishment than provided in the sanction of the article of the Special Part of the CC. It

342. Švedas G. European Union criminal law and its influence on the institutes of the General Part of Lithuanian criminal law // Lithuanian legal system under the influence of European Union law, Vilnius, 2014, p. 158–159.

should be noted that application of the special sentencing rules, according to the jurisprudence of the Supreme Court of Lithuania, is a discretionary right of the court (but not an obligation).[343]

A. Mitigating Circumstances

614. Article 59 of the CC provides an illustrative list of the mitigating circumstances:

(1) the offender has provided assistance to the victim or otherwise actively avoided or attempted to avoid more serious consequences;
(2) the offender has confessed to commission of an act provided for by a criminal law and sincerely regrets or has assisted in the detection of this act or identification of the persons who participated therein;
(3) the offender has voluntarily compensated for or eliminated the damage incurred;
(4) the act has been committed due to a very difficult financial condition or desperate situation of the offender;
(5) the act has been committed as a result of mental or physical coercion, where such a coercion does not eliminate criminal liability;
(6) the commission of the act has been influenced by a provoking or venturesome behaviour of the victim;
(7) the act has been committed at the request of the victim, who is in a desperate situation;
(8) the act has been committed in violation of conditions of detention of a person who has committed the criminal act, immediate necessity, discharge of professional duty or performance of an assignment of law enforcement institutions, conditions of industrial or economic risk or lawfulness of a scientific experiment;
(9) the act has been committed by exceeding the limits of self-defence, where a criminal law provides for liability for exceeding the limits of self-defence;
(10) the act has been committed in a state of extreme agitation caused by unlawful actions of the victim;
(11) the act has been committed by a person of diminished capacity;
(12) the act has been committed by a person intoxicated by alcohol or drugs against his will;
(13) a voluntary attempt to renounce commission of the criminal act has been unsuccessful.

343. Ruling of the Supreme Court of Lithuania in criminal case No. 2K-7-287/2009.

615. Since the list is illustrative, the court may also recognise other circumstances as mitigating, which have not been indicated in this list, for example, voluntary compensation of the part of the incurred damage,[344] careless behaviour of the victim,[345] excessive duration of the criminal prosecution[346] and difficult personal or family situation,[347] etc.

616. When imposing a punishment, a court shall not take into consideration a mitigating circumstance, which is provided for in the law as constituting element of the definition of the criminal act.

B. Sentencing Rules Permitting to Mitigate the Punishment

1. Imposition of a More Lenient Punishment than Provided for by a Law

617. The imposition of a more lenient punishment than provided for by the law is an exceptional sentencing rule allowing to impose the type of the punishment or size of imprisonment, which is more lenient than provided in the sanction of the article of the Special Part of the CC. The Constitutional Court, recognising the necessity of such a sentencing rule, has noted that:

> the legislature, by choosing the way of creation of the sanction for the commission of a criminal act when the article itself, establishing liability for the specified criminal act, provides such minimum punishment of imprisonment which is strict, alongside must establish by law the legal regulation according to which a court, by imposing a punishment for this criminal act, must have an opportunity to take account of all circumstances of the case mitigating criminal liability, as well as of those which have not been expressis verbis established by law, and to impose a milder punishment than that provided for by law.[348]

618. Article 62 of the CC provides three grounds, in which a court may impose a more lenient punishment than provided for by the law for every criminal act:

(1) where a person who has committed a criminal act freely and voluntarily gives himself/herself up or reports this act, confesses to the commission thereof and sincerely regrets and (or) assists pretrial investigators and a court in detecting the criminal act and has fully or partially compensated for or eliminated the incurred property damage;

---

344. Ruling of the Supreme Court of Lithuania in criminal case No. 2K-127/2011.
345. Ruling of the Supreme Court of Lithuania in criminal case No. 2K-433/2011.
346. Rulings of the Supreme Court of Lithuania in criminal cases No. 2K-274-788/2019 and No. 2K-75-222/2020.
347. Rulings of the Supreme Court of Lithuania in criminal cases No. 2K-112/2003 and No. 2K-274-788/2019.
348. Decision of the Constitutional Court of Lithuania of 10 Jun. 2003, *Valstybės žinios*, 2003, No. 57-2552.

(2) in the case of the presence of mitigating circumstances, at least partial compensation for or elimination of property damage, if any has been incurred, and where:
   (a) the offender maintains disabled persons or persons suffering from a grave illness and no one else can look after them, or
   (b) the offender maintains young children and there would be no one to look after them if the punishment provided for by the law was imposed; or
   (c) the offender as an accomplice had only a secondary role in the commission of the criminal act; or
   (d) the act was discontinued at the stage of preparation to commit the crime or at the stage of an attempt to commit the criminal act; or
   (e) the act has been committed by exceeding the limits of self-defence, or
   (f) the act has been committed in violation of conditions of detention of the person who has committed the criminal act, immediate necessity, discharge of professional duty or performance of an assignment of law enforcement institutions, conditions of an industrial or economic risk or lawfulness of a scientific experiment;

(3) where a person who participated in the commission of an intentional murder, makes a confession regarding all the criminal acts committed by him/her and actively assists in detecting an intentional murder committed by members of an organised group or criminal association and where:
   (a) the murder has been committed as a result of a threat or coercion; or
   (b) the offender as an accomplice had only a secondary role in the commission of the murder; or
   (c) the act has been discontinued at the stage of preparation for the commission of the murder or at the stage of attempting to commit the murder.

619. In the presence of the indicated conditions, a court may:

(1) impose a more lenient punishment than the minimum punishment provided for in the sanction of an article of the CC for a criminal act committed; or
(2) impose a more lenient fine than the minimum fine provided in the General Part of the CC or a more lenient punishment for dangerous repeat offender, or
(3) impose a more lenient type of punishment than provided for in the sanction of an article of the CC for a criminal act committed.

620. It should be noted that, in the doctrine of the Lithuanian criminal law, very strict conditions for the imposition of a more lenient punishment than provided for by the law were criticised.[349]

349. Dapšys A., Misiūnas J., Čaplinskas A. Bausmės individualizavimo teisinės problemos, Vilnius, Teisės institutas, 2008, p. 62–63.

2. Imposition of a Punishment Upon Hearing a Case Under the Simplified Procedure or upon Conducting a Summary Examination of Evidence

621. The imposition of a punishment upon hearing a case under the simplified procedure or upon conducting a summary examination of evidence is an exceptional sentencing rule allowing to reduce the imposed punishment. This sentencing rule provides that 'upon hearing a criminal case under the accelerated procedure or upon conducting a summary examination of evidence, also when criminal proceedings are terminated by a penal order, the convict shall be imposed a punishment which, by the same judgment, shall be reduced by one-third' (Article 64(1) of the CC). The specified rule shall be applicable solely in cases when a person pleads guilty.

3. Imposition of a Punishment Applying the Principle of Justice

622. The imposition of a punishment by applying the principle of justice is an exceptional sentencing rule, which provides that where imposition of the punishment provided for in the sanction of an article of the Special Part of the CC is evidently in contravention to the principle of justice, a court may impose, taking into consideration the purpose of the punishment, a commuted punishment subject to a reasoned decision. This sentencing rule allows the court to impose the general minimum of any type of punishment, which is more lenient than provided in the sanction of an article of the Special Part of the CC for the committed criminal act.

623. When explaining this sentencing rule, the Supreme Court of Lithuania emphasised that

> court‘s decision to apply the principle of justice may be made by taking into consideration, in particular, a set of factors (circumstances) identified in a specific case. Basically, there has to be such a set of factors/circumstances, according to which the punishment, though formally meeting all basic principles of the imposition of a punishment (it may be even minimum of the sanction), does not fulfil all the purposes, or vice versa – it basically fulfils just one – the punishing of the offender.[350]

IV. Concurrence of Offences

624. The CC does not provide a legal definition of the single criminal act and their forms as well as the concurrence of criminal acts and their forms; the jurisprudence of the Supreme Court of Lithuania and the doctrine of the Lithuanian criminal law are in charge of it.

---

350. Rulings of the Supreme Court of Lithuania in criminal cases No. 2K-P-18-648/2016 and No. 2K-111-511/2021.

625. The concurrence of criminal acts, according to the jurisprudence of the Supreme Court of Lithuania, is a situation when the offender commits two or more criminal acts until the adoption of the judgment, and there are no legal barriers for the realisation of the criminal liability for committed criminal acts.[351]

626. There are two types of the concurrence of the criminal act – concurrence by one criminal act (ideal concurrence) and concurrence by more criminal acts (real concurrence). The type of the concurrence of the criminal act determines sentencing rules for the imposition of a final combined punishment: punishment consolidation is applicable in the case of ideal concurrence, and the cumulation of punishments as a rule – in the case of real concurrence.

627. A person shall not be considered to have committed several criminal acts where he/she has committed a continuous or continued criminal act.

A. Concurrence by One Act

628. According to the jurisprudence of the Supreme Court of Lithuania, a concurrence of criminal acts by one act (ideal concurrence) occurs if the offender commits more than one criminal act provided in different articles of the Special Part of the CC by the same act.[352]

B. Real Concurrence of Offences

629. According to the jurisprudence of the Supreme Court of Lithuania, a concurrence of criminal acts by more acts (real concurrence) occurs if the offender realises more than one criminal act provided in the same or different articles of the Special Part of the CC by more acts committed in different time periods.[353]

C. Continued or Collective Offences

630. A single criminal act corresponds to one *corpus delicti* of the criminal act provided in one article of the Special Part of the CC. The single criminal act may have forms, which are comparable to the concurrence of the criminal acts, such as continuous criminal act and continued criminal act (on continuous and continued criminal act *see* paragraphs 217–220).

631. Commission of two or more criminal acts should form the concurrence of criminal acts (*see* paragraphs 624–629).

---

351. Rulings of the Supreme Court of Lithuania in criminal cases No. 2A-7-4-699/2015 and No. 2K-P-78/2012.
352. Ruling of the Supreme Court of Lithuania in criminal case No. 2A-7-4-699/2015.
353. Ruling of the Supreme Court of Lithuania in criminal case No. 2K-138-976/2015.

D. Sentencing Rules for the Commission of Several Criminals Acts

632. The Lithuanian criminal law provides special sentencing rules when several criminal acts (concurrence of criminal acts) have been committed. These rules cover two situations: (1) where several criminal acts have been committed; and (2) where a new criminal act has been committed before serving an imposed punishment, or where a new criminal act has been committed during the period of suspension of the execution of the punishment or conditional release from correctional institution. It should be noted that in both situations a final combined punishment may consist of two punishments.

633. Where several criminal acts have been committed, a court shall impose a punishment for each criminal act separately and subsequently – a final combined punishment. When imposing a final combined punishment, the court may impose either a consolidated punishment or a fully or partially cumulative punishment. A consolidated punishment means that a more severe punishment imposed shall cover a more lenient punishment and the final combined punishment shall be equal to the most severe punishment imposed for all the separate criminal acts. A court must impose a consolidated punishment where: (1) there is an ideal concurrence of criminal acts; (2) where the committed criminal acts differ markedly in their degree of dangerousness and are assigned to different types or categories of criminal acts (e.g., misdemeanour and less serious, serious or grave crime, minor and serious or grave crime, etc.[354]); (3) where an imprisonment for a period of twenty years or a life imprisonment has been imposed for the commission of one of the criminal acts.

634. A fully cumulative punishment means that all more lenient punishments which have been imposed shall be added to the most severe punishment imposed for one of the committed criminal acts. Meanwhile, a partially cumulative punishment means that more lenient punishments imposed shall be added in part to the most severe punishment imposed for one of the committed criminal acts. The reasons for choosing part of each added punishment must be indicated. The added part of the punishment may not be less than the minimum amount of the type of punishment, except when the added punishment is lower than this amount.

635. Where imposing a final combined punishment a part of the imposed punishments may be consolidated, whereas others may only be fully or partially accumulated, a court may combine punishments by the way of consolidation and accumulation of punishments. A court shall make a choice of the procedure for combining punishments upon assessing the nature and dangerousness of the committed criminal acts.

354. Rulings of the Supreme Court of Lithuania in criminal cases No. 2K-P-193/2007, No. 2A-7-8-697/2015.

636. A final combined punishment may not exceed a twenty-year of imprisonment, whereas in the cases when a punishment of another type is imposed, the punishment may not exceed the maximum punishment established for this kind of punishment, when a punishment is imposed for several criminal acts.

637. A punishment shall be imposed according to these sentencing rules also in the cases when following the passing of a judgment it is established that a person has committed one more crime or misdemeanour prior to the passing of the judgment in the first case. In this case, the fully or partially served punishment imposed by the previous judgment shall be included in the term of the punishment.

638. Where a new criminal act has been committed before serving an imposed punishment, or where a new criminal act has been committed during the period of suspension of the execution of the punishment or conditional release from correctional institution, a court shall impose a punishment for a new criminal act separately and subsequently – a final combined punishment. When imposing a final combined punishment, the court may impose a fully or partially cumulative punishment.

639. A fully cumulative punishment means that a court shall add an entire part of the punishment not served yet to a punishment imposed by a new judgment. Meanwhile, when imposing a partially cumulative punishment, a court shall add a part of the term of a punishment not served yet to a punishment imposed by a new judgment. Where the part of the not-served term of the punishment is larger, a part of the punishment imposed by the new judgment shall be added to the former part. The reasons for choosing part of each added punishment must be indicated. The added part of the punishment may not be less than the minimum amount of the type of punishment, except when the added punishment is lower than this amount.

640. A final combined punishment may not exceed a twenty-five-year of imprisonment, whereas in the cases when a punishment of another type is imposed, the punishment may not exceed the maximum punishment established for this kind of punishment, when a punishment is imposed according to these rules.

641. Where the punishment of a life imprisonment is imposed for one of the crimes committed, punishments shall be combined by consolidation and the final combined punishment shall be a life imprisonment.

V. Combination of Sentencing Rules

642. In most criminal cases, the sentencing rules are applied in combination, but the CC does not specify the hierarchy of sentencing rules. Meanwhile, the jurisprudence of the Supreme Court of Lithuania and the doctrine of the Lithuanian criminal law indicate certain interrelations between the concrete sentencing rules. For example, the Supreme Court of Lithuania has stated that:

imposition of a punishment by applying the principle of justice (paragraph 3, Article 54 of the CC) may be applicable only in a case where are no legal grounds for applying the rule of the imposition of a more lenient punishment than provided for by the law (Article 62 of the CC).[355]

643. The doctrine of the Lithuanian criminal law[356] has presented similar recommendations that the imposition of a punishment by applying the principle of justice and the imposition of a punishment upon hearing a case under the simplified procedure or upon conducting a summary examination of evidence cannot be applied together.

355. Ruling of the Supreme Court of Lithuania in criminal case No. 2K-179-699/2016.
356. Švedas G., Veršekys P., Levon J., Prapiestis D. Lietuvos Respublikos baudžiamojo kodekso bendrosios dalies vientisumo ir naujovių suderinamumo iššūkiai, Vilnius, Vilniaus universiteto leidykla, 2017, p. 188.

Part II. Criminal Procedure

Chapter 1. Principles, Institutions, Stages

§1. The Judicial Organisation

644. The judicial organisation in Lithuania was described within the overview of the judicial system (*see* paragraphs 17–24). The rules on territorial jurisdiction, competence of courts in criminal matters as well as composition of the courts mainly are contained in the Code of Criminal Procedure, the Law on Courts and the Law on the Establishment of District Courts.[357] Also, some rules on the jurisdiction of the courts in criminal matters are prescribed in the CC. These rules define main principles concerning the validity of criminal laws with respect to space (*see* paragraphs 161–166).

645. The territory of the activity of the district and regional courts is established in the Law on the Establishment of District Courts and the Law on the Establishment of the Supreme Court of Lithuania, Appeal Court of Lithuania, Regional Courts and Determination of the Territory of the Activity of the Regional Courts.[358] The Supreme Court of Lithuania and the Court of Appeal of Lithuania shall exercise jurisdiction over the whole territory of the Republic.

I. Trial Jurisdictions

646. According to Article 233 of the Code of Criminal Procedure, every criminal case must be heard by a court of the same composition. If any of the judges may no longer be present, for any reason, during the hearing, he/she must be replaced by another judge, and the hearing of the case, as a rule, must start from the beginning.

647. If the hearing of a criminal case may take a long time, an alternate judge may be appointed. The alternate judge must be present in the courtroom from the start of the hearing of the case, and where the examining judge cannot be present

357. Lietuvos Respublikos apylinkių teismų įsteigimo įstatymo Nr. I-2375 pakeitimo įstatymas, TAR, 2016-06-30, No. 2016-17973.

358. Dėl Lietuvos Aukščiausiojo Teismo, Lietuvos apeliacinio teismo, apygardų teismų įsteigimo, apygardų teismų veiklos teritorijų nustatymo ir Lietuvos Respublikos prokuratūros reformavimo, *Valstybės žinios*, 1994, No. 50-932.

during the hearing of the case the alternate judge shall replace him/her. If the alternate judge does not request the court proceeding to be renewed or if the case is heard only by one judge who does not make such a decision, the case shall continue to be heard without the renewal.

648. The composition of the courts depends on the instance at which they are proceeding and on the type of the court. The Code of Criminal Procedure and the Law on Courts provide that in district courts criminal cases shall be heard by one judge, with the exception when a Chairman of the court composes a chamber of three judges. In regional court, criminal cases also shall be heard by one judge. The exception is criminal cases where persons are charged with committing grave crimes (for which life imprisonment may be imposed) as well as cases where the accused were, during the commission of the crime, the President of the Republic of Lithuania, members of the *Seimas* or the government, justices of the Constitutional Court, judges or prosecutors. These cases shall be heard by a chamber of three judges of a regional court.

649. In the Appeal Court criminal cases shall be heard by the chamber of three judges.

650. In the Supreme Court criminal cases shall be heard by the chamber of three judges, or an extended chamber of seven judges, or the plenary session (also, *see* paragraph 121).

651. It should be noted that all judges are professionals in Lithuania. However, on 11 October 2016 Seimas has adopted the Conception on the establishment of the institute lay judges,[359] which provides for the establishment of lay judges who shall participate in trials of certain categories of criminal cases. It should be noted that amendments to the Constitution will be necessary for the implementation of this conception.

652. The trial jurisdictions can be divided into first instance, appellate instance and cassation instance jurisdictions. The Code of Criminal Procedure determines the substantive competence of the district and regional courts as the courts of the first instance. The main criterion establishing the substantive competence is the seriousness of the criminal act, but it may also be the status of the offender. All criminal cases, with the exception of those, which come within the jurisdiction of a regional court, are under the jurisdiction of a district court. This rule means that the district court has jurisdiction to decide criminal cases where charges are against persons who committed misdemeanours, negligent crimes, minor and less serious crimes and few serious crimes.[360] Criminal cases where charges are against persons who committed serious and grave crimes (with the exception of these serious and grave

359. Lietuvos Respublikos Seimo 2016 m. spalio 11 d. nutarimas Nr. XII-2676 ‘Dėl Visuomeninių teisėjų (tarėjų) instituto teismuose koncepcijos patvirtinimo’, TAR, 2016, No. 25101.
360. Goda G., Kazlauskas M., Kuconis P. Baudžiamojo proceso teisė, Vilnius, Registrų centras, 2011, p. 365.

crimes (severe health impairment (paragraph 1, Article 135 of the CC), rape (paragraphs 1, 2 and 3, Article 149 of the CC), sexual assault (paragraphs 1, 2 and 3, Article 150 of the CC), theft (paragraph 3 Article 178 of the CC), robbery (paragraphs 2 and 3, Article 180 of the CC), swindling (paragraph 2, Article 182 of the CC) and unlawful possession of narcotic or psychotropic substances for the purpose of distribution thereof or unlawful possession of a large quantity of narcotic or psychotropic substances (paragraphs 1 and 2, Article 260 of the CC) which are assigned to the jurisdiction of the district court), as well as cases where the accused were, during commission of the crime, President of the Republic of Lithuania, members of the *Seimas* or the government, justices of the Constitutional Court, judges or prosecutors shall come within the jurisdiction of a regional court.

653. A regional court shall have the right to take any criminal case coming within the jurisdiction of the district court in the territory of this regional court.

654. The rules on territorial jurisdiction determine which of the courts have the competence to decide the criminal case. The main rule concerning the territorial jurisdiction of courts on each level of the courts' system is the principle of *forum delicti commissi.* It means that a criminal case shall come within the jurisdiction of the court of the territory where a criminal act was committed. Where criminal acts have been committed in the territories under the jurisdiction of several courts, a criminal case shall be heard by the court in the territory in which most criminal acts were committed. If the number of committed criminal acts is equal, a criminal case shall be heard by the court in the territory in which the last criminal act was committed. Where a criminal act was committed on board of a sea vessel or an aircraft of the Republic of Lithuania and the mentioned rule of place of the committed criminal act cannot be applied, the case shall come within the jurisdiction of the court of the territory where the registration port of the vessel or aircraft is situated.

655. Another rule concerning territorial jurisdiction is the principle of *forum dimicili.* It means that if it is impossible to establish the place where a criminal act was committed or where a criminal act was committed abroad, the case shall come within the jurisdiction of the court of the territory where the accused has permanent residence. If the accused has no permanent residence in the Republic of Lithuania, the case shall come within the jurisdiction of the court of the territory where the pre-trial investigation was completed.

656. Where a case involving charges against one or several persons who have committed several criminal acts comes within the jurisdiction of a regional court in respect of at least one criminal act or one suspect, it shall be heard by a regional court.

657. Article 227 of the Code of Criminal Procedure provides that a court, upon establishing prior to the trial, that the criminal case received does not come under its jurisdiction, shall refer the case according to jurisdiction. The court, upon establishing that the case which is being heard comes within the jurisdiction of another court of the same category shall continue the hearing until the disposition of the case, without referring it to another court. It shall not be permitted to refer a case to a district court, if the trial proceeding is commenced at the regional court. A district court, upon establishing during the trial that the case comes within the jurisdiction of a regional court shall refer it, in all cases, according to its jurisdiction.

658. Article 229 of the Code of Criminal Procedure states that in order to protect the essential interests of the State security, public order or administration of justice, a criminal case may be referred from the court with jurisdiction over the case to another court. Referral of the criminal case from the court with jurisdiction over to another court shall be permitted only before it is submitted for trial. The issue of referral of the criminal case from one court to another shall be decided as follows: (1) where the case is referred from one district court to another district court – by the Chairman of the regional court of the territory where the district courts belong or the Chairman of a criminal division of this court; (2) where the case is referred from a district court of one regional court to a district court of another regional court or from one regional court to another regional court – by the Chairman of the Court of Appeals of Lithuania or the Chairman of the criminal division of this court; (3) where the case is referred from one territorial chamber to another chamber of the same district court – by the Chairman of the district court.

659. The Chairman of a superior court or the Chairman of a criminal division of this court is obliged to settle all raised disputes over jurisdiction issue.

II. Investigating Jurisdictions

660. Investigation jurisdictions (i.e., court competence regarding the outcome of the pretrial investigation or the question of indictment) do not exist in the criminal justice system of Lithuania. Following the legal tradition of the continental European countries (e.g., Germany), the prosecutor in Lithuania is a full 'owner' of the pretrial investigation. Article 118 of the Constitution prescribes that only the prosecutor shall prosecute criminal cases on behalf of the State, shall carry out a pretrial investigation, and shall supervise the activities of pretrial investigators and institutions. These constitutional provisions are laid down more explicitly in the Law on the Prosecution Office,[361] which prescribes that prosecutors shall: (1) organise and lead pretrial investigations;[362] (2) conduct pretrial investigations or separate investigative actions; (3) control the procedural and intelligent activities of the pretrial investigative bodies; (4) sustain a criminal charge before the court; (5) supervise the execution of judgments; (6) coordinate the activities of pretrial investigative bodies; etc.

361. Lietuvos Respublikos prokuratūros įstatymas, *Valstybės žinios*, 2003, No. 42-1919.
362. The Prosecutor General has adopted a methodological recommendations on this issue: Generalinio prokuroro įsakymas 'Dėl Rekomendacijos dėl prokuroro veiklos organizuojant ikiteisminį tyrimą ir jam vadovaujant', *Valstybės žinios*, 2008, No. 72-2783.

661. The criminal procedure of Lithuania also provides a pretrial judge (*see* paragraphs 48, 909, 910). According to the doctrine of the Lithuanian criminal procedure, the pretrial judge is a passive participant of the pretrial investigation, i.e., he/she has no rights to perform any investigative actions on his/her own initiative. The main role of the pretrial judge is to apply coercive procedural measures, to provide judicial control over the prosecutor's and pretrial investigator's actions and decisions during the pretrial investigation and to control the taking of evidence (e.g., examination of witness, victim or suspect), etc.[363]

662. It should be noted that the Lithuanian law on criminal procedure establishes the rules concerning the place of the pretrial investigation and the substantive competence of the pretrial investigation institutions. Article 174 of the Code of the Criminal Procedure provides that a pretrial investigation shall be conducted by a prosecutor or a pretrial investigation institution, which have jurisdiction of the territory where a criminal act has been committed. With a view to ensuring a speedier and exhaustive investigation of a criminal act, a prosecutor or a pretrial investigation institution of another location may be tasked with conducting the pretrial investigation. A prosecutor or a pretrial investigation of another location shall be tasked to conduct pretrial investigation of a criminal act by a superior prosecutor.

663. Where it is necessary to conduct investigative actions in another location, a prosecutor or a pretrial investigation institution may conduct these actions themselves or they may direct an appropriate prosecutor or a pretrial investigation institution to conduct them. A prosecutor shall have the right to direct a prosecutor or any pretrial investigation institution of another location to conduct investigative actions.

664. The substantive competence of the pretrial investigation institutions (police, State Border Guard Service, the Special Investigations Service, the Military Police, the Financial Crimes Investigations Service, the State Fire Prevention Service, the Customs, etc.) is prescribed in laws and the Prosecutor General Recommendation on distribution of the pretrial investigation of criminal acts between pretrial investigation authorities[364] establishing the lists of criminal acts, for which a concrete institution should commence the pretrial investigation.

---

363. Goda G., Kazlauskas M., Kuconis P. Baudžiamojo proceso teisė, Vilnius, Registrų centras, 2011, p. 296–298.
364. Generalinio prokuroro rekomendacija 'Dėl nusikalstamų veikų tyrimo paskirstymo ikiteisminio tyrimo įstaigoms', *Valstybės žinios*, 2008, No. 94-3712.

§2. The Stages of the Penal Process

I. Two Basic Distinctions

665. Lithuanian criminal procedure is divided into the process stages. The Code of Criminal Procedure and doctrine of the Lithuanian criminal procedure[365] distinguish these stages of the criminal procedure: pretrial investigation, criminal proceedings before the court of first instance, criminal proceedings before the Court of Appeal, execution of the judgment or ruling that came into effect and criminal proceedings before the cassation court. All process stages are either mandatory (which are necessary for the criminal procedure, e.g., pretrial investigation, court trial) or optional (appeal and cassation procedure, etc.).

666. Pretrial investigation is a first stage of the criminal procedure in Lithuania. The pretrial investigation starts from the date of opening a pretrial investigation and ends with the transfer of the indictment, or any other final procedural act to the court.[366] The main tasks of the pretrial investigation are to: (a) promptly and properly identify all the circumstances of the criminal act; (b) identify the person who committed the criminal act; (c) enable a proper examination of the case in the court; (d) take necessary measures to ensure the right to damages and other rights for the participants in criminal proceedings. When these challenges are fulfilled, the pretrial investigation has to be completed, and the criminal procedure passes to the second phase: trial in the Court of First Instance. The preparation of an indictment (the traditional function of the prosecutor) is not considered as a separate and independent phase of a criminal process, and it is an integral part of the pretrial investigation. The prosecutor chooses the moment of the indictment. The prosecutor, in organising, leading or conducting the pretrial investigation actions himself/herself, has to determine when the tasks of the pretrial investigation are fulfilled. Such decision is made by the prosecutor only when he/she considers that the circumstances of the committed criminal act are identified, there is no more need of any investigative actions and it is clear that the trial court will be able to prove the guilt of the suspect.[367] Furthermore, it should be stressed that the institute of judicial inquiry does not exist in the Lithuanian criminal procedure and the pretrial investigation is a unified stage without any substantive subdivisions.

667. The second major stage of the criminal procedure is the criminal proceedings before the court of first instance. This is a procedural stage of activity, starting from the receipt of a criminal case in the court and ending with the adoption and publication of a final procedural act of the court (normally the court's judgment, and

365. Ažubalytė R., Jurka R., Zajančkauskienė J. Baudžiamojo proceso teisė. Bendroji dalis. I knyga, Vilnius, Registrų centras, 2016, p. 44.
366. Goda G., Kazlauskas M., Kuconis P. Baudžiamojo proceso teisė, Vilnius, Registrų centras, 2011, p. 286.
367. Goda G., Kazlauskas M., Kuconis P. Baudžiamojo proceso teisė, Vilnius, Registrų centras, 2011, p. 342.

sometimes its ruling). At this stage, the court must resolve the criminal case substantially and answer to the question of whether the accused is guilty of the criminal act with which he/she is charged.[368] In case the accused is found guilty, the court also must decide about the punishment or other form of realisation of the criminal liability.

668. The third stage of the criminal procedure is criminal proceedings before the Court of Appeal. The appeal process is a control stage of the criminal proceedings arising after the examination of criminal cases at first instance. This phase of the procedure is optional, since it occurs only if the participants in the criminal proceedings or the prosecutor appeal the judgment or ruling of the first instance court, and ends after the Court of Appeal instance adopts and declares a judgment or ruling. The main purpose of an appeal is to check the legality and feasibility of the judgment or ruling of the first instance court, and if necessary to correct its errors.

669. The fourth major stage of the criminal procedure is the execution of the judgment or ruling that came into effect. In this phase of the procedure the court executes the judgment itself (e.g., the acquittal judgment, etc.), or passes the judgment to be executed by penal institutions.

670. The fifth stage of the criminal procedure is criminal proceedings before the cassation court. The cassation process is the stage of the criminal procedure, in which under the cassation appeal of the participants in the criminal proceedings or the prosecutor, the judgment or the ruling (that came into effect) is verified as to aspects of law only. Proceedings of cassation form the uniform case law interpreting and applying laws and other legal acts.

671. The last stage of the criminal procedure is a resurrection of the criminal proceedings, which provides an opportunity for some exceptional cases to verify the legality and legitimacy of the final court judgment or ruling. The criminal proceedings may be resurrected on the newly emerged circumstances, for a clearly improper use of the CC and for the decisions of the United Nations (UN) Committee on Human Rights or the ECtHR, or Constitutional Court of Lithuania.

II. The Preparatory Inquiry

A. *Pretrial Investigation*

1. The Police and the Prosecution Service

672. The relationship between prosecution (prosecutor) and a pretrial investigation institution (pretrial investigator) is regulated in the Code of Criminal Procedure. It was mentioned before that the main actor of the pretrial investigation is the

368. Ažubalytė R., Jurka R., Zajančkauskienė J. Baudžiamojo proceso teisė. Bendroji dalis. I knyga, Vilnius, Registrų centras, 2016, p. 45.

prosecutor. The Code of Criminal Procedure provides that the prosecutor has the right to conduct the whole of the pretrial investigation or its separate actions by himself/herself. Where the pretrial investigation or its separate actions are conducted by institutions of the pretrial investigation the prosecutor shall be obliged to supervise the course of the pretrial investigation conducted by these institutions.

673. The prosecutor shall give mandatory instructions to the pretrial investigators, rescinding their unlawful or unfounded resolutions. The prosecutor also has the right to order the application of the actions of the criminal intelligence. Where the pretrial investigation or its separate actions are conducted by pretrial investigators, the prosecutor shall be obliged to supervise the course of the pretrial investigation.

674. Reviewing (controlling) the pretrial investigation, the prosecutor has the right to specify when the pretrial investigator must present him/her with the material of the criminal case. The prosecutor also has the right to order a pretrial investigation period, to which the pretrial investigation must be completed, or the date on which the pretrial investigator must submit a short written report about the actions of the pretrial investigation it carried out, or to attend the discussion on the pretrial investigation. The pretrial investigator also must present to the prosecutor the material of the criminal case, if there are no suspects in the case after two months (or another period specified by the prosecutor) from the start of the pretrial investigation. The prosecutor must be informed separately when the pretrial investigator submits a suspicion notice for the suspect. On the conclusion of all the actions of the pretrial investigation (or when the pretrial investigation was completed), the pretrial investigator must transmit the criminal case file to the prosecutor. Upon the receipt of this information the prosecutor then decides either: a) to close the criminal case, or b) to acknowledge that there are grounds and to prepare the indictment.

675. The following decisions in the pretrial investigation may be issued only by the prosecutor: (1) on the joinder and separation of the pretrial investigation; (2) on a temporary stay of the proceeding; (3) on the discontinuation of the proceeding; (4) on the termination of the pretrial investigation; and (5) on the termination of the proceeding by drawing up the indictment. Only the prosecutor may make an application to the pretrial judge in respect of the conduct of steps within his/her competence.

676. Meanwhile, the pretrial investigation institutions (investigators), when conducting a pretrial investigation, shall have the right to perform all the actions provided for in the Code of Criminal Procedure, with the exception of those which may be performed solely by the prosecutor or a pretrial judge. The pretrial institutions (investigators) must: (1) conduct all necessary pretrial investigative actions for the disclosure of the committed criminal act; (2) comply with all the instructions of the prosecutor; and (3) report to the prosecutor at the time he/she appoints the course of the pretrial investigation.

2. The Beginning and Closing of the Pretrial Investigation

677. The legality principle applies for the pretrial investigation and the prosecution in Lithuania. This conclusion may be inferred from the Article 2 of the CCP, which states that a prosecutor and a pretrial investigator must institute criminal proceedings in every case, in which the elements of a criminal act come to light, and shall take all measures to conduct, as soon as possible, the pretrial investigation to disclose the criminal act. The legality principle in Lithuania's criminal justice system means that pretrial investigators and prosecutors must react to all information concerning the commission of criminal acts, and must adopt all necessary pretrial investigative decisions and conduct all necessary pretrial investigative actions for the detection of criminal acts.[369] It must be noted that, in the doctrine of Lithuanian criminal procedure, the principle of legality was criticised, especially in cases when the pretrial investigation of minor crimes involves the application of expensive pretrial investigative actions, for example, the European Arrest Warrant (EAW), etc.[370]

a. The Beginning of the Pretrial Investigation

678. Article 166 of the Code of Criminal Procedure specifies that any pretrial investigation shall be commenced: (1) upon the receipt of a complaint, application or report about a criminal act; (2) upon the receipt of a victim's complaint; and (3) upon establishing elements of a criminal act and drawing up of an official notice by a prosecutor or a pretrial investigator.

679. The pretrial investigation concerning these criminal acts – negligent minor harm to health (paragraph 1, Article 139 of the CC), beating or minor harm to health (paragraph 1, Article 140 of the CC), threatening to murder or causing a severe health impairment to a person or terrorisation of a person (Article 145 of the CC), restriction of freedom of a person's actions (Article 148 of the CC), illegal persecution of a person (Article 148(1) of the CC), simple rape (paragraph 1, Article 149 of the CC), simple sexual assault (paragraph 1, Article 150 of the CC), simple sexual abuse (paragraph 1, Article 151 of the CC), sexual harassment (Article 152 of the CC), slander (Article 154 of the CC), unlawful violation of inviolability of a person's dwelling (Article 165 of the CC), unauthorised disclosure or use of information about a person's private life (Article 168 of the CC), theft (paragraphs 1 and 4, Article 178 of the CC), unlawful use of energy and communications services (paragraphs 1 and 3, Article 179 of the CC), swindling (paragraphs 1 and 3, Article 182 of the CC), misappropriation of property (paragraphs 1 and 3, Article 183 of the CC), squandering of property (paragraphs 1 and 3, Article 184 of the CC), causing property damage by deceit (Article 186 of the CC), destruction of or damage to

---

369. Goda G., Kazlauskas M., Kuconis P. Baudžiamojo proceso teisė, Vilnius, Registrų centras, 2011, p. 15–16.
370. Čepas A., Švedas G. Tarptautinė teisminė pagalba baudžiamosiose bylose. Asmenų, įtariamų padarius nusikalstamą veiką, išdavimas baudžiamajam persekiojimui (ekstradicija, perdavimas Tarptautiniam baudžiamajam teismui arba pagal Europos arešto orderį), Vilnius, TIC, 2008, p. 88–90.

property (paragraphs 1 and 3, Article 187 of the CC), destruction of or damage to property through negligence (Article 188 of the CC), self-willed conduct (paragraph 1, Article 294 of the CC) and contempt for the memory of the deceased (Article 313of the CC), shall be commenced only if there is a victim's complaint or an application of his/her lawful representative. In these cases pretrial investigation may also be commenced by a prosecutor's request, the committed criminal act is of public importance or if criminal act inflicted damage to a person who for compelling reasons cannot defend his/her legitimate interests and there is no victim's complaint.

680. If the criminal acts show signs of domestic violence, the pretrial investigation will be initiated even if there is no complaint from the victim or a statement by his/her legal representative.

681. When the prosecutor receives a complaint, an application or communication about a criminal act or where the prosecutor himself/herself establishes elements of a criminal act he/she shall start the pretrial investigation at the earliest opportunity. After the start of the pretrial investigation the prosecutor either performs the actions of the pretrial investigation himself/herself, or directs a pretrial investigation institution to perform them.

682. According to Article 168 of the Code of Criminal Procedure and the Prosecutor General's recommendations,[371] following the receipt of a complaint, an application or a report, and, where necessary, its updated version, the prosecutor or the pretrial investigator may refuse to commence a pretrial investigation only where the facts stated in the complaint, application or the report about the criminal act are obviously disinterested, or the circumstances, which are established in the law of the criminal procedure and make the criminal procedure unavailable, are clear. It should be noted that in the course of updating a complaint, an application or a report, the prosecutor or the pretrial investigator may gather additional information, for example, by asking the person who has filed the complaint, by taking documents from the State institutions, etc.

683. In case of a refusal to commence a pretrial investigation, the prosecutor or the pretrial investigator shall draw up a reasoned resolution. A copy of the resolution to refuse commencement of the pretrial investigation shall be sent to the person who has filed the complaint, application or report. The pretrial investigator shall, within 24 hours, send a copy of the resolution to the prosecutor. The resolution of the pretrial investigator not to commence the pretrial investigation may be appealed against the prosecutor, and the prosecutor's resolution may be appealed to the pretrial judge, and the ruling of the pretrial judge may be appealed to the region court.

684. A pretrial investigation must be carried out in an expedited manner and not later than: (1) three months for the investigation of the misdemeanour; (2) six

371. Generalinio prokuroro įsakymu patvirtinta rekomendacija 'Dėl ikiteisminio tyrimo pradžios ir jos registravimo tvarkos', *Valstybės žinios*, 2008, No. 94-3713.

months for the investigation negligent crime, minor and less serious crimes; (3) nine months for the investigation of the serious and grave crimes. These terms may be extended by the decision of the superior prosecutor due to the complexity, high volume or other relevant circumstances of the case. The pretrial investigation must be a priority in cases where suspects are arrested, as well as cases in which suspects or victims are minors.

b. The Closing of the Pretrial Investigation

685. The pretrial investigation may be closed under the condition that all the necessary pretrial investigation actions provided by the Code of Criminal Procedure have been conducted, and the case has been sufficiently clarified that the prosecutor may decide (a) to file the indictment, or (b) to terminate the pretrial investigation.

C. The Judicial Inquiry

686. As it was mentioned before, the investigating jurisdictions and judicial inquiry stage do not exist in the Lithuanian criminal procedure. The inquiry in court is a part of the trial (the criminal proceedings before the court of first instance).

III. The Prosecution

687. As it was mentioned before, the prosecution and preparation of an indictment did not create a separate stage of the criminal procedure and is a part of a pretrial investigation stage.

A. The Attribution and the Object of the Right to Prosecute

688. The Lithuanian criminal procedure provides only one type of prosecution—State prosecution.

689. The State prosecution is maintained by the State prosecutor. Where the prosecutor is satisfied that sufficient evidence has been gathered during the pretrial investigation as to the culpability of the suspect for committing a criminal act, he/she shall notify the suspect, his/her defence counsel, the victim, the plaintiff and the accused in the civil action and their representatives that the pretrial investigation is finished and they have a right to examine the case file and make motions for additional pretrial investigation actions. The prosecutor must pass a reasoned decision on any motions for additional pretrial investigation actions. Where the pretrial investigation or the majority of its actions was conducted by a pretrial investigation institution, the prosecutor may order that the pretrial investigation institution submit a short written report about the pretrial investigation he/she carried out.[372] Afterwards the prosecutor shall draft the indictment. The indictment shall state: (1) the name of the court which will hear the criminal case; (2) the name, surname, date of birth, marital status, profession, workplace of the suspect, and, at the prosecutor's discretion, any other personal information; (3) a brief description of the criminal act: the place, time, forms, motives, consequences and other important circumstances; information about the victim; extenuating or aggravating circumstances for the suspect; (4) the basic information on which the prosecution is based; (5) the article (paragraph and sub-paragraph) of the CC creating liability for the committed act; (6) the name and surname of the defence counsel of the suspect if he/she had a counsel during the pretrial investigation; (7) the account of the suspect, if he/she rejects the accusation.[373] The prosecutor shall also give or forward to the accused a copy of the indictment.

690. It should be noted that the Lithuanian criminal procedure has provided an institute of private prosecution and granted the victim powers to prosecute in case of ten minor crimes (e.g., negligent minor harm to health (Article 139 of the CC), beating or minor harm to health (Article 140 of the CC), etc.), but the *Seimas* abolished this institute from 1 October 2017.[374]

B. The Suspension of the Right to Prosecute

691. The suspension of the pretrial investigation means a temporary pause of the pretrial investigation that is not included in the term of the pretrial investigation. The Lithuanian criminal procedure currently provides one discretionary ground for the suspension of the pretrial investigation. When all the necessary pretrial investigation actions were carried out and all possibilities to determine the offender were exhausted, but that person has not been established, a pretrial investigation may be suspended by the reasoned decision of the prosecutor. The prosecutor's decision to suspend a pretrial investigation may be appealed against the superior prosecutor within seven days after the service of a copy of the decision to the victim or his/her representative. If the superior prosecutor dismisses the complaint, his/her decision may be appealed against with the pretrial judge.

---

372. The Prosecutor General has adopted methodological recommendation on this issue: Generalinio prokuroro įsakymas 'Dėl Rekomendacijos dėl ataskaitos, pateikiamos baigus ikiteisminį tyrimą (Baudžiamojo proceso kodekso 218 straipsnis), surašymo', *Valstybės žinios*, 2003, No. 39-1805.
373. The Prosecutor General has adopted methodological recommendation on this issue: Generalinio prokuroro įsakymas 'Dėl Rekomendacijos dėl kaltinamojo akto surašymo ir perdavimo teismui', TAR, 2015, No. 08536.
374. Lietuvos Respublikos baudžiamojo proceso kodekso 3, 22, 57, 58, 167, 256, 293, 312, 317, 320, 322, 324 straipsnių pakeitimo ir 34 straipsnio ir XXX skyriaus pripažinimo netekusiais galios įstatymas, TAR, 2017, No. 12575.

692. If the ground for the suspension of the pretrial investigation ceased, the pretrial investigation must be renewed without a separate decision by performing at least one pretrial investigative action.

C. The Dissolution of the Right to Prosecute

693. Article 3 of the Code of Criminal Procedure, provides that the criminal procedure may not be instituted, and, if instituted, must be terminated in the following cases: (1) where there are no elements of a crime or misdemeanour in the act; (2) where the period of limitation for criminal liability has expired; (3) where a person, at the moment of commission of a criminal act, has not yet reached the age of criminal responsibility; (4) in the absence of a victim's complaint or an application of his/her lawful representative, or a prosecutor's order to institute the proceeding; (5) where the accused is dead, with the exception of cases when the proceeding is necessary for the rehabilitation of the dead person or for the reopening of a case involving other persons, when new circumstances are discovered; (6) where a court judgment against a person for the same charge or a court ruling, or a prosecutor's decision to terminate the procedure for the same reason have become effective; (7) where there is a circumstance removing criminal liability (e.g., self-defence, necessity, etc.);[375] (8) where criminal prosecution has been terminated on the grounds provided in the Law on Prevention of Organised Crime.[376] If during the hearing the referred circumstances are discovered, the court shall hear the case until the end and shall hand down an acquittal.

694. Furthermore, Article 3(2) of the Code of Criminal Procedure provides a special ground for the termination of criminal procedure for the person who has immunities based on national or international law (*see* paragraphs 183–194). If the criminal act was committed by the person, who has immunities based on national or international law, the criminal proceedings are started, but a notice of suspicion cannot be written, the person cannot be questioned as a suspect or recognised as a suspect, also he/she cannot be arrested or otherwise restricted in his/her freedom. If after the completion of all not prohibited investigative actions the competent authority does not permit a person to prosecute, or the person has immunity from criminal jurisdiction, the criminal proceedings should be terminated. Criminal proceedings may be renewed when the competent authority gives the permission to prosecute or the person otherwise loses the immunity, or it is necessary to carry out the investigative actions, which are not prohibited by the laws of the Republic of Lithuania or international law.

695. Meanwhile, Article 212 of the Code of Criminal Procedure states that the pretrial investigation (and prosecution) shall be terminated: (1) where it transpires

---

375. Review of the Criminal Division of the Supreme Court of Lithuania of 7 Jun. 2010, Teismų praktika, No. 33.
376. Lietuvos Respublikos organizuoto nusikalstamumo prevencijos įstatymas, TAR, 2020-06-29, No. 14343.

during the pretrial investigation that there are circumstances provided for in Articles 3 and 3(2) of the CCP; (2) where insufficient information is gathered during the pretrial investigation to prove the suspect's culpability in committing a criminal act; (3) where the accused was released from criminal liability when a person or criminal act loses its dangerousness (Article 36 of the CC); (4) where the accused was released from criminal liability due to minor relevance of a crime (Article 37 of the CC); (5) where the accused was released from criminal liability upon reconciliation between the offender and the victim (Article 38 of the CC); (6) where the accused was released from criminal liability on bail (Article 40 of the CC); (7) where the accused was released from criminal liability when a person actively assisted in detecting the criminal acts committed by members of an organised group or a criminal association (Article 39(1) of the CC); (8) where the accused was released from criminal liability as a whistle-blower (Article 39(2) of the CC); (9) where the accused was released from criminal liability under the grounds provided in Articles of the Special Part of the CC; (10) where, under the CC, there are circumstances removing criminal liability (e.g., self-defence, necessity, etc.); (11) where several criminal acts are committed; (12) where the duration of the pretrial investigation is too long.

696. The pretrial investigation shall be terminated by the prosecutor's decision or by the prosecutor's decision, which must be confirmed by the pretrial judge. Termination of the pretrial investigation shall be communicated by sending the copies of the decision to the suspect, his/her representative, defence counsel, victim and other parties to the proceeding. The Code of Criminal Procedure prescribes that where the pretrial investigation is terminated by the prosecutor's decision, this decision may be appealed by the suspect, his/her representative, defence counsel, victim and other parties to the proceedings to a higher prosecutor, then to a pretrial judge and, eventually, to a higher court. If the prosecutor's decision to terminate the pretrial investigation has been approved by the pretrial judge, the decision of the pretrial judge to approve the prosecutor's decision may be directly appealed to a higher court. The decision of the higher court is final in all cases.

697. According to the complaints of participants in the criminal proceedings, or on his/her own initiative, the prosecutor may renew a pretrial investigation if there is a basis for doing so. The pretrial investigation, which was terminated according to the resolution of the prosecutor and that termination was confirmed by the pretrial judge, can be renewed when the pretrial judge confirms the decision of the prosecutor to renew the pretrial investigation. On the renewal of the pretrial investigation the suspect, his/her representative, defence counsel, victims and civil claimant and their representatives have to be reported. These individuals have the right to appeal the ruling to renew the pretrial investigation. If the superior prosecutor dismisses the complaint, his/her decision may be appealed against with the pretrial judge. The decision on the appeal of the pretrial judge can be appealed against with the superior court. The decision of the superior court is final and not subject to appeal.

1. Abolition of Penal Provision, Grant of Amnesty, Death of the Accused

698. The Code of Criminal Procedure did not explicitly provide the abolition of penal provision as the ground for the termination of the criminal procedure or pretrial investigation (and prosecution). On the contrary, if the abolition of penal provision relates to the *corpus delicti* of the criminal act, the criminal procedure as well as the pretrial investigation (and prosecution) may be terminated on the ground that 'where there are no elements of a crime or misdemeanour in the act' (Article 3 of the CCP).

699. The amnesty and clemency did not create the ground for the termination of the criminal procedure or pretrial investigation (and prosecution), because they are linked only to the release from the execution of the imposed punishment (but not a release from the criminal liability).

700. The death of the accused is the ground for the termination of the criminal procedure or pretrial investigation (and prosecution) with the exception of cases when the proceeding is necessary for the rehabilitation of the dead person or for the reopening of a case involving other persons, when new circumstances are discovered. The Supreme Court of Lithuania has noted that the criminal procedure or pretrial investigation (and prosecution) cannot be terminated due to death of the accused if continuation of the criminal procedure creates preconditions for the defence of unreasonably convicted or accused of a deceased person's honour and dignity.[377]

2. Too long Duration of the Pretrial Investigation

701. The Code of Criminal Procedure provides discretionary ground for the termination of the pretrial investigation and prosecution in case when the pretrial investigation lasts too long. Article 215 of the CCP provides that 'if within six months after the first interrogation of the suspect the pretrial investigation is not completed, the suspect, his/her representative or defence counsel may file a complaint with the pretrial judge for the termination of the pretrial investigation due to long duration of the pretrial investigation'. The pretrial judge for the examination of the complaint shall organise the hearing, in which suspect, his/her defence counsel and the prosecutor must participate. The pretrial judge shall adopt one of the following rulings: (1) to dismiss the complaint; (2) to order the prosecutor to complete a pretrial investigation within the time limit; or (3) to terminate the pretrial investigation.

377. Ruling of the Supreme Court of Lithuania in criminal case No. 2K-P-444/2011.

3. Commission of the Several Criminal Acts

702. The Code of Criminal Procedure provides a discretionary ground for the termination of the pretrial investigation and prosecution in case when several criminal acts were committed. Article 213 of the CCP provides that 'where the suspect is suspected of having committed several criminal acts one or several of which are misdemeanours or minor crimes while the other act or acts are serious or grave crimes, the prosecutor may terminate the pretrial investigation of misdemeanours or minor crimes'.[378] This decision may be adopted, if the prosecutor considers that in this case the criminal proceeding of serious and grave crimes will be accelerated. The pretrial investigation of misdemeanours and minor crimes cannot be terminated, if the civil action for the compensation of the damage caused by these criminal acts was brought.

4. Limitation by Time

703. The Lithuanian criminal law foresees two types of the statute of limitations of criminal liability: (1) statute of limitations of a judgment of conviction, and (2) statute of limitation for the execution of a judgment of conviction. The statute of limitations of a judgment of convictions is a circumstance barring the pretrial investigation and prosecution. It should be mentioned that, in 2010, Seimas made the important changes of the statute of limitations of a judgment of conviction, which significantly extended the terms of the period of the statute of limitations of a judgment of conviction, established the suspension of these terms due to procedural reasons, etc.[379] These changes as unfounded and inappropriate were criticised in the doctrine of the Lithuanian criminal law.[380]

704. The statute of limitations of a judgment of convictions is unconditional; the prosecutor and court must apply it, if it sets up all conditions.[381] When explaining the essence of the statute of limitations of a judgment of convictions, the Supreme Court of Lithuania stated that 'upon the expiration of the terms of the statute of limitations, the criminal proceedings cannot be carried out'.[382]

---

378. The Prosecutor General has adopted a methodological recommendation on this issue: Generalinio prokuroro įsakymas 'Dėl ikiteisminio tyrimo nutraukimo pagal naujojo Baudžiamojo proceso kodekso 213 straipsnį (kai yra padarytos kelios skirtingo sunkumo nusikalstamos veikos)', *Valstybės žinios*, 2003, Nr. 39-1805.
379. Lietuvos Respublikos baudžiamojo kodekso 95 straipsnio pakeitimo bei papildymo, Kodekso papildymo 170(2) straipsniu ir Kodekso priedo papildymo įstatymas, *Valstybės žinios*, 2010, No. 75-3792.
380. For example, Piesliakas V., Riaubaitė E. Apkaltinamojo nuosprendžio priėmimo senatis teorijoje ir teismų praktikoje, Justitia, 2010, Nr. 2, p. 11–12; Bikelis S. Senaties institutas baudžiamojoje justicijoje, Teisės institutas, 2012, p. 80, etc.
381. Lietuvos Respublikos baudžiamojo kodekso komentaras. Bendroji dalis (1-98 straipsniai), Vilnius, TIC, 2004, p. 492–493, 497.
382. Ruling of the Supreme Court of Lithuania in criminal case No. 2K-7-233/2007.

705. The statute of limitations of a judgment of conviction is, in criminal law, a set period of time, after which the person who has committed a criminal act cannot be convicted. A person who has committed a criminal act cannot be subject to a judgment of conviction where there are three conditions simultaneously:

(1) the following period has elapsed:
  (a) three years, in the event of commission of a misdemeanour;
  (b) eight years, in the event of commission of a negligent or minor intentional crime;
  (c) twelve years, in the event of commission of a less serious intentional crime;
  (d) fifteen years, in the event of commission of a serious crime;
  (e) twenty-five years, in the event of commission of a grave crime;
  (f) thirty years, in the event of commission of a crime relating to an intentional homicide; and
(2) within the indicated period the person did not hide from pretrial investigation or a trial; and
(3) within the indicated period the person did not commit a new criminal act.

706. The statute of limitations starts from the commission of a criminal act and runs until the passing of a judgment. The time of the commission of a criminal act is the time of an act (or omission) or the time of occurrence of the consequences provided for by the criminal law, where the occurrence of those consequences was desired at a different time. When explaining the time of the commission of a continued and continuous criminal act and its relation with the statute of limitations, the Supreme Court of Lithuania has stated that 'the moment, from which the term of the statute of limitations of a judgment of convictions starts, is the time when the continuous criminal act has been terminated or the last act of the continued criminal act has been committed'.[383]

707. The CC provides a special rule 'if a minor suffers from the criminal acts provided for in Chapters XVIII 'Crimes against Human Health,' XX 'Crimes against Human Liberty,' XXI 'Crimes and misdemeanours against freedom of a person's sexual self-determination and inviolability,' XXIII 'Crimes and misdemeanours against a child and a family' and XLIV 'Crimes and misdemeanours against morality' of the CC, the statute of limitations may not run out before the person reaches the age of twenty-five years', which implements the requirements of Directive 2011/92/EU of the European Parliament and of the Council of 13 December 2011 on combating the sexual abuse and sexual exploitation of children and child pornography, and replacing Council Framework Decision 2004/68/JHA.[384]

383. Ruling of the Supreme Court of Lithuania in criminal case No. 2K-P-267/2011.
384. Directive 2011/92/EU of the European Parliament and of the Council of 13 Dec. 2011 on combating the sexual abuse and sexual exploitation of children and child pornography, and replacing Council Framework Decision 2004/68/JHA, *OJ L 335, 17.12.2011, p. 1–14.*

708. Where a person who has committed a criminal act hides from the pretrial investigation or a trial, the statute of limitations shall not run. The statute of limitations shall resume running from the day when the person is detained or when he/she appears before a pretrial investigation officer, a prosecutor or the court. However, a judgment of conviction may not be passed where twenty-five years have lapsed since the commission of the criminal act by the person and thirty years have lapsed since the commission of a crime relating to an intentional homicide, and the statute of limitations has not stopped running due to commission of a new crime. When explaining the content of hiding from the pretrial investigation and trial, the Supreme Court of Lithuania has emphasised that:

> concealment is a conscious action that is carried out by a person aiming to avoid prosecution after the commission of a criminal act. These actions can be attributed to the change of residence, moving systematically from one location to another, going abroad, living without documents or false documents acquisition, the name or surname change, change in appearance, etc.[385]

709. Where a person who has committed a criminal act enjoys, under laws of the Republic of Lithuania or international legal norms, immunity from criminal liability and the competent authority does not allow his/her prosecution, the statute of limitations stops running. The statute of limitations shall resume running from the receipt of the competent authority's permission to prosecute the person who has committed the criminal act or after he/she loses the immunity by other means. In this case, a judgment of conviction cannot be passed where an established period exceeding five years has lapsed since the commencement of the statute of limitations.

710. In the course of hearing of a case before the court, the statute of limitations stops running for a period for which the court announces a break: (1) in the hearing before the court or postpones the hearing of the case due to the absence of the accused or his/her defence counsel; or (2) in the hearing before the court pending an expert examination or a professional investigation assigned by the court or satisfaction of a request for legal assistance submitted to a foreign State; or (3) in the hearing before the court and charges a prosecutor or a pretrial investigation judge with taking the procedural actions provided for in the CCP of Lithuania; or (4) in the hearing before the court for the new defence counsel of the accused to familiarise with the case file.

711. Where a person commits a new intentional criminal act before the expiry of the indicated terms, the statute of limitations stops running. In such a case, the statute of limitations in respect of the first criminal act shall start running from the commission of a new crime or misdemeanour.

385. Ruling of the Supreme Court of Lithuania in criminal case No. 2K-7-371/2011.

712. According to the international treaties of Lithuania,[386] the following crimes have no statute of limitations: (1) genocide (Article 99 of the CC), (2) treatment of persons prohibited under international law (Article 100 of the CC), (3) enforced disappearance (Article 100(1) of the CC), (4) torture (Article 100(3) of the CC), (5) killing of the persons protected under international humanitarian law (Article 101 of the CC), (6) deportation or transfer of civilians (Article 102 of the CC), (7) causing bodily harm to, torture or other inhuman treatment of the persons protected under international humanitarian law or violation of protection of their property (Article 103 of the CC), (8) forcible use of civilians or prisoners of war in the armed forces of the enemy (Article 105 of the CC), (9) destruction of protected objects or plunder of national valuable properties (Article 106 of the CC), (10) aggression (Article 110 of the CC), (11) prohibited military attack (Article 111 of the CC), (12) use of prohibited means of warfare (Article 112 of the CC) and (13) negligent performance of the commander's duties (Article 113(1) of the CC).

5. *Non bis in idem* (Provisions Against Double Jeopardy)

713. The principle *non bis in idem* is provided in the Constitution, the CC and the Code of Criminal Procedure. This principle means a prohibition that no person may be punished for the same violation of law twice. In the Lithuanian criminal procedure the principle *non bis in idem* requires to terminate the criminal procedure or pretrial investigation (and prosecution), where a court judgment against a person for the same charge or a court ruling, or a prosecutor's decision to terminate the procedure for the same reason have become effective (also, *see* paragraph 139).

§3. The Legal Position of the Accused and the Civil Party

I. Introductory Remarks

714. In the doctrine and law of the Lithuanian criminal procedure several terms to designate the defendant are used. The term defendant is used only in the doctrine of the Lithuanian criminal procedure and includes all possible legal statuses of the person who has committed a criminal act. The Code of Criminal Procedure distinguishes these terms of the person who has committed a criminal act depending on the stage of the criminal procedure: suspect, accused, convict (convicted or acquitted person). The defendant may be a physical person or a legal entity which is represented in the criminal procedure by a head or an employee of the legal entity also an advocate authorised by a legal entity to represent it at the criminal procedure.

386. Tarptautinio baudžiamojo teismo Romos statutas, priimtas 1998 m. liepos 17 d. Jungtinių Tautų diplomatinėje įgaliotųjų atstovų konferencijoje, skirtoje Tarptautinio baudžiamojo teismo įsteigimui, *Valstybės žinios*, 2003, No. 49-2165; Konvencija dėl senaties termino netaikymo už karo nusikaltimus ir už nusikaltimus žmoniškumui, *Valstybės žinios*, 2002, No. 23-856.

715. The suspect is a participant of the pretrial investigation. According to Article 21 of the Code of Criminal Procedure, the person detained on suspicion of having committed a criminal act or a person questioned about a criminal act he/she has committed, or a person for whom a suspicion notice was drawn and who was summoned for questioning shall be held a suspect. The doctrine of the Lithuanian criminal procedure[387] has noted that a 'person must be recognised as a suspect if there are facts which justify the minimal possibility that the person committed a criminal act and the prosecutor subjectively believes in it'. When a person is in hiding or his/her location is unknown, he/she may be recognised as a suspect only by the decision of a prosecutor or pretrial judge order (ruling), or in urgent cases – by the decision of the pretrial investigator. The Supreme Court of Lithuania also has noted that 'there is no barrier to recognise the real procedural position of the person as a suspect even before he/she was questioned as a witness'.[388]

716. The accused shall be a party to judicial proceedings. According to Article 22 of the Code of Criminal Procedure, the accused shall be a person against whom an indictment has been brought by the prosecutor, or for whom there is a prosecutor's application to punish the person pursuant to a penal order, also a person against whom a case is heard in an accelerated procedure.

717. The accused against whom a conviction has been rendered shall become the convicted person, and the person against whom an acquittal has been brought shall become the acquitted person.

718. It should be noted that since 2008 in the Lithuanian criminal procedure a possibility to examine a person, who could testify about his/her own possible criminal act, as a witness in the pretrial investigation stage has been introduced. Such a witness is called a 'special witness'. His/her procedural situation is intermediate between that of a disinterested witness, and the suspect's procedural status. A person may be questioned as a special witness if there are facts in the case to suggest that there was potentially a criminal act and that it was committed by a specific person, but there is insufficient information for the status of the suspect to be awarded to that person.[389] The status of a special witness is recommended to apply in cases in which the pretrial investigation is carried out to determine whether the criminal act was actually committed, as well as when some investigations of the criminal act are not sufficiently clear: for example, possible violations of road safety or vehicle operating rules; and in cases involving State officials and civil servants, when the law restricts the pretrial investigation of such persons, etc. A liability for false testimony (Article 235 of the CC) does not apply for the suspect (the accused) and special witnesses, as well as procedural measures of compulsion for the avoidance or refusal to give a testimony. The doctrine of the Lithuanian criminal procedure has

---

387. Merkevičius R. Baudžiamasis procesas: įtariamojo statusas, Vilnius, Registrų centras, 2008, p. 198–199.
388. Ruling of the Supreme Court of Lithuania in criminal case No. 2K-281/2006.
389. The Prosecutor General has adopted methodological recommendation on this issue: Generalinio prokuroro įsakymas 'Dėl rekomendacijos dėl liudytojo apklausos Baudžiamojo proceso kodekso 80 ir 82 straipsnių nustatyta tvarka', *Valstybės žinios*, 2008, No. 6-234.

criticised this procedural status because it does not produce any result, as such a person must later be recognised as a witness or suspect.[390]

II. The Legal Position of the Accused

A. The Provisions in the Code of Criminal Procedure

719. The Code of Criminal Procedure provides that the suspect has the following rights: (1) to know with the commission of what criminal act he/she is suspected; (2) to inform consular authorities and one person; (3) to receive urgent medical assistance; (4) to know the maximum time limit, how many hours (days) his/her freedom may be restricted before the beginning of the trial; (5) to submit requests; (6) from the moment of his/her apprehension or first interrogation to have a defence counsel; (7) to receive an oral and written translation; (8) to give explanations in the pretrial investigation or to remain silent; (9) to give documents and other material relevant to the pretrial investigation; (10) to lodge requests; (11) to lodge challenges; (12) to get access to the case-file of the pretrial investigation; (13) to appeal against the actions and decisions of a pretrial investigator, prosecutor or pretrial judge; (14) to be accompanied by a legal representative at court hearings and other procedural actions, as well as the right to privacy when the suspect is a minor.

720. The Code of Criminal Procedure provides that the accused has the following rights: (1) to be informed of the charges and to be provided with a transcript of the indictment; (2) to inform consular authorities and one person; (3) to receive urgent medical assistance; (4) to examine the materials of the case in court; (5) to make copies of case documents; (6) to have a defence counsel; (7) to receive an oral and written translation; (8) to lodge requests; (9) to lodge challenges; (10) to give evidence and to be present during the examination of the evidence; (11) to ask questions during the hearing; (12) to provide explanations about the circumstances of the case which is being heard and to express his/her opinion about the motions made by the other parties to the proceedings; (13) to take part in the arguments where there is no defence counsel; (14) to address the court with the final speech; (15) to be accompanied by a legal representative at court hearings and other procedural actions, as well as the right to privacy when the suspect is a minor; (16) to appeal the judgment and court rulings.

721. The lists of the above-mentioned rights of the suspect and accused are not exhaustive, since different institutes of the criminal procedure may provide also other rights of the suspect or accused. Furthermore, it should be noted that the Criminal Division of the Supreme Court of Lithuania has adopted a review on court

390. Goda G. Vertybiniai prioritetai baudžiamajame procese, Vilnius, Registrų centras, 2014, p. 116.

practice on the application of the suspect and accused rights,[391] in which the content of such rights as the right to know the charge, the right to remain silent, the right to impartial and independent court, the right to translation, the right to examine the case file, the right to question witnesses and victims, the right to have the criminal case examined within the shortest possible time, etc. has been disclosed.

722. According to the Code of Criminal Procedure, the legal entity, which is suspected or accused in the commission of a criminal act, enjoys all the rights and duties of the suspect or the accused. These rights and duties of the legal person devolve upon the representative of a legal entity.

723. Further the content of several main rights of the suspect and the accused shall be revealed.

1. The Right to Know the Suspicion and the Charge

724. The suspect and accused have the right to know the suspicion and the charge. The Code of Criminal Procedure, in accordance with the requirements of the Directive 2012/13/EU of the European Parliament and of the Council of 22 May 2012 on the right to information in criminal proceedings,[392] sets forth that before the start of the first questioning, the suspect shall receive a suspicion notice which must contain information about the criminal act (place of commission, date, other circumstances; the law which provides criminal responsibility for this criminal act), as well as the rights of the suspect.[393]

725. Once the pretrial investigation is finished, the prosecutor shall draft an indictment and also hand in or forward to the accused a copy of the indictment. The indictment shall state: (1) the name of the court which will hear the criminal case; (2) the name, surname, date of birth, marital status, profession, workplace of the suspect, and, at the prosecutor's discretion, any other personal information; (3) a brief description of the criminal act: the place, time, forms, motives, consequences and other important circumstances; information about the victim; mitigating or aggravating circumstances for the suspect; (4) the basic information on which the prosecution is based; (5) the article (paragraph and sub-paragraph) of the CC creating liability for the committed act; (6) the name and surname of the defence counsel of the suspect if he/she had a counsel during the pretrial investigation; (7) the

391. Review of the Criminal Division of the Supreme Court of Lithuania of 15 Dec. 2016, Teismų praktika, No. 45; Review of the Criminal Division of the Supreme Court of Lithuania of 6 Apr. 2017, Teismų praktika, No. 46.
392. Directive 2012/13/EU of the European Parliament and of the Council of 22 May 2012 on the right to information in criminal proceedings, *OJ L 142, 1.6.2012, p. 1–10.*
393. The Prosecutor General has adopted methodological recommendation on this issue: Generalinio prokuroro įsakymas 'Dėl rekomendacijos dėl pranešimo apie įtarimą parengimą ir nusikalstamų veikų perkvalifikavimo ikiteisminio tyrimo metu', TAR, 2014, No. 2014-10494.

account of the suspect, if he/she rejects the accusation; (8) the opinion of the prosecutor concerning possibility to carry out the shortened examination of the evidence.[394]

726. It should be mentioned that a failure to respect the right of the suspect to be informed about charges during any action of the pretrial investigation (e.g., questioning of the suspect, etc.) would be considered a breach of the data collection procedure resulting in the denial or substantial constraint of the rights of the suspect (or the accused). In addition, the Supreme Court of Lithuania has pointed out that 'in case the indictment does not state or incorrectly states all relevant factual circumstances, which shall be consistent with all the elements of the criminal act (the place, time, methods, consequences of the act, etc.) leading to the interference with the right of the accused to defence, it should be considered that the indictment does not conform to the requirements of the CCP'.[395]

2. The Right to Legal Assistance

727. The suspect or the accused has a full right to a defence counsel. Article 44 of the Code of Criminal Procedure states that 'everyone may defend himself/herself in person or through legal assistance of his/her own choosing or, if he/she has no sufficient means to pay for legal assistance, to be given it free in accordance with the procedure provided for by the law regulating the provision of legal aid guaranteed by the State'. The suspect himself/herself expresses his/her own wish to have or not to have the defence counsel in the record.

728. According to the Code of Criminal Procedure, a defence counsel shall be obligatory: (1) in cases where the suspect or accused is a minor; (2) in cases involving blind, deaf, mute and other persons who because of physical or mental disabilities are not able to exercise their right to the defence counsel; (3) in cases involving persons who do not know the language of the proceedings; (4) when there is a conflict of interests between the defence of the suspects where at least one of the suspects has a defence counsel; (5) in cases involving crimes punishable by life imprisonment; (6) during the court hearing when the accused person is *in absentia*; (7) in cases involving pretrial detention or where the accused is in the pretrial detention; (8) in case of extradition, surrender to the International Criminal Court or EAW; (9) during the court hearing in expedited procedure, etc. The pretrial investigator, the prosecutor or the court shall have the right to determine that the participation of defence counsel is obligatory where, in their opinion, the rights of the suspect or the accused will not be adequately defended without legal assistance. The suspect or the accused shall be entitled to waive the right to defence counsel, or by reasoned request to ask to replace the appointed defence counsel at any stage of the

394. The Prosecutor General has adopted methodological recommendation on this issue: Generalinio prokuroro įsakymas 'Dėl Rekomendacijos dėl kaltinamojo akto surašymo ir perdavimo teismui', TAR, 2015, No. 2015-08536.
395. Ruling of the Supreme Court of Lithuania in criminal case No. 2K-393/2010.

procedure, with the exception of cases where the court hearing is *in absentia*. Waiver of the right to defence counsel shall be permitted only on the initiative of the suspect or the accused. Waiver of this right shall be entered in the record.

729. A declaration waiving the right to defence counsel made by a minor or a person who, because of physical and mental disabilities, is unable to exercise his/her right to defence, or by a person who does not know the language in which the proceedings are conducted, or by a person who is charged for the commission of a serious or grave crime, need not be binding – on the pretrial investigator, the prosecutor or the court. A refusal to have a defence counsel shall not deprive the suspect, the accused or the convicted person of the right to have a defence counsel again at any stage of the procedure.

730. Article 48 of the CCP states that the defence counsel shall have the right: (1) to examine the record of the arrest of the suspect or EAW; (2) to be present during the questioning of the suspect and meet with the suspect before the questioning or a court hearing; (3) to meet, from the very first questioning of the suspect, with the arrested or detained suspect without the presence of any other person, without any limitations on the number or duration of meetings; (4) to take part in gathering evidence during the pretrial investigation actions involving the suspect as well as during the pretrial investigation actions conducted on the motion of the suspect or his/her defence counsel; (5) by leave of the pretrial investigator, the prosecutor or the judge, to take part in any other actions of gathering evidence, etc. According to the CCP, a defence counsel need not participate in pretrial investigation actions involving the suspect apart from those cases when it is obligatory (e.g., imposition of pretrial detention, questioning a juvenile suspect, confrontation with juvenile suspect, etc.). In all other instances, the defence counsel has the right to participate in pretrial investigation actions involving the suspect.

731. According to the Law on the Bar and the Code of Criminal Procedure, the defence counsel has the right to gather independently the data necessary for the defence which may be obtained by the counsel without procedural coercive measures: to obtain from enterprises, institutions, organisations and individuals documents and objects necessary for the defence, to talk with individuals about the circumstances of the incident known to them, to inspect and take photos of the scene of the criminal act or means of transport, or record in any other way the information necessary for the defence. It is noted in interpretation of this right, in the doctrine of the Lithuanian criminal procedure, that the defence counsel may collect, capture and submit such data acquitting the defendant and mitigating his/her criminal responsibility, which has been lawfully obtained without recourse to procedural coercive measures. The defence counsel has the right to receive documents or other information from State institutions, municipalities, private or legal persons, etc., as well as the right to talk, for example, with witnesses, experts, victims and other parties to the criminal case, irrespective of whether they have been questioned by any pretrial investigator, prosecutor or pretrial judge.[396] The Supreme Court of Lithuania case law corroborates the above-mentioned theoretical provisions and states that 'privately made sound recording, which confirms the circumstances relevant to the case, may be recognised as evidence'.[397]

732. The doctrine of the Lithuanian criminal procedure[398] has noted that national legal provisions concerning the scope of the right of access to a lawyer in criminal procedure and lawyers' rights correspond to the requirements of the Directive 2013/48/EU of the European Parliament and of the Council of 22 October 2013 on the right of access to a lawyer in criminal proceedings and in European arrest warrant proceedings, and on the right to have a third party informed upon deprivation of liberty and to communicate with third persons and with consular authorities while deprived of liberty.[399]

3. The Right to Lodge Requests, to Give Explanations or to Remain Silent in Pretrial Investigation

733. The right to lodge requests, *inter alia*, includes a request to carry out the pretrial investigative action. The Code of Criminal Procedure stipulates that the suspect and/or his/her defence counsel shall have the right to request the prosecutor in writing to carry out the pretrial investigative actions. Upon receipt of such a request, the prosecutor may: (1) perform such actions himself/herself; (2) instruct the pretrial investigation institution to perform the requested actions; (3) decline to perform the requested actions. If declining to perform the requested actions, the prosecutor should document it in the form of a decision. The person who submitted a request shall have the right, within seven days from receiving it, to lodge a complaint against the decision to the pretrial judge. The pretrial judge should examine the complaint within three days. The decision of the judge shall be final. If the judge decides that the actions requested by the suspect (or defence counsel) should be performed, the prosecutor should perform the actions without any delay or direct the pretrial investigation institution to perform them.

734. The Code of Criminal Procedure directly (*expressis verbis*) provides for the right to silence of the suspect or the accused during the pretrial procedure or trial. Following the doctrine of the Lithuanian criminal procedure, the right to silence (e.g., right to refuse answering questions and producing documents, etc.) stems from the understanding of the suspect's right to present his/her statements with respect to charges brought against him/her and to give evidence, according to which the right

396. Goda G., Kazlauskas M., Kuconis P. Baudžiamojo proceso teisė, Vilnius, Registrų centras, 2011, p. 107.
397. Ruling of the Supreme Court of Lithuania in criminal case No. 2K-12/2010.
398. Goda G. Vertybiniai prioritetai baudžiamajame procese, Vilnius, Registrų centras, 2014, p. 86.
399. Directive 2013/48/EU of the European Parliament and of the Council of 22 Oct. 2013 on the right of access to a lawyer in criminal proceedings and in European arrest warrant proceedings, and on the right to have a third party informed upon deprivation of liberty and to communicate with third persons and with consular authorities while deprived of liberty, *OJ L 294, 6.11.2013, p. 1–12.*

to present statements, to give evidence or produce documents is in the full and absolute disposition of the suspect or the accused.[400] Neither the law, nor judicial jurisprudence lays down any liability or sanctions in case the suspect or the accused gives no evidence, refuses to answer questions or to produce documents. The suspect or the accused has the right to maintain an absolute passivity in these procedural actions, which require the will of the suspect or the accused, for example, the suspect or the accused has the right to refuse to provide voice or handwriting samples, etc.

735. The suspect and the accused must obey provisional or other procedural coercive measures, which are applicable for him/her, and may not illegally influence the progress or result of the procedure (e.g., he/she cannot destroy or conceal evidence of criminal acts, or influence witnesses, etc.).

4. The Right to Access to the Case-File During Pretrial Investigation and Trial

736. Article 181 of the Code of Criminal Procedure provides for the right to have access to the file during the pretrial investigation or trial for the suspect or the accused and his/her defence counsel.

737. At any moment during the pretrial investigation, the suspect and his/her defence counsel shall have the right to examine the material of the pretrial investigation, as well as make copies of or relevant extracts from the material of the pretrial investigation. Where the suspect is in custody, only his/her defence counsel shall have the right of access to the material of the pretrial investigation. The suspect or his/her defence counsel shall submit an application to grant access (make copies or relevant extracts) to the material of the pretrial investigation to the prosecutor. The prosecutor shall allow access to all the material of the pretrial investigation as well as allowing the making of copies of (relevant extracts from) the material of the pretrial investigation when the pretrial investigation is finished and an indictment is under preparation.

738. It is possible to postpone access to the case-file during the pretrial investigation. The prosecutor shall have the right to deny the suspect or his/her defence counsel access to all or part of the material of the pretrial investigation during the pretrial investigation, if (according to the jurisprudence of the Supreme Court of Lithuania[401]) such an examination is likely to undermine the favourable results of the pretrial investigation. To refuse access to the whole or part of the material of the pretrial investigation, the prosecutor shall pass a decision which may, within seven days, be appealed by the suspect or his/her defence counsel with the pretrial judge. The pretrial judge shall examine such an appeal within three days and adopt the decision (ruling), which shall be final.

400. Merkevičius R. Baudžiamasis procesas: įtariamojo statusas, Vilnius, Registrų centras, 2008, p. 470–527, etc.
401. Ruling of the Supreme Court of Lithuania in criminal case No. 2K-525/2010.

739. When the case file has been received at the court, the prosecutor, the accused, his/her legal representative and the defence counsel shall have the right of access to all the materials of the case-file and shall be allowed to make copies of the material, or appropriate extracts, from the pretrial investigation. If the accused is in detention, his/her defence counsel shall have the right to examine the case and make copies or appropriate extracts. If the accused has no defence counsel or has refused to have a defence counsel, he/she shall have the right of access to the case file as well as the right to make copies of or extracts from the material of the case file.

740. The Prosecutor General Recommendations[402] state that a request for access may be dismissed due to likely damage to the pretrial success, if there are contradictions between the testimony of the parties; if the pretrial data has not been formalised yet; if the application relates to access to data on juvenile victims and suspects; if the application relates to access to data on the use of coercive measures (secret pretrial investigative actions); if the application relates to access to the data and locations of witnesses, victims, experts, specialists and others, etc. Copies or extracts of the material of the pretrial investigation can be made and transmitted to the suspect (accused).

741. Furthermore, it should be noted that Article 177 of the Code of Criminal Procedure provides that 'information about the pretrial investigation shall not be made public. It may be made public only subject to a prosecutor's leave and only to such an extent as is determined as permissible. It is prohibited to make public information about juvenile suspects and victims'.[403] etc.

5. The Right to have Another Person Informed About Arrest or Detention

742. The Code of Criminal Procedure provides the right of the suspect or accused person concerning information about his/her arrest or detention.

743. When a person is arrested or pretrial detention is ordered, the prosecutor should notify a family member or close relative, or other person indicated by the arrested or detained person. If the arrested or detained person does not specify a particular person, the prosecutor should notify any family member or close relative on his/her own initiative. The prosecutor has the right to postpone the notification, if it may damage the success of the pretrial investigation or the arrested or detained person explicitly states that such notification might endanger his/her family members,

402. The Prosecutor General has adopted methodological recommendation on this issue: Generalinio prokuroro įsakymas 'Dėl Rekomendacijos dėl proceso dalyvių susipažinim su ikiteisminio tyrimo medžiaga patvirtinimo', TAR, 2018, No. 2330.

403. The Prosecutor General has adopted methodological recommendation on this issue: Generalinio prokuroro įsakymas 'Dėl ikiteisminio tyrimo duomenų skelbimo rekomendacijų patvirtinimo', TAR, 2017, No. 13412; Lietuvos Respublikos generalinio prokuroro įsakymas 'Dėl Ikiteisminio tyrimo duomenų teikimo ir panaudojimo ne baudžiamojo persekiojimo tikslais ir ikiteisminio tyrimo duomenų apsaugos rekomendacijų patvirtinimo', TAR, 2017, No. 13413.

close relatives or other persons. The arrested or detained person should also be afforded an opportunity to inform his/her family member or close relatives himself/herself.

744. When pretrial detention was ordered for the citizen of other State, the prosecutor must immediately notify Ministry of Foreign Affairs of the Lithuania and, if detained person wishes so, – diplomatic mission or consulate of state of his/her citizenship.

B. Other Applicable Laws

745. It should be noted that some rights of the suspect and accused are defined also in other laws.

746. Law on the State Language[404] (also the Code of Criminal Procedure) lays down safeguards for suspects or other parties who do not know the Lithuanian language. The Law on the State Language states that participants in the legal proceedings, who do not know the state language (Lithuanian), shall be provided with the services of an interpreter free of charge. The Constitution and the CCP guarantee them a right to make statements and explanations, lodge requests and appeals, as well as speak in their native language or the language they know. When consulting the case file, they shall have the right to the services of an interpreter free of charge. The costs of interpretation (translation) shall be paid by the State. All case file documents served on the suspect, accused or third party (if they do not know the State (Lithuanian) language) have to be translated into their native language or into the language they know. The Supreme Court has acknowledged that 'the rights of the accused have been violated because she was unable to present arguments in the Russian language during the trial; besides, she has not received the court's decision on the appeal in the Russian language'.[405]

747. The doctrine of the Lithuanian criminal procedure[406] has indicated that national legal provisions concerning the safeguards for the suspects or other parties who do not know the Lithuanian language are more favourable than the requirements of the Directive 2010/64/EU of the European Parliament and of the Council of 20 October 2010 on the right to interpretation and translation in criminal proceedings.[407]

748. The Law on Pretrial Detention[408] stipulates that detained persons shall have the right (upon arrival at the pretrial detention centre) to receive written information

---

404. Lietuvos Respublikos valstybinės kalbos įstatymas, *Valstybės Žinios*, 1995, No. 15-344.
405. Ruling of the Supreme Court of Lithuania in criminal cases No. 2K-620/2006.
406. Goda G. Vertybiniai prioritetai baudžiamajame procese, Vilnius, Registrų centras, 2014, p. 87–88.
407. Directive 2010/64/EU of the European Parliament and of the Council of 20 Oct. 2010 on the right to interpretation and translation in criminal proceedings, *OJ L 280, 26.10.2010, p. 1–7.*
408. Lietuvos Respublikos suėmimo vykdymo įstatymas, *Valstybės žinios*, 2008, No. 81-3172.

about the welfare procedures and confinement conditions in the pretrial detention establishment, about the rights, obligations and restrictions that apply to them. This information shall be communicated in Lithuanian or in the mother tongue or other language that the detainee can understand. In addition, the administration of a remand prison should ensure that the information defined by laws and regulations of Lithuania regarding detainees' rights, obligations, prohibitions and agenda should be available in each cell. Employees of the remand prison visiting the cells of the arrested should clarify the procedures and conditions, rights, obligations and restrictions that apply to the detainees, if necessary.

III. The Legal Position of the Victim and the Civil Party

A. General Observations

749. The Code of Criminal Procedure regulates a definition and legal status of the victim and injured party in criminal procedure.

750. The person who due to commission of the criminal act sustains physical, property or moral damage shall be recognised as the victim. The victim also may be recognised as a family member or close relative of a physical person who died from the criminal act, if they suffered physical, material or moral damage due to that person's death. Only a physical person may be recognised as a victim. A person is recognised as a victim by a pretrial investigator, a prosecutor's decision or a court ruling.

751. A person who due to committed criminal act has sustained material or moral damage shall be entitled to bring a civil action in a criminal case against the suspect or the accused, or the person who bears material responsibility for the actions of the suspect or the accused. The notion of the injured party is larger and it includes not only the victim, but also any other physical person or a legal entity who requests, in a criminal case, compensation for damage to his/her property, physical or moral damage caused to him/her by the criminal act of a suspect or the accused. Such physical person or legal entity shall be held by the plaintiff by a decision of the prosecutor or by a court ruling. Furthermore, a prosecutor who acts in the criminal case must bring a civil action during the trial, if it has not yet been entered where damage has been caused by a criminal act to the State or a person who, because of minority, illness, dependence upon the accused or any other reasons, is incapable to protect his/her lawful interests in court.

752. The judge, the prosecutor and the pretrial investigator must inform the victim and injured party about their procedural rights and ensure a possibility for them to exercise these rights.

B. The Rights of the Victim

753. The victim and his/her representative have the following rights: (1) to receive information on the state of the criminal procedure concerning him/her; (2) to adduce evidence; (3) to lodge requests and challenges; (4) to participate in the assessment of his/her special protection needs; (5) to examine in court the materials of the case; (6) to take part in the court hearing; (7) to appeal against the decisions and actions of a pretrial investigator, a prosecutor, a pretrial judge and of the court; (8) to address the court with the final speech; (9) to appeal the judgment or a court ruling; (10) to have an accompanying person during criminal procedure; etc. The victim also has the right to refuse access to information on his/her status in the criminal procedure, unless such refusal would infringe the rights of the suspect or accused person.

754. The victim shall be summoned and examined as a witness. The victim must testify on oath and will be held responsible for committing any perjury as a witness.

755. It may be pointed out that, in accordance with the requirements of the Directive 2012/29/EU of the European Parliament and the Council of 25 October 2012 establishing minimum standards on the rights, support and protection of victims of crime, and replacing Council Framework Decision 2001/220/JHA[409] and the Code of Criminal Procedure of Lithuania, the prosecutor or pretrial investigator during the first questioning must identify specific protection needs of the victim. In the context of this assessment, particular attention should be paid to victims who have suffered considerable harm due to the severity of the crime; victims who have suffered a crime committed with a bias or discriminatory motive which could, in particular, be related to their personal characteristics; victims whose relationship to and dependence on the offender make them particularly vulnerable; also victims of terrorism, organised crime, human trafficking, gender-based violence, violence in a close relationship, sexual violence, exploitation or hate crime, and victims with disabilities, etc. Taking into consideration above requirements (besides the rights guaranteed to all victims) additional rights are provided for some categories of victims – a juvenile victim under 18, victim of the sexual criminal act and victim of the less serious, serious or grave crime and there is a threat of real danger to his/her life, health, freedom or property. Juvenile victims under 14 shall be examined by the pretrial judge, accompanied, if so requested, by their representative, defence counsel or prosecutor.[410] Juvenile victims who are under 18 shall, as a rule, be examined during a pretrial investigation not more than once. A video and audio recording must be made during their examination. Victims younger than 18 shall be called to a trial hearing only in exceptional cases. Victims of the less serious, serious or grave crime

409. Directive 2012/29/EU of the European Parliament and the Council of 25 Oct. 2012 establishing minimum standards on the rights, support and protection of victims of crime, and replacing Council Framework Decision 2001/220/JHA, *OJ L 315, 14.11.2012, p. 57–73.*

410. The Prosecutor General has adopted methodological recommendation on this issue: Generalinio prokuroro įsakymas 'Dėl Rekomendacijos dėl nepilnamečio liudytojo ir nukentėjusiojo apklausos', *Valstybės žinios*, 2009, No. 112-4806.

and there is a threat of real danger to their life, health, freedom or property may be granted to non-disclosure of their identity,[411] etc. Victims of the sexual criminal act may request that their examination shall be conducted by a person of the same sex.

756. Moreover, after recognition of a person as the victim of a violent crime, he/she immediately should be informed by the pretrial investigator or a prosecutor about their right to the compensation under the Law on Compensation for the Victims of Violent Crimes.

757. Furthermore, a prosecutor or a pretrial investigator must notify the victim of the suspect's detention with a view to ascertaining whether the victim wants to be informed of the prospect of a suspected release from a place of detention or imprisonment.

758. The doctrine of the Lithuanian criminal procedure[412] has noted that national legal provisions concerning the legal possibilities to represent and defend the rights of the victim are fully compatible with the requirements of the above-mentioned Directive 2012/29/EU.

C. The Rights of the Injured Party

759. The plaintiff (injured party) has the following rights: (1) to submit explanations on the substance of a civil action; (2) to provide evidence; (3) to lodge requests and challenges; (4) to examine the materials of the case, to have extracts or copies of the documents he/she needs; (5) to take part during the court hearing; (6) to lodge a complaint against the actions and to appeal against the decisions of the pretrial investigator, the prosecutor, the judge or the court to the extent they relate to the civil action; (7) to take part during the court hearing in the appeal instance.

760. The plaintiff (injured party) must: (1) be present during the hearing of the case by the Court of First Instance; (2) submit, at the court's request, documents in his/her possession, which are relevant for the civil action brought; (3) observe the rules of procedure established by court.

761. A civil action may be brought by filing a claim with the pretrial investigator, the prosecutor or the court at any stage of the criminal procedure but not later than before the examination of the evidence in the court hearing. The victim who has failed to file a civil action in a criminal case shall be entitled to enter a claim

---

411. The Constitutional Court has emphasised that 'non-disclosure of victim or witness identity must be an exceptional measure for the protection of their safety' (*see* decision of the Constitutional Court of Lithuania of 19 Sep. 2000, *Valstybės žinios*, 2000, No. 80-2423). The Prosecutor General has adopted methodological recommendations on this issue: Generalinio prokuroro įsakymas 'Dėl Rekomendacijos dėl anonimiškumo ir dalinio anonimiškumo nukentėjusiajam ar liudytojui suteikimo ir šio sprendimo procesinio įforminimo', TAR, 2014, No. 6146.

412. Goda G. Vertybiniai prioritetai baudžiamajame procese, Vilnius, Registrų centras, 2014, p. 183–184, 197.

under the civil procedure. A civil action entered in a criminal case shall be exempt from the stamp duty. When civil action was brought during pretrial investigation stage, the pretrial investigator and prosecutor must collect data, which proves the legal ground and size of the civil action. During the criminal procedure, a pretrial investigator, a prosecutor or the court must invoke remedies for the pending civil action: to discover property belonging to a suspect or an accused, or person who bears material responsibility for the actions of the suspect or the accused and impose a temporary limitation of the property. The civil action shall be heard by the court together with the criminal case. A plaintiff may withdraw his/her claim before the court leaves for the consideration of the judgment.

762. It should be noted that dismissal of a civil action by a judgment in a criminal case shall deprive the plaintiff of the right to bring the same civil action under the civil procedure (and *vice versa*).

763. When rendering a judgment of conviction, the court shall grant the claim filed (in full or in part) or dismiss it. When granting the civil action, the court may not adhere to the extent of the claim if its amount does not affect the qualification of the criminal act and the size of the punishment. When rendering a judgment of acquittal the court shall (1) reject the civil action unless the participation of the accused in the commission of a criminal act has been proved; (2) not proceed with the civil action where the accused is acquitted on the grounds of absence of *corpus delicti* of a criminal act. In this case the civil action may be re-entered in the civil procedure.

§4. The Rules of Evidence

764. The Code of Criminal Procedure of Lithuania provides that:

> evidence in criminal procedure shall be the material obtained in the manner prescribed by law. Admissibility of the material obtained shall be determined in every case by the court or judge who is seized of the case. Only material which proves or disproves at least one circumstance relevant for a fair disposition of the case may be regarded as evidence.

The Supreme Court of Lithuania, in accordance with the CCP, also has noted that 'the admission of the data collected during pretrial investigation as evidence is an exclusive competence of the court'[413] and 'only material which is obtained by lawful means and that may be validated by the procedural actions laid down in the CCP may be considered as evidence'.[414]

765. The doctrine of the Lithuanian criminal procedure divides the evidences into direct and indirect; personal and items; charging and justifying, etc. The direct

413. Ruling of the Supreme Court of Lithuania in criminal case No. 2K-251/2010.
414. Ruling of the Supreme Court of Lithuania in criminal case No. 2K-239/2010.

evidence relates directly to the fact which is being tested (e.g., the testimony of the accused about committed criminal act, etc.), the indirect evidence relates indirectly, through interim fact, to the existence of the fact which is being tested (e.g., DNA samples of the accused on the knife that was the mean of the murder, etc.). Personal evidences are evidences, when the information is persisted in the person's consciousness and transmitted by speech or in writing. Items are the evidences, which transmit the information, persisted in material objects.[415]

I. The Principles of Evidentiary Law

766. The main principles of the Lithuanian criminal procedure which also concern the evidentiary law are the principle of presumption of innocence, the principle *in dubio pro reo,* the principle of lawfulness of evidentiary procedure, the principle of immediacy and the principle of free assessment of evidence.

767. Article 31 of the Constitution of Lithuania states that 'every person shall be presumed innocent until proven guilty according to the procedure established by law and until declared guilty by an effective court sentence'. A similar rule is contained in the CCP, which sets up that 'everyone charged with a criminal act shall be presumed innocent until proven guilty in accordance with the procedure prescribed by this Code and established by an effective court sentence'. This principle puts the burden of proof on the prosecutor. Furthermore, the court and other state institutions must observe this requirement during the whole criminal procedure. When investigating the case, neither the court, nor the pretrial investigator or prosecutor shall have the right to cast the burden of proof upon the suspect or the accused. The doctrine of the Lithuanian criminal procedure also states that 'the burden of proof [...] lies with state officials. The suspect (accused) or his/her defence counsel may not be forced to prove innocence (e.g., to provide evidence of innocence, etc.)'.[416]

768. Following the provisions of the CCP and the case law, the next important principle of evidentiary law is the principle *in dubio pro reo*. This principle means that the suspect or the accused will always receive the benefit of the doubt. The Senate of the Supreme Court has noted that 'any doubts are treated in favour of the defendant, if the court, having exhausted all possibilities cannot remove them'.[417] These rules are strictly observed in court jurisprudence, and the Supreme Court of Lithuania has stated that 'conviction cannot be based on conjecture or assumptions. It can be based on the evidence which is sufficient to draw indisputable conclusions about the guilt. All the doubts that cannot be removed during court hearings are treated in favour of the defendant'.[418]

---

415. Goda G., Kazlauskas M., Kuconis P. Baudžiamojo proceso teisė, Vilnius, Registrų centras, 2011, p. 185–186.
416. Goda G., Kazlauskas M., Kuconis P. Baudžiamojo proceso teisė, Vilnius, Registrų centras, 2011, p. 172.
417. Decision of the Senate of the Supreme Court of Lithuania of 20 Jun. 2003, Teismų praktika, No. 19, p. 202–239.
418. Ruling of the Supreme Court of Lithuania in criminal case No. 2K-374/2010.

769. The principle of lawfulness of evidentiary procedure requires that only material which is obtained by lawful means and may be validated by the procedural actions laid down in the CCP may be considered as evidence. According to the Review of the Criminal Division of the Supreme Court regarding the application of the rules on evidence, 'data can be recognised as evidence, if it has been obtained in accordance with the CCP, other laws (e.g., the Law on Police, the Law on the Bar, etc.) or legal acts implementing the laws'.[419] Moreover, the Supreme Court has noted that 'the judgment shall be based solely on the evidence which has been tested and verified at trial'.[420]

770. The evidentiary procedure in the trial stage is strongly determined by the principle of immediacy (which is closely related to the other trial principles such us publicity, orality, etc.). This principle means that the Court of First Instance shall directly examine evidence in a criminal case: question defendants, victims, witnesses, listen to specialists and expert findings and explanations, inspect items (material evidence), read out records and any other documents. Persons questioned during the pretrial investigation in a trial hearing shall give their testimony and explanations orally. Meanwhile, the principle of orality means that the persons who gave testimony during the pretrial investigation should be called to give testimony at a court hearing. However, there are certain exceptions to this main rule. Testimony given earlier by the defendant, victim or witness to a pretrial judge or at a court hearing may be read out at the trial hearing, and audio and video recordings of such inquiries may be played if this defendant, victim or witness: (1) is dead, or absent from the trial hearing due to important reasons; (2) refuses to give or avoids giving evidence, or submits that he/she does not remember some circumstances that were previously testified; (3) at the hearing, gives evidence, which is substantially different from that given during the pretrial investigation or earlier at the hearing. The Supreme Court of Lithuania has noted that 'the testimony that is read aloud is not an independent source of evidence – it can help to verify other evidence of the case'.[421]

771. In addition, the testimony of a person questioned in court after the postponement or adjournment of the case hearing, as well as the testimony given during the pretrial investigation to the pretrial judge by a witness not called by a court ruling to the trial hearing by reason of anonymity or because he/she has not attained the age of 18, may be read out in the trial hearing.

772. When the earlier judgment or court order (ruling) is quashed, or when proceedings are again pending before the court, the victims and witnesses earlier questioned in the court hearing shall not be invited for repeated questioning except the case when it requires the interests of justice.

---

419. Review of the Criminal division of the Supreme Court of Lithuania of 28 Jun. 2007, Teismų praktika, No. 27, p. 322, 325.
420. Ruling of the Supreme Court of Lithuania in criminal case No. 2K-393/2010.
421. Ruling of the Supreme Court of Lithuania in criminal case No. 2K-179/2010.

773. The principle of free assessment of evidence requires that judges shall assess the evidence according to their inner conviction based on a scrupulous and objective review of all the circumstances of the case in accordance with the law. The Senate of the Supreme Court of Lithuania has pointed out that 'judgment shall be lawful and reasonable. The judgment is reasonable, when the court makes its findings as to the criminal act, the defendant's guilt or innocence, punishment, etc. based on the fully and impartially investigated and properly assessed evidence'. The court's opinion in assessing the evidence should be well-founded. The Senate of the Supreme Court of Lithuania, in accordance with the CCP, also has noted that 'the court's judgment may not be based solely on a confession of the accused or on the testimony of classified victims or witnesses, if they have not been validated by other evidence'[422]. In addition, the Supreme Court of Lithuania has stressed that 'no evidence is given any priority in accordance with the provisions of the CCP'[423] and 'each evidence must be evaluated separately and as a whole'.[424]

II. The Means of Proof

774. The Code of Criminal Procedure provides the exhaustive list of the admissible means of proof (according to the doctrine of the Lithuanian criminal procedure – the kinds of evidence[425]): testimony of the suspect and the accused; testimony of the victim; testimony of the witness; expert report; specialist conclusion; item as an evidence; document as an evidence.

A. The Testimony of the Suspect and Accused

775. The suspect must be questioned at least once during the pretrial investigation, before drawing up the indictment. The suspect must always be questioned before imposing a remand measure on him/her. Article 187 of the Code of Criminal Procedure provides that before the start of the first questioning, the suspect must receive the suspicion notice (*see* paragraph 724).

776. It should be noted that upon receiving the appropriate notification from the prosecutor, which may be filed on the initiative of the suspect, his/her defence counsel or the prosecutor, during the pretrial investigation the suspect may be questioned by the pretrial judge. On the application of the suspect the prosecutor must bring him/her before the pretrial judge within a reasonable time after filing such an application. On the initiative of the prosecutor the suspect shall be brought before the pretrial judge for questioning if it is thought that during the trial the accused may

---

422. Decision of the Senate of the Supreme Court of Lithuania of 20 Jun. 2003, Teismų praktika, No. 19, p. 202–239.
423. Ruling of the Supreme Court of Lithuania in criminal case No. 2K-218/2010.
424. Ruling of the Supreme Court of Lithuania in criminal case No. 2K-173-648/2017.
425. Goda G., Kazlauskas M., Kuconis P. Baudžiamojo proceso teisė, Vilnius, Registrų centras, 2011, p. 186.

change his/her testimony or exercise his/her right not to testify. The prosecutor and defence counsel must be present during the questioning held on the application of the suspect. The questioning of the suspect shall open by inviting the suspect to disclose the circumstances on the ground of which he/she wished to be questioned by the pretrial judge. After that, the defence counsel and the prosecutor may put questions to the suspect. The Supreme Court of Lithuania has emphasised that 'the testimonies given to the pretrial judge are evidence even in case when the person did not approve them during the hearing'.[426]

777. In all cases, at the start of the questioning the suspect shall be asked whether he/she pleads guilty to the charge of a criminal act of which he/she is suspected; after that he/she shall be invited to make a testimony about the basic points of the suspicion. Finally, he/she may be asked questions. The testimony of the suspect shall be entered in the record in first person singular and be recorded verbatim as far as possible. Where necessary, the questions put to the suspect and his/her replies shall be noted.

778. A free suspect receives the summons for questioning. The suspect who cannot be present at the place of questioning, also a provisionally arrested or detained suspect may be questioned by the videoconferencing system.

779. At the trial, after the accused has submitted a response to the charges, the presiding judge shall inform him/her of his/her right to give explanations, to respond to questions or to refuse to do any of the above. The judge shall also explain that the accused is entitled to put questions to the persons being examined and give explanation about the evidence under examination. Where there is more than one accused, all of whom wish to give testimony, the order of priority for giving testimony shall be laid down by the court. Each accused shall be heard separately. The examination of the accused shall start with the proposal of the presiding judge to give testimony about the charge and the known circumstances of the case.

B. The Testimony of the Witness and Victim

780. Any person of whom there is evidence that he/she has knowledge of any circumstances relevant to the case may be summoned as a witness. The Supreme Court has noted that 'witness testimony is legally obtained data that can be verified by the procedural actions provided in the CCP; they cannot be false'.[427] A witness shall have the right: (i) to testify in his/her mother tongue and to make use of the services of an interpreter if the examination is conducted in a language he/she does not know; (ii) to examine the record of his/her testimony and make revisions in it; (iii) to request sound and video recording during his/her testimony; (iv) to provide protection from undue interference; (v) to be reimbursed for the expenses he/she has incurred; (vi) to have a representative.

426. Ruling of the Supreme Court of Lithuania in criminal case No. 2K-7-48/2009.
427. Ruling of the Supreme Court of Lithuania in criminal case No. 2K-30/2006.

781. The victim shall be summoned and examined as a witness (on the status of the victim *see* paragraphs 750–758).

782. A person who, under a certificate of a medical institution or a conclusion of a psychiatrist or medical examiner, is unable, owing to his/her physical or mental disability, to form a clear understanding of the facts relevant to the case, and cannot, therefore, testify about them, is precluded from being witness. Circumstances due to which persons shall be precluded from being witnesses: (a) a person who can testify about a criminal act he/she himself/herself committed; (b) a judge having knowledge of a secret of the deliberation room; (c) the defence counsel of the suspect and the accused, representatives of the plaintiff and the defendant in a civil action owing to the circumstances which came to their knowledge in their capacity as counsel or representatives, also the translator – for the circumstances which came to their knowledge in their capacity as translator; (d) clergymen – because of the secrets of the confessional; (e) producers, disseminators of information for the public, the publishers and/or disseminators of information for the public, journalists for the reason of confidentiality of the source of information under the Law on Providing Information to the Public.[428]

783. Members of the family or close relatives of the suspect and the accused (according to the constitutional ban to compel to give evidence against family members or close relatives) may refrain from giving evidence, or from replying to some of the questions put to them. The pretrial investigator, prosecutor, pretrial judge or court must inform members of the family or close relatives[429] of the suspect and the accused before questioning about their right to refuse to testify or to reply to some of the questions put to them. The Supreme Court of Lithuania strictly observes this requirement in court practice, for example, the court noted that 'questioning the suspect's mother without her consent violates the requirements of the CCP'.[430] It must be noted that in the case law of Lithuanian courts (which is supported by the doctrine of the Lithuanian criminal procedure[431]), the members of the family are treated in a broad sense and include persons whose family relations are *a priori* or *post factum*.

428. Lietuvos Respublikos visuomenės informavimo įstatymas, *Valstybės žinios*, 2000, No. 75-2272.
429. According to the Criminal Code of Lithuania, close relatives shall be parents (adoptive parents), children (adopted children), brothers, sisters, grandparents and grandchildren. Family members of the perpetrator shall be the parents (adoptive parents), children (adopted children), brothers, sisters and their spouses living together with him/her, the spouse of the perpetrator or the person living with him/her in common law (partnership), parents of the spouse, person with whom the marriage was agreed and former spouses.
430. Ruling of the Supreme Court of Lithuania in criminal case No. 2K-514/2000.
431. Jurka R. Liudytojas ir jo procesiniai interesai baudžiamajame procese, Vilnius, Registrų centras, 2009, p. 205–208.

784. The President of the Republic of Lithuania may testify only with his/her consent and at the residence of president before a pretrial judge.

785. A juvenile witness or a victim who is under 14 years of age shall be examined by the pretrial judge, accompanied, if so requested, by his/her representative, defence counsel or prosecutor.[432] A juvenile witness and a victim who are under 18 shall, as a rule, be examined during the pretrial investigation not more than once and in special room, adapted for children. A video and audio recording must be made during their examination. If a suspect or his/her defence counsel is present at the questioning of a witness or victim younger than 18 years of age, the pretrial judge shall ensure that such witness or victim is not subjected to any unauthorised influence. Witnesses or victims younger than 18 shall be called to a trial hearing only in exceptional cases. If the suspect may have an influence on a witness or victim who is less than 18 years, the pretrial judge adopts the decision to refuse the participation of the suspect in such examination. Also, the pretrial judge has the right to prohibit the suspect and other participants of the procedure (except a psychologist or a representative of the State institution for the protection of the rights of the child) to be present in the premises where examination of the juvenile witness or victim is conducted if it is required by the interests of the juvenile. In this case, the suspect and other participants are given the opportunity to observe and hear the examination, and they can ask questions through the pretrial judge.

786. The victim or the witness may request that the prosecutor or a pretrial investigator grant them non-disclosure of their identity. The prosecutor or the pretrial investigator will do so where there are necessary grounds. The non-disclosure of the identity of the victim and witness may arise where there are the following grounds: (1) there is a threat of a real danger to the life, health, freedom or property of the victim, the witness or members of their family or close relatives; (2) the evidence of the victim or the witness is of great importance to the criminal case; (3) the victim or the witness are taking part in a case relating to a less-serious, serious or grave crime. The pretrial judge shall question the victim or the witness subject to the non-disclosure of the identity with these exceptions. The pretrial judge may determine that the questioning must be conducted in the absence of the defence counsel at the place where the questioning is taking place. In such a case, after questioning, the judge shall inform the defence counsel of the testimonies obtained. After that, the defence counsel shall have the right to put questions to the victim or the witness through the pretrial judge. If the questions asked could reveal the identity of the person subject to questioning, the pretrial judge shall have the right not to ask the questions, or reformulate them. The answers to the defence counsel questions shall be entered in the record of the questioning, which the defence counsel shall be entitled to examine after questioning. If the person who is to make

432. The Prosecutor General has adopted methodological recommendation on this issue: Generalinio prokuroro įsakymas 'Dėl Rekomendacijos dėl nepilnamečio liudytojo ir nukentėjusiojo apklausos', *Valstybės žinios*, 2009, No. 112-4806.

identification is a person subject to the non-disclosure of the identity, the identification parade shall be conducted by providing acoustic and visual obstacles, to conceal the identity of the identifier.

787. Every person summonsed as a witness or a victim must appear before the pretrial investigator, the prosecutor or the court and give truthful testimony as to his/her knowledge of the circumstances, which are relevant for the case. A witness or a victim who fails to appear before the pretrial investigator without a lawful excuse, may be brought in person. If a witness or a victim fails, for no good reason, to appear before the pretrial investigator, the prosecutor or the court, or refuses, without a lawful cause, to give evidence, procedural coercive measures – a fine – shall be applied against him/her. Where a witness or a victim fails to appear before the court or, with no lawful basis, refuses to give evidence, the judge or the court may also order his/her arrest. A witness and a victim shall be held liable for perjury under the CC.

C. The Expert Report

788. Expert examination shall be ordered where the pretrial judge or the court determines that a special examination requiring scientific, artistic or any other special knowledge must be carried out in order to establish the circumstances of a criminal act.

789. Article 84 of the Code of Criminal Procedure provides that an expert is a person who has special knowledge in a particular field and whose name is on the Experts' List of the Republic of Lithuania.[433] Where no experts in a field needed are to be found on the Experts' List, a person whose name is not on the Experts' List may be appointed an expert.

790. An expert shall have a right: (1) to examine the materials of the case relating to the subject of expert examination; (2) to request to be provided additional information necessary for presenting a report; (3) to be present when investigative actions related to the subject of expert examination are performed, and during the hearing. An expert shall refuse to present his/her report if the materials submitted to him/her are insufficient for the purpose required or are outside the scope of his/her special knowledge. In these cases, the expert shall make a written statement that he/she is not able to present a report. The doctrine of the Lithuanian criminal procedure[434] has noted that national legal provisions concerning the functions and status of the forensic expert (specialist) are fully compatible with the requirements

433. Requirements for the expert, procedure and other aspects is regulated by Law on Forensic Examination (*see*: Lietuvos Respublikos teismo ekspertizės įstatymas, *Valstybės žinios*, 2002, No. 50-4969; TAR, 2020-06-19, No. 13466).

434. Paužaitė-Kulvinskienė J., Juodkaitė-Granskienė G., Pajaujis V. Teismo eksperto pareigos, atsakomybė ir iš jos kylančios sankcijos. Lietuvos kontekstas ir Europos perspektyvos // Baudžiamoji justicija ir verslas, Vilnius, 2016, p. 339–344.

provided in the European Commission for the Efficiency of Justice (CEPEJ) Guidelines on the role of court-appointed experts in judicial proceedings of Council of Europe's Member States Document adopted by CEPEJ at its twenty-fourth Plenary meeting (Strasbourg, 11 – 12 December 2014),[435] which define minimum requirements for a forensic expert, general principles of ordering and performing a forensic examination, limits of the role of forensic expert in the court, etc.

791. On the ordering procedure of the expert examination, *see* paragraphs 866–871.

D. The Specialist Conclusion

792. Article 89 of the Code of Criminal Procedure provides that a specialist shall be a person who has adequate special knowledge and skills, and who has been appointed by a pretrial investigation institution to conduct examination of tangible objects and submit a conclusion on the issues within his/her competence (e.g., forensic pathologists shall be specialists conducting an examination of a human body or a cadaver; forensic psychiatrists – examination of a person's mental condition, etc.). Upon completing the examination of the items assigned to him/her, a specialist shall submit his/her conclusion. A specialist's conclusion may be included in the record of the conducted investigative action. Where it is necessary to examine the items in a laboratory, a specialist's conclusion shall be drawn in the form of a separate document. It should be noted that the Supreme Court of Lithuania has stated that 'the scientific opinion which presents the interpretation of the legal norm, relationship of this legal norm with the international legal acts, etc. is not a specialist report in terms of evidence'.[436]

793. If the conclusion given by the specialist at the pretrial investigation is sufficiently clear and comprehensive, it shall be read out during the hearing in the absence of the specialist. The specialist shall be summoned to the hearing for questioning only when the court recognises that his/her testimony is necessary for explaining or supplementing the conclusion.

794. A specialist must, when called upon, appear before the court and present an objective conclusion about the matters put to him/her. Where a specialist, for no good reason, fails to appear before the court, or where he/she refuses to perform his/her duty without a lawful ground, a fine may be applied. A specialist shall be held liable for giving a false report under the CC of Lithuania.

---

435. https://wcd.coe.int/ViewDoc.jsp?Ref=CEPEJ(2014)14&Language=lanEnglish&Ver=original&BackColorInternet=DBDCF2&BackColorIntranet=FDC864&BackColorLogged=FDC864.

436. Ruling of the Supreme Court of Lithuania in criminal case No. 2K-7-1-693/2017.

E. The Item (as an Evidence)

795. Objects relevant for the pretrial investigation of a criminal act and the hearing, shall be physical items which were instruments for or means of committing a criminal act or upon which traces of a criminal act have been left, or which were targets of criminal acts committed by the offender, as well as all other items which may be instrumental in detecting a criminal act and the offenders, or in disproving the charge or mitigating the liability.

796. Objects which must be subjected to examination shall be inspected and described in the conclusion of a specialist. Objects relevant for the investigation of a criminal act and the trial shall be kept and submitted together with the file of the pretrial investigation of a criminal act. If any of the objects, because of their bulk or other reasons, may not be kept and submitted together with the file of the pretrial investigation of a criminal act, they must be, where possible, photographed, sealed and kept at a place indicated by the pretrial investigator, the prosecutor or the court.

797. A judgment, a ruling or a decision to terminate proceedings must determine the issue of objects relevant for the investigation of a criminal act and the trial

F. The Document (as an Evidence)

798. Documents relevant for the pretrial investigation of a criminal act and the hearing shall be objects in which an enterprise, agency, organisation, an official or a physical person record by appropriate signs information which enables to detect a criminal act and determine the circumstances related to the act.

799. Documents relevant for the investigation of a criminal act and the court hearing shall be as follows: (1) records of the survey, search, seizure, identification parade, verification of evidence, reconstruction of the crime, the experiment and other investigative actions as well as records of the trial; (2) documents of agencies, enterprises, and organisations: written instruments, certificates, accounting reports, minutes of meetings and other official documents; (3) private papers, statements, applications, complaints, letters, diaries and other writings of a private nature of physical persons; (4) magnetic, laser and electronic recordings: audio and video recordings, compact discs and other electronic forms of recording information; (5) other physical objects bearing information recorded graphically or in other signs which are relevant for the pretrial investigation of a criminal act and the hearing.

800. Documents, records and other entries shall be considered items where they have characteristics of the object relevant for the pretrial investigation of a criminal act and the hearing.

III. The Exclusion of Evidence

801. As it was mentioned above, the court as evidence may consider only material which is obtained by lawful means and may be validated by the procedural actions laid down in the CCP.

802. Following the requirements of the Lithuanian criminal procedure and jurisprudence of the Supreme Court of Lithuania, when deciding whether to accept data as evidence, the court should determine whether the means by which the data has been obtained are in conformity with the requirements of law and check whether they have been verified by procedural actions provided for in the CCP.[437] If the relevant data has been provided by private parties (e.g., the suspect, defence counsel, the victim or his/her representative, or any other physical person or legal entity), the court should ascertain whether the means to obtain the data are not prohibited by law. Information provided by private individuals shall not be recognised as evidence only when it has been received in a manner directly prohibited by law. In cases where the relevant data has been collected by public authorities or a pretrial investigator, prosecutor, pretrial judge or the court, it is necessary to determine whether it has been obtained in the manner prescribed by law without any breach of the procedure for obtaining data established by law.[438] Data collected by public authorities or officials by means which are not provided for in law, shall not be recognised as evidence, no matter how persuasive it may be determining the circumstances relevant for the criminal case.

803. A breach of the data collection procedure *per se* does not mean that such data may no longer be recognised as evidence. In this case, it is necessary to assess: (1) whether the violation affected the reliability of the data and (2) whether the violation deprived or restricted the rights of the accused.[439] The data received in breach of the procedure for their collection, which raises doubts as to their reliability and such doubts cannot be eliminated by performing other actions envisaged in the CCP, shall not be recognised as evidence. The court may recognise as evidence data received in breach of procedural violations, if it does not affect the reliability of the data and does not deprive the accused of his/her rights or constrain such rights substantially.[440] If data collection irregularities deny the accused his/her rights, or limit them substantially, such data shall not be recognised as evidence, regardless that there is no doubt as to its reliability. Although the CCP does not formulate *expressis verbis*, the data collected contrary to the legal rules of evidence shall nevertheless be considered as inadmissible evidence. The court cannot rely on such data in conviction. The CCP does not specify any general procedure as to what should be done

437. Review of the Criminal division of the Supreme Court of Lithuania of 28 Jun. 2007, Teismų praktika, No. 27, p. 328.
438. Review of the Criminal division of the Supreme Court of Lithuania of 28 Jun. 2007, Teismų praktika, No. 27, p. 329.
439. Goda G., Kazlauskas M., Kuconis P. Baudžiamojo proceso teisė, Vilnius, Registrų centras, 2011, p. 168.
440. Review of the Criminal division of the Supreme Court of Lithuania of 28 Jun. 2007, Teismų praktika, No. 27, p. 330–331.

with the data recognised as inadmissible evidence. However, in some cases, the CCP lays down special rules, for example, in the case of unauthorised seizure of articles or documents, they shall be returned to the person from whom they came, and cannot be relied on in conviction.

Chapter 2. Powers, Rights and Duties in the Pretrial Investigation

§1. Powers, Rights and Duties of the Prosecutor and Pretrial Investigator

804. The powers and duties of the prosecutor and the pretrial investigator (police, Special Investigation Service, Financial Crimes Investigation Service, etc.) during pretrial investigation stage are prescribed not only in the Code of Criminal Procedure, but also in the Law on Prosecution, the Law on Police, the Law on Special Investigation Service, the Law on Financial Crimes Investigation Service, the Law on Criminal Intelligence and other legal acts.

I. Introductory Remarks

805. According to the Lithuanian criminal procedure, the prosecutor and the pretrial investigator may secretly or publicly collect data, which is necessary for the establishment of the committed criminal act and the person who has committed this criminal act.

806. The Lithuanian criminal procedure distinguishes two forms of secret data collection. The secret data collection may be executed by the state authorities for the purpose of the future criminal procedure (proactive investigation) and for the purposes of national security. The secret data collection for the purpose of the national security is regulated by the Law on Intelligence.[441] Meanwhile, the secret data collection for the purpose of future criminal procedure is provided for in the Law on Criminal Intelligence.[442] According to the Law on Criminal Intelligence, a criminal intelligence investigation shall be started before the pretrial investigation, if: (1) there is an information about the preparation of or commission of a less-serious, serious or grave crime, or on a person who prepares or commits abovementioned crime; (2) the suspect, accused or convicted is hidden; (3) the person has disappeared; (4) the protection of individuals from criminal activity is carried out. During the investigation of criminal intelligence State authorities may apply such methods of secret data collection as questioning; controlled delivery, actions simulating a criminal act, covert surveillance, secret operation, use of technical means, etc.

807. If a criminal intelligence investigation reveals the *corpus delicti* signs of a criminal act, the pretrial investigation is immediately initiated.[443] The Supreme

441. Lietuvos Respublikos žvalgybos įstatymas, *Valstybės žinios*, 2012, No. 129-6463.
442. Lietuvos Respublikos kriminalinės žvalgybos įstatymas, *Valstybės žinios*, 2012, No. 122-6093.
443. The Prosecutor General has adopted methodological recommendation on this issue: Generalinio prokuroro įsakymas 'Dėl Rekomendacijų dėl Kriminalinės žvalgybos įstatymo, Baudžiamojo proceso kodekso normų taikymo ir kriminalinės žvalgybos informacijos panaudojimo baudžiamajame procese patvirtinimo', *Valstybės žinios*, 2013, No. 2-83.

Court has noted that criminal intelligence must be turned into a pretrial investigation as soon as possible since the Code of Criminal Procedure requires the pretrial investigation to be carried out and the criminal act to be revealed in the shortest time.[444] During the pretrial investigation, a pretrial investigator and a prosecutor may carry out procedural coercive measures and investigative actions provided in the Code of Criminal Procedure. The Code of Criminal Procedure establishes the exhaustive list of these procedural coercive measures and investigative actions, which means that the pretrial investigator, prosecutor, pretrial judge and the court may apply only them. This list provides such procedural coercive measures and investigative actions as provisional arrest, committal of the suspect to a medical institution, bringing in person, taking of samples for a comparative analysis, search, seizure, temporary limitation of the property rights, temporary removal from the office, prosecutor rights to request information, taking photographs, filming, taking measurements, fingerprints and samples for genetic dactyloscopy, actions of the officers of a pretrial investigation institution without disclosing their identity, simulation of a criminal act, covert surveillance, etc.

II. Covert Policing Methods

808. When the pretrial investigation is started, the pretrial judge or the prosecutor may order to apply covert (secret) investigative actions provided in the Code of Criminal Procedure. The Code of Criminal Procedure provides these covert (secret) investigative actions: actions of the officers of a pretrial investigation institution without disclosing their identity (Article 158 of the CCP), simulation of a criminal act (Article 159 of the CCP) and covert surveillance (Article 160 of the CCP).

809. A prosecutor, upon receiving information from a person about a plan to commit a crime or to participate in such a crime, may file with a pretrial judge an application to authorise the person to commit actions simulating a criminal act in order to detect the persons who commit crimes. This measure may be applied only for the crimes provided in the CC.

810. When performing actions simulating a criminal act it shall be prohibited to incite a person to commit a criminal act.[445] It must be noted that the case law of the ECtHR,[446] as well as the jurisprudence of the Supreme Court of Lithuania,[447] contain examples of the improper implementation of this requirement in Lithuania. This measure is executed by the officer of the pretrial investigation institution. In special cases, when there are no other possibilities of detecting the persons committing crimes, this measure may be also conducted by persons who are not officers of the pretrial investigation.

---

444. Ruling of the Supreme Court of Lithuania in criminal case No. 2K-7-85-696/2016.
445. Ruling of the Supreme Court of Lithuania in criminal case No. 2K-251/2007.
446. Goda G., Kazlauskas M., Kuconis P. Baudžiamojo proceso teisė, Vilnius, Registrų centras, 2011, p. 276–277.
447. Rulings of the Supreme Court of Lithuania in criminal cases No. 2A-P-6/2008 and No. 2A-P-2/2009.

811. When authorising actions simulating a criminal act, the pretrial judge must make a ruling specifying the following: (1) the person authorised to commit actions simulating a criminal act; (2) the person against whom such actions are to be performed; (3) information about the criminal act of that person; (4) the authorised actions; (5) the result sought.

812. Actions of the officers of a pretrial investigation institution without disclosing their identity must be authorised by a ruling of the pretrial judge and on condition that there is sufficient information about criminal activities of the person who is subject to the pretrial investigation. These officers may also use a mode of conduct simulating a criminal act. If such actions restrict the inviolability of the home or the secrecy of the correspondence, they may be applied only when investigating less-serious, serious and grave crimes. Officers of a pretrial investigation institution when conducting actions without disclosing their identity shall be prohibited from inciting or inducing a person to commit a criminal act,[448] also they cannot resort to procedural coercive measures where a separate decision or a ruling relating to what has not been made. This measure is executed by the officer of the pretrial investigation institution. In special cases when there are no other possibilities to detect the persons committing crimes, this measure may be also conducted by persons who are not officers of the pretrial investigation. A prosecutor must apply for the authorisation of this measure. The pretrial judge ruling authorising officers of a pretrial investigation institution to perform actions without disclosing their identity must be written and reasoned and must indicate the following: (1) the persons who will perform the undercover actions; (2) the person against whom undercover actions must be performed; (3) information about the criminal act of the person; (4) the authorised actions; (5) the result sought; (6) the duration of undercover actions.

813. A pretrial judge, upon receiving an appropriate application from a prosecutor, may order (acoustic and visual) covert surveillance of a person or a motor vehicle or other object (e.g., houses, flats, administrative premises, etc.[449]). An official who has taken part in secret surveillance may be questioned as a witness. If necessary, the rules of non-disclosure of the identity of the witness (official) may be applied. The ruling of a pretrial judge or the decision of a prosecutor or a pretrial investigator for surveillance of a person, a motor vehicle or an object must specify the following: (1) the person, the motor vehicle or the object of the surveillance; (2) the reason for such a measure; (3) the duration of surveillance. If a video or audio recording or filming is wanted (intended) during the surveillance this must also be provided for in the ruling of the pretrial judge, or the decision of the prosecutor or the pretrial investigator.

814. In cases of utmost urgency, all these covert (secret) investigative actions may be also applied by a decision of a prosecutor or a pretrial investigator; however, if this is the case, within three days from the start of these actions the consent

448. Ruling of the Supreme Court of Lithuania in criminal cases No. 2K-313/2010.
449. Goda G., Kazlauskas M., Kuconis P. Baudžiamojo proceso teisė, Vilnius, Registrų centras, 2011, p. 278.

of the pretrial judge must be sought. If such a consent is not forthcoming, the actions that have been initiated must be cancelled and all collected data must be destroyed.

815. The record of the actions simulating a criminal act, actions of the officers of a pretrial investigation institution without disclosing their identity and secret surveillance shall be made and must be added to the case file.

III. The Powers to Check and Search

816. The powers of the police to check and identify the person are regulated by the mentioned Law on Police. The police officer shall have these general rights: (1) having a reasonable suspicion that a criminal act has been carried out, to check documents of the person who is related to it, documents of the means of transport, freight documents and to seize them temporarily, until the adoption of a decision; (2) to detain and bring offenders to official premises of the police or other law-enforcement institutions for the purpose of establishing their identity, drawing up records, statements and reports and examining the persons and their possessions, etc. While investigating a criminal act or possessing information that such an act is being planned, is carried out or has been carried out, the police officer shall have the right: (1) to inspect economic and commercial as well as financial or other activities of the enterprises, agencies and organisations of all types, the state of protection of material valuables and goods, the legality of their acquisition, production, utilisation, and sale, and the premises of production, administration and other spheres, including sealed premises; (2) to inspect vehicles entering or leaving the territory of enterprises, agencies and organisations, as well as the freight and goods carried by means of transportation belonging to natural or legal persons; (3) to order and carry out inventory, auditing, check measurements and other inspections; to examine, review and seize documents concerning book keeping, personnel, inspections and audits, other documents, as well as samples of raw materials, products, and goods, other items; to demand that book keeping be in order; (4) to obtain information and explanatory statements concerning criminal acts from managers, officers and persons who are materially responsible and others; (5) to inspect the means of transportation, individuals and their personal luggage at check posts of all kinds; etc.

817. In principle the same powers and duties to check and search for the officers of the Special Investigation Service provides the Law on Special Investigation Service, for the officers of the Financial Crimes Investigation Service – the Law on Financial Crimes Investigation Service, etc.

818. Article 155 of the Code of Criminal Procedure also provides the right of the prosecutor, having obtained the consent of a pretrial judge, to request any State, public or private agency, enterprise or organisation to facilitate the examination of the necessary documents or any other appropriate information, and make recordings or copies of documents and information, if this is necessary for the investigation of a criminal act. The doctrine of the Lithuanian criminal procedure indicates that under this procedure it is impossible to get information from any individual even if he/she has it.[450] The prosecutor may only use the information gathered in the specified manner for the pretrial investigation of a criminal act. The prosecutor must immediately destroy any information that is not necessary for the investigation of a criminal act.

IV. The Powers of Entry, Search and Seizure

819. The Law on Police, the Law on Special Investigation Service, the Law on Financial Crimes Investigation Service, etc. provide the powers for the officers of the police, Special Investigation Service, Financial Crimes Investigation Service, etc. while in the pursuit of suspects or absconding criminals, or in an attempt to prevent a criminal act from being carried out, or in carrying out the pretrial investigation to enter, at any time of day, residential or non-residential premises, territories of physical persons and legal entities, as well as to halt and enter any means of transportation; to enter the premises of enterprises, agencies or organisations of all types during working hours or during non-working hours (with an administrative representative, a representative of the owner or the owner of the enterprise, agency or organisation); etc.

820. According to the Code of Criminal Procedure, the pretrial investigator or the prosecutor may carry out a seizure, if it is necessary to seize tangible objects, documents, also postal or telegraphic communications, which is needed for the pretrial investigation, and if it is known where and in whose possession they are.

821. Only the prosecutor, the judge or the court shall have the right to examine the content of postal or telegraphic correspondence.

822. Upon reasonable belief that there are, in some premises or other place, instruments of a criminal act, tangible objects obtained or acquired in a criminal way, or other objects or documents that might be relevant for the pretrial investigation, a pretrial investigator or a prosecutor may carry out a search with a view to discovering and seizing them. A search may also be carried out with the purpose of finding fugitives or bodies. The Supreme Court of Lithuania has noted that 'data must be realistic, reasonable and may be obtained from procedural actions (e.g., victim or witness testimony, etc.) or the investigation of criminal intelligence'.[451]

823. A personal search may be carried out subject to the same rules as a search of a flat, house or other premises. A personal search, without a prior order relating to the search, may be carried out: (1) when effecting a provisional arrest or a pretrial detention; (2) when there are substantial grounds for believing that a person

450. Lietuvos Respublikos baudžiamojo proceso kodekso komentaras. I dalis, Vilnius, TIC, 2003, p. 392.
451. Ruling of the Supreme Court of Lithuania in criminal case No. 2K-141/2007.

present on the premises or any other place where a seizure or a search are being carried out is hiding tangible objects or documents relevant to the case.

824. A pretrial investigator or a prosecutor shall have the right to carry out a body search of a suspect, a victim or any other person when there is a need to find traces of the criminal act or any special marks on his/her body, where medical examination is not necessary. Where the person objects to being subjected to a body search, an order to this effect from a pretrial investigator or a prosecutor is required.

825. It is prohibited to effect seizures or searches at night, with the exception of cases of the utmost urgency. An officer conducting a seizure or a search must limit himself/herself to the seizure only of those objects or documents, which may be of relevance for the pretrial investigation.

826. Tangible objects and documents the circulation whereof is prohibited by law must be seized irrespective of whether they are relevant or not for the investigation.

827. A personal search may be carried out only by someone of the same sex. If the search involves exposure of the person's body, it will be carried out by a pretrial investigator, a prosecutor or a medical doctor of the same sex as the person searched. When carrying out a personal search on a person, actions humiliating his/her dignity or which are detrimental to his/her health shall not be permitted.

828. A seizure or search must be carried out in the presence of the owner, tenant, manager of the flat, house or other premises where the search is being conducted, a member or their family or a close relative, and where a search is being carried out in business premises or an office, in the presence of a representative of that business or office. When it is not possible to arrange the presence of the above persons, a search shall be carried out in the presence of any other two persons or a representative of a municipal institution. Where appropriate, guests may be invited to participate in the search and in other cases.

829. Searches of land, forestry or bodies of water can take place without the participation of the owner, tenant or manager, but after the search these persons have to be informed of the search in writing.

830. Seizures and searches of premises occupied by a diplomatic mission, or where members of the diplomatic mission and their families live, may be effected only subject to a request by, or with the consent of diplomatic representatives.

831. An officer effecting a seizure or search must take measures to prevent disclosure of the circumstances of private life, unrelated to the case, of a person living in the premises and other persons which come to light during the seizure or search.

832. Persons in possession of tangible objects or documents subject to seizure must not interfere with the officers carrying out a seizure. Failure to comply with this requirement may result in them being fined.

833. Before starting a seizure or a search, a pretrial investigator or prosecutor must read out a decision or a ruling relating to the search, after which he/she must request that the tangible objects or documents specified in the decision or the ruling be surrendered, or the place where the person is in hiding be disclosed. When effecting a seizure or a search, a pretrial investigator or prosecutor shall have the right to gain entry; when doing this he/she must avoid unnecessary damage to locks, doors or other objects. A pretrial investigator or prosecutor shall have the right to forbid those persons present at the premises or place where a seizure or a search is taking place, and also those persons who come to the premises or place, from leaving the premises or the place, or from communicating among themselves or with other persons, until the seizure or the search is over. The premises or the place where a seizure or a search takes place may be surrounded by officers.

834. If persons having possession of the tangible objects or documents subject to seizure do not agree to surrender these objects and documents voluntarily, seizure may be effected by force.

835. The pretrial judge ruling ordering seizure or search must be written and reasoned. In case of a search, the ruling must indicate what objects will be searched for.

836. In cases of utmost urgency, a seizure or search may be effected under a decision of the pretrial investigation officer or the prosecutor; however, in such cases, within three days, approval of the pretrial judge must be sought with regard to the lawfulness of such a seizure or search. If this approval is denied, all objects and documents which had been taken shall be returned to those from whom they were taken, and cannot be referred to as evidence later in the criminal procedure.

837. A record about the seizure or search shall be drafted. The record must specify the objects and documents seized, and their main features must be described. If no objects or documents were seized during the search, this must also be indicated in the record. A copy of the record of a seizure and search shall be left with the person at whose place the seizure or search was conducted. All the seized tangible objects and documents must be shown to the persons present and must be listed in the record of a seizure or search, or in a list attached to it, indicating their quantity, measurements, weight, individual marks and their physical condition.

V. The Powers of Arrest

838. The Lithuanian criminal procedure provides four forms of the temporary deprivation of the person's freedom during pretrial investigation: bringing in person, a provisional arrest, pretrial detention and committal to the medical institution.

These forms differ in duration and the procedure and purpose of imposition, for example, bringing in person may be imposed on a person who fails to appear before the pretrial investigator, a provisional arrest may be imposed where the grounds for the pretrial detention, etc. exist.

839. The suspect, the accused, the victim and any other person summoned as a witness must appear before the pretrial investigator, the prosecutor or the court. The suspect, the accused, the victim or the witness who fails to appear before the pretrial investigator, the prosecutor or the court without good cause may be brought in person. The person shall be brought in by the police by a decision of the pretrial investigator, the prosecutor or a ruling of the pretrial judge or court.

VI. The Powers for the Temporary Limitation of the Property Rights

840. A temporary limitation of the property rights of a suspect or a physical person who is financially responsible for the actions of the suspect, or of other physical persons who have possession of the property received or acquired by criminal means, may be imposed by a decision of a prosecutor. The temporary limitation of the property rights of the legal entity also may be imposed with the view to securing a civil claim or the confiscation of property. According to the doctrine of the Lithuanian criminal procedure[452] a temporary limitation of the property rights is a procedural coercion measure, which fulfils a preventive function.

841. A temporary limitation on the property rights may be imposed together with or separately from a seizure or search. A temporary limitation of the property rights shall be cancelled by the decision of a prosecutor or a court ruling where the measure is no longer necessary.

842. A prosecutor's decision on a temporary limitation of the property rights may not be for longer than for a period of six months. This term may be extended, but for not more than one period of six months by the ruling of the pretrial judge. However, the number of extensions in cases involving serious and grave crimes or when a suspect is in hiding shall not be subject to any limits.

843. The property of a person for whom a temporary limitation of property rights is being imposed, shall be charged. All the property charged must be shown to the persons present. The charging list must indicate the quantity of the objects charged and their individual features. Where a temporary limitation is imposed on bank deposits, all transactions involving them shall be suspended, if the decision on a temporary limitation of the property rights does not provide otherwise.

---

452. Bilius M., Stonys J. Laikino nuosavybės teisių apribojimo problematika baudžiamajame procese: optimalaus sprendimo beieškant // Baudžiamoji justicija ir verslas, Vilnius, 2016, p. 389.

844. A person on whom a temporary limitation of the rights of property has been imposed shall be entitled to appeal against the decision of a prosecutor to the pretrial judge. Such an appeal must be examined by the pretrial judge within three days from the receipt of the appeal. The decision of the pretrial judge may be appealed against a higher court, the decision whereof shall be final and not subject to appeal.

VII. The Powers to Interview the Suspect and Witness

A. The Powers to Interview the Suspect

845. As it was mentioned before, the suspect must be questioned at least once during the pretrial investigation, before drawing up the indictment. The suspect must be always questioned before imposing a remand measure on him/her.

846. The suspect must arrive to the questioning, but he/she may refuse to give testimony. It should be noted that the suspect cannot be held liable for giving false testimony.[453] At the start of the questioning, the suspect shall be asked whether he/she pleads guilty to the charge of a criminal act of which he is suspected. After that, he/she is invited to make a testimony about the essence of the suspicion. Finally, he/she may be asked additional questions. The testimony of the suspect shall be entered in the record in first person singular and be as much verbatim as possible. Where necessary, the questions put to the suspect and his/her replies shall be noted. Moreover, if during the questioning, the suspect has exercised his/her right to remain silent or refuse to testify about his/her own alleged crime, this shall be noted in the record.

B. The Powers to Interview the Witness

847. Article 182 of the Code of Criminal Procedure provides that a person shall be called for questioning by a summons which shall indicate the person to be summoned and for what purpose, the place and to whom he/she is being summoned, the day and hour when he/she has to present himself/herself, the consequences of a failure to present himself/herself. A person may also be summonsed for questioning by telephone or any other way, except that if such is the case, procedural coercive measures may not be applied for the failure to present himself/herself.

848. Before commencing the questioning of a witness, a prosecutor or a pretrial investigator shall determine the identity of the witness, obtain the necessary information about the character of the witness and his/her relations with the suspect, inform him/her about his/her rights and responsibilities. Before the first questioning, the witness is warned about the responsibility for giving false testimony, and he/she confirms this with his/her signature in the record. Before starting another

453. Goda G., Kazlauskas M., Kuconis P. Baudžiamojo proceso teisė, Vilnius, Registrų centras, 2011, p. 317.

questioning, the witness is reminded that he/she has been warned about the responsibility for giving false testimony, and this is indicated in the record.

849. The examination shall open with an invitation to the witness to tell everything he/she knows about the circumstances relevant to the disposition of the case. Afterwards the witness may be asked questions. The testimony of the witness shall be recorded in first person and verbatim as much as possible. Where necessary, the question put to the witness and his/her replies shall be recorded.

C. The Powers for Confrontation, Identification Parade, Verification of the Testimonies on the Site and Experiment

850. Two previously questioned persons whose testimonies show essential contradictions may be brought for the confrontation in order to discover the reasons for the contradictions and to eliminate them. When questioning the persons brought for the confrontation, general rules of questioning of a witness and a suspect must be followed.

851. When starting the questioning of the persons brought for the confrontation they shall be questioned whether they know each other and in what relation they are to each other. After that, the persons shall be asked in turn to testify about the circumstances for the reason of whose discovery they have been brought for confrontation. After the testimony of each of the persons questioned, they may be asked additional questions. If a person questioned during the confrontation changes his/her earlier testimony, he/she must be asked about the reasons for changing his/her earlier testimony. The persons brought for the confrontation may put questions to each other. The other persons present during the confrontation may also put questions to the persons brought for the confrontation.

852. It shall be permitted to make the testimonies of the participants of the confrontation contained in the records of previous questionings public as well as to review the audio and video recordings of those questionings only after their testimonies during the confrontation and after entering them in the record.

853. With a view to verifying the testimony of a questioned person about a certain person, article or any other tangible object, an identification parade may be held. The person who is to be identified shall be shown to the identifying person together with other person of the same sex who by their appearance has greater similarity with the person to be identified. The overall number of the persons shown during the identification parade must be at least three (this requirement shall not apply when identifying a body). Before starting the identification parade, the person to be identified shall be invited to take any position among the persons shown during the identification parade, making a note accordingly in the record.

854. If the person cannot be shown, the identification parade can be made with the help of his/her photo or video recording which shall be shown together with the photos or video recording of at least three other persons. The Supreme Court of Lithuania has noted that 'an identification parade by photo can only be made when the person himself/herself cannot be shown'.[454]

855. In order to identify an unknown suspect, tangible object or any other item, a witness or a victim also may be shown collections of people's photos, files of video recordings, objects or any other items gathered at a pretrial investigation institution.

856. Before the identification parade, the person who is to make identification must be questioned about the circumstances under which he/she saw or took notice in any other way of the person, article or any other tangible object subject to identification as well as about the marks and features according to which he/she may identify this person, article or any other tangible object. After the identification parade the person who participates at the identification parade may be questioned and invited to explain according to what features or characteristics he/she identified this person, object or any other item or explain the differences between the persons, objects or any other items shown to him/her for identification and referred in his/her testimony.

857. The Lithuanian criminal procedure also provides that with a view to verifying and revising the testimony given by a witness, a victim or a suspect, with regard to the site or the situation of the incident, the actions of the participants in the incident or other circumstances relevant to the investigation of a criminal act, the site indicated by the person whose testimony is being verified or revised may be visited and comparison of the testimony subject to verification with the circumstances on the site may be effected. The person whose testimony is subject to verification shall voluntarily indicate the place about which he/she gave testimony, explain the testimony given previously, demonstrating their connection with the circumstances on the site and answers the questions put to him/her.

858. With a view to verifying the testimonies and versions of the witnesses, victims and the suspects, it is possible to reconstruct the situation of the event under investigation, its environment, the actions of the persons or any other circumstances and to conduct the appropriate tests.

VIII. Miscellaneous

A. The Powers at the Scene of the Offence

859. Article 205 of the Code of Criminal Procedure provides that in order to examine the traces of a criminal act and other items relevant to the disposition of the case, to uncover the circumstances of the criminal act and other facts pertinent to the case, an examination of the scene of the criminal act, the human body, the

454. Ruling of the Supreme court of Lithuania in criminal case No. 2K-250-942/2016.

location, premises (there are some restrictions to access to residential and work areas of diplomats, members of the *Seimas*, judges, etc.), documents and other items may have to be conducted.

860. 'Crime scenes' or other places, as well as tangible objects relevant to the pretrial investigation of a criminal act, or any items which do not have to be examined, shall be inspected by the prosecutor, a pretrial investigator or a specialist. A record of the inspection shall be made which shall specify in detail the 'crime scene', other places or items and their features relevant to the establishment of the circumstances of a criminal act. Such places or items shall be photographed as required.

861. An exhumed body must be identified by the persons who knew him/her, or identified in some other way. Family members or close relatives of the dead person shall have the right to be present during the exhumation.

862. Examination of items shall be carried out by specialists. Examination of a human body shall be carried out by a medical examiner or any other doctor. Examination of the mental state of a person shall be carried out by a forensic psychiatrist.

863. Tangible objects, documents and other items shall be examined at the site of their discovery. Where the examination of tangible objects, documents or other items takes a long time or where technical facilities are needed, they may be examined at a laboratory or other place having adequate facilities.

864. Exhumation of an officially buried body and examination of a person's residence or work premises which are not the scene of the criminal act without the consent of the owners or the representatives of an enterprise, institution, or organisation are subject to the written and reasoned ruling of the pretrial judge.

865. Upon completing the examination of the places or items assigned to him/her, a specialist shall submit the report. A specialist's report may be included in the record of the examination conducted.

B. The Powers to Call in Experts

866. According to the Lithuanian criminal procedure, an expert examination shall be ordered where the pretrial judge or the court determines that a special examination requiring scientific, artistic or any other special knowledge must be carried out for establishing the circumstances of a criminal act.

867. Upon establishing that it is necessary to order expert examination during pretrial investigation, the prosecutor shall duly inform in writing the suspect, his/her defence counsel and other parties to the proceedings interested in the findings of expert examination and shall indicate the period during which the aforesaid persons may make requests on questions to the expert, appointment of a specific expert and submit additional material for expert examination. If the suspect is not in the territory of the Republic of Lithuania, the information concerning expert examination must be sent in accordance with the international agreements of the Republic of Lithuania to the central institutions of a foreign state. Thereafter the prosecutor shall file an application to the pretrial judge.[455] Requests of the parties to the proceeding or a notice that no requests have been received shall be attached to the application. The pretrial judge ruling on having expert examination must be written and reasoned. The ruling shall indicate: the circumstances of a criminal act; the grounds for ordering expert examination; the expert institution or the expert who will undertake the expert examination; the questions put to the expert; and the materials submitted to the expert.

868. Upon carrying out appropriate examinations, an expert shall draw up a report of expert examination, which, *inter alia*, shall formulate answers to the questions that have been submitted. The conclusions of the expert may not go beyond the scope of his/her special knowledge. Upon receiving the expert's report, the prosecutor shall send a notification in writing to the suspect, his/her defence counsel and other parties to the proceedings who have requested expert examination or who made requests for ordering expert examination, and indicate in it the time and place where the report may be studied. A report shall be made to evidence that the expert's report has been studied.

869. If it is necessary, the court by the same procedure may order expert examination during the trial.

870. If the expert examination was performed during the pretrial investigation and the report of expert examination presented to the court is sufficiently clear and comprehensive, the report shall be read out during the hearing in the absence of the expert. The expert shall be summoned to the hearing for questioning only after the court recognises that his/her testimony is necessary for explaining or supplementing the expert report.

871. An expert must, when called upon, appear before the court and present an objective report about the matters put to him/her. Where an expert, for no good reason, fails to appear before the court, or where he/she refuses to perform his/her duty without a lawful ground, a fine may be applied. An expert shall be held liable for giving a false report under the CC of Lithuania.

455. The Prosecutor General has adopted methodological recommendation on this issue: Generalinio prokuroro įsakymas 'Dėl Rekomendacijų dėl užduočių specialistams ir ekspertams skyrimo patvirtinimo', *Valstybės žinios*, 2011, No. 8-379.

§2. POWERS, RIGHTS AND DUTIES WITHIN THE FRAMEWORK OF THE PRETRIAL DETENTION

I. Introductory Remarks

872. Article 20 of the Constitution of Lithuania provides that

> no person may be arbitrarily arrested or detained. No person may be deprived of freedom except on the bases, and according to the procedures, which have been established in laws. A person detained in flagrante delicto must, within 48 hours, be brought to court for the purpose of determining, in the presence of the detainee, the validity of the detention. In the event that the court does not pass a decision to arrest the person, the detained individual shall be released immediately.

These constitutional requirements, also provisions of Article 5 of the ECHR and case law[456] of the ECtHR are very important for the regulation and application of the procedural coercive measures, especially those related to the restriction of personal freedom.

873. The Code of Criminal Procedure provides four procedural coercive measures, which relate to the restriction of personal freedom – bringing in person, a provisional arrest, a pretrial detention and a committal of the suspect or accused to the medical institution.

II. The Warrants of Attachment and of Arrest

A. The Warrant of Attachment

874. According to Article 140 of the CCP, a provisional arrest can be ordered and enforced by any person, pretrial investigator or prosecutor, if the person concerned is apprehended either in the criminal act (*in flagrante delicto*) or immediately after the criminal act. The police must be informed immediately if the person was arrested by any other person.

875. Unless the person is caught red-handed, only the prosecutor, or pretrial investigator in exceptional cases, may decide upon provisional arrest, provided that a ground for it exists: (1) there are grounds for pretrial detention; (2) there is a need immediately to restrict the freedom; (3) there are no possibilities of bringing the person before a pretrial judge for the imposition of pretrial detention.

876. A prosecutor must be notified in any case of the provisional arrest of a person, by means of a copy of the written provisional arrest protocol. The Code of

456. Goda G., Kazlauskas M., Kuconis P. Baudžiamojo proceso teisė, Vilnius, Registrų centras, 2011, p. 235, 238–239.

Criminal Procedure regulates the time limits for provisional arrest. The arrested person must be questioned as suspect within 24 hours, by pretrial investigator or prosecutor. This provision contains no such wording as 'as soon as possible', but the provision has to be read in connection with another rule, which provides that provisional arrest shall not last longer than is necessary for identification of a person and for performing indispensable investigative actions. The maximum term for provisional arrest is 48 hours. As an exception to this rule, the maximum term for provisional arrest is 24 hours if a person has already been questioned as suspect earlier in the process (however, a prosecutor has the right to extend this term up to 48 hours). If the prosecutor is of the opinion that pretrial detention is necessary, the arrested person must be brought, within 48 hours, before a pretrial judge. Provisional arrest (in the case of a person apprehended in the criminal act (*in flagrante delicto*) or immediately after the criminal act) may be enforced for any criminal act provided in the CC. In other cases, the provisional arrest may be ordered and enforced in exceptional cases only for a crime punishable by more than one year of imprisonment (meaning the abstract (legal) order of the punishment, provided in the sanction of the Article of the Special Part of the CC).

877. In every case of provisional arrest, the pretrial investigator or prosecutor as soon as possible must file the written protocol of the provisional arrest of the person.

878. The arrested person must be released immediately if: (1) the suspicion was not confirmed that he/she had committed a criminal act; (2) it is established that there are no grounds and conditions for the pretrial detention or the pretrial detention is not necessary; (3) the provisional arrest period provided by law has expired; (4) the court decides to refuse to impose the pretrial detention.

879. Time of provisional arrest shall be included into the time of pretrial detention and punishment.

B. The Warrant of Pretrial Detention

880. According to Article 120 of the Code of Criminal Procedure, pretrial detention is one of the provisional measures. The pretrial detention may be applied only if a 'reasonable ground' exists that justifies to believe that a suspect committed a criminal act. When deciding upon applying for or ordering the pretrial detention, the prosecutor, pretrial judge or court have to take into account the gravity of the crime committed by a suspect, his/her personality, whether he/she has a permanent residence and a job or any other legal means of livelihood, his/her age, the condition of his/her health, his/her marital status and other circumstances which might be pertinent when determining this issue. The wording 'reasonable ground' is not defined any further; according to the Senate of the Supreme Court of Lithuania,[457] the court must examine whether there is any reasonable evidence that the suspect could have committed the crime.

881. Article 122 of the Code of Criminal Procedure gives four grounds for the pretrial detention:

(1) the risk of escape. The pretrial detention is possible if there is a probable cause to believe that a suspect might escape (go into hiding) from the pretrial investigator, prosecutor or court. According to this provision, not only must the personal circumstances such as marital status, place of residence, etc. be taken into account, but also the record of convictions. The CCP does not provide for an automatic connection between the risk of absconding and a person's status as a foreigner, or lack of a fixed abode;
(2) the risk of obstruction of the process or the risk of obscuring evidence by the suspect or the accused. With respect to the risk of collusion, the pretrial detention is possible when there is evidence that a suspect himself/herself, or through other persons, might make an attempt to approach victims, witnesses, experts, other suspects or convicted persons, or to destroy, conceal or forge tangible objects and documents relevant to the case;
(3) the risk of committing new crimes. When there is a reasonable ground to believe that a suspect will commit new crimes, the pretrial detention might be imposed when a person is suspected or accused of having committed one or several serious or grave crimes, or aggravated theft, robbery, extortion or aggravated damaging of property, and might, before rendering of the judgment, commit a new grave crime or one of the crimes mentioned above. The same is possible when there is evidence that while at large, the suspect, suspected of a threat or an attempt to commit a crime, might actually commit any crime;
(4) a request for extradition, surrender to the International Criminal Court or EAW.

882. The Senate of the Supreme Court of Lithuania has noted[458] that the seriousness of a crime and the gravity of the possible sanction may be sufficient ground for the pretrial detention. However, in court jurisprudence, this remark has not lead to the practice of the pretrial detention being applied automatically after a serious or grave crime; other factors such as prior convictions, sources of living, family relations, etc. are taken into account as well.[459]

883. The pretrial detention may be ordered only for a crime, which is punishable by more than one year of imprisonment (meaning the abstract (legal) order of

457. Decision of the Senate of the Supreme Court of Lithuania of 30 Dec. 2004, Teismų praktika, No. 22, 2004.
458. Decision of the Senate of the Supreme Court of Lithuania of 30 Dec. 2004, Teismų praktika, No. 22.
459. Ruling of the Appeal Court of Lithuania in criminal case No. 1S-33/2008.

the punishment, provided in the sanction of the Article of the Special Part of the CC) and where a less severe provisional measure cannot achieve the purposes of the provisional measures.

884. For determining the issue of imposition of the pretrial detention during pretrial investigation, the prosecutor has to file an application and the competent pretrial judge or the judge of the region court must hold a hearing, in which participation of the suspect is obligatory; a defence counsel and a prosecutor may be present and take part in questioning of the suspect.

III. The Continuation of Pretrial Detention

885. Article 127 of the Code of Criminal Procedure provides the time limits for pretrial detention in the pretrial investigation stage of the case: the pretrial detention may not be applied for more than six months. A definite term shall be determined by the pretrial judge who imposes the pretrial detention. However, initially the pretrial detention may not be imposed for a period longer than three months and two months for juveniles. An extension of the pretrial detention, but for a period not longer than up to six months, may be authorised by the same pretrial judge or another pretrial investigation judge of the same district court or another district court.

886. The six months period of the pretrial detention can be extended: if the case is very complex or has a particularly large scope, the judge of a region court can grant incremental extensions of three months or two months for juveniles, but the overall duration may not exceed nine months for adults and six months for juveniles during the pretrial investigation stage. In cases involving serious or grave crimes, as well as in cases where suspects or accused persons are members of a group of accomplices, an organised group or a criminal association, or when persons are arrested or detained in a foreign State, the term of the pretrial detention may not last for more than eighteen months and twelve months for juveniles during the pretrial investigation stage.

887. In accordance with Article 127 of the Code of Criminal Procedure, for determining the issue of the extension of the pretrial detention during pretrial investigation, the prosecutor has to file an application and a competent pretrial judge or a judge of the region court must hold a hearing to which he/she summons a defence counsel and a prosecutor (whose presence is obligatory). If needed, the suspect may be brought to the hearing as well; this is mandatory when the pretrial detention lasts for more than six months or four months for the juvenile. The participation of the suspect in the hearing may be ensured by a videoconferencing system.

888. Once the pretrial investigation has been finished and procedure has progressed to the trial stage, the possibility of further extensions is without limit. On the contrary, during the entire criminal procedure, the pretrial detention cannot last more than two-thirds of the maximum punishment of imprisonment, provided in the sanction of the Article of the Special part of the CC for the most serious crime that is under the investigation and trial.

IV. The Lifting of the Warrant of Arrest or Pre-trial Detention

889. During the pretrial investigation, a prosecutor shall have the right to release the detained suspect if the ground for the pretrial detention has disappeared or its conditions have changed. The prosecutor must notify the pretrial judge or the court, which imposed the pretrial detention or extended its term about such a decision.

V. The Appeals to the Court of Appeal and the Court of Cassation

890. An appeal against imposition or an extension of the pretrial detention may be filed by the detainee or his/her defence counsel within twenty days from the moment of deciding to impose or extend the pretrial detention. The appeal should be filed through the court that imposed or extended the pretrial detention. The court must communicate the appeal, without delay, to a higher court. A panel of three judges of the higher court must consider the appeal within seven days from the receipt of the appeal. A hearing shall be held to consider the appeal against the imposition or extension of the pretrial detention, and the detainee and his/her legal counsel or only the counsel shall be summonsed to the hearing. The presence of the prosecutor during such hearing is obligatory. The participation of the suspect in the hearing may be ensured by a videoconferencing system. Practically, the suspect (accused) and his/her defence counsel get the chance to have their pretrial detention examined twice every three months.

891. A complaint against the non-imposition, or non-extension of the pretrial detention, also the release of the detainee from the pretrial detention may be filed by the prosecutor within three days from the moment of deciding to non-impose or non-extend the pretrial detention, etc. The appeal should be filed through the court that did not impose or extend the pretrial detention. The court must communicate the appeal, without delay, to a higher court. A panel of three judges of the higher court must consider the complaint within seven days from the receipt of the complaint. A hearing shall be held to consider the complaint against the imposition or extension of the pretrial detention, and the suspect or the accused and his/her legal counsel shall be summonsed to the hearing. The presence of the defence counsel and the prosecutor during such hearing is obligatory.

892. The decision of the panel of three judges of a higher court concerning the appeal or complaint is definitive and not subject to appeal.

VI. The Committal the Suspect or Accused to the Medical Institution

893. Where during the pretrial investigation or hearing of a criminal case, there is a need for a medical or psychiatric expert examination of a suspect or accused, he/she shall be committed by a pretrial judge's or court ruling to the examining institution until the report of expert examination is submitted to a prosecutor or the court. The time spent at the institution shall be included in the term of the pretrial detention. If it is established that the suspect or the accused, because of his/her mental disorder, may be dangerous for the public, a judge may order an extension of his/her stay at an examining institution or the suspect or the accused may be transferred to another special institution until the court decides upon the issue on employing compulsory medical measures. A suspect or accused shall be committed to an examining institution and his/her period of the stay at the institution shall be determined and extended following the same procedure provided for when applying or appealing against the pretrial detention. During the pretrial investigation stage, the detained suspect shall be committed to an examining institution by the decision of a prosecutor.

VII. An Alternative to the Pretrial Detention: Freedom and Release Under Conditions

894. The Code of Criminal Procedure provides the following separate provisional measures (which may be called as alternatives to the pretrial detention): an intensive supervision, a house arrest, a bail, an obligation to reside separately from the victim and (or) prohibition to approach the victim closer than a prescribed distance, a seizure of documents, a suspension of a special right, an injunction to report periodically to the police and a recognizance.[460] A provisional measure for a soldier may be an observation by the command of the military unit where he/she is doing his/her service, and for a minor – a committal to the supervision of the parents, or foster parents or the administration of a children's institution.

895. Provisional measures may be imposed with a view of securing the presence of a suspect during the proceedings, unhindered pretrial investigation, court hearing, the execution of the judgment and the prevention of commission of new criminal acts.

896. Provisional measures may be imposed only where there is a probable cause that a suspect committed a criminal act. A prosecutor, a pretrial judge or the court, when deciding whether there is a need to impose a provisional measure and selecting its type, must take into account the gravity of the criminal act committed by a suspect, his/her personality, whether he/she has a permanent residence and a job or

460. The Prosecutor General has adopted methodological recommendation on application of these provisional measures: Generalinio prokuroro įsakymas 'Dėl Rekomendacijų dėl kardomųjų priemonių, išskyrus suėmimą, skyrimo ikiteisminio tyrimo metu tvarkos ir nustatytų sąlygų laikymosi kontrolės patvirtinimo', TAR, 2015, No. 19096.

any other legal source of livelihood, his/her age, condition his/her of health, his/her marital status and other circumstances which might be pertinent when determining this issue. Several provisional measures less severe than the pretrial detention may be imposed at the same time. Moreover, a more severe provisional measure may be imposed upon the suspect who violates an imposed provisional measure.

897. An intensive supervision, a house arrest and an obligation to reside separately from the victim and (or) prohibition to approach the victim closer than a prescribed distance may be imposed only by the ruling of the pretrial judge or the court; other provisional measures – by the prosecutor's decision or the ruling of the pretrial judge or the court. It should be noted that in urgent cases such provisional measures as a seizure of documents, a suspension of a special right, an injunction to report periodically to the police, a recognizance, an observation by the command of military unit and a committal to the supervision of the parents, or foster parents or the administration of a children's institution may be imposed by the decision of the pretrial investigator. The pretrial investigator must immediately inform the prosecutor about it.

898. A provisional measure may also be imposed for an accused and the convicted person.

899. A house arrest shall be an obligation for a suspect during the prescribed time to stay at home, not to attend public places and not to have contacts with certain people. When applying this provisional measure, the term and conditions of house arrest shall be determined in the ruling of the pretrial judge or the court. Initially, the house arrest may not be imposed for a period longer than six months; this term may be extended for three months. Number of extensions is unlimited. A suspect shall be informed that the intensive supervision or the pretrial detention may be applied against him/her, for the breach of the conditions of house arrest.

900. An intensive supervision shall be the control of the suspect by the electronic means of surveillance. Initially, the intensive supervision may not be imposed for a period longer than six months; this term may be extended for three months. Number of extensions is unlimited. A suspect shall be informed that the pretrial detention may be applied against him/her, for the breach of the conditions of intensive supervision. The suspect must be aware of the electronic monitoring device and adhere to the established schedule, also he/she is not allowed to remove, damage or destroy an electronic monitoring device.

901. A suspect may be obliged to reside separately from the victim and (or) prohibited to approach the victim closer than a prescribed distance. Moreover, the suspect may also be obliged not to communicate in any form and to seek contact with the victim and persons who are living with the victim or to visit the specified places where the victim or persons who are living with the victim are at present. The suspect must leave the house, where he/she lived with the victim.

902. A bail shall be an amount of money paid by a suspect, his/her family members or relatives, also by other persons, enterprises or institutions into a deposit account of the prosecution office or the court. The amount of cash shall be determined by the official or the court, who imposes this provisional measure, taking into consideration the nature of the committed criminal act, the extent of the impending punishment, the financial situation of the accused and the person who gives bail and their character. When the bail is accepted, the person who pays must be informed that if the suspect does not fulfil his/her obligation the bail shall pass to the State.

903. A seizure of documents as a provisional measure may be applied by a decision of a prosecutor. The passport, the identity card, the driver's licence may be seized from the suspect. After the seizure of the documents, the suspect shall be issued a certificate stating which document has been taken from him/her.

904. The exercise of a special right is prohibited during the suspension of that special right. Upon a person who has breached this provisional measure, a more stringent provisional measure may be imposed.

905. A suspect may be obligated to report regularly to the police. The decision must contain the address of the police institution, the days of the week and the month, and the time when the suspect must report to the police institution. Where the suspect fails to appear at the police institution at the prescribed time, an officer of the police institution must promptly notify the prosecutor and take measures to establish the whereabouts of the suspect.

906. A recognizance shall be a written obligation by a suspect not to leave his/her place of residence or temporary residence without permission to leave of a prosecutor, a judge or the court. The suspect may also be obliged not to visit certain places and not to communicate and to seek out contact with certain persons.

907. Placing of the suspect who is a soldier under the observation by the command of a military unit shall be application of measures provided by the military service statute[461] with a view to ensuring a proper behaviour of the suspect and his/her appearance when summonsed by the pretrial investigator, the prosecutor, the pretrial judge or the court. The command of a military unit shall report in writing about the course of observation to the prosecutor, the pretrial judge or the court, who have imposed this provisional measure.

908. A committal of a juvenile suspect into care of his/her parents, foster parents also placing him/her under observation by the administration of a children's institution shall be a written undertaking by any of the aforesaid persons or of the administration of a children institution to ensure a proper behaviour of a juvenile suspect and his/her appearance when summonsed by the pretrial investigator, the prosecutor and the court.

---

461. Lietuvos Respublikos karo tarnybos statutas, *Valstybės žinios*, 2008, No. 30-1057.

§3. THE POWERS AND DUTIES OF THE INVESTIGATING JUDGE IN THE PRE-TRIAL INVESTIGATION

I. Introductory Remarks

909. As it was mentioned before, the investigating jurisdictions and judicial inquiry stage do not exist in the Lithuanian criminal procedure and the pretrial judge does not investigate. The main role of the pretrial judge is to apply coercive procedural measures and investigative actions, to provide judicial control over the prosecutor's and pretrial investigator's actions and decisions during the pretrial investigation and to control the taking of evidence. According to Article 173 of the Code of Criminal Procedure, during pretrial investigation the pretrial judge has the competence:

(1) to impose and order the application of procedural coercive measures and investigative actions: pretrial detention, home arrest, obligation to reside separately from the victim and (or) prohibition to approach the victim closer that a prescribed distance, committal of the suspect to the medical institution, actions of the officers of a pretrial investigation institution without disclosing their identity, simulation of a criminal act, covert surveillance, search, seizure of postal communication, temporary removal from the office, prosecutor rights to request information, expert examination, interception, recording, collection and monitoring of the telephone conversations, other information transmitted via telecommunications networks, procedural fine and arrest;
(2) to swear and examine the witnesses and the victims;
(3) to examine the suspects;
(4) to adopt or approve the prosecutor's decisions to terminate a pretrial investigation; (5) to approve the prosecutor's decisions to resume the terminated pretrial investigation; (6) to examine the complaints of parties to the proceeding concerning the actions of the pretrial investigation officers and the prosecutor.

910. These procedural actions shall be performed by the pretrial judge subject to an appropriate request from the prosecutor who shall submit it either on its own initiative or on the initiative of a party to the proceeding. The pretrial judge may not decline to examine the prosecutor's requests. The pretrial judge shall also perform procedural actions upon a request of the trial court. The pretrial judge has no right to perform any actions on his/her own initiative.

II. The Powers to Trace Telephonic Communications

911. Where there is a prosecutor's request, and permission of the pretrial judge in the form of a ruling, a pretrial investigator may intercept telephone conversations, to record and collect them, monitor other information transmitted via telecommunications networks and make recordings if there are grounds to believe that in this way information may be obtained about a less serious, serious or grave crime in preparation, being committed or committed, or if there is a danger that violence, coercion or other illegal actions may be used against a victim, witness or other parties to the proceedings or their relatives.

912. The doctrine of the Lithuanian criminal procedure accepts that this procedural measure can be applied either to the participants of criminal proceedings or to other persons (this is an exception).[462]

913. This measure may be applied when investigating: (1) less-serious, serious or grave crimes; or (2) minor crimes: grooming of a person under the age of 16 (Article 152(1) of the CC); incitement against any national, racial, ethnic, religious or other group of persons; (Article 170 of the CC), unlawful disposal of installations, software, passwords, login codes and other data (Article 198(2) of the CC); possession of pornographic material displaying a young child (Article 309 of the CC); or (3) there is a danger that violence, coercion or other illegal actions may be used against a victim, witness or other parties to the proceedings or their relatives. The Criminal Division of the Supreme Court of Lithuania has adopted a review on the application of the interception and control of the telecommunications,[463] in which the legal and factual grounds, objects and term of the application of the interception and control of the telecommunications, etc. have been disclosed.

914. It is possible to intercept telephone conversations and monitor other information transmitted via telecommunications networks (except its content), if there are grounds to believe that in this way, information may be obtained about these minor crimes: violation of a person's correspondence (Article 166 of the CC), unlawful connection to an information system (Article 198(1) of the CC) and possession of pornographic material (Article 309 of the CC). The doctrine of the Lithuanian criminal procedure[464] does not discuss what level or degree of suspicion is necessary in order to monitor electronic communications networks and transmission of information, except its content. On the contrary, the doctrine states that in the written request of the prosecutor to allow the coercive measures, there must be described the background and the motivation of application of this measure to a particular person.[465]

915. Interception of telephone conversations and the recording and monitoring of other information transmitted via telecommunication networks, may not last for longer than that of other six months. When investigating a complicated or large-scale criminal act, however, such measures may be extended once for a further three months.

---

462. Goda G., Kazlauskas M., Kuconis P. Baudžiamojo proceso teisė, Vilnius, Registrų centras, 2011, p. 268.
463. Review of the Criminal division of the Supreme Court of Lithuania of 25 Jun. 2015, *Teismų praktika*, No. 43.
464. Lietuvos Respublikos baudžiamojo proceso kodekso komentaras. I dalis, Vilnius, TIC, 2003, p. 388.
465. Lietuvos Respublikos baudžiamojo proceso kodekso komentaras. I dalis, Vilnius, TIC, 2003, p. 388.

916. The Code of Criminal Procedure, in accordance with the case law of the ECtHR,[466] forbids the interception, recording or monitoring of telephone conversations between defence counsel and the suspect or accused, or of other communications from these persons transmitted via telecommunications networks.

917. Interception and recording of telephone conversations of victims, witnesses or other parties to the proceedings, and monitoring and recording of other communications of these persons transmitted via telecommunications networks, may be effected at the request of these persons[467] or with their consent even where there is no ruling of the pretrial judge, and where the services and facilities of a communications business are not used.

918. Audio recordings that are immaterial for the case shall not be attached to the case file and shall be destroyed forthwith, and an appropriate statement shall be drawn up by a decision of a prosecutor.

919. In cases of extreme urgency, these actions may be also applied by a decision of a prosecutor; however, if this is the case, within three days from the start of these actions the consent of the pretrial judge must be obtained. If such consent is denied, the actions that have been initiated must be cancelled and all records immediately destroyed.

920. Any record made by a pretrial investigator about monitoring of information transmitted via the telecommunications networks shall outline only the contents of an audio recording relevant for the criminal case. In the case of monitoring of telecommunication traffic data, a separate record is not drawn up. The documents about telecommunication traffic data obtained from telecommunication companies must be added to the case file.

III. The Powers to Interview the Accused and Witnesses

A. *The Interviewing of the Accused*

921. According to the Code of Criminal Procedure, upon receiving an application from the prosecutor, which may be filed on the initiative of the suspect, his/her defence counsel or the prosecutor, during the pretrial investigation the suspect may be questioned by the pretrial judge. According to the doctrine of the Lithuanian criminal procedure,[468] initiative of the suspect or his/her defence counsel to give testimony for the pretrial judge must be always accepted regardless of the reasons. On

466. Goda G., Kazlauskas M., Kuconis P. Baudžiamojo proceso teisė, Vilnius, Registrų centras, 2011, p. 268.
467. Ruling of the Supreme Court of Lithuania in criminal case No. 2K-510/2005.
468. Goda G., Kazlauskas M., Kuconis P. Baudžiamojo proceso teisė, Vilnius, Registrų centras, 2011, p. 318.

the application of the suspect the prosecutor must bring the detained suspect before the pretrial judge as soon as possible and participate in his/her questioning.

922. On the initiative of the prosecutor the suspect shall be brought before the pretrial judge for questioning when it is thought that during the trial the accused may change his/her testimony or exercise his/her right not to testify.

923. At the request of the suspect, his/her defence counsel must be present at the questioning. The questioning of the suspect shall open by inviting the suspect to tell about the circumstances on the ground of which he/she wanted to be questioned by the pretrial judge. After that, the defence counsel and the prosecutor may put questions to the suspect.

924. A suspect who is not able to appear in a questioning held by the pretrial judge or is held in detention or at a correctional institution may be questioned by a videoconferencing system.

B. The Interviewing of Witnesses

925. According to Article 184 of the Code of Criminal Procedure, a prosecutor shall apply to the pretrial judge to have the witnesses questioning, where it is thought that: (1) it will not be possible to examine the witness during the trial; (2) the witness may change his/her testimony during the trial or exercise his/her right to refuse to testify; (3) the witness shall give a more detailed testimony to the pretrial judge.

926. Before starting the questioning of a witness the pretrial judge must put the person to be questioned under oath. A prosecutor must participate in the questioning of a witness conducted by the pretrial judge. During the examination the prosecutor shall have the right to put to the person under questioning additional questions.

927. According to the requirements of the Article 6 of the ECHR, the pretrial judge must notify the suspect and his/her defence counsel about the place and time of the questioning to be conducted. The detained suspect shall be brought to the place of the questioning. The suspect and his/her defence counsel have the right to participate in such a questioning and put questions to the person under questioning, and after the close of the questioning – to study the record of the questioning and make comments about it. According to the jurisprudence of the Supreme Court of Lithuania, failure of a suspect who is not in pretrial detention and his/her defence counsel to appear during the questioning of a witness shall not prevent proceeding with such action.[469]

469. Ruling of the Supreme Court of Lithuania in criminal case No. 2K-P-221/2008.

Chapter 3. The Inquiry in Court

§1. The Trial

928. The trial stage is a central stage of the criminal procedure when the court examines the indictment and decides the question whether the accused is guilty in committing a criminal act. If the accused is found guilty, the court must also resolve the question on realisation of criminal liability[470] (e.g., by releasing from criminal liability or imposing a punishment, etc.).

929. The trial stage consists of two parts: the preparation of hearing and hearing. Meanwhile, the hearing has the parts of the preparation of the hearing, the examination of the evidence, final speeches and the last word of the accused and the adoption and promulgation of the judgment.

930. It should be noted that the Code of Criminal procedure provides special forms of the court procedure that may be applicable in alternative to the hearing: penal order and expedited procedure. Also, the Lithuanian criminal procedure establishes special rules for the hearing *in absentia*, hearing in case of application of the compulsory medical measures and hearing in case of prosecution of the legal entity.

931. Punishment may be imposed by a penal order[471] in case of criminal acts, which are punishable by all the types of punishment, except the cases when the sanction of the article of the Special Part of the CC provides only imprisonment or life imprisonment. The Constitutional Court of Lithuania has noted that:

> under the CCP, it is permitted to deviate from the model of general criminal procedure and the criminal procedure can be finished by means of a court penal order only when there are all these conditions: (1) the culprit redeems or removes the inflicted damage, if the damage was inflicted, or commits to redeeming or removal of such damage; (2) the prosecutor brings forth an initiative to end the procedure by means of a court penal order, and the accused does not oppose to this initiative; (3) the victim does not lodge a complaint against the decision of the prosecutor to end the procedure by means of a court penal order, and if he/she lodges it, the judge of pre-trial investigation does not grant this complaint; (4) the circumstances of the case are clear, otherwise (if the circumstances were not sufficiently clear and if the existing doubts could be removed only during the consideration in court) the judge would, by means of a ruling, have to refer the case for consideration in court, i.e., to enter the model of general criminal procedure; (5) the accused agrees to the imposition

470. Goda G., Kazlauskas M., Kuconis P. Baudžiamojo proceso teisė, Vilnius, Registrų centras, 2011, p. 351.
471. The Prosecutor General has adopted methodological recommendation on this issue: Generalinio prokuroro įsakymas 'Dėl Rekomendacijų dėl proceso užbaigimo baudžiamuoju įsakymu patvirtinimo', TAR, 2015, No. 08532.

of the fine by means of a court penal order and does not demand the consideration of the case in court under general procedure.[472]

The judge shall be entitled to draw up the penal order upon receipt of the prosecutor's application. The penal order must be served on the accused person. If the accused person objects to the imposition of the punishment by the penal order, he/she has the right to file an application at the court which issued the penal order within fourteen days following the service thereof requesting the court to hold a hearing. If the accused submits an application for a hearing, the penal order does not acquire legal force. If the accused person fails to exercise this right, the penal order shall become effective.

932. If the circumstances of commission of a criminal act are clear and the case in respect of the commission of the criminal act is subject to be heard before the district court, the prosecutor may on the day of commission of the criminal act or within fourteen days from starting the pretrial investigation apply to the court which has jurisdiction over the case with an application to hear the case in an expedited procedure.[473] In such a case, the prosecutor shall not draw up the indictment, but submits the application and the pretrial investigation material (if pretrial investigative actions were commenced) to the court. The prosecutor together with the pretrial investigation institution also must inform the accused, his/her defence counsel, the victim, the plaintiff, the civil defendant and their representatives and witnesses about the time and place of the hearing, which will deal with the case in expedited procedure. The victims, plaintiffs and civil defendants questioned during the pretrial investigation are also informed that their absence without valid reasons is considered as consent to hearing the case without being present and does not preclude a hearing, unless the court recognises that their participation is necessary.

933. When a court receives an application from a prosecutor on the expedited procedure, a court hearing is to be held or other date and time of the hearing, which must be organised not later than within fourteen days, are announced and the prosecutor is informed. At the beginning of the hearing, the prosecutor issues his/her application. After that, the judge asks the accused whether he/she understands the charges brought by the prosecutor and agrees to be tried immediately, or if he/she wants to have the hearing later. An accused's request to hold a hearing later may be justified only on the grounds that he/she needs time to prepare for the defence. The hearing in the expedited procedure is going in accordance with general rules, only instead of the indictment the prosecutor reads his/her application for the expedited procedure.

472. Decision of the Constitutional Court of Lithuania of 24 Jan. 2008, *Valstybės žinios*, 2008, No. 11-338.

473. The Prosecutor General has adopted methodological recommendation on this issue: Generalinio prokuroro įsakymas 'Dėl Rekomendacijų dėl proceso baigimo pagreitinto proceso tvarka patvirtinimo', TAR, 2015, No. 08538.

I. The Preparation of the Hearing

934. The preparation of the hearing is performed by the sentencing court. According to Article 231 of the Code of Criminal Procedure, the Chairman of the court, the deputy chairman or the Chairman of the criminal division shall, within two days after receiving the case by the court, appoint the judges who will prepare the case for the hearing, and after its referral for trial – will hear the case. If the case during the trial must be heard before a three-judge panel, the other judges as well as the alternate judge may be appointed afterwards but not later than seven days before the opening of the trial.

935. Upon examining the case, the judge may enter a ruling: (1) to submit the criminal case for the hearing; (2) to refer the case according to its jurisdiction, to separate or to consolidate a case or to defer the case; (3) to postpone the case; (4) to refer the case to the prosecutor; (5) to order the pretrial judge or prosecutor to perform an investigative action; and (6) to terminate the case.

936. The judge, upon having examined the case and determined that there are no obstacles shall refer the case for the hearing. The issue of separation or consolidation of a case may also be solved while referring the case for the hearing. When referring the case for the hearing, the judge shall formulate the decision in the ruling to refer the case for the hearing, indicate the name and surname of the accused, the criminal law under which his/her criminal act has been qualified, the date and place of the hearing and decide the issue of the persons who are to be summoned to the hearing as the accused, his/her legal representative, the victim, the plaintiff and the defendant in a civil action and their representatives, the witnesses and experts. This ruling may also indicate the place and time of the hearing or the decision to hear the case according to a pre-agreed and established timetable for the hearing.

937. If the accused has expressed his/her consent to a shortened examination of the evidences, the judge may decide to summon only the accused and his/her defence counsel to the hearing, and only inform the other participants of the proceedings about the time and place of the hearing and their right to attend the hearing.

938. By the same ruling the judge must decide on the received requests, appointment of the defence counsel, invitation of an interpreter, imposition, extension, change or lifting of a provisional measure (with the exception of pretrial detention) and on the hearing *in camera*. The issue relating to the imposition or extension of a pretrial detention may be decided only in the court hearing, in which the prosecutor, accused and defence counsel must participate. The participation of the accused in the hearing may be ensured by a videoconferencing system.

939. The issue of the referral of the case for the hearing must be determined by the judge within fifteen days from the date of the receipt of the case by the court – where the accused is in pretrial detention, and within one month – where the accused is free. The case must go for the hearing within twenty days from rendering the ruling by the judge to refer the case for the hearing. The complex or large cases, also cases where the hearing shall proceed according to a pre-agreed and established timetable must go for the trial within three months from rendering the ruling by the judge to refer the case for the hearing.

II. The Attendance of the Parties

940. The Code of Criminal Procedure contains strict rules on the participation at the hearing and prescribes whose participation is mandatory at the hearing and who is to be summoned to the hearing, as well as on who shall be only notified of the hearing.

941. The hearing shall take place with the participation of the prosecutor, the victim and his/her representative, the accused and his/her representative and defence counsel, the plaintiff and the defendant and their representatives. During the hearing several prosecutors may be present, one accused may be defended by several defence counsels.[474] The court, when investigating evidence, may allow victims, their representatives, plaintiffs and defendants, their representatives, experts and specialists not to take part and not to be present at the hearing.

942. In the Court of First Instance the case shall be heard with the accused present. The presence of the accused shall be obligatory. Hearing of the case shall be allowed in the absence of the accused (*in absentia*) only in the case, where the accused is not on the territory of the Republic of Lithuania and avoids appearing in the trial. In the event of non-appearance of the accused at the trial, the court shall make a break or defer the hearing. The court has the right to bring the accused in person or to change the provisional measure for him/her.

943. Non-appearance of a legal representative of a juvenile accused shall not stay the hearing of the case if the court finds that his/her presence is not obligatory.

944. In the event of non-appearance of the prosecutor or defence counsel and where there is no possibility to replace them during the hearing, the court shall make a break or defer the hearing. It should be noted that the defence counsel who fails to appear in court may be replaced by another defence counsel. The prosecutor or the defence counsel, who joins the case must be given time to prepare for the participation in the hearing.

945. In the event of non-appearance of the victim or his/her representative, the court shall determine the issue whether to proceed with the hearing or whether to defer the hearing, with account of whether, in the event of non-appearance of the

474. Lietuvos Respublikos baudžiamojo proceso kodekso komentaras, II dalis, Vilnius, TIC, 2003, p. 79.

victim or his/her representative, all the circumstances of the case may be examined thoroughly and the interests of the victim may be protected.

946. In the event of the non-appearance of the plaintiff or his/her representative the court shall not proceed with the civil action. In this case the person who sustained damage as a result of a criminal act shall have the right to bring a claim under the civil procedure. It should be noted that the court shall have the right to hear a civil action in the absence of the plaintiff, if it finds it necessary or if there is an application of the plaintiff to proceed with the hearing of the claim without his/her participation.

947. The non-appearance of the defendant or his/her representative shall not suspend the hearing of a civil claim.

III. The Course of the Trial

948. Article 241 of the Code of Criminal Procedure provides that hearing shall be presided over by the presiding judge who in collegially heard cases shall be appointed by the Chairman of the court or the Chairman of the criminal division. If the case is heard by one judge, he/she shall have all the rights and duties of the presiding judge. The presiding judge shall make use of all the measures provided by law for a comprehensive examination of all the material circumstances of the case. He/she must dismiss from the hearing everything that is not related to the case and what might cause an unnecessary delay of the hearing. The court must ensure that a criminal case is tried in the shortest possible time and that the case must be tried in a way that minimises numbers of breaks of the hearing.

949. When hearing the case, the Court of First Instance must make a direct examination of the evidence of the case: to question the accused, victims, witnesses, hear the conclusion of the experts and report of the specialists, inspect the material evidence, read out the records and other documents. Testimonies and explanations of the persons questioned during the hearing (as a general rule) shall be oral.

950. According to Article 255 of the Code of Criminal Procedure, the hearing shall involve only those accused and only those criminal acts on the grounds of which the case is committed for the hearing. The Criminal Division of the Supreme Court of Lithuania has adopted a review on court practice on the scope of the court trial,[475] in which the scope of the court trial, the possibility to change the qualification of the criminal act or the facts of the case, etc. have been disclosed. The accused may not be found guilty for a requalified criminal act or another criminal act, facts of which are essentially different from those set out in the indictment, if, during the hearing, he/she was not informed about this possibility in advance. The prosecutor, the victim has the right to lodge a written request for the requalification

475. Review of the Criminal division of the Supreme Court of Lithuania of 25 Jun. 2009, Teismų praktika, No. 31.

of the criminal act under a different criminal law or for the change of the facts which are essentially different from those set out in the indictment[476] (during the hearing, but before the end of the examination of the evidence). When the court receives such a request or in case there are grounds to believe that the criminal act referred to in the indictment may be requalified or the facts which are in the indictment may be changed by essentially different facts, it must immediately inform the accused and other parties about the possibility of the requalification of the criminal act or the change of the facts which are essentially different from those set out in the indictment., . In these cases (even in situation when the charge is changed into less strict[477]), the accused or his/her defence counsel has the right to request a break in the hearing for additional preparation for defence.

A. *The Preparation of the Hearing*

951. The Code of Criminal Procedure provides that at the time set for the hearing of a criminal case the presiding judge shall open the trial proceedings and announce the case that will be heard. Having been given the floor by the presiding judge, the clerk of the court shall announce to the court the appearance of the parties, also of witnesses, experts and interpreters, and the reasons for non-appearance of the persons who did not arrive at the hearing.

952. The presiding judge shall inform the interpreter of his/her duty to translate to persons taking part in the proceedings, who cannot understand or speak Lithuanian, the content of the testimony, statements, documents read out in the court, as well as of the orders of the presiding judge and decisions of the court. In addition, the presiding judge shall warn the interpreter of the responsibility for refusal, without good reasons, to perform his/her duty and of the liability for false or knowingly incorrect interpretation (Article 235 of the CC). Thereafter the interpreter, who has not been sworn, shall be sworn.

953. The witnesses who have appeared shall be removed from the courtroom. The presiding judge shall take measures to ensure that the witnesses examined by the court do not communicate in the court building with the witnesses who have not yet been examined.

954. The presiding judge shall establish the identity of the accused ascertaining his/her name, surname, year, month and day of birth, place of birth, place of residence, occupation, education, family status, also other information relevant to the identity of the accused.

---

476. The rules in the Code of Criminal Procedure concerning the requalification of the criminal act under a different criminal law or for the change of the facts which are essentially different from those set out in the indictment has been revised in accordance with the ruling of the Constitutional Court of Lithuania (*see* decision of the Constitutional Court of Lithuania of 15 Nov. 2013, *Valstybės žinios*, 2013, No. 119-6005).
477. Ruling of the Supreme Court of Lithuania in criminal case No. 2K-7-228/2008.

955. In case of non-appearance at the hearing of the accused, his/her legal representative, the prosecutor or the defence counsel, the victim, the plaintiff, the defendant or their representative, the court shall decide, whether to continue the hearing.

956. If a witness or expert fails to appear at the hearing, the court shall decide whether to hear the case or to defer the hearing, considering, whether it is possible to make a full and comprehensive examination of the case in the absence of the said persons, or shall make the break to summon the persons. In this regard, the court must assess whether the testimony of a witness who fails to appear is essential for the case, or he/she was questioned by pretrial judge during pretrial investigation, etc.[478]

957. If the court has made a ruling to defer the proceedings, it may examine the witnesses, experts, specialists, plaintiffs, defendants and their representatives who have appeared. They shall be summoned to the subsequent hearing only in case of necessity.

958. The presiding judge shall announce the names of the judges, prosecutors, defence counsels, experts, interpreters and clerks of the hearing and inquire about the opinion of the parties as regards the disqualification of any of the said persons and, if any, resolves the requests for disqualification.

959. The presiding judge shall inform the accused, his/her legal representative, the victim, the plaintiff, the defendant and their representatives of their rights and duties provided in the CCP. If the participant declares that he/she has not understood the issue, the rights must be explained repeatedly, more specifically by revealing the content of the unclear rights.[479]

960. The presiding judge shall inform the expert and specialist of their rights and duties and shall also warn them on the responsibility for refusal without good reasons to perform their duty and for making a false conclusion (Article 235 of the CC). Thereafter the expert and specialist who have not been sworn, shall be sworn.

961. Completing the preparation of the hearing, the presiding judge shall inquire of the parties, whether they have requests to summon new witnesses, experts or to demand other evidence. Having presented his/her request, a party must specify the circumstance for the establishment whereof new evidence is required. The court shall rule on every request. The court may also at its discretion decide to summon new witnesses, experts, also insist upon submission of new evidence.

---

478. Goda G., Kazlauskas M., Kuconis P. Baudžiamojo proceso teisė. – Vilnius, Registrų centras, 2011, p. 411.
479. Goda G., Kazlauskas M., Kuconis P. Baudžiamojo proceso teisė. – Vilnius, Registrų centras, 2011, p. 413.

B. The Examination of the Evidence

962. The examination of the evidence is the main part of the hearing during which the examination of all circumstances of the case is carried out.[480] The examination of the evidence starts by the reading of the indictment (*see* paragraph 725). The indictment shall be read out by the prosecutor. If the indictment is large in volume (more than five pages[481]), the prosecutor may give a summary of its contents, indicating the substance of the charge (place, time, consequences of the criminal act, main data on which the charge is based, article of the CC which provides liability for the committed criminal act, mitigating and aggravating circumstances). Thereafter the presiding judge shall ask the accused whether he/she understood the charge, as necessary, shall explain the accused the substance of the charge and inquire whether he/she pleads guilty. The accused shall have the right to substantiate his/her answer.

963. After the accused has submitted a response to the charges, the presiding judge shall inform him/her of his/her right to give explanations, to respond to questions or to refuse to do any of the above. The judge shall also explain that the accused is entitled to put questions to the persons being examined and give explanation about the evidence under examination. Where there is more than one accused, all of whom wish to give testimony, the order of priority for giving testimony shall be laid down by the court after it has asked the submissions of the accused and their defence counsels. The examination of the accused shall start with a proposal of the presiding judge to give testimony about the charge and the known circumstances of the case.

964. Article 273 of the Code of Criminal Procedure provides that if the accused, who is not charged with a grave crime, after the announcement of the indictment offers an admission of guilt and wishes to give testimony forthwith, also agrees to waive the examination of other evidence, the examination of the evidence may be terminated, provided that the circumstances of commission of the criminal act are beyond doubt and the prosecutor and defence counsel do not object to the shortened examination of the evidences. If there are more than one accused charged with the commission of one or several crimes, shortened examination of the evidences may be conducted only where the above-mentioned conditions are applicable with respect to all the accused. It should be noted that even in case of the shortened examination of the evidences, the judgment may be based only on the evidence which has been reviewed at the hearing.[482]

480. Goda G., Kazlauskas M., Kuconis P. Baudžiamojo proceso teisė, Vilnius, Registrų centras, 2011, p. 415.
481. Goda G., Kazlauskas M., Kuconis P. Baudžiamojo proceso teisė, Vilnius, Registrų centras, 2011, p. 417.
482. Goda G., Kazlauskas M., Kuconis P. Baudžiamojo proceso teisė, Vilnius, Registrų centras, 2011, p. 446.

965. The prosecutor, the victim, the plaintiff, the defendant and their representatives, the defence counsel, legal representative of the accused and the accused shall be entitled to pose questions to the accused, victims, witnesses, experts and specialists under examination in the hearing. Where a witness is summoned to the court at the request of one of the parties, the party shall be entitled to question that witness first. The judges have the right to pose questions to persons questioned at any phase of the examination of the evidence. The judges and, with the consent of the presiding judge, the parties shall pose questions to the persons questioned directly. The presiding judge may deprive the parties who abuse direct questioning of the above right and permit to pose questions through him/her. Questions to the juvenile victims and witnesses shall be posed only through the presiding judge or, if necessary, – through their representative. The presiding judge shall reject questions, which are irrelevant to the case. It should be noted that the Lithuanian criminal procedure prohibits putting questions with a suggestive answer.[483]

966. According to the Code of Criminal Procedure, the testimony of the accused, victim and witness, given to the pre-trial judge or during the previous stage of the hearing before the court may be read out at the present stage of the hearing; also audio-video recorded questioning may be heard out or viewed when the accused, victim and witness: (1) is dead or is absent from the hearing for good reasons, and, for the accused, also in the cases when hearing is conducted *in absentia*; (2) refuses or avoids to give testimony, in addition, when he/she declares himself/herself unable to recall certain circumstances he/she previously gave testimony about; (3) gives testimony at the hearing, which differs in essence from the testimony given at the pretrial investigation or previously before the court.

967. In addition, at the hearing may be read out the testimony given by the witness, questioned in the court after the break or deferral of the hearing, the testimony given during the pretrial investigation by the anonymous witness who has not been summoned to the court, also the testimony of the juvenile witness.

968. Before hearing and viewing the video-audio recordings, the testimony given by the accused, the victim or the witness, placed in the appropriate records of the questioning carried out by the pretrial judge or in the records of the hearing shall be read.

969. Witnesses shall be examined individually, with the witnesses who have not yet been questioned to be absent from the courtroom. The presiding judge shall ascertain the relationship between the witness, the accused and the victim and suggest that the witness inform the court of all the matters relating to the case that are in his/her knowledge, refraining from recounting any matters the source whereof is unknown to him/her. Thereafter the witness shall be put questions. The witnesses who have been questioned shall remain in the courtroom until the closure of the

483. Goda G., Kazlauskas M., Kuconis P. Baudžiamojo proceso teisė, Vilnius, Registrų centras, 2011, p. 421.

hearing. Having heard the submissions of the parties, the court may allow the questioned witness to leave the courtroom even before the closure of the hearing. At the request of the parties to the proceedings or on the initiative of the court the questioned witness may be subjected to additional examination.

970. When giving testimony, the witness may refer to his/her records where the testimony relates to any numerical or other data difficult of committing to memory. At the request of the presiding judge or other parties, the records must be presented for their inspection. The witness shall be allowed to read the documents in his/her possession, if they concern the given testimony. The documents shall be presented to the presiding judge and the parties and by the court ruling may be attached to the case material.

971. The anonymous witness shall be questioned *in camera*, using the technical means enabling the alteration of pictures or voice, thereby preventing the parties from establishing the identity of the questioned person.[484]

972. The victim shall be questioned and his/her testimony shall be read out in compliance with all rules applicable to the questioning of witnesses and reading out of their testimony. Where there are several victims who are to be questioned, the court shall establish the order of succession according to which they will be questioned.

973. If the specialist report or the expert conclusion given at the pretrial investigation is sufficiently clear and all-embracing, it shall be announced at the hearing in the absence of the specialist or the expert. The specialist or the expert shall be summoned to the hearing for questioning only when the court recognises that his/her testimony is necessary for clarifying or supplementing the report or conclusion. The specialist and expert shall be questioned in accordance with the rules laid down for the questioning of witnesses.

974. In the course of the hearing, the court shall be entitled to take any procedural investigative actions provided in the CCP. If it is impossible for any reason to perform these procedural investigative actions in the court, or these procedural investigative actions cause unnecessary obstruction of the trial, the court may instruct the prosecutor or the pretrial judge to perform these investigative actions.[485]

484. The Prosecutor General has adopted methodological recommendation on this issue: Generalinio prokuroro įsakymas 'Dėl Rekomendacijų dėl anonimiškumo ir dalinio anonimiškumo nukentėjusiajam ar liudytojui suteikimo ir šio sprendimo procesinio įforminimo patvirtinimo', TAR, 2014, No. 06146.

485. Lietuvos Respublikos baudžiamojo proceso kodekso komentaras, II dalis, Vilnius, TIC, 2003, p. 166–167.

975. In the course of the examination of the evidence, the prosecutor may request permission to provide him/her with additional evidence by carrying out procedural investigative actions. The court, having satisfied this request of the prosecutor, makes a break in the hearing.

976. The material evidence shall be reviewed by the court and shall also be demonstrated to the parties. As necessary, the material evidence shall also be shown to the witnesses and the expert. The review of the material evidence, whether on the court's own initiative or upon the request of the parties, may be conducted at any phase of the examination of evidence. Persons who are shown the material evidence may bring certain circumstances, related to the review, to the court's notice. The material evidence which cannot be delivered to the court shall be reviewed by the court, as necessary, at the site of location of the material evidence.

977. In the course of the examination of the evidence, the presiding judge shall announce all relevant documents which have been obtained during the pretrial investigation and the trial. When it is necessary for a thorough examination of the circumstances of the case, at the request of the parties or at the initiative of the court, these documents or parts of them shall be made public by reading and inspecting them. Video-audio recordings made in the course of the pretrial investigation may be listened to and viewed during the hearing.

978. Upon reviewing all evidence contained in the case the presiding judge shall offer the parties the opportunity to add anything they may wish. Having examined the applications, if any, and, as necessary, having carried out additional investigative actions, the presiding judge shall announce termination of the examination of the evidence.

C. The Final Speeches and Last Word of the Accused

979. Article 293 of the Code of Criminal Procedure states that after the examination of the evidence, the court shall hear the final speeches and the last word of the accused. The final speeches shall comprise the statements made by the prosecutor, the victim or his/her representative, the plaintiff and the defendant in a civil action or their representatives, the defence counsel or the accused, if he/she has waived his/her right to have defence counsel.

980. The parties to the criminal procedure shall not be entitled to the submission of evidence not reviewed at the hearing. After the parties have made their statements, they shall be entitled, with leave of the presiding judge, to rebuttal or rejoinder arguments as well as commentaries in respect to prior statements. The defence counsel, or, in his/her absence, the accused shall be the last in sequence to present his/her rejoinder arguments and commentaries. The court may not restrict the time of the statements by fixing the time limit, however, the presiding judge shall be entitled to interrupt the parties if they manifestly go beyond the limits of the case.

981. After the closure of the final speeches the presiding judge shall allow the accused the last word. Posing of questions to the accused during the presentation of his/her last word shall not be allowed. The court may not limit the last word of the accused in time, however, the presiding judge shall be entitled to interrupt the accused if he/she speaks of the circumstances that are clearly of no relevance to the case.

982. If the persons who presented their statements or the accused in his/her last word bring to light any new circumstances which are relevant for the case, the court upon the request of the parties or *proprio motu* may resume the examination of the evidence.

983. After the last word of the accused, the court shall inform of the date and place of the pronouncement of the judgment and retire to the deliberation room for the deliberation.

IV. The Judgment of the Case

984. According to Article 297 of the Code of Criminal Procedure, the courts of the Republic of Lithuania shall render the judgment in the name of the Republic of Lithuania. The doctrine of the Lithuanian criminal procedure states that the judgment must be legitimate, fair, reasoned and convincing.[486] The judgment shall be rendered by the judges in a deliberation room. Only the judges of the court in which the case is heard may be present at the time in the room. When the cases are heard collegially, deliberations and voting of the judges presided over by the presiding judge shall take place in the course of rendering of the judgment. Disagreements regarding the procedure of deliberations and voting shall be resolved by the court *in corpore*. The judges shall deliberate and vote separately on whether guilt has been proved beyond reasonable doubt, on the legal qualification of the criminal act, on the imposition of the punishment and other issues. The presiding judge shall formulate the questions to be settled in such a manner that they could be answered either in the affirmative or in the negative way. The first to vote shall be the judge with the shortest record of service of the judge. The presiding judge shall be the last to vote irrespective of his/her length of service record. The judge, who voted against the finding of guilt has the right to abstain from voting on the imposition of the punishment. In such a case, the vote of the judge shall be put down to the opinion of the judge in favour of the accused. All matters shall be resolved by majority vote. However, the life imprisonment punishment may be imposed on the accused only unanimously. The judge, who has a dissenting opinion when the judgment is rendered, shall be entitled to express it in writing. The dissenting opinion shall not be read during the promulgation of the judgment but shall be appended to the case.

---

486. Goda G., Kazlauskas M., Kuconis P. Baudžiamojo proceso teisė, Vilnius, Registrų centras, 2011, p. 455.

985. After considering and determining the issues necessary for the rendering of judgment, the court shall draw up the judgment. The court shall base the judgment only on the evidence which has been reviewed at the hearing. In accordance with the CCP and case law of the ECtHR,[487] the judgment of conviction may not be based only on the testimony given by the anonymous victims and witnesses. The judgment of conviction may be based on the testimony given by the above persons only in case the testimony is confirmed by other evidence. The judgment shall be signed by all judges. The dissenting judge shall also sign the judgment.

986. The judgment rendered by the court may be that of conviction or of acquittal. In addition, the court may render a judgment of termination of a case. By a judgment of conviction the accused is found guilty of commission of a criminal act stipulated in the criminal law and a punishment is imposed on him/her. If, before the rendition of the judgment, the accused falls ill with a grave incurable disease due to which the serving of the punishment would be too difficult, the court renders the judgment of conviction and may release the convicted person from the execution of the imposed punishment. The court shall render a judgment of termination of a case where there are grounds for releasing the accused person from criminal liability, provided for in the CC of Lithuania. The court shall render the judgment of acquittal if: (1) a criminal act was not committed; (2) participation of the accused in the commission of the criminal act has not been proved. If, after the judgment of acquittal is rendered on the ground that participation of the accused in the commission of the criminal act has not been proved and the person who committed the act remains undetected and the judgment becomes effective, the court must transfer the case to the prosecutor, so that he/she should take measures to determine the person who committed the criminal act.

987. The judgment must be composed of the introductory, descriptive and operative parts. The Criminal Division of the Supreme Court of Lithuania has adopted a review on the content of the judgment,[488] in which the content of each part of the judgment, also the content of the judgment of the appeal instance and penal order, etc. have been disclosed.

988. The judgment must be pronounced not later than within fourteen days from the date of notification of its pronouncement time and place. If the case is complex and large, within the time limit set by the court for the shortest possible time, but not later than forty-five days. The court or the judge of the panel pronounces the judgment by reading the introductory and operative parts of the judgment. In accordance with the ruling of the Constitutional Court of Lithuania, the court also has to

487. Goda G., Kazlauskas M., Kuconis P. Baudžiamojo proceso teisė, Vilnius, Registrų centras, 2011, p. 52–54.
488. Decision of the Senate of the Supreme Court of Lithuania of 20 Jun. 2003, Teismų praktika, No. 19.

explain orally the reasons for the conviction, which may be supplemented by reading separate parts of the judgment.[489] The judgment must be pronounced in the presence of the accused, the prosecutor and the defence counsel. All persons present in the courtroom shall hear the judgment standing. Having pronounced the judgment, the judge must explain to the parties the procedure and the time limits for the appeal against the judgment and shall also explain to the accused the specific features of the execution of the imposed punishment.

989. A transcript of the judgment immediately after the pronouncement is served to the acquitted or convicted person or the person to whom the case is terminated. If these persons were absent when the judgment was pronounced or not accepted the transcript of the judgment immediately after the pronouncement, a transcript of the judgment shall be served on or sent to these persons within five days from the pronouncement of the judgment.

§2. The Legal Remedies

I. Introductory Remarks

990. The right to appeal is a one of the fundamental human rights guaranteed by the international and national law. For example, Article 1 of the seventh Additional Protocol to ECHR[490] provides that 'everyone convicted of a criminal offence by a tribunal shall have the right to have his/her conviction or sentence reviewed by a higher tribunal. The exercise of this right, including the grounds on which it may be exercised shall be governed by law'. Article 30 of the Constitution of Lithuania also states that 'any person whose constitutional rights or freedoms are violated shall have the right to appeal to court'. According to the Constitutional Court of Lithuania:

> the constitutional right of the person to apply to court and the instance system of courts imply that the law must establish such legal regulation so that it could be possible to appeal against the final act adopted by a court of general jurisdiction or a specialised court […] at least in one court of higher instance. Justice is implemented by always leaving an opportunity to rectify a possible mistake or change the judgment in the light of new circumstances.

The Constitutional Court of Lithuania also has noted that:

> the law must establish not only the right of the party to the proceedings to lodge an appeal with at least one court of higher instance against any final act

489. Decision of the Constitutional Court of Lithuania of 21 Sep. 2006, *Valstybės žinios*, 2006, No. 102-3957.
490. Žmogaus teisių ir pagrindinių laisvių apsaugos konvencijos Protokolas Nr. 7, iš dalies pakeistas Protokolu Nr. 11, *Valstybės žinios*, 2011, No. 156-7394.

which was adopted in a case by a court of first instance, but also it must establish a procedure of such appeal, which would permit correcting possible mistakes of the court of first instance.[491]

991. The Lithuanian criminal procedure establishes three ordinary legal remedies: (1) appeal against the judgment of the court of first instance (appellate procedure),[492] (2) cassation appeal against the judgment of the court of second instance (cassation procedure) and (3) appeal against the rulings of the lower courts (unless such appeal is explicitly banned by the CCP).

992. Furthermore, the Lithuanian criminal procedure provides three extraordinary legal remedies: (1) reopening of the criminal case if new circumstances are discovered, (2) reopening of the criminal case due clear improper application of the criminal law and (3) reopening of the criminal case due to the decision of the European Court on Human Rights or UN Human Rights Committee or Constitutional Court of Lithuania.

II. The Ordinary Legal Remedies

A. Appeal Against the Judgment of the First Instance Court

993. According to the Lithuanian criminal procedure, an appeal against the ineffective judgment and ruling of the first instance court may be based on grounds of fact and (or) law. The ineffective judgment or ruling may be appealed before the county courts as courts of appellate instance and before the Court of Appeal of Lithuania. The county court shall review, by appeal, cases which have been heard at the district courts and the Court of Appeal of Lithuania shall review, by appeal, cases which have been heard by the county Court of First Instance. An appeal shall be examined in the written procedure or the hearing before the panel of three judges of county court or Court of Appeal of Lithuania.

994. The prosecutor, the accused, the person to whom the case has been terminated, his/her defence counsel and legal representative, the victim and his/her representative have the right to file, on any grounds and for any reasons, appeals against the judgment before it becomes effective. The acquitted person, his/her defence counsel and legal representative have the right to file appeals against the judgment to the extent it is related to the reasons and the grounds for acquittal. The plaintiff, the defendant and their representatives have the right to file appeals against that part of the judgment, which is connected with the civil action. The bail payer and person whose property or a corresponding sum of money was seized, also their representatives can appeal the judgment only on this decision. The defence counsel

491. Decision of the Constitutional Court of Lithuania of 24 Jan. 2008, *Valstybės žinios*, 2008, No. 11-338.
492. Decision of the Senate of the Supreme Court of Lithuania of 23 Jun. 2005, Teismu praktika, No. 23.

of the convicted or acquitted person has the right to file an appeal only when this is in conformity with the will of the convicted or acquitted person expressed in writing. The defence counsel of a person who is unable to exercise his/her right to defence due to his/her physical or mental deficiencies, or the defence counsel of the person to whom the case has been terminated or the defence counsel of the convicted or acquitted juvenile or the representatives are not bound by the will of the convicted or acquitted person.

995. Article 313 of the Code of Criminal Procedure provides that an appeal against the court judgment, which has not yet become effective shall be recorded in writing and shall be signed by the appellant. The appeal must state: the name of the appellate court; the case with respect to which the appeal has been filed; the merits of the part of the judgment appealed against; grounds of and reasons for the appeal against the judgment; the appellant requests concerning the evidence, their scope and investigation procedure, etc. The appeal shall be filed with the appellate court through the court, which rendered the judgment within twenty days from the day the judgment was pronounced. For a detained person the time limit for the filing of an appeal shall run from the day he/she is served a transcript of the judgment. For the accused who did not participate in the hearing the time limit for filing an appeal shall run from the day a transcript of the judgment is sent to him/her.

996. Persons who have the right to file an appeal, for whom, however, the time limit for appeal has elapsed, shall be entitled to apply to the trial court with a request to grant restoration of the time limit. An application for the granting of restoration of the time limit for filing an appeal may not be filed after the expiry of more than six months from the pronouncement of the judgment.

997. The court shall review the case within the limits of the appeals and only in relation to the persons with respect to whom the appeals have been filed. However, if in the course of hearing of the case the court determines essential violations of the Code of Criminal Procedure, the court shall examine whether this had a negative influence on the judgment delivered not only against the person whose appeal is heard, but also on the judgment against other convicted persons who have not filed an appeal.

998. The principle of *non-reformatio in peius* is an important principle of the proceedings before the superior criminal courts in Lithuania.[493] The court of appellate instance may aggravate the legal position of the convicted or acquitted person only in case when such requirement has been filed in the appeal of the prosecutor, the victim and the plaintiff. The position of the convicted, acquitted person or the person to whom the case has been terminated may not be aggravated to more than it is requested in the appeal. The Supreme Court of Lithuania has noted that legal position of the convicted shall be aggravated, for example, in cases when the court during the appeal procedure imposes a penal measure together with the punishment,

---

493. Goda G., Kazlauskas M., Kuconis P. Baudžiamojo proceso teisė, Vilnius, Registrų centras, 2011, p. 478.

increases amount awarded to pay the damages, etc.[494] If the appellate court mitigates the judgment for the convicted persons in respect of whom appeals have been taken, it may also mitigate the judgment to the other convicted persons insofar as the grounds for the mitigation of the judgment for the former are also applicable to the latter.

999. The main form of the examination of the appeal is hearing. The prosecutor and the defence counsel shall participate in the hearing. The convicted person, the acquitted person, the person to whom the case has been terminated, their representatives, the person on whom was imposed or not imposed compulsory medical measures, the victim, the plaintiff, the defendant and their representatives have the right to take part in the hearing. It should be noted that the absence of these persons from the hearing, provided they were timely informed, shall not suspend the hearing of the case.

1000. The hearing of the case shall start by a statement of one of the judges where he/she states the merits of the case (e.g., the main conclusions of the judgment rendered by the Court of First Instance, grounds for the appeals or arguments in respect of the appeals, etc.). On the initiative of the court or upon the application of the parties, the judgment of the Court of First Instance and other judgments or rulings made in the course of the proceedings as well as the trial record of the court or parts thereof may be read out. If additional material is submitted to the court, the Chairman of the panel or another judge shall read it and hand over to parties for examination (if they request so). The court of the appellate instance may perform the examination of the evidence. The Supreme Court of Lithuania has noted that the appellate court must carry out the examination of evidence if the first instance court did it incompletely or insufficiently.[495]

1001. If the pretrial investigation does not establish the circumstances which have not been established also by the Court of First Instance and the establishment thereof at the hearing of the appellate court, the appellate court may direct that the pretrial judge or prosecutor performs the appropriate procedural investigative actions.

1002. The hearing is completed by the final speeches and last words of the convicted person, acquitted person or person to whom the case is terminated. After the last word, the appellate court shall inform of the date and place of the pronouncement of the judgment and retire to the deliberation room for the deliberation. The appellate court judgment or ruling shall be pronounced by the Chairman of the panel or another judge in the courtroom.

1003. A transcript of the appellate court judgment or ruling shall be submitted immediately after the pronouncement to the appellant as well as the acquitted person, the convicted person or the person to whom the case has been terminated. If

---

494. Ruling of the Supreme Court of Lithuania in criminal case No. 2K-151-648/2017.
495. Ruling of the Supreme Court of Lithuania in criminal case No. 2K-66-942/2017.

these persons did not participate during the pronouncement of the judgment or ruling, the transcript of the judgment or ruling shall be submitted or sent to them within five days from the pronouncement of the judgment or the ruling. The other appellants shall be delivered a transcript of the judgment or ruling within five days from the request.

1004. The appeal may be examined in the written procedure, if the appeal requests: (1) to quash the judgment and terminate the criminal case due to existence of the circumstances for which the proceedings is not possible or grounds for the release of the accused from criminal liability; (2) to change the judgment due to incorrect application of the criminal law, incorrect imposition of the punishment or other errors of the judgment. A case cannot be dealt by the written procedure, when: (1) an appeal is filed on the grounds of an aggravating situation of the convicted or acquitted person, or (2) the party is requesting the hearing, or (3) it is necessary to carry out the examination of the evidence, or (4) the panel of three judges of the regional court was the first instance court.

1005. The appellate court with respect to the appealed judgment shall adopt a following decision: (1) to dismiss the appeal; (2) to quash the judgment and terminate the case; (3) to change the judgment; (4) to quash the judgment and return the case to the hearing in the first instance court; (5) to quash the judgment and return the case to the prosecutor. The appellate court has the right to quash or change the judgment for individual convicted persons or in respect of separate criminal acts.

1006. The judgment or ruling of the appellate court together with the criminal case, the appeal and additionally submitted material shall be within seven days from the date of pronouncement shall be referred for execution to the first instance court which rendered the judgment. The judgment of acquittal and the judgment to terminate the case shall be executed immediately. The convicted person kept in custody, who has been participating in the hearing, shall be released from custody in the courtroom. If the convicted person who is in custody has been absent in the hearing, a transcript of the judgment releasing the convicted person from custody shall be dispatched directly to the administration of the place of confinement for the execution. The administration of the place of confinement must within one day notify the first instance court, which had delivered the judgment of the execution of the judgment rendered by the appellate court.

B. Cassation Appeal Against the Judgment of the Second Instance Court

1007. According to the Lithuanian criminal procedure, an appeal against the effective judgment and ruling of the first instance court and the appellate court may be based on ground of law. The Supreme Court of Lithuania has noted that during the cassation procedure the court verifies legality on the basis of the facts already established and without re-evaluating the evidence.[496] The Supreme Court of Lithuania shall review by way of cassation procedure cases relating to effective judgments or rulings of the first instance courts and the appellate courts. The cassation cases shall be reviewed at the hearing by the panel of three judges, or the extended panel of seven judges of the Criminal Division of the Supreme Court of Lithuania or by the plenary session of the Supreme Court of Lithuania (*see* paragraph 121).

1008. The cassation appeal against the effective judgment or ruling may be filed by the prosecutor, the victim, his/her representative, the convicted person, his/her defence counsel, the acquitted person, his/her defence counsel, the person to whom the criminal case was terminated, their defence counsels and representatives, person to whom compulsory medical measures was imposed (not imposed), his/her defence counsel, representative, family members or close relatives, also plaintiff, defendant and their representatives, bail payer and person whose property or corresponding sum of money were seized.

1009. The defence counsel of the convicted or acquitted person and the person to whom the criminal case was terminated have the right to file cassation appeal only when this is in conformity with the will of the convicted or acquitted person expressed in writing. The defence counsel of the person who is unable to exercise his/her right to defence due to his/her physical or mental deficiency or defence counsel of a person to whom the criminal case has been terminated, also the defence counsel of the juvenile have the right to file the cassation appeal without paying any heed to the will of the defended person. The plaintiff, the defendant and their representatives have the right to file appeals against that part of the judgment which is connected with the civil action. The bail payer and person whose property or a corresponding sum of money was seized, also their representatives can appeal the judgment only on this decision.

1010. Article 368 of the Code of Criminal Procedure provides that the cassation appeal must state: the name of the cassation court; the appealed judgment or ruling; grounds and reasons for the cassation appeal against the judgment or ruling; the requests of the appellant in cassation. The cassation appeal shall be signed by the appellant in cassation. The appellant in cassation has the right to withdraw his/her cassation appeal in writing. The cassation appeal filed by the prosecutor may be withdrawn by a superior prosecutor.

1011. The cassation appeal may be filed within three months period from the date when judgment or ruling comes into force. The persons who have been prevented from observing a time limit for filing a cassation appeal due to essential reasons may apply to the Supreme Court of Lithuania with the request to grant the restoration of the time limit. An application for the restoration of the time limit for filing cassation appeal shall not be admissible after the lapse of over one year when the judgment or ruling comes into force.

---

496. Ruling of the Supreme Court of Lithuania in criminal case No. 2K-135-648/2016.

1012. It should be noted that the Supreme Court of Lithuania shall not accept the cassation appeals against the effective judgment and rulings which were not reviewed by the appellate court. Furthermore, the cassation appeal is possible only for aspects which were examined in the court of the appellate instance. The cassation appeal filed on the same ground for the second time is inadmissible and shall not be subject to review.

1013. The CCP provides only two grounds for the cassation appeal against an effective judgment or ruling: (1) incorrect application of a criminal law; (2) essential violation of the Code of Criminal Procedure. The incorrect application of the criminal law shall be considered an incorrect application of the norms of the General Part of the CC of Lithuania as well as qualification of the criminal acts not under the articles, paragraphs and sub-paragraphs of the CC under which they should have been qualified. The essential violations of the requirements of the Code of Criminal Procedure shall be considered violations which resulted in the restriction of the rights of the accused guaranteed by law (e.g., the right to trial before the fair and impartial court, the right to speak in native language, etc.[497]) or which obstructed a thorough and objective trial of the case by the court and prevented the rendering of a fair judgment or ruling.

1014. An effective judgment or ruling in cassation procedure may be verified only in the aspect of the application of law, i.e., legality of the judgment or ruling.[498] Where several persons have been convicted in a criminal case, the court shall review the case of the person in respect of whom a cassation appeal has been filed. In case, however, the incorrect application of the criminal law and essential violations of the Code of Criminal Procedure could have also had an effect on the other convicted persons, the court shall also review the lawfulness of the judgment rendered in respect of the other convicted persons who have not appealed.

1015. In the course of the hearing of the cassation appeal, the court may apply a law providing for the *corpus delicti* of a less serious criminal act or terminate the criminal case. The court shall be authorised to apply a law providing for a more serious crime if a cassation appeal has been filed on the issue. The court may impose a heavier punishment if the unfair punishment was imposed due to incorrect application of the criminal law. The court may impose a heavier punishment only in case if a cassation appeal has been filed on the issue. Even in this case the court cannot impose the life imprisonment punishment. When applying another criminal law or imposing a new punishment, the Supreme Court shall rely on the evidence examined at the first instance court and the court of appellate instance.

1016. The cassation appeal shall be filed with the Supreme Court of Lithuania. After verifying that the cassation appeal has been filed within the prescribed time

497. Goda G., Kazlauskas M., Kuconis P. Baudžiamojo proceso teisė, Vilnius, Registrų centras, 2011, p. 533.
498. Goda G., Kazlauskas M., Kuconis P. Baudžiamojo proceso teisė, Vilnius, Registrų centras, 2011, p. 527.

limit, it is not repeated, etc., it is forwarded to the selection panel of three judges of the Supreme Court. The selection panel decides on the issue of an acceptance of the cassation appeal by a written procedure. A cassation appeal is deemed to have been accepted if at least one of the members of the selection panel voted for it. The selection panel also decides whether the case is to be dealt with by oral or written procedure.

1017. According to Article 374(2) of the Code of Criminal Procedure, the case must be dealt by the oral procedure, when: (1) an appeal is filed on the grounds of an aggravating situation of the convicted or acquitted person, or a person to whom the case has been terminated; (2) the case shall be reviewed by the extended panel of seven judges or plenary session of the Supreme Court of Lithuania; (3) the panel of three judges of the county court was the first instance court; (4) the appellate court quashes the judgment of the first instance on the grounds (a) the first instance court has rendered the judgment of conviction, whereas the court of appellate instance concludes at the hearing that the participation of the accused person in the commission of the criminal act has not been proved or that there is no *corpus delicti* of the criminal act in the act of the accused; (b) the first instance court has rendered the judgment of acquittal whereas the court of the appellate instance concludes at the hearing that the judgment of conviction must be rendered; (c) the first instance court has rendered the judgment which terminates criminal cases whereas the court of the appellate instance concludes at the hearing that the judgment of conviction or acquittal must be rendered; and a new judgment shall be adopted; (5) the selection panel or the sentencing panel of judges decides that it is necessary to hear oral explanations of the parties. When several cassation appeals are to be dealt with in the case, the case is dealt with in the oral procedure, if at least one of them has decided to hear the case in the oral procedure. In other cases, the cassation appeal is reviewed in the written procedure.

1018. When a ruling to hear the cassation appeal is made, the court may stop the execution of any court judgment or ruling or part of it, until the cassation case shall be resolved.

1019. During the trial of the cassation case in a written procedure, the parties are not summoned to a hearing. The prosecutor must and other parties may submit the responses to the cassation appeal. Failure to submit responses to the cassation appeal from other parties does not prevent the trial in written procedure. The court ruling is not pronounced in the courtroom; a transcript of the ruling shall be sent to the parties.

1020. During the trial of the cassation case in an oral procedure the prosecutor and defence counsel must participate in the hearing. Furthermore, the victim, his/her representative, the convicted person, acquitted person, the person to whom the criminal case was terminated, their representatives, person to whom compulsory medical measures was imposed (not imposed), his/her representative, family members or close relatives, also plaintiff, defendant and their representatives, bail payer and person whose property or corresponding sum of money were seized may participate in the hearing. Where the cassation appeal is filed on the grounds aggravating the position of the convicted person, the convicted person detained in custody shall be delivered to the court. The convicted person who is free or the acquitted person shall be summoned to the hearing. It should be noted that non-appearance by the persons who were timely informed or summoned to the hearing shall not suspend the hearing of the case.

1021. The hearing of the case shall start by a statement of one of the judges where he/she states the merits of the case. After it, the parties of the hearing have the right to give main and additional explanations. The last additional explanation is given by the convicted person, the acquitted person or the person to whom the case was terminated, or his/her defence counsel or representative. Upon hearing the explanations the Chairman of the panel shall inform of the date and place of the pronouncement of the ruling and retired to the deliberation room for the deliberation. The ruling of the cassation court shall be pronounced by the Chairman of the panel or another judge in the courtroom. If, upon reviewing the cassation appeal, the convicted person must be released from custody, the ruling shall be transferred for the execution on the day of its pronouncement.

1022. Having heard the cassation appeal the court shall make the following decision: (1) to dismiss the cassation appeal; (2) to quash the judgment and the subsequent rulings and terminate the proceedings; (3) to quash the judgments of the first instance and appellate court and return the case to the hearing in the first instance court; (4) to quash the judgment or ruling of the appellate court and affirm the judgment or ruling of the first instance court (with or without the amendments); (5) to quash the judgment or ruling of the appellate court and refer the case for the hearing in the appellate court; (6) to change the court judgment or ruling.

C. Appeal Against the Rulings of the Lower Courts to the Superior Courts

1023. The parties and other persons have the right to appeal to superior courts against the rulings of the lower courts, except in the cases where the Code of Criminal Procedure explicitly prohibits such an appeal or provides for special procedure of appeal against separate court rulings.

1024. An appeal may be filed to a superior court against a ruling of the lower court, if parties or other persons believe that their rights and legitimate interests have been infringed by the ruling adopted by a lower court. Appeals against the rulings of the district court shall be filed with the county court, against the rulings of the county court – with the Court of Appeal of Lithuania within seven days from the day of the receipt of the ruling. The appeal shall be filed through the court, which issued the ruling.

1025. The appeal shall be examined at the superior court hearing or written procedure within seven days from the receipt of the appeal at the court or the deadline of the submission of the responses. The appeals concerning imposition of the home arrest as a provisional measure or the imposition of a compulsory medical measure, also appeals which require to aggravate legal status of the parties may be examined at the hearing. At the hearing a prosecutor and an appellant may participate. If the appeal is filed by an accused or convicted person who is kept in custody, his/her defence counsel shall participate at the hearing. The non-appearance of the above persons, provided they have been notified in due time of the date of the hearing, shall not suspend the examination of the appeal. The appellant, the defence counsel of the detained accused or convicted person may give explanations in order to revise or supplement the arguments of the appeal as well as present documents connected to the appeal. The superior court having examined the appeal shall make the following decision: (1) to dismiss the appeal; (2) to quash the court ruling and adopt a new ruling; (3) to change the court ruling. The county court or the Court of Appeals of Lithuania ruling on the appeal shall become effective from the date of its adoption and shall not be subject to appeal.

III. The Extraordinary Legal Remedies

1026. The Lithuanian criminal procedure provides three extraordinary legal remedies: (1) reopening the criminal case if new circumstances are discovered; (2) reopening the criminal case due to the decision of the ECtHR or Human Rights Committee of the UN or Constitutional Court of Lithuania; and (3) reopening the criminal case due to clear improper application of the criminal law.

A. Reopening the Criminal Case if New Circumstances are Discovered

1027. The Supreme Court of Lithuania may quash an effective court judgment or ruling and reopen the criminal case if new circumstances are discovered. New circumstance, the discovery whereof gives ground for the renewal of a criminal case, shall be as follows: (1) the effective court judgment established that the testimony given by the witness or victim or the expert conclusion was knowingly false, also that other evidence whereon the court judgment or ruling was forged; (2) the effective court judgment established a case of criminal abuse by the judges; (3) the effective court judgment established a case of criminal abuse by the persons who carried out the pretrial investigation of the case, which resulted in the rendering of an illegal and unreasonable judgment; (4) other circumstances which were not known and could not have been known to the court when the judgment or ruling were adopted, although the pretrial investigation and trial have been complete and through and which, taken separately or together with the circumstances established earlier prove that the convicted person is innocent or that he/she committed a criminal act less or graver than the one he/she has been convicted of, also which proves that the person who has been acquitted or whose case has been terminated is guilty.

1028. The Supreme Court may review a court judgment or ruling on the ground of circumstances that have been newly discovered within one year from the day of discovery of the said circumstances.

1029. The convicted person, the acquitted person, their defence counsels and legal representatives, the plaintiff and the defendant and their representatives may submit to the chief county prosecutor or Prosecutor General an application regarding the newly discovered circumstances. Upon completion of examination of the newly discovered circumstances and provided there is ground to reopen the criminal case, the prosecutor shall transfer the examination material accompanied by his/her conclusion to the Chairman of the Supreme Court.

1030. In the Supreme Court the issue of reopening the criminal case due to newly discovered circumstances shall be considered and determined in the hearing by the panel of three judges of the Criminal Division. Upon considering the prosecutor's conclusion presented with the examination material, the court shall make the following decision: (1) to quash the court judgment or ruling, reopen the case and refer it for renewed pretrial investigation or reopening of the trial; (2) to quash the court judgment or ruling and to terminate the case; (3) to refuse to reopen the case. The court shall have the authority to stop the execution of any court judgment or ruling, if the decision to reopen the case has been adopted.

B. *Reopening the Criminal Case due to the Decision of the European Court on Human Rights or Human Rights Committee of the United Nations or Constitutional Court of Lithuania*

1031. The criminal cases decided by the courts of the Republic of Lithuania may be reopened if the UN Human Rights Committee or ECtHR rules that the judgment of conviction has been rendered in violation of the International Covenant on Civil and Political Rights (ICCPR) or the ECHR or the Additional Protocols. The legal ground for the case reopening is the character and gravity of the violations, which causes reasonable doubts concerning the conviction of the person and the persistent violations may be rectified only by reopening the case.[499] Criminal cases decided by the courts of the Republic of Lithuania also may be reopened if Constitutional Court of Lithuania declares that the law or other legal act on the basis of which the judgment was adopted contradict the requirements of the Constitution of Lithuania.

1032. The application to reopen a criminal case may be filed by a person with respect to whom violations of the ICCPR or the ECHR or the Additional Protocols or the Constitution of Lithuania have been committed, his/her legal successor, their representative or the Prosecutor General of Lithuania. The Chairman of the Supreme Court of Lithuania may request to reopen a criminal case even if no application of the above-mentioned persons has been filed.

---

499. Lietuvos Respublikos baudžiamojo proceso kodekso komentaras, II dalis, Vilnius, TIC, 2003, p. 568.

1033. An application or request to reopen a criminal case, with the attached appropriate decision of the UN Human Rights Committee or the ECtHR, shall be filed within six months from the day of delivery of the final decision of the UN Human Rights Committee or the ECtHR or the Constitutional Court of Lithuania with the Supreme Court of Lithuania. An application or request filed on the same ground for the second time shall be inadmissible.

1034. If the application complies with the requirements, the panel of the Supreme Court of Lithuania shall refer the case to: (1) the panel of three judges of the Criminal Division (if the case has not been reviewed by way of cassation procedure), or (2) the plenary session of the Supreme Court of Lithuania (if the case has been reviewed by way of cassation procedure). Having decided to reopen the criminal proceedings, the court may stay the execution of judgments and rulings in the case.

1035. A hearing for the reopened criminal case of the panel of judges or the plenary session of the Criminal Division of the Supreme Court shall be held within the possible shortest time. The person who has filed the application for the reopening of the criminal case shall have the right to participate in the hearing. The prosecutor and the defence counsel must participate in the hearing. Notice of the hearing shall be given to the convicted person, the victim and their representative. If the ground for reopening the case concerns the issues determined in the cassation ruling, all persons who were entitled to take part in the hearing of the cassation case shall be notified thereof. The non-appearance of the persons, notified in the appropriate manner of the place and time of the hearing of the reopened case, shall not suspend the hearing of the case.

1036. At the beginning of the hearing one of the judges shall state the merits of the case, the content of the judicial decisions and of the application or request to reopen the case. After the statement made by the judge the person who filed the application for the reopening of the case shall be given an opportunity to speak. Thereafter the court shall hear other persons participating in the hearing of the case. The person who filed the application shall be entitled to give additional explanations last.

1037. Having heard the statements and additional explanations, the court shall retire to the deliberation room to issue a ruling. If after the hearing of the reopened case the convicted person must be released from the place of imprisonment, the ruling shall be transmitted for execution on the same day of its pronouncement.

1038. Having heard the reopened criminal case, the court shall make the following decision: (1) to dismiss the application or request and affirm the decisions made by the court; (2) to quash the judgment and subsequent rulings and dismiss the case; (3) to quash the judgment and subsequent rulings and refer the case for the new pretrial investigation or hearing at the Court of First Instance; (4) to quash the appellate court judgment or ruling and affirm the judgment made by the first instance court (either with or without amendments); (5) to quash the appellate court judgment or ruling and refer the case for the new hearing by the appellate court; (6) to quash the cassation court ruling and issue a new ruling; (7) to amend court judgments or rulings. Having heard a reopened criminal case, the court also may quash the judgments or rulings in part. Above-mentioned court rulings shall be final and not subject to appeal.

C. Reopening the Criminal Case due to Clear Improper Application of the Criminal Law

1039. The Supreme Court may quash an effective court judgment or ruling and reopen the criminal case if according to the circumstances specified in the judgments and rulings, there are grounds for assuming that the application of the criminal law was clearly improper and, as a result, it is necessary to mitigate the legal status of the sentenced person[500] by: (a) quashing the judgment and subsequent rulings and terminating the criminal case; (b) to requalifying a criminal act pursuant to another article of a Special Part of the CC of Lithuania, which provide criminal liability for a less serious criminal act; (c) correcting the violations of the provisions of the imposition of the final punishment and reducing the final punishment; (d) releasing the convicted person from the punishment due to statute of limitations, or (e) correcting improper application of the act of amnesty and reducing the final punishment or releasing convicted person from the punishment.

1040. The application to reopen a criminal case may be filed by a convicted person, his/her representative or defence counsel, also the Prosecutor General of Lithuania. The Chairman of the Supreme Court may request to reopen a criminal case even if no application of the above-mentioned persons has been filed. The application or request may be filed only until convicted person serves his/her judgment. An application or request filed on the same ground for the second time shall be inadmissible.

1041. If the application complies with the requirements, the panel of the Supreme Court of Lithuania may reopen the criminal case and refer the case to: (1) the panel of three judges of the Criminal Division (if the case has not been reviewed by way of cassation procedure); or (2) the extended panel of the seven judges of the Criminal Division (if the case has been reviewed by way of cassation procedure by the panel of three judges of the Criminal Division); or (3) the plenary session of the Supreme Court of Lithuania (if the case has been reviewed by way of cassation procedure by the extended panel of seven judges of the Criminal Division). Having decided to reopen the criminal proceedings, the court may stay the execution of judgments and rulings in the case.

---

500. Goda G., Kazlauskas M., Kuconis P. Baudžiamojo proceso teisė, Vilnius, Registrų centras, 2011, p. 621.

1042. A hearing for the reopened criminal case of the panel or the extended panel of judges or the plenary session of the Criminal Division of the Supreme Court shall be held within the possible shortest time. The prosecutor and the defence counsel must participate in the hearing. Notice of the hearing shall be given to the convicted person, the victim and their representative. The non-appearance of the persons, notified in the appropriate manner of the place and time of the hearing of the reopened case, shall not suspend the hearing of the case.

1043. At the beginning of the hearing one of the judges shall state the merits of the case, the content of the judicial decisions and of the application or request to reopen the case. After the statement made by the judge the court shall hear other persons participating in the hearing of the case.

1044. Having heard the statements and additional explanations, the court shall retire to the deliberation room to issue a ruling. If after the hearing of the reopened case the convicted person must be released from the place of imprisonment, the ruling shall be transmitted for execution on the same day of its pronouncement.

1045. Having heard the reopened criminal case, the court shall make the following decision: (1) to dismiss the application or request to reopen the case; (2) to quash the judgment and subsequent rulings and to terminate the case; (3) to quash the judgment and subsequent rulings of the appellate and cassation courts and affirm the judgment of the Court of First Instance; (4) to quash the judgment or ruling of the cassation court and to affirm the judgment of the first instance and appellate court (either with or without amendments); (5) to amend court judgments or rulings.

Part III. Execution and Extinction of Sanctions

Chapter 1. Sources of Penitentiary Law and Nature of Regulations

1046. The Lithuanian punishment execution law is a branch of the public law, which regulates the execution of all punishments provided in the CC. Penitentiary law is a part of the punishment execution and regulates the execution of the imprisonment and life imprisonment punishments.

1047. The Constitution of Lithuania is a source of punishment execution (and penitentiary) law. For example, Article 48 of the Constitution provides a special rule for the penitentiary law according to which 'labour which is performed by convicts in places of confinement and which is regulated by law shall not be deemed as forced labour either'. Furthermore, the Constitutional Court of Lithuania in 2003 and 2015 has adopted two decisions concerning the compatibility of the punishment execution law to the constitutional requirements. In the first case, the Constitutional Court has declared that 'obligatory censorship of the correspondence of persons serving a sentence of imprisonment without providing by law the grounds for such censorship was in conflict with Article 22 of the Constitution of the Republic of Lithuania'.[501] In the second case the Constitutional Court of Lithuania has decided that the rule of the Code of Punishment Execution which has stated that 'correspondence between convicts detained in pretrial detention, arrest, and correctional institutions is prohibited in the cases where they are not spouses or close relatives' is in conflict with the requirements of the Constitution of Lithuania and the constitutional principle of a State under the rule of law.[502]

1048. The main source of the punishment execution law is the Code of Punishment Execution. This Code regulates the basic principles of the punishment execution, the rights and obligations of the sentenced persons, as well as the rules of the execution of all punishment, etc. Besides the CPE, the Law on Probation regulates execution of the suspension of the execution of the imprisonment and conditional release from a correctional institution; the Law on Activities of Correctional Officers – the legal status (functions, rights and obligations) of the correctional officers

501. Decision of the Constitutional Court of Lithuania of 24 Mar. 2003, *Valstybės žinios*, 2003, No. 29-1196.
502. Decision of the Constitutional Court of Lithuania of 26 Feb. 2015, TAR, 2015, No. 03023.

of the system of punishment execution. It should be noted that in accordance with the CPE, Law on Probation, Statute on Service in the Prison Department under the Ministry of Justice of Lithuania, etc., there are numerous legal acts regulating various aspects of the punishment execution adopted by the government,[503] Ministry of Justice,[504] jointly by the Ministry of Justice and the Ministry of Internal Affairs,[505] Prison department,[506] etc. It should be noted that according, for example, to the CPE, State institutions may adopt legal acts on punishment execution issues only in cases directly provided for in this Code. In addition, these legal acts may establish only the procedure for limiting the rights and freedoms, also the procedure for realisation of duties of the convicted persons provided for in the laws of the Lithuania.

1049. Lithuanian punishment execution law has strongly been influenced by binding and recommendatory international legal acts. The main mandatory international sources are ICCPR (1991),[507] ECHR (1995),[508] EU Charter of Fundamental Rights, 1984 UN Convention against Torture and other Cruel, Inhuman and Degrading Treatment or Punishment (1991),[509] 1987 European Convention for the Prevention of Torture and other Cruel, Inhuman and Degrading Treatment or Punishment and its additional protocols (1998),[510] etc. Recommendatory legal acts should also be mentioned – the Council of Europe recommendations on various imprisonment and probation issues, for example: Rec(2006)2 of the Committee of Ministers to Member States on the European Prison Rules, Rec R(89)12 of the Committee of Ministers to Member States on education in prison, Rec R(82)16 of the Committee of Ministers to Member States on prison leave, Rec(92)12 of the Committee of Ministers to Member States on the European rules on the community sanctions and measures, Recommendation Rec(2003)23 of the Committee of Ministers to Member States on the management by prison administrations of life sentence and other long-term prisoners, CM/Rec(2012)12 of the Committee of Ministers to Member States concerning foreigner prisoners, CM/Rec(2014)3 of the Committee of Ministers to Member States concerning dangerous offenders, etc.

1050. The jurisprudence of the ECtHR is also a very important source, because the ECtHR has brought several decisions on various punishment execution matters

503. For example, Lietuvos Respublikos Vyriausybės nutarimas 'Dėl suimtųjų ir nuteistųjų bendrojo ugdymo ir profesinio mokymo organizavimo', TAR, 2016-01-20, No. 1243, etc.
504. For example, Lietuvos Respublikos teisingumo ministro įsakymas 'Dėl Areštinių vidaus tvarkos taisyklių patvirtinimo', TAR, 2015, No. 2015-12468, etc.
505. For example, Lietuvos Respublikos teisingumo ministro ir Lietuvos Respublikos vidaus reikalų ministro įsakymas 'Dėl Probacijos tarnybų ir policijos bendradarbiavimo vykdant laisvės apribojimo bausmę taisyklių patvirtinimo', *Valstybės žinios*, 2012, No. 88-4632, etc.
506. For example, Lietuvos Respublikos Kalėjimų departamento prie teisingumo ministerijos direktoriaus įsakymas 'Dėl Kardomojo kalinimo ir laisvės atėmimo vietų įskaitos tarnybų darbo instrukcijos patvirtinimo', *Valstybės žinios*, 2002, No. 47-1832, etc.
507. Tarptautinis pilietinių ir politinių teisių paktas, *Valstybės žinios*, 2002, No. 77-3288.
508. Žmogaus teisių ir pagrindinių laisvių apsaugos konvencija, iš dalies pakeista protokolais No. 11 ir Nr. 14, *Valstybės žinios*, 2011, No. 156-7390.
509. Konvencija prieš kankinimą ir kitokį žiaurų, nežmonišką ar žeminantį elgesį ar baudimą, *Valstybės žinios*, 2006, No. 80-3141.
510. Europos konvencija prieš kankinimą ir kitokį žiaurų, nežmonišką ar žeminantį elgesį ir baudimą bei jos pirmasis ir antrasis protokolai, *Valstybės žinios*, 1998, No. 86-2393.

against Lithuania, for example, matters concerning living conditions,[511] medical treatment,[512] education,[513] secrecy of the correspondence,[514] prohibition of the long-term visits for the detained persons,[515] non-possibility to review the life imprisonment,[516] inappropriate conduct of the correctional institution staff,[517] private life aspects[518] in the correctional institutions.

1051. It is also important to bring the attention to the significance of the reports of the Council of Europe's Committee for the Prevention of Torture and Inhuman or Degrading Treatment or Punishment (CPT) to the punishment execution law as well as the practice of the correctional institutions and officials. The CPT has visited Lithuania during periodic visits in 2000, 2004, 2008, 2012 and 2016, also during ad hoc visits in 2010 and 2018.

---

511. ECtHR decision *Valašinas v. Lithuania*, No. 44558/98; ECtHR decision *Karalevičius v. Lithuania* No. 53254/99, ECtHR decision *Savenkovas v. Lithuania* No. 871/02, ECtHR decision *Kasperovičius v. Lithuania* No. 54872/08; ECtHR decision *Mironovas and others v. Lithuania* Nos 40828/12, 29292/12, 69598/12, 40163/13, 66281/13, 70048/13, 70065/13; ECtHR decision *Aleksandravičius and others v. Lithuania* Nos 32344/13, 43576/13, 49516/13, 65956/13, 71139/13, etc.
512. ECtHR decision *Valašinas v. Lithuania*, No. 44558/98; ECtHR decision *Bagdonavičius v. Lithuania* No. 41252/12, etc.
513. ECtHR decision *Valašinas v. Lithuania*, No. 44558/98; ECtHR decision *Jankovskis v. Lithuania* No. 21575/08, etc.
514. ECtHR decision *Valašinas v. Lithuania*, No. 44558/98; ECtHR decision *Puzinas v. Lithuania*, Nr. 44800/98 ECtHR decision *Karalevičius v. Lithuania* Nos 53254/99, ECtHR decision *Čiapas v. Lithuania* No. 4902/02, etc.
515. ECtHR decision *Varnas v. Lithuania* No. 42615/06; etc.
516. ECtHR decision *Matiošaitis and others v. Lithuania* Nos 22662/13, 51059/13, 58823/13, 59692/13, 59700/13, 60115/13, 69425/13 and 72824/13.
517. ECtHR decision *Česnulevičius v. Lithuania* Nos 13462/06; ECtHR decision *Tautkus v. Lithuania* No. 29474/09.
518. ECtHR decision *Biržietis v. Lithuania* No. 49304/09; etc.

Chapter 2. General Principles Concerning the Execution of Sentences and Orders

1052. The Code of Punishment Execution provides these principles of the punishment execution: (1) principle of legality, (2) principle of non-discrimination, (3) principle of humanism, (4) principle of individualisation of punishment execution and public participation in correction of convicted persons and (5) principle of the progressive execution of the punishment, etc. It should be noted that the principles of the punishment execution are important not only for the legislative process, but also for practical aspects since the Code of Punishment Execution and the Law on Probation provide that in case of the gaps in the law penal institutions and officials must act in accordance with the requirements of these principles.

1053. The content of the principle of legality has several aspects. First of all, a legal basis for the enforcement of the punishment may be only a valid judgment of conviction of the court of Lithuania. In the cases provided for by international treaties of the Republic of Lithuania and laws of Lithuania, the valid judgment of conviction of a foreign State court (e.g., Norway, Russia, Belarus, etc.) or an international judicial authority (e.g., International Criminal Court) may also be a legal basis for the punishment enforcement in Lithuania. Second, the restrictions on the rights and freedoms of the convicted person, also the duties of the convicted person shall be determined only by the laws of the Republic of Lithuania. It also means that legal acts, which must implement the law cannot establish a new limitation of the rights or special duties for the convicted person.[519] Third, the conduct of the convicted person may be restricted only by prohibition or duty. Meanwhile, the punishment enforcement authority or official may act only in ways and in the manner directly prescribed by law.

1054. The principle of non-discrimination means that the enforcement of punishments is guided by the rule that all convicted persons are equal regardless of their origin, gender, social or property status, nationality or race, political views and parity, education, language, religion or other beliefs, genetic features, disability, sexual orientation, type and nature of activity, place of residence and other circumstances, which are unforeseen in the laws of Lithuania.

1055. The content of the principle of humanism has several aspects. First, during the execution of a punishment, it is prohibited to expose the convicted person to the torture or to the behaviour which is cruel or detrimental to the human dignity. Second, the CPE provides prohibition of any medical, biological and other scientific experiments with a convicted person whose freedom is restricted, even with his/her consent. Third, it is prohibited, except in cases provided for in the laws of Lithuania, to film or photograph a convicted person whose freedom is restricted

519. Švedas G. Bausmių vykdymo teisė. Bendroji dalis, Vilnius, Registrų centras, 2013, p. 111.

without his/her prior consent. The doctrine of the Lithuanian punishment execution[520] has also noted that principle of humanism requires during the execution of the punishment to apply only positive and legitimate corrective measures such as education, professional training and work, psychological effect, social rehabilitation programmes, etc.

1056. The principle of individualisation of punishment execution and public participation in correction of convicted persons means that corrective measures shall be applied to the convicted persons according to their personality and conduct during the execution of the punishment, as well as the gravity and nature of the committed criminal act. This principle requires that the punishment execution law shall provide different corrective measures, also different forms and methods of influence on convicted persons (e.g., mass, group or individual work).[521] Non-governmental organisations, religious communities, their members and other natural and legal persons have the right to participate in the process of the correction of the convicted persons.

1057. The principle of the progressive execution of the punishment requires that the legal status of the convicted persons shall be mitigated or aggravated in accordance with the procedure established by the CC, the Code of Criminal Procedure and the Code of Punishment Execution, taking into account their behaviour during the execution of the punishment, compliance with established obligations and prohibitions, their attitude to work, education and professional training, their response to psychological effect and measures of social rehabilitation. The doctrine of the Lithuanian punishment execution has noted that mitigation or aggravation of the legal status of the convicted person must correspond to the requirements of proportionality, for example, the better behaviour of the convicted person and the longer it lasts, the more additional rights and freedoms must be given to the convicted person.[522]

1058. The doctrine of the Lithuanian punishment execution points out the principle of the development of convicted person initiative, which means that the convicted person must be not only the object of the corrective measures but also an active participant of the preparation and implementation of the whole correctional process.[523]

---

520. Švedas G. Bausmių vykdymo teisė. Bendroji dalis, Vilnius, Registrų centras, 2013, p. 118.
521. Blaževičius J., Švedas G., Usik D. Lietuvos Respublikos bausmių vykdymo kodekso komentaras, I-V dalys (1-183 straipsniai), Vilnius, TIC, 2004, p. 47.
522. Švedas G. Bausmių vykdymo teisė. Bendroji dalis, Vilnius, Registrų centras, 2013, p. 122–123.
523. Švedas G. Bausmių vykdymo teisė. Bendroji dalis, Vilnius, Registrų centras, 2013, p. 126–127.

Chapter 3. The Prison System

§1. Organisational Structure

I. Prison Administration and Classification of Penitentiaries

1059. The system of Lithuanian correctional institutions has been described in the General Introduction (*see* paragraphs 51–54).

1060. According to the Code of Punishment Execution, all correctional institutions may be classified into institutions of punishment execution (including central prison hospital) and pretrial detention institutions; institutions for juveniles and institutions for men and for women. According to the security level, institutions of punishment execution may be classified into prisons (high security), correctional houses (medium security) and open prisons (minimum security).[524] Furthermore, a prison as its composite part has medium and high security units, correctional houses for adults – high, medium and minimum security units, correctional houses for juveniles – medium and minimum security units. It should be noted that the main institutions for the execution of the imprisonment are correctional houses where approximately 95% of all convicted persons are serving their punishment.

1061. The order of the director of the Prison department under the Ministry of Justice provides that the maximum number of inmates in the correctional institution should not exceed: Vilnius correctional house – 642; Alytus correctional house – 965; Marijampolė correctional house – 1050; Pravieniškių correctional house-open prison – 2660; Panevėžys correctional house – 425; Kaunas pretrial detention centre-correctional house for juveniles – 324; Šiauliai pretrial detention centre – 440; Central prison hospital – 380, etc.[525]

1062. The internal rules of the correctional institutions also provide that the minimum living space per person shall not be less than: 3.1 m^2 – in the premises of dormitories of the correctional institutions; 3.6 m^2 – in the premises of confinement of the correctional institutions; 4.1 m^2 – in the living premises of the Kaunas juvenile pretrial detention centre and correctional house; 7 m^2 – in the living premises of the central prison hospital.[526]

524. Švedas G. Lithuania. Criminal Justice Systems in Europe and North America, Helsinki, HEUNI, 2000, p. 38.
525. Kalėjimų departamento prie Lietuvos Respublikos teisingumo ministerijos departamento direktoriaus įsakymas ‘Dėl didžiausio laisvės atėmimo vietų įstaigose leidžiamų laikyti asmenų skaičiaus ir minimalaus ploto, tenkančio vienam asmeniui, nustatymo’, TAR, 2021, No. 20141.
526. Kalėjimų departamento prie Lietuvos Respublikos teisingumo ministerijos departamento direktoriaus įsakymas ‘Dėl didžiausio laisvės atėmimo vietų įstaigose leidžiamų laikyti asmenų skaičiaus ir minimalaus ploto, tenkančio vienam asmeniui, nustatymo’, TAR, 2021, No. 20141.

II. Classification of Prisoners

1063. The classification of inmates is the precondition of the implementation of the principle of individualisation of punishment execution.[527] The CPE provides that the purposes of the inmates separate or isolated custody is to: (1) distinguish between convicted persons who, due to the nature of their crimes or personal characteristics, may have a negative influence on other convicts; (2) facilitate the social rehabilitation of the convicts; (3) help ensure the supervision of the convicts and their safety; (4) help ensure compliance with the requirements of security and management of correctional institutions.

1064. The Lithuanian law on punishment execution provides mandatory and discretionary criteria for the classification of inmates.[528] The mandatory criteria, which the administration of the correctional institutions must follow, are: gender of the inmate; age of the inmate; health of the inmate; previous convictions of the inmate, etc. The Code of Punishment Execution requires that men and women, adults and minors, inmates of different groups must be kept in separate correctional institutions or isolated from each other in the same correction institution. Furthermore, isolated from each other in the same correction institution (or in separate correctional institutions if there is such a possibility) must be kept: former or existing State officials for the first time sentenced to imprisonment; persons for the first time sentenced for minor and less serious crimes to imprisonment; persons sentenced for intentional and negligent crimes; dangerous repeat offenders sentenced for serious and grave crimes; persons with active pulmonary tuberculosis; persons sentenced to life imprisonment. Men and women may be kept together in open prisons and transitional (halfway) houses.

1065. The discretionary criteria, which the administration of the correctional institutions may follow and keep isolated from other inmates, are: former or existing civil servants; disabled persons with a 0–40% capacity for work or with a high or medium-level of special needs; working and good behaviour inmates; inmates who violate the regime of a correctional institution, etc.

1066. In addition, according to the principle of progressive execution of the punishment, in each correctional institution inmates are divided into certain groups according to their behaviour during imprisonment. According to the CPE, the prison has ordinary and disciplinary groups, the correctional house – ordinary, disciplinary and soft groups, the correctional house for the juveniles – ordinary and soft groups. The legal status (i.e., rights and obligations) of the inmates who are in the disciplinary group is most restricted, and inmates who are in the soft group – the mildest.

527. Švedas G. Bausmių vykdymo teisė. Bendroji dalis, Vilnius, Registrų centras, 2013, p. 124.
528. Švedas G. Nuteistųjų laisvės atėmimo bausme klasifikavimo probleminiai aspektai Lietuvoje // Bausmių vykdymo sistemos teisinis reguliavimas ir perspektyvos Lietuvos Respublikoje, Vilnius, 2010, p. 164.

All new inmates who arrived at the correctional institution are assigned to an ordinary group. Further, taking into account the inmate's behaviour during the execution of the punishment, compliance with established obligations and prohibitions, attitude to work, education and professional training, response to psychological effect and measures of social rehabilitation, the administration of the correctional institution may encourage (or punish) the inmate and transfer him/her to the soft (or disciplinary) group. The transfer to the disciplinary group may be imposed from three to twelve months, after which the inmate must be returned to the ordinary group.

1067. In the central prison hospital men and women, adults and minors, also persons sentenced to life imprisonment must be kept separate from each other.

§2. The Penitentiary Regime

I. Introduction

1068. According to Article 111 of the Code of Punishment Execution, the corrective measures which are applicable to the inmates include regime of the imprisonment execution, employment of inmates and social rehabilitation. The regime of the imprisonment execution is a set of differentiated conditions for the execution of an imprisonment and the rules of the conduct of inmates. The main requirements of the regime are: (a) obligatory separation of the convicted persons from the outside world and permanent supervision of their conduct; (b) requirement for the convicted persons to perform their duties accurately and coherently; (c) formation of the different conditions for the imprisonment execution in accordance with the severity and nature of the crime committed by the convicted person, the personality and the conduct of the convicted person during the execution of the punishment. The inmates who serve an imprisonment wear their own clothes or clothes provided by the correctional institution. The inmates are allowed to have food, essential accessories and other items the list of which is established by the internal rules of the correctional institutions.[529] The inmates also are allowed to buy food and other necessary items in the shops of correctional institutions, to get visits, to send and receive correspondence, parcels and small packages, to receive and send money remittances, to make telephone calls, to walk in open air, etc.

1069. The Code of Punishment Execution provides that measures to ensure regime of the correctional institutions are: protection of correctional institutions; prevention and investigation of violations of law; the order of entering and leaving the correctional institutions; internal order of the correctional institutions; daily routine; actions of the administration of correctional institution when inmates goes on

529. Lietuvos Respublikos teisingumo ministro įsakymas 'Dėl Pataisos įstaigų ir tardymo izoliatorių vidaus tvarkos taisyklių patvirtinimo', TAR, 2020, No. 911.

hunger strike, refuses to work or to perform orders and instructions of the administration, or severely violates the internal procedure of the correctional institution, etc.

II. Aspects of Living Conditions

A. *Visits, Correspondence and Telephone*

1070. The right to visits, correspondence (including small package) and telephone calls are provided in the Code of Punishment Execution. These rights are a very important element for keeping normal social relationships with a family, close relatives and the outside world, also for the prevention of the detrimental effects of imprisonment.

1071. The inmates have the right to visits, which may take place under the supervision of the administration of the correctional institution or without supervision. Inmates have the right to choose the form of the visit. Visits under the supervision of the administration may happen in the following ways: (1) remotely – up to two hours; (2) in special premises of a correctional institution without physical contact between visitors and an inmate – for up to two hours; (3) in the premises of a correctional institution with physical contact between visitors and an inmate – for up to three hours. Visits without the supervision of the administration may take place in special premises of correctional institutions and may last up to 24 hours. The frequency and types of the visits depend on the type of the correctional institution (prison, correctional house, etc.) and the group in which imprisonment is being served, for example, inmate who serves imprisonment in the ordinary group of prison have the right to two visits during one month, inmate who serves imprisonment in the ordinary group of correctional house – four visits during one month, etc. The Code of Punishment Execution allows the inmate to replace visit to the two-four telephone calls. For inmates who are serving imprisonment in the soft group of the correctional institution, additional visits for their social contacts may be granted by the director of the correctional institution.

1072. Physical contact is allowed during visits with the spouse, cohabitee, close relatives and the person with whom the inmate has a common child. Visit under the supervision takes place in front of the representative of the correctional institution, but the conversation is not heard. Visits without supervision are allowed only with the spouse, cohabitee or the person with whom the inmate has a common child and take place in special rooms arranged for the living. The visit must be immediately terminated if the inmate or visitors violate the visit procedure.

1073. The director of the correctional institution must allow a visit by the spouse, cohabitee, close relatives or the person with whom the convict has a common child the inmate, who has a serious illness endangering his/her life. These visits are not counted into the established limit of visits.

1074. Furthermore, the Code of Punishment Execution provides that lawyer's meetings with the inmates are not limited and these meetings are not counted into the established limit of visits. Each meeting with the lawyer takes place at the working time of the administration of correctional institution and cannot last more than 8 hours.

1075. For convicted spouses, both of whom are serving prison terms, visits also may be granted. Convicted spouses can get a visit, if both have the right to the desired visit. The location of these visits is determined by the directors of correctional institutions where the spouses are serving their punishment. The costs of the transfer are paid by the inmates themselves.

1076. The inmates are allowed to send and receive an unlimited number of letters. The administration of the correctional institution must serve a letter received on behalf of the inmate to the inmate and a letter submitted by the inmate must be sent to the addressees no later than within three working days. The costs of sending letters are paid by the inmate himself/herself. It should be noted that the letters received and sent by the inmates may be checked by a resolution of the director of the correctional institution or by a ruling of the judge in order to prevent the commission of criminal acts or other violations of law or to protect the rights and freedoms of other persons, also it may temporarily suspend (up to three months) the expulsion and service of the letters. The resolution of the director of the correctional institution or the ruling of the judge shall specify the reasons, length, mode and other circumstances for the checking of the letters or the suspension of service and other circumstances, for which the letters need to be checked or the service of them to be suspended.

1077. The inmates have the right to apply with requests, petitions and complaints to officials and civil servants of State and municipal institutions, non-governmental organisations and international institutions. The requests, petitions and complaints addressed to the officials and civil servants of State and municipal institutions are not checked and must be sent within one working day. Answers to the inmate requests, petitions and complaints are served to the inmates within two working days (answers from international institutions – within one working day). It should be noted that inmates are prohibited from sending anonymous or collective complaints to the State and municipal institutions and officials, also on behalf of other inmates or not through the administration of the correctional institution.

1078. The inmates have the right to telephone calls. The frequency of the telephone calls depends on the type of correctional institution (prison, correctional house, etc.) and the group in which imprisonment is being served, for example, inmate who serves imprisonment in the disciplinary group of prison have the right to call twice a month, inmate who serves the prison sentence in the ordinary group of prison – twice a week, and inmate who serves imprisonment in the soft group of correctional house – three times a day, etc. It should be noted that the director of the correctional institution has the right to allow an additional one-time telephone call if the inmate so requests because of important circumstances. One telephone call cannot last more than 15 minutes. The telephone conversation may be terminated if the inmate violates the calling procedure.

B. Information and Media

1079. The administration of the correctional institutions is obliged to assure the possibility for inmates to access the information and media through the State equipment in common rooms. Meanwhile, the CPE provides that the inmates (except those who serve their punishment in the disciplinary group) have the right to use their own portable TVs and radios, computers, video recorders, computer game machines, compact disc players, etc. during free time.

1080. All correctional institutions have libraries which should be equipped with a sufficient number of books, newspapers and magazines. The inmates (except inmates of a disciplinary group) have the right to purchase unlimited quantities of literature and stationery, as well as to subscribe the newspapers and magazines. In addition, the right to subscribe newspapers and magazines for inmates is provided to their spouses, cohabitees and close relatives, as well as other natural and legal persons. The inmates are prohibited from obtaining, acquiring, storing, distributing or subscribing to violent or cruelty-related publications as well as pornographic publications.

C. Prison Labour

1081. Labour is one of the corrective measures for the inmates. An inmate of the correctional institution must work if he/she is offered the labour by the administration of the correctional institution. The administration of the correctional institution must ensure that the inmate is recruited according to his/her working capability and, to the extent possible, to the possessed speciality. The disabled inmates may be included in the labour only with their written consent, provided there is a doctor's conclusion and job vacancies. Usually, the inmates work in the correctional institutions and State enterprises under the correctional institutions. The activity of correctional institutions and State enterprises under correctional institutions, in which inmates are involved, must serve only the main objective of teaching the inmates to pursue their life goals through legitimate means. These activities may be financed from the State budget (including the European Union and other international financial assistance funds). The Report of the Prison department under the Ministry of Justice of Lithuania has noted that approximately 1671 (or 32%) inmates were employed in 2020.[530]

530. Kalėjimų departamento prie Lietuvos Respublikos teisingumo ministerijos 2020 metų veiklos ataskaita, Vilnius, 2021.

1082. The CPE provides that the term of inmates' work may not be more than 8hours per day. The work of the inmates may not be less than 80 hours per month. The inmates are given two days of rest per week.

1083. Furthermore, the working inmates have the right to the remuneration proportionate to the quantity and quality of the work and the right to vacation.

1084. Education and professional training are also corrective measures of the inmates. Inmates below the age of 16 must attend a secondary school. Other inmates are involved in secondary education only if they wish so. Furthermore, the professional training of the inmates may be organised in the correctional institutions and State enterprises under the correctional institutions. The inmates have the right to choose a profession (speciality) that they will study according to the list provided by the administration of the correctional institution and the available training base. The Report of the Prison department under the Ministry of Justice of Lithuania has noted that approximately 934 (or 17.6%) inmates were involved in secondary education and 849 (or 16%) – in professional training in 2020.[531]

D. Disciplinary Measures

1085. The rules of the disciplinary liability – disciplinary measures, disciplinary procedure and legal remedies are provided in the Code of Punishment Execution. Disciplinary offences may be divided into the offences and serious offences. Offences are violations of the regime of the imprisonment execution. The disciplinary measures for offences are a (1) reprimand, (2) reduction of the maximum amount of money for which inmates may purchase personal belongings per month by the amount of one basic social benefit to three months; (3) a ban on the purchase of personal items for one month (except for the purchase of hygiene items and stationery); (4) a contribution to the fund of social support for inmates in the amount of one basic social benefit. Serious offences are systematic or severe violations of the regime of the imprisonment execution. The disciplinary measures for serious offences are: solitary confinement for up to thirty days for adults and up to five days for juveniles. The transfer to the solitary confinement and to the cell type premises cannot be applicable to pregnant women and mothers with a child until 3 years of age, as well as inmates for the medical reasons.

1086. The disciplinary procedure is initiated and the disciplinary measure is imposed by the director of the correctional institution or delegated official. The disciplinary measure may be imposed only on the inmate who has committed a disciplinary offence. For several disciplinary offences committed simultaneously, one disciplinary measure is imposed. When imposing the disciplinary measure, due account shall be taken of the circumstances of the commission of the disciplinary offence, the amount and nature of the disciplinary measures already imposed, as

531. Kalėjimų departamento prie Lietuvos Respublikos teisingumo ministerijos 2020 metų veiklos ataskaita, Vilnius, 2021.

well as the written explanation of the inmate. The disciplinary measure to be imposed must be proportionate to the gravity and nature of the disciplinary offence committed. The disciplinary measure imposed must be executed immediately and no later than within one month after its imposition. The inmate has the right to appeal the imposed disciplinary measure to a higher official. The filing of a complaint does not stop the execution of the imposed disciplinary measure.

E. Leave from Prison

1087. The Code of Punishment Execution provides several types of leave from correctional institutions during the execution of the punishment, such as: (a) short-term leave from the correctional institution to the place of domicile; (b) leave from the correctional institution for serious reasons; (c) leave without guardianship outside the territory of the correctional institution for the education, professional training, work or social rehabilitation, etc. Most of these short-term leaves from correctional institutions may be used as a means of encouragement for good behaviour of the inmates during the execution of the imprisonment.[532]

1088. The short-term leave from the correctional institution to the place of domicile which is in the territory of the Republic of Lithuania may be granted to the inmates who are serving their punishment in the soft group of the correctional institutions and who have completed at least from six up to two years of the punishment imposed by the court. This type of leave from the correctional institution may be once every one-four months for three days. The time of this short-term leave is counted into the time of execution of the punishment. The right to short-term leave from the correctional institution to the place of domicile does not have: (a) dangerous repeat offenders; (b) inmates from whom this right has been deprived for the commission of the violations; (c) inmates with dangerous and extremely dangerous communicable diseases that are dripping through the air, etc. The permission for a short-term leave from the correctional institution to the place of domicile is given by the director of the correctional institution on the basis of the personality of the inmate and his/her conduct during the imprisonment, also the part of the imprisonment executed. The control of the conduct of the inmates who were granted the short-term leave from the correctional institution to the place of domicile may be carried out by means of electronic monitoring. Travel costs are paid by the inmate himself/herself or his/her close relatives.

1089. The inmates (except those serving a life imprisonment punishment) may be allowed the leave from the correctional institutions on the territory of the Republic of Lithuania for a maximum period of ten days due to the death or serious illness of a spouse, cohabitee or close relative, as well as a natural disaster that has caused material damage to the inmate or his/her spouse, cohabitee or close relatives. The time of this type of leave is counted into the time of execution of the punishment.

532. Blaževičius J., Švedas G., Usik D. Lietuvos Respublikos bausmių vykdymo kodekso komentaras. I-V dalys (1-183 straipsniai), Vilnius, TIC, 2004, p. 279–280.

The permission to leave the correctional institution for serious reasons is given by the director of the correctional institution on the basis of the personality of the inmate and his/her conduct during the imprisonment, also the part of the imprisonment executed. The inmates' leave from correctional institutions is carried out with or without escort, and juveniles – only escorted; adult inmates may be handcuffed. The control of the conduct of the inmates whom the leave from the correctional institution for serious reasons was granted also may be carried out by means of electronic monitoring. Travel costs are paid by the inmate himself/herself or his/her close relatives.

1090. The inmates may be allowed to leave the territory of the correctional institution without guardianship if: (a) a punishment is served in the soft group of correctional institution; (b) the risk of criminal behaviour is low or medium and progress has been made in reducing this risk; (c) at least one-fourth of a punishment has been served (in case when the imposed punishment is up to ten years) or there was no more than one year left until his/her possible transfer to a transitional (halfway) house (in case when the imposed punishment is more than ten years). This type of leave may be granted if this is necessary for the education, professional training, work being performed or participation in the implementation of social rehabilitation measures. This type of leave means that the inmate has the opportunity to be present in a particular area at the time of implementation of work, education, professional training or social rehabilitation measures or to go on a certain route. The control of the conduct of the inmates whom this type of leave was granted may be carried out by means of electronic monitoring. The right to this type of leave does not have: (a) dangerous repeat offenders; (b) inmates from whom this right has been deprived for the commission of the violations; (c) inmates with dangerous and extremely dangerous communicable diseases that are dripping through the air, etc.

1091. Furthermore, the CPE establishes the possibility for juvenile inmates during the visit up to 8 hours to be outside the territory of juvenile correctional house with parents, close relatives or other persons of trust. In addition, the inmates who are well-behaved may be allowed to go to the cinema, theatre, concert, sports or other events organised outside the correctional institution together with the staff of the correctional institution.

III. Forms of Alternative Execution of the Prison Sentence

1092. The Lithuanian law does not provide for the alternative execution of the imposed imprisonment punishment. On the contrary, the CPE foresees a milder imprisonment execution regime for pregnant women and mothers of children under 3 years of age, as well as for inmates who are under intensive preparation for the conditional release from the correctional institution.

1093. The administration of the correctional house for pregnant women and mothers of children under 3 years of age may allow to live outside the correctional house until the child reaches 3 years of age if it requires the interests of child. These women are placed in residential premises near the correctional house and are regularly monitored by the administration of the correctional house. Women have the right: (1) to have cash and to use them without limit; (2) to make telephone calls, receive and send an unlimited number of letters, small packages, postal items and to have visits; (3) to go freely within the area designated by the director of the correctional house at the appointed time. Convicted persons are informed about the limits of the defined territory. Upon the expiry of the period of dismissal from work due to pregnancy and childcare, these women have to take up a job specified by the administration of the correctional house. It should be noted that the control of the conduct of the women whom the possibility to live outside the correctional house was granted may be carried out by means of electronic monitoring. The right of women to live outside the correctional house who systematically or extremely maliciously violate the rules of a prescribed regime or rules of conduct by the decision of the director of the correctional house shall be abolished and these women shall be transferred to the correctional house to continue the execution of the imprisonment.

1094. The inmates may be transferred to a special unit of the correctional institution – a transitional (halfway) house. The inmates for which conditional release from correctional institution is not applicable (*see* paragraph 1108), inmates who must serve their imprisonment in the prison and some other categories of inmates did not have the right to be transferred to the transitional (halfway) house.[533]

1095. The main task of the transitional house is intensive preparation of the inmates for the conditional release from correctional institutions. The inmates of the transitional house have the right: (1) to have cash and to use them without limit; (2) to make telephone calls, receive and send an unlimited number of letters, small packages, postal items and to have visits; (3) to leave up to 14 hours the territory of the transitional house with the permission of the administration if this is necessary for the education, medical treatment or work to be performed; (4) once a week, up to two non-working days to return to their domicile which are on the territory of Lithuania; etc.

§3. Prisoners' Rights, Complaints Procedures and Judicial Control

1096. Article 10 of the Code of Punishment Execution states that a person who serves his/her punishment has all the rights, freedoms and obligations with the restrictions provided in the laws of Lithuania and court judgment. The doctrine of

533. Kalėjimų departamento prie Lietuvos Respublikos teisingumo ministerijos direktoriaus įsakymas 'Dėl nuteistųjų perkėlimo į Pusiaukelės namus tvarkos aprašo patvirtinimo', TAR, 2016, No. 6061.

Lithuanian punishment execution states that the convicted person has general and special rights and freedoms, also general and special obligations and prohibitions.[534]

1097. All convicted persons have general rights and freedoms, for example, the right to receive written information about the order of the execution of the imposed punishment, etc. Meanwhile, only persons to whom a certain type of the punishment is imposed have special rights for example, only persons who are sentenced to arrest, imprisonment and life imprisonment punishments have the right for a visit, etc. The Code of Punishment Execution attributes these rights and freedoms to the group of general rights and freedoms: (1) right to receive written information about the order of the execution of the imposed punishment; (2) right to apply with complaints, requests and petitions to the punishment execution or other State institution or official, also international institution or official; (3) right to receive medical treatment; (4) right to receive legal assistance; (5) right to solve citizenship issues; (6) right to participate in elections and referendum, and (7) freedom of conscience and religion. It should be noted that the implementation of some general rights may differ depending on the punishment imposed, for example, in case of arrest or imprisonment punishment the right to receive legal assistance and meet with the lawyer shall be realised only in the correctional institution, such a meeting may be only during working hours of the administration of the correctional institution, etc.

1098. The Code of Punishment Execution to the group of special rights of the persons who were sentenced to imprisonment punishment attributes these rights: (1) right to contacts with outside world (visits, telephone calls, correspondence, etc.); (2) right to buy food, literature, stationery and other items in the shop of the correctional institution; (3) right to use electrical appliances and other items; (4) right to have watches, to wear own clothes and footwear; (5) right to receive and send money transfers; (6) right to spent at least 2 hours in fresh air; (7) right to conclude civil transactions; (8) right to marriage; (9) right to short-term leave from the correctional institution; (10) right of foreigners to contact representatives of their countries; (11) right to accommodation, meal, etc.

1099. According to Article 110 of the Code of Punishment Execution, all convicted persons have few general obligations – they must comply with the requirements of the Constitution and laws and rules of conduct, also they must carry out instructions and orders of the correctional institutions or officials. Meanwhile, special obligations established for the persons serving imprisonment punishment are: (1) to clean living premises; (2) to keep the property of the correctional institution safe; etc. Besides it, these prohibitions are established for the persons serving imprisonment punishment: (1) to organise pickets, demonstrations, riots and other illegal activities and to participate in them; (2) to establish political parties and organisations and participate in their activities; (3) to acquire, manufacture, distribute or consume alcoholic beverages or their surrogates, narcotic, psychotropic or

534. Švedas G. Bausmių vykdymo teisė. Bendroji dalis, Vilnius, Registrų centras, 2013, p. 305, 326-328.

other psychoactive substances, to use medical substances without the permission of a doctor; (4) to acquire or transfer in any way their own, other inmates, and State property to other inmates or the administration of correctional institutions, as well as provide paid or otherwise remunerated services to other inmates or the administration of correctional institutions; (5) to make tattoos for yourself and other persons; (6) to distribute manuscripts and other publications without the permission of the administration of the correctional institution; (7) to incite other inmates to refuse to comply with the requirements of the administration of correctional institutions; (8) to demand any service from another inmate or to provide them, to use physical or mental violence against other persons; (9) to have tobacco in the premises of cell type, as well as in the places of health services of the correctional institutions.

1100. According to the Code of Punishment Execution, the supervision of the lawfulness of the activities of the correctional institutions and officials is carried out by the courts, prosecutors, *Seimas* controllers (ombudsmen), the Ministry of Justice and other State institutions in accordance with the laws of the Republic of Lithuania. Furthermore, in accordance with the international treaties of Lithuania, the supervision of the lawfulness of the activities of the correctional institutions and officials may be carried out by the international institutions, for example, EHtHR, CPT, etc.[535]

1101. The inmates have the right to file complaints against actions and decisions of the correctional institution and officials before the head of the correctional institution. The director of the correctional institution must take a decision concerning complaint within twenty working days. The decision of the director of the correctional institution may be appealed within one month before the director of the Prison department under the Ministry of Justice. The director of the Prison department must take a decision concerning complaint within twenty working days. The decisions and actions of the director of the Prison department may be appealed before the region administrative court within twenty days.

1102. It should be noted that the inmates have the right to apply directly to the President of the Republic, member of the *Seimas* or Government, prosecutor, *Seimas* Controller (ombudsmen) or representative of the Ministry of Justice at the time of their visit to correctional institutions.

§4. Early Release

I. Conditional Release

1103. According to the doctrine of punishment execution of Lithuania, the conditional release from the correctional institution is a very important institute which has to prepare a convicted person for life after serving the punishment and release

535. Blaževičius J., Švedas G., Usik D. Lietuvos Respublikos bausmių vykdymo kodekso komentaras. I-V dalys (1-183 straipsniai), Vilnius, TIC, p. 41.

from the correctional institution.[536] The substantive conditions of the conditional release from correctional institution is prescribed in the Code of Punishment Execution, procedure for conditional release from the correctional institution – in the Code of Criminal Procedure and the implementation of the conditions of the conditional release from correctional institution – in the Law on Probation.

1104. A convicted person serving his/her imprisonment punishment in the correctional institution, who (1) has served at least one-third, one-half or two-thirds of the punishment depending on the length of the imposed imprisonment, (2) has complied with the measures provided in the individual social rehabilitation plan, and (3) the risk whose criminal behaviour is low, and/or (4) the progress in eliminating the risk of criminal behaviour constitutes reasonable grounds to believe that he/she will comply with the laws and will not commit any crime, may be conditionally released from the correctional institution. The doctrine of the Lithuanian punishment execution[537] has criticised the mechanism and grounds for conditional release from correctional institution since the number of conditionally released persons, for example, from 1082 (or 31% of all persons released from correctional institutions) in 2015 to 826 (or 30% of all persons released from correctional institutions) in 2016 significantly reduced. In 2020, 984 persons were conditionally released from correctional institutions.

1105. In accordance with the Code of Punishment Execution, conditional release from correctional institutions is applied by the Commission on Conditional Release from Correctional Institutions. For a convict who has already had parole revoked, conditional release from a correctional institution shall be applied by the district court, which approves the decision of the Commission to apply conditional release from correctional institutions.

1106. Until 2019, the CPE provided special requirements for the conditional release from correctional institutions for the pregnant women and mothers of children under 3 years of age. These inmates had the right for conditional release from the correctional institution without observing the requirements for the duration of the served imprisonment. Meanwhile, from 2019, the pregnant women and mother with the child under 3 years of age may be conditionally after serving at least one-third, one-half or two-thirds of the punishment depending on the length of the imposed imprisonment (*see* paragraph 1104). The decision to apply the conditional release from the correctional institution for the pregnant women and mother with the child under 3 years of age had to be taken in accordance with the interests of the mother and the child.

---

536. Švedas G. Bausmių vykdymo teisė. Bendroji dalis, Vilnius, Registrų centras, 2013, p. 303.
537. Vosyliūtė A. Lygtinis paleidimas kaip integracijos prielaida: teismų sprendimų problemos // Bausmių taikymo ir vykdymo tarptautinis palyginimas, tendencijos ir perspektyvos Lietuvoje, Vilnius, 2017, pp. 212–213.

1107. The convicted person, who agrees to be subject to intensive supervision, may be conditionally released from the correctional institution not earlier than six months before he/she has actually served the above-mentioned minimum part of the imposed imprisonment.

1108. It should be noted that the following persons shall not be conditionally released from correctional institutions: (1) persons convicted for the crimes against the independence, territorial integrity and constitutional order of the State of Lithuania (XVI Chapter of the CC); (2) persons convicted for the crimes against freedom of a minor's sexual self-determination and/or inviolability (XXI Chapter of the CC); (3) persons whose death punishment was replaced with life imprisonment under the pardon or amnesty procedure as well as persons who are sentenced to life imprisonment; (4) persons who are convicted for intentional crimes committed in arrest houses, correctional institutions or pretrial detention institutions; (5) persons who have less than three months left until the fulfilment of the imprisonment.

1109. The Commission for Conditional Release from Correction Institution must preliminarily examine and assess substantive conditions and other specific circumstances (such as personality of the convicted person, prior life and previous convictions, the conduct during the execution of the imprisonment and implementation of the measures of the individual program, etc.) concerning the possibility of the conditional release from the correctional institution. After it, the Commission adopts a reasoned resolution to apply or not apply the conditional release from correctional institution and (if needed) forwards it to the court. It should be noted that in case a correctional institution has received a statement that the victim prefers to be notified about the forthcoming release of the convicted person, the Commission for Conditional Release from Correctional Institution shall notify the victim of his/her right to lodge a reply regarding the convicted person's request.

1110. The decision of the Commission on Conditional Release from Correctional Institution may be appealed before the district court.

Chapter 4. Extinction of Sanctions or Sentences

1111. The Code of Punishment Execution provide these grounds for the extinction of the punishment: (1) completion of the imposed punishment; (2) amnesty; (3) clemency; (4) cancellation of the sentence and termination of the pretrial investigation; (6) other grounds provided in the laws of Lithuania, for example, the statute of limitations of the execution of the judgment of conviction, severe incurable illnesses, etc.

1112. After the completion of the imprisonment and arrest or due to the other grounds for the extinction of the punishment, the convicted person is released from the correctional institution on the first half of the last day of the punishment and, if released on other grounds – on the day the correctional institution receives the necessary documents. If the necessary documents are received no more than three hours before the end of the working day, the convicted person is released in the morning of the next day. When the punishment ends on the day of rest or celebration, the sentenced person is released on the working day before the day of rest or celebration. Identity documents, personal items, the money kept in the personal account, as well as the documents certifying the execution of the punishment are issued to the person on the day of release. Furthermore, the head of the penal institution or his/her deputy must explain to the released person his/her rights and duties. Released minors are sent to the parents, close relatives or guardians. These minors must be accompanied by a staff member of the correctional institution, parents, close relatives or guardians.

§1. Pardon, Amnesty, Illness

1113. The pardon, amnesty and release from the punishment due to illness of the convicted person is regulated by the CC.

1114. A person who commits a criminal act may be released from serving the entire length of the sentence or a part thereof by an amnesty act passed by the *Seimas*. The amnesty act lays down the grounds, conditions and procedure for granting amnesty. During the independence period the *Seimas* has adopted eight amnesty acts. Most of these amnesties were of limited scope and only the amnesty of 2000[538] was applied to a larger number of convicted persons – 2,271 was released from imprisonment and to 4897 – the term of imprisonment[539] was shortened.

1115. A convicted person may be released from serving the entire length of the sentence or a part thereof where the President of the Republic of Lithuania grants

538. Lietuvos Respublikos įstatymas dėl amnestijos akto, *Valstybės žinios*, 2000, No. 35-973.
539. Švedas G. Baudžiamosios politikos pagrindai ir tendencijos Lietuvos Respublikoje, Vilnius, TIC, 2006, p. 211.

his/her clemency plea. It should be noted that the pardon cannot be granted before the judgment becomes final and the convicted person starts the execution of the imposed punishment.

1116. A person who committed a criminal act may be released from a punishment where, before a judgment is passed by the court, he/she contracts a serious incurable illness rendering him/her unable to serve the punishment. In such a case, the court shall, when passing a judgment of conviction, impose a punishment upon this person and release him/her from serving the punishment. The court shall decide on this issue taking into consideration the gravity of the committed criminal act, the personality of the convict and the nature of the illness.

1117. A person who contracts a serious incurable illness following the passing of a judgment may be released from serving the undischarged term of the punishment. The court shall decide on this issue taking into consideration the gravity of the committed criminal act, the personality of the convicted person, his/her conduct while serving the punishment, the nature of the illness and the period of the sentence already served. The court must also assess the impact of the serious incurable disease on punishment execution as well as possibilities of such disease treatment in correctional institution.[540] The Supreme Court of Lithuania has ruled that release offender from punishment due to serious incurable illness is the discretionary right of the court, and not an obligation.[541]

1118. A person who, following the commission of a criminal act or imposition of a punishment, starts to suffer from a mental disorder rendering him/her incapable of understanding the nature of his/her actions or controlling them shall be released from serving the undischarged term of the sentence. In releasing this person from a punishment, the court shall decide whether to impose upon him/her a compulsory medical measure. In the event of convalescence of this person, he/she may be ordered to serve the undischarged term of the sentence. In such a case, the period during which the person was undergoing compulsory medical measure shall be included in the term of an imprisonment on a day-to-day basis.

§2. The Limitation of the Penalty by Time

1119. The statute of limitations of the execution of the judgment of conviction is provided in the CC of Lithuania. This kind of the statute of limitations are also unconditional; the court must apply them, if it sets up all their conditions.[542]

1120. The essence of the statute of limitations for the execution of a judgment of conviction is, in criminal law, a set period of time, after which the judgment of

---

540. Ruling of the Supreme Court of Lithuania in criminal case No. 2K-133-677/2015.
541. Ruling of the Supreme Court of Lithuania in criminal case No. 2K-524/2013.
542. Lietuvos Respublikos baudžiamojo kodekso komentaras. Bendroji dalis (1-98 straipsniai), Vilnius, TIC, 2004, p. 492-493, 497.

conviction cannot be executed and a convicted person must be released from the execution of the imposed punishment.[543] The doctrine of the Lithuanian criminal law has noted that the CC of Lithuania does not provide the statute of limitations for the execution of a judgment of conviction for penal and reformative measures explicitly.[544] A judgment of conviction shall not be executed where there are three conditions simultaneously:

(1) it was not executed within:
  (a) two years following imposition of a punishment for a misdemeanour; or
  (b) three years following imposition of a non-custodial sentence or of an imprisonment for a term not exceeding two years; or
  (c) five years following imposition of an imprisonment for a term not exceeding five years; or
  (d) ten years following imposition of an imprisonment for a term not exceeding ten years; or
  (e) fifteen years following imposition of an imprisonment for a term exceeding ten years or imposition of a life imprisonment; and
(2) during the specified period the convict did not evade the serving of the sentence; and
(3) during the specified period the convict did not commit a new criminal act.

1121. The statute of limitations for execution of a judgment of conviction shall run from the coming into effect of the judgment until the commencement of execution of the judgment.

1122. Where, after a judgment becomes effective, the convict evades the serving of the sentence, the statute of limitations shall stop running. In this case, the period shall resume running from the day when the convict arrives to serve the sentence or is detained. However, the judgment may not be executed where fifteen years have elapsed since its coming into effect, and twenty years have elapsed in the case of imposition of an imprisonment for a term exceeding ten years or of a life imprisonment, and the statute of limitations has not stopped running due to commission of a new criminal act.

1123. Where the convict commits a new criminal act before the expiry of the statute of limitations for execution of a judgment of conviction, the statute of limitations shall stop running. In this case, the statute of limitations for execution of the judgment of conviction shall run from the commission of a new crime or misdemeanour. When imposing a punishment for a new criminal act, the court shall apply the rules of imposition of punishment where a new criminal act has been committed before serving an imposed punishment.

---

543. Lietuvos Respublikos baudžiamojo kodekso komentaras. Bendroji dalis (1-98 straipsniai), Vilnius, TIC, 2004, p. 497.
544. Švedas G., Veršekys P., Levon J., Prapiestis D. Lietuvos Respublikos baudžiamojo kodekso bendrosios dalies vientisumo ir suderinimo iššūkiai, Vilnius, Vilniaus universiteto leidykla, 2017, p. 222.

§3. Deletion of the Conviction and Rehabilitation of Offenders

1124. According to the CC, a person convicted of commission of a crime in respect of whom a judgment of conviction passed by a court of the Republic of Lithuania or another Member State of the EU has become effective shall be considered as a person having a previous conviction. The person convicted of commission of a crime in a non-EU Member State, provided that a notice of the coming into effect of a judgment of conviction passed by a court of that State is received under international treaties of the Republic of Lithuania, shall also be considered as a person having a previous conviction. The previous conviction may be a basis for restricting only those rights and freedoms of a person whose restriction is provided for by laws of the Republic of Lithuania, for example, according to the Law on the Bar[545] a person who has the previous conviction cannot become an advocate or according to the Law on the Banks[546] – head of the bank, or according to the Law on the Control of Firearms and Ammunition – to buy and have some categories of firearms,[547] etc.

1125. The following persons shall be considered as having a previous conviction: (1) the persons given a suspended execution of the punishment – during the period of suspension; (2) the persons convicted of negligent crimes – during the period of serving the sentence; (3) the persons convicted of intentional crimes who have actually served the imposed sentence – during the period of serving the sentence and during the following period commencing after they have served the sentence or have been released from serving the sentence:

(a) for three years if convicted of a minor or less serious crime;
(b) for five years if convicted of a serious crime;
(c) for eight years if convicted of a grave crime;
(d) for ten years if they are dangerous repeat offenders or persons whose life imprisonment has been commuted to a custodial sentence.

1126. These terms shall be calculated from the full serving of the imposed sentence or release from serving the sentence. The above-mentioned terms of validity of previous conviction following the serving of the sentence or release from serving the sentence in respect of the juveniles shall be reduced by half. After the lapse of at least one-half of the term of conviction, a court may, at the request of the convicted person, reduce the term of conviction or expunge the conviction. Upon the expiry of the mentioned terms, the previous conviction shall expire and the persons shall be considered as having no criminal record.

1127. Where a person who has a previous conviction commits a new crime or misdemeanour, calculation of the term until the expiry of previous conviction shall cease. In such a case, calculation of the term until the expiry of the conviction for

545. Lietuvos Respublikos advokatūros įstatymas, *Valstybės žinios*, 2004, No. 50-1632.
546. Lietuvos Respublikos bankų įstatymas, *Valstybės žinios*, 2004, No. 54-1832.
547. Lietuvos Respublikos ginklų ir šaudmenų kontrolės įstatymas, TAR, 2019, No. 10570.

the previous criminal act shall commence from the serving of the penalty for the new crime or misdemeanour. The person shall be considered as having the previous conviction for each criminal act until the expiry of conviction for the most serious of the acts.

1128. The data on the suspected, accused and convicted persons, the criminal act and punishment, the judgment and its revision in appeal and cassation instance, are all contained in the registry of the suspected, accused and convicted persons. The procedure for conducting this registry, as well as the rules of the removal of persons from this registry, is regulated by the Law on Registry of Suspected, Accused and Convicted Persons[548] and Rules on registration of the suspected, accused and convicted persons and submission of the data.[549]

1129. A person whose term of the conviction has expired shall be rehabilitated and have the same legal status as the person who has not been sentenced for the commission of a criminal act.

§4. Revision of Sentences

I. Conditions Relating to the Nature of the Sanction Imposed

1130. The possibility of revision of final sentences is regulated by the provisions of the CCP on the reopening of criminal procedure, which is an extraordinary legal remedy (paragraphs 1026–1045). Furthermore, a final judgment may be revised without reopening of criminal procedure in these instances: (a) resolution of execution of several judgments that have not been executed; (b) resolution of doubts and ambiguities arising in the course of execution of the judgment; (c) resolution of certain issues arising in the course of execution of the judgment; (d) resolution of the application of the milder criminal law.

II. Circumstances Justifying Revision of the Sentence

A. Inconsistency Between Distinct Convictions

1131. Lithuanian criminal procedure provides the rule for the resolution of the execution of several judgments that have not been executed. This rule states that

> where there are other judgments rendered with respect to the convicted person, which have not been executed in full or in part and of the existence whereof the court which rendered the last judgment could not have been aware of, the same court or any other court of the same instance or any superior court

548. Lietuvos Respublikos įtariamųjų, kaltinamųjų ir nuteistųjų registro įstatymas, *Valstybės žinios*, 2011, No. 86-4145.
549. tariamųjų, kaltinamųjų ir nuteistųjų registro nuostatai, TAR, 2019, No. 6970.

according to the place of execution of the last judgment shall make an order on the procedure of enforcement of punishments provided for by the judgments which have not been executed in full or in part.

B. False Statement, New Facts or New Circumstances

1132. New facts or new circumstances (including a false statement) are not a circumstance justifying revision of the sentence without reopening of criminal procedure, but a reason for reopening of criminal case (paragraphs 1027–1030).

C. Resolution of Doubts and Ambiguities Arising in the Course of Execution of Judgment

1133. A final judgment may be revised without a reopening of the criminal case for the reason of the resolution of doubts and ambiguities arising in the course of execution of the judgment. According to the Lithuanian criminal procedure, the court shall be authorised to resolve, in the course of execution of the judgment, the doubts arising due to the defects of the judgment, provided that the resolution of the above doubts does not affect the substance of the judgment. The court shall be authorised to make decisions regarding: (1) revocation of the order for the application of provisional measures in the cases where the fact of revocation of the order for the application of provisional measures is not indicated in the judgment when the accused is acquitted or convicted and relieved of punishment; (2) revocation of the order for the application of measures for securing civil action, or confiscation of property, or extended confiscation of property where the appropriate order is not revoked by the judgment when the judgment of acquittal is rendered or the claim is refused or confiscation of property is not ordered; (3) crediting the time spent in pretrial detention into the term of the punishment, if the convicted person has not been given credit on his/her sentence for the time that he/she has spent in pretrial detention or if the credit given has not been accurately assessed; (4) crediting the served punishment, where the punishment is imposed by several judgments, if the judgment has not given credit to the convicted person for the term of the served punishment or the term credited has not been correctly assessed; (5) rectification of errors in the judgment – incorrect spelling of the name or surname of the convicted person, or errors arising due to incorrect presentation of biographical data of the convicted person as well as clerical errors and errors in calculation; etc. The court may also eliminate the ambiguities that have emerged after the rendering of the judgment if there has been a change in the circumstances prior to the execution of the judgment. The court may make a decision: (1) on the confiscation of the subsequently discovered property which has been acquired by the convicted person prior to the rendering of the judgment and is subject to confiscation pursuant to law; (2) on the revision of the list of objects and instruments subject to confiscation under the court judgment where it is specified in the judgment that the part of the property owned by the convicted person is subject to confiscation; as well as other ambiguities.

D. Resolution of Certain Issues Arising in the Course of Execution of Judgment

1134. A final judgment may be revised without a reopening of criminal case for the reason of resolution of certain issues arising in the course of execution of the judgment. According to the Lithuanian criminal procedure, the court shall be authorised to resolve, in the course of execution of the judgment, these issues relating to: (1) relieving the convicted person from punishment due to illness; (2) converting or relieving from the community service, fine or restriction of liberty punishments; (3) converting one penal measure to another penal measure; etc.

E. Resolution of the Application of the Milder Criminal Law

1135. A final judgment may be revised without a reopening of criminal case for the reason of resolution of the application of the milder criminal law, which was adopted during the execution of the judgment.

III. Procedure

1136. A final judgment may be revised by the court, which rendered the judgment or the court of the place where the imposed punishment is executed without reopening of criminal case, either upon the request of prosecutor, defence counsel, sentenced person or other parties or the representative of the institution executing the punishment. The procedure depends on the ground for the revision of the judgment and may be oral hearing or written procedure. As necessary, the court shall invite the prosecutor, the defence counsel, sentenced person and other parties to the court hearing, however, failure by the above persons to appear shall not impede the hearing of the case.

General Conclusions

1137. Lithuanian criminal law belongs to the family of civil law (continental) systems and has been significantly influenced by the German model. In Lithuania, substantive and criminal procedural laws were codified relatively late – the CC of 2000, the Code of Criminal Procedure of 2002 and the Code of Punishment Execution of 2002 were the first codified national laws in the legal framework of the independent State of Lithuania that reinforced the national legal fundamentals underpinning the criminal policy of the state. The codes were in the process of development for almost ten years. In the final stage of drafting, they were significantly influenced by the conventions of the Council of Europe and by the legal acts of the European Union.

1138. The Lithuanian criminal law may be generally seen as modern. The substantive criminal law follows the latest trends of criminalisation at the European level and introduces a highly individualised system of criminal liability (punishments, penal and reformative measures, institutions for the release from criminal liability and punishment, etc.). Meanwhile, the criminal procedure aims to meet the international human rights requirements, while also trying to increase the efficiency in pretrial investigation, prosecution and trial. The numerous amendments and supplements of the CC and Code of Criminal Procedure, during 2003–2021, were made to comply with the new requirements of the international treaties of Lithuania and EU legal acts, decisions of the CJEU and ECtHR, the case law of the Lithuanian Constitutional and Supreme Courts. However, the quality of some amendments and supplements to the CC and Code of Criminal Procedure is questionable.

Selected Bibliography

§1. Legal Acts of Lithuania

Lietuvos Respublikos Konstitucija. – Valstybės žinios, 1992, No. 33-1014.
Lietuvos Respublikos Konstitucijos papildymo Konstituciniu aktu 'Dėl Lietuvos Respublikos narystės Europos Sąjungoje' ir Lietuvos Respublikos Konstitucijos 150 straipsnio papildymo įstatymas. – Valstybės žinios, 2004, No. 111-4123.
Lietuvos Respublikos baudžiamasis kodeksas. – Valstybės žinios, 2000, No. 89-2741.
Lietuvos Respublikos baudžiamojo proceso kodeksas. – Valstybės žinios, 2002, No. 37-1341.
Lietuvos Respublikos bausmių vykdymo kodeksas. – Valstybės žinios, 2002, No.73-3084.
Lietuvos Respublikos administracinių nusižengimų kodeksas. – TAR, 2015, No. 2015-11216.
Lietuvos Respublikos teismų įstatymas. – Valstybės žinios, 2002, No. 17-649.
Lietuvos Respublikos prokuratūros įstatymas. – Valstybės žinios, 2003, No. 42-1919.
Lietuvos Respublikos advokatūros įstatymas. – Valstybės žinios, 2004, No. 50-1632.
Lietuvos Respublikos policijos įstatymas. – TAR, 2015, No. 2015-10818.
Lietuvos Respublikos probacijos įstatymo Nr. 1860 pakeitimo įstatymas. – TAR, 2019, Nr. 11184.
Lietuvos Respublikos kriminalinės žvalgybos įstatymas. – Valstybės žinios, 2012, Nr. 122-6093.
Lietuvos Respublikos įstatymas dėl Europos Sąjungos valstybių narių sprendimų baudžiamosiose bylose tarpusavio pripažinimo ir vykdymo. – TAR, 2014, No. 2014-17299.
Lietuvos Respublikos antstolių įstatymas. – Valstybės žinios, 2002, No. 53-2042.
Lietuvos Respublikos suėmimo vykdymo įstatymas, *Valstybės žinios*, 2008, No. 81-3172.
Lietuvos Respublikos organizuoto nusikalstamumo prevencijos įstatymas, TAR, 2020-06-29, No. 14343.
Lietuvos Respublikos teisėkūros pagrindų įstatymas, *Valstybės žinios*, 2012, No. 110-5564.

§2. Jurisprudence of the Constitutional Court of Lithuania

Konstitucinio Teismo 1993 m. gruodžio 13 d. nutarimas 'Dėl Lietuvos Respublikos baudžiamojo kodekso 148 straipsnio 2 dalies ir Lietuvos Respublikos baudžiamojo proceso kodekso 93 straipsnio 1 ir 2 punktų atitikimo Lietuvos Respublikos Konstitucijai'. Valstybės žinios, 1993, Nr. 70-1320.

Konstitucinio Teismo 1998 m. liepos 9 d. nutarimas 'Dėl 1996 m. liepos 2 d. ir 1997 m. sausio 9 d. įstatymų, kuriais buvo padaryti Lietuvos Respublikos baudžiamojo kodekso 310 straipsnio pakeitimai ir papildymai, atitikimo Lietuvos Respublikos Konstitucijai'. Valstybės žinios, 1998, Nr. 63-1827;

Konstitucinio Teismo 1998 m. gruodžio 9 d. nutarimas 'Dėl Lietuvos Respublikos baudžiamojo kodekso 105 straipsnio sankcijoje numatytos mirties bausmės atitikimo Lietuvos Respublikos Konstitucijai'. Valstybės žinios, 1998, Nr. 109-3004;

Konstitucinio Teismo 2001 m. sausio 11 d. nutarimas 'Dėl Lietuvos Respublikos baudžiamojo kodekso 7 straipsnio 2 dalies atitikties Lietuvos Respublikos Konstitucijai'. Valstybės žinios, 2001, Nr. 5-143;

Konstitucinio Teismo 2003 m. birželio 10 d. nutarimas 'Dėl Lietuvos Respublikos baudžiamojo kodekso 45 straipsnio (1998 m. liepos 2 d. redakcija) ir 312 straipsnio 3 dalies (1998 m. vasario 3 d. redakcija) atitikties Lietuvos Respublikos Konstitucijai'. Valstybės žinios, 2003, Nr. 57-2552;

Konstitucinio Teismo 2009 m. birželio 8 d. nutarimas 'Dėl Lietuvos Respublikos baudžiamojo kodekso 20 straipsnio 1, 2, 3 dalių (2000 m. rugsėjo 26 d. redakcija), 20 straipsnio 5 dalies (2004 m. liepos 5 d. redakcija), 43 straipsnio 4 dalies (2000 m. rugsėjo 26 d. redakcija) atitikties Lietuvos Respublikos Konstitucijai'. Valstybės žinios, 2009, Nr. 69-2798.

Konstitucinio Teismo 2012 m. birželio 4 d. nutarimas 'Dėl Lietuvos Respublikos baudžiamojo kodekso 129 straipsnio 2 dalies 3 punkto (2008 m. birželio 12 d. redakcija), 135 straipsnio 2 dalies 3 punkto (2008 m. birželio 12 d. redakcija) atitikties Lietuvos Respublikos Konstitucijai'. Valstybės žinios, 2012, Nr. 64-3246.

Konstitucinio Teismo 2014 m. kovo 18 d. nutarimas 'Dėl Lietuvos Respublikos baudžiamojo kodekso kai kurių nuostatų, susijusių su baudžiamąja atsakomybe už genocidą, atitikties Lietuvos Respublikos Konstitucijai'. TAR, 2014, Nr. 2014-03226.

Konstitucinio Teismo 2016 m. birželio 27 d. nutarimas 'Dėl Lietuvos Respublikos baudžiamojo proceso kodekso 3 straipsnio 1 dalies nuostatos, 235 straipsnio 1 dalies, 254 straipsnio 4 dalies, 327 straipsnio 1 punkto atitikties Konstitucijai'. – TAR, 2016, Nr. 2016-17705.

§3. Resolutions of the Senate of the Supreme Court of Lithuania and Reviews of the Criminal Division of the Supreme Court of Lithuania

LAT Senato 2002 m. gruodžio 20 d. nutarimas Nr. 38 Dėl teismų praktikos taikant Baudžiamojo kodekso normas, reglamentuojančias baudžiamųjų įstatymų galiojimą laiko atžvilgiu // Teismų praktika, Vilnius, No. 18.

LAT Senato 2003 m. birželio 20 d. nutarimas Nr. 40 'Dėl teismų praktikos, taikant Baudžiamojo proceso kodekso nuostatas, reglamentuojančias nuosprendžio surašymą' // Teismų praktika. 2003, No. 19.

LAT Senato 2004 m. birželio 18 d. nutarimas Nr. 46 'Dėl teismų praktikos nusikaltimų žmogaus gyvybei bylose' // Teismų praktika, Vilnius, No. 21.

LAT Senato 2004 m. gruodžio 30 d. nutarimas Nr. 49 'Dėl teismų praktikos išžaginimo ir seksualinio prievartavimo baudžiamosiose bylose' // Teismų praktika, Vilnius, No. 22.

LAT Senato 2005 m. birželio 23 d. nutarimas Nr. 52 'Dėl teismų praktikos vagystės ir plėšimo baudžiamosiose bylose' // Teismų praktika, Vilnius, No. 23.

LAT Senato 2005 m. gruodžio 29 d. nutarimas Nr. 55 'Dėl teismų praktikos nusikalstamų veikų finansų sistemai baudžiamosiose bylose (BK 214, 215, 219, 220, 221, 222, 223 straipsniai)' (Lietuvos Aukščiausiojo Teismo senato 1997 m. gruodžio 22 d. nutarimo Nr. 13 naujoji redakcija) // Teismų praktika, Vilnius, No. 23.

LAT Baudžiamųjų bylų skyriaus 2007 m. sausio 4 d. 'Teismų praktikos nusikaltimu ir baudžiamųjų nusižengimų valstybės tarnybai ir viešiesiems interesams baudžiamosiose bylose (BK 225, 226, 227, 228, 229 straipsniai) apibendrinimo apžvalga' // Teismų praktika, Vilnius, No. 26.

LAT Baudžiamųjų bylų skyriaus 2007 m. vasario 22 d. 'Teismų praktikos nusikalstamo susivienijimo baudžiamosiose bylose apibendrinimo apžvalga' // Teismų praktika, Vilnius, No. 26.

LAT Baudžiamųjų bylų skyriaus 2007 m. vasario 22 d. 'Teismų praktikos sukčiavimo baudžiamosiose bylose (Baudžiamojo kodekso 182 straipsnis) apžvalga' // Teismų praktika, Vilnius, No. 26.

LAT Baudžiamųjų bylų skyriaus 2007 m. birželio 28 d. 'Teismų praktikos skiriant bausmes (BK 54–64 straipsniai) apžvalga' // Teismų praktika. – Vilnius, Nr. 2007, No. 27.

Lietuvos Aukščiausiojo Teismo Baudžiamųjų bylų skyriaus 'Baudžiamojo proceso kodekso normų, reglamentuojančių įrodinėjimą taikymo teismų praktikoje apžvalga' // Teismų praktika, No. 27.

LAT Baudžiamųjų bylų skyriaus 2008 m. vasario 15 d. 'Teismų praktikos taikant bausmių vykdymo atidėjimą BK 75 ir 92 straipsnių apžvalga' // Teismų praktika, Vilnius, No. 28.

LAT Baudžiamųjų bylų skyriaus 2008 m. gegužės 16 d. 'Teismų praktikos skiriant bausmes už nužudymus (BK 129 straipsnis) apžvalga' // Teismų praktika, Vilnius, No. 28.

LAT Baudžiamųjų bylų skyriaus Senato 2009 m. kovo 24 d. 'Teismų praktikos keliu transporto eismo saugumo ar transporto priemonių eksploatavimo taisyklių pažeidimo (BK 281 straipsnis) baudžiamosiose bylose apžvalga' // Teismų praktika, Vilnius, No. 30.

LAT Baudžiamųjų bylų skyriaus 2010 m. vasario 18 d. 'Teismų praktikos taikant turto konfiskavimą (BK 72 straipsnis) apžvalga' // Teismų praktika, Vilnius, No. 32.

LAT Baudžiamųjų bylų skyriaus 'Baudžiamojo proceso kodekso normų, nustatančiu aplinkybes, dėl kurių baudžiamasis procesas negalimas, teismų praktikoje apžvalga' // Teismų praktika, No. 33.

LAT Baudžiamųjų bylų skyriaus 2010 m. spalio 18 d. 'Teismų praktikos skiriant bausmes už kontrabandą (BK 199 straipsnis) tyrimas' // Teismų praktika, Vilnius, No. 34.

LAT Baudžiamųjų bylų skyriaus 2011 m. vasario 10 d. 'Teismų praktikos skiriant bausmes už nusikalstamas veikas valstybės tarnybai ir viešiesiems interesams

(BK 225, 226, 227 ir 228 straipsniai) tyrimas' // Teismų praktika, Vilnius, No. 34.
LAT Baudžiamųjų bylų skyriaus Senato 2012 m. birželio 29 d. 'Teismų praktikos nusikaltimų žmoniškumui ir karo nusikaltimų baudžiamosiose bylose apžvalga (BK 99, 100 ir 102 straipsniai)' // Teismų praktika, Vilnius, No. 37.
LAT Baudžiamųjų bylų skyriaus 2014 m. birželio 9 d. 'Teismų praktikos nusikalstamų veikų, susijusių su neteisėtu disponavimu narkotinėmis, psichotropinėmis medžiagomis ar pirmos kategorijos šių medžiagų pirmtakais (prekursoriais) (BK 259–261, 263–264, 266 straipsniai) apžvalga' // Teismų praktika, Vilnius, No. 40.
LAT 2016 m. rugpjūčio 23 d. Teismų praktikos nagrinėjant baudžiamąsias bylas dėl sudėtingų pavienių nusikalstamų veikų ir nusikalstamų veikų sutapčių apžvalga Nr. AB-44-1. Teismų praktika. 2016, No. 44.

§4. Books

Baudžiamoji teisė. Specialioji dalis. Pirma knyga. Vilnius: Eugrimas, 2000.
Baudžiamoji teisė. Specialioji dalis. Antra knyga. Vilnius: Eugrimas, 2001.
Baudžiamoji teisė. Bendroji dalis. Vilnius: Eugrimas, 2003.
Lietuvos Respublikos baudžiamojo proceso kodekso komentaras. I dalis. Vilnius, TIC, 2003.
Lietuvos Respublikos baudžiamojo proceso kodekso komentaras. II dalis. Vilnius, TIC, 2003.
BLAŽEVIČIUS J., ŠVEDAS G., USIK D. Lietuvos Respublikos bausmių vykdymo kodekso komentaras. I-V dalys (1-183 straipsniai). Vilnius, TIC, 2004.
Lietuvos Respublikos baudžiamojo kodekso komentaras. Bendroji dalis. (1-98 straipsniai). Vilnius, TIC, 2004.
ABRAMAVIČIUS A., MICKEVIČIUS D., ŠVEDAS G. Europos Sąjungos teisės aktų įgyvendinimas Lietuvos baudžiamojoje teisėje. Vilnius, V Teisinės informacijos centras, 2005.
ŠVEDAS G. Baudžiamosios politikos pagrindai ir tendencijos Lietuvos Respublikoje. Vilnius, V Teisinės informacijos centras, 2006.
BARANSKAITĖ A. Taikos sutartis baudžiamojoje teisėje: atleidimas nuo baudžiamosios atsakomybės kaltininkui ir nukentėjusiajam susitaikius. Vilnius, V Teisinės informacijos centras, 2007.
MERKEVIČIUS R. Baudžiamasis procesas: įtariamojo statusas. Vilnius, Registrų centras, 2008.
Lietuvos Respublikos baudžiamojo kodekso komentaras. Specialioji dalis (99-212 straipsniai). II dalies 1 knyga. Vilnius, Registrų centras, 2009.
Lietuvos Respublikos baudžiamojo kodekso komentaras. Specialioji dalis (213–320 straipsniai). II dalies 2 knyga. Vilnius, Registrų centras, 2010.
Lietuvos Respublikos baudžiamajam kodeksui – 10 metų. Vilnius, 2011.
ŠVEDAS G. Bausmių vykdymo teisė. Bendroji dalis. Vilnius, Registrų centras, 2013.
GODA G., KAZLAUSKAS M., KUCONIS. Baudžiamojo proceso teisė. Vilnius, Registrų centras, 2011.
Globalizacijos iššūkiai baudžiamajai justicijai. Vilnius, Registrų centras, 2014.
Lithuanian legal system under the influence of European Union law. Vilnius, 2014.

GODA G. Vertybiniai prioritetai baudžiamajame procese. Vilnius, Registrų centras, 2014.
Šiuolaikinės baudžiamosios teisės tendencijos. Vilnius, 2015.
Baudžiamoji justicija ir verslas. Vilnius, 2016.
AŽUBALYTĖ R., JURKA R., ZAJANČKAUSKIENĖ J. Baudžiamojo proceso teisė. Bendroji dalis. I knyga. Vilnius, Registrų centras, 2016.
ŠVEDAS G., VERŠEKYS P., LEVON J., PRAPIESTIS D. Lietuvos Respublikos baudžiamojo kodekso bendrosios dalies vientisumo ir naujovių suderinimo iššūkiai. Vilnius, Vilniaus Universiteto leidykla, 2017.
Lietuvos baudžiamoji teisė. Bendroji dalis. 1 knyga. Vilnius, Vilniaus universiteto leidykla, 2019.
Lietuvos baudžiamoji teisė. Bendroji dalis. 2 knyga. Vilnius, Vilniaus universiteto leidykla, 2020.

§5. Law Journals

Teisė (Law)
Jurisprudencija (Jurisprudence).
Teisės problemos (Law problems);
Justitia
Socialinių mokslų studijos (Studies of social sciences)
Teisės apžvalga (Law review)

Selected Bibliography

Index

The numbers here refer to paragraph numbers.

Accomplice, *see* Complicity
Accused
  general, 714–718
  interview, 845, 846, 921–924
  position and rights, 719–748
Actus reus, 201–222
Administrative violations, 28
Aggravating circumstances, 603, 604
Amnesty, 585, 1113, 1114
Analogy, 138
Appeal, *see* Remedies
Arrest, *see* Penalties
Attempt
  definition and kinds, 340–341
  impossibility, 351, 352
  intention, 342

Bail, 902
Bar, 55–61
Body Search, 824
Burden of proof, *see* Evidence

Clemency (pardon), 586, 1111, 1115
Community service, *see* Penalties
Compulsory medical measures, 564–570
Complicity, 354–360
  abettor, 371–373
  instigator, 369–370
  organiser, 367–370
  perpetrator, 361–366
Conditional release, *see* Prison system
Confrontation, *see* Witness
Concurrence of offences, 624–629
Consent of the victim, *see* Justifications
Consequences, 212–216
Continuous offences, 218–220
Corporate liability, *see* Legal person
Court of Appeal, *see* Judicial system
Covert policing
  actions of the officers without disclosing their identity, 812
  covert surveillance, 813–815
  general, 808–810
  simulation of criminal act (including controlled delivery), 811
Criminal law, 25–33
  characteristics, 34, 35
  history, 77–101
  sources, 102–123
Criminal offences
  classification, 197
  concept, 196, 198–200
  kinds, 204–222
Criminal association, *see* Forms of complicity
Culpability, 223–225
Custodial penalties, *see* Penalties

Death penalty, 487, 488
Detention
  bringing in person, 838
  committal to the medical institution, 893
  provisional arrest, 874–879
  pretrial detention, 880–892
District court, *see* Judicial system
Dolus directus, 233
Dolus eventualis, 234

Entrapment, 381
Entry and search, 819–837
Evidence
  burden of proof, 767
  documents, 798–800
  exclusion of evidence, 801–803
  expert report, 788–791

illegally obtained evidence, 769, 773, 801–803
item, 795–797
means of proof, 774
principles, 766–773
specialist conclusion, 792–794
testimony of suspect or accused, 775–779
testimony of witness and victim, 780–787
Excuses
diminished capacity, 311–314
force majeure and coercion, 318–319
ignorance and mistake, 320–324
insanity, 303–310
intoxication, 315–317
minority, 299–302

Fine, *see* Penalties
Forensic examination, 866–871
Forms of complicity
criminal association, 374, 377–378
group of accomplices, 374–375
organised group, 374, 376

Guilt, 223–225

House arrest, 899

Identification parade, *see* Witness
Ignorance and mistake, *see* Excuses
Illegally obtained evidence, *see* Evidence
Immediacy (principle of), 766, 770
Immunities, 183–194
Imprisonment, *see* Penalties
Indictment, 666
Intent, 226–237
Interpretation of criminal law, 140–141
Intoxication, 315–317
Insanity, 303–314

Judicial system, 17–24, 49–50, 644, 645
Judgment, 984–989
Jurisdiction
extraterritorial, 167–168
personal, 169–171
protection, 172–174
territorial, 161–166
universality, 175–176
Justifications
apprehension of a person who committed a criminal act, 282–284
consent of the victim, 278–281
justifiable professional or economical risk, 289–290
necessity, 273–277
performance of an assignment of a law enforcement institution, 285–288
public duty or order of the authorities, 256–259
realisation of his/her rights, 295–296
scientific experiment, 291–294
self-defence, 260–271

Legal person
liability, 247–253
sanctioning system, 485
Legal consequences of conviction, 1124–1129
Legality (principle of), 134–139

Minority, 299–302
Mistake (of fact; of law), *see* Excuses
Misdemeanour, 196
Mitigating circumstances, 614–616

Non bis in idem, 713
Nulla poena sine culpa, 142–145
Necessity, *see* Justifications
Negligence, 238–244

Oath, 754
Omission (offences of), 206–209

Penalties
arrest, 490–492
community service, 510–514
concept and purpose, 480, 481
fine, 500–503
imprisonment, 493–495
life imprisonment, 496–499
liquidation of legal person, 517
restriction of liberty, 504–509
restriction of operation of legal person, 515, 516
system and types, 482–486
Penal measures
general, 518–524
separate types, 525–549
Pretrial judge, 48, 909, 910
Preparation to commit a crime, 335–339
Presumption of innocence, 766, 767
Pretrial detention, *see* Detention
Prison system

classification, 1059–1067
complaint, 1101–1102
communication, correspondence, visits and telephone, 1070–1080
conditional release, 1103–1110
disciplinary measures, 1085–1086
leave, 1087–1091
principles, 1052–1058
regime, 1068–1069
work, 1081–1084
Prohibition of retroactivity, 150–153
Proportionality (principle of), 146–148
Prosecution
dissolution of the right to prosecute, 693–708
general, 688–690
powers, 672–676
principle of state prosecution, 688–690
suspension of the right to prosecute, 691–692
Prosecution service, 43–47
Provisional measures, 894–908
Punishment, *see* Penalties

Recidivism, 605–612
Regional court, 18, 19, 49, 645, 648, 652, 653, 656–658
Reformative measures
general, 550–554
separate types, 555–563
Release from criminal liability
general, 457–459
separate types, 460–479
Release from punishment, 581–586
Remedies
appeal (against first instance judgment), 993–1006
appeal (against second instance judgment), 1007–1022
appeal (against decisions), 1023–1025
extraordinary remedies, 1026–1045
general, 990–992
Retroactivity
milder statute, 154–157
stricter statute, 158, 159

Search and seizure, 819–837
Self-defence, *see* Justifications
Sentencing
general, 587–601
increasing punishment, 602–612
mitigating punishment, 613–623

for several criminal acts, 632–641Statute of limitations, 703–712, 1119–1123

Supreme Court, *see* Judicial system
Suspect
interview, 845–846
position and rights, 715, 719–748
Suspension of the execution of punishment, 971–980

Territorial principle, 161–166
Temporal limitation of the property rights, 840–844
Trial, 928–933
Trial courts, 646–659

Victim
general, 749–752
plaintiff rights, 759–763
position and rights, 753–758

Witness
confrontation, 850–852
identification parade, 853–856
verification of the testimonies of the site, 857–858

Index

www.ingramcontent.com/pod-product-compliance
Ingram Content Group UK Ltd.
Pitfield, Milton Keynes, MK11 3LW, UK
UKHW020134290926
15471UKWH00003B/475

9 789403 547